*James Gamble Rogers
and the Architecture of Pragmatism*

The Architectural History Foundation
New York, New York

The MIT Press, Cambridge, Massachusetts, and London, England

James Gamble Rogers
and the Architecture of Pragmatism

Aaron Betsky

Library of Congress Cataloging–in–Publication Data
Betsky, Aaron
    James Gamble Rogers and the architecture of pragmatism / by Aaron Betsky.
        p.   cm.
    Includes bibliographical references.
    ISBN 0-262-02381-4
    1. Rogers, James Gamble—Criticism and interpretation. I. Title.
NA737.R59B48 1994
720'.92—dc20   94-7081 CIP

This book was edited by David G. De Long, Chairman of the Graduate Program in Historic Preservation, University of Pennsylvania.

This book was made possible thanks to a Revolving Fund established with the help of The Ahmanson Foundation, The Equitable Life Assurance Company, The Graham Foundation for Advanced Studies in the Fine Arts, Mrs. Agnes Gund, The Henry Luce Foundation, Paul Mayen, Mrs. Barnett Newman, The Nate B. and Frances Spingold Foundation, and Dave and Reba Williams.

Aaron Betsky is an architectural designer and critic living in Los Angeles.

Designed and typeset by Bessas & Ackerman.

Contents

Acknowledgments   vii

Foreword by Paul Goldberger   ix

Introduction   1

CHAPTER ONE   Foundations   9

CHAPTER TWO   The Architecture of Pragmatism   39

CHAPTER THREE   Civic Architecture   67

CHAPTER FOUR   Building the New Yale   103

CHAPTER FIVE   Bright College Years   139

CHAPTER SIX   Cities Set Upon a Hill   163

CHAPTER SEVEN   Rational Fortresses   211

Notes   235

Chronology   261

Index   269

Illustration credits   275

Acknowledgments

This project came about as a result of a challenge by Victoria Newhouse, publisher of the Architectural History Foundation. I had written a review of several books in the American Monograph series, and Mrs. Newhouse dared me to *do* rather than criticize. I am extremely grateful that she did, and the help she and David G. De Long have offered me in this long process of discovery, writing, and editing has been invaluable.

After agreeing to write this book, I discovered that James Gamble Rogers had produced a great deal more work than was evident at first, and that both the documentation and the actual buildings were spread throughout the eastern part of the United States. I needed to find the time and the wherewithal to do the necessary research. The Graham Foundation made this possible with a generous grant. I am grateful to the foundation and to Carter H. Manny, Jr., its director emeritus. I subsequently received a grant from the Rockefeller Archive Center, which allowed me to use its extensive archives on Edward Harkness and the Commonwealth Fund.

Librarians, archivists, and research assistants wherever I went guided me through their collections with great skill and generosity, and I am grateful to all of them. I would, however, like to thank especially Patrick Quinn at the Northwestern University Archives, Bill Massa at Yale, and Tom Rosenbaum at the Rockefeller Archive Center. The family of James Gamble Rogers, particularly Pauline Rogers and Mrs. Van Sluyck, were also very generous with their time and information.

I was lucky enough to be aided in my efforts by Joe Day, without whose knowledge, persistence, and research acumen I would not have survived. Tony Hurtig, Peter Lipson, and Matt Kupritz also helped in my efforts to research and photograph the work of James Gamble Rogers. Robert Bruegmann was willing to listen to all of my unformed ideas and helped me put Rogers in a historical context. Patrick Pinnell went so far as to edit my manuscript, as well as provide me with sound advice. Sylvia Lavin and Celia McGee also edited and refined parts of the manuscript with their usual skill and clarity. Their help turned this project into a book.

Finally, I must thank Vincent Scully and John Hall for first making me look at the work of James Gamble Rogers; Jaime Rua, who helped me to articulate the philosophical ideas that I hope are evident in some of this book; John Nelson and Celia and Henry McGee, who gave me a roof over my head as I researched this book in the Chicago and New York areas; and Peter Christian Haberkorn, for his support and encouragement over the last five years.

Foreword: James Gamble Rogers   PAUL GOLDBERGER

One is tempted, after reading the life of James Gamble Rogers, to wonder if he was not born as much before his time as after it. He spent much of his career as an anachronistic figure, an architect whose work was conservative, even reactionary, in its determined indifference to Modernism. In his lifetime he was a rear-guard figure, and proud of it. Now, nearly half a century after Rogers' death, the world has turned: Modernism has lost the potency that it had in the 1920s and 1930s, the vital spark that made Rogers and his peers seem so distant from the most ambitious architectural thought of their time, and the traditional, eclectic, highly derivative architecture Rogers practiced is taken, once again, with some seriousness.

It is not only that Rogers himself is viewed with more respect today than he was a generation or two ago, it is that no small number of architects today are producing architecture that might be called Rogersian in its sensibility. The children of James Gamble Rogers seem now to be all about, making buildings that are frankly derivative of historical styles, a calling they, like Rogers, pursue less with the goal of singling out any one style as an ideologically correct way of making architecture than with the objective of creating elegant, picturesque compositions. The elevation of comfort over intellectual challenge that characterized so much architecture of the 1980s—from the houses of Robert A. M. Stern and Jaquelin T. Robertson to the office towers of Philip Johnson and Kohn Pedersen Fox to the civic buildings of Thomas Beeby—is very much in the Rogers mold: it seems to emerge out of an intuitive sense of what assemblage of traditional elements will make a visually pleasing composition, not out of any ideological or theoretical imperative.

The line of descent of which Rogers is such an important part is not merely that of historicist architects, and, indeed, it can exclude many architects whose designs are motivated primarily by a stylistic dogma. Peers though they may have been, Rogers had little in common with a polemical Gothic Revivalist such as Ralph Adams Cram, who deeply believed in the moral rightness of Gothic architecture and saw his stylistic choice as something of a moral crusade. Rogers embraced no such crusade: he could switch with utter ease from Classical to Gothic to Colonial—indeed, in one of the most astonishing flaunts to ideological purity in all of American architecture, he once managed to shift from Southern Colonial to Gothic on two sides of a single building.

Rogers was pragmatic: he designed what worked, so long as it was within a broad vocabulary of precedent. To him architecture was a matter of cultivation, of education, of propriety, and of manners. He was no more interested in inventing a new style of building than he was in inventing a new way to dress or a new way to set the dinner table—he believed that the modes that had been handed down by previous generations were not only acceptable but preferable to anything his generation might invent, and that as an architect it was as much his duty to speak the language that had been bequeathed to him as it was his duty as a dinner guest to speak the language of his hostess.

I mean the analogy not at all casually. Creative conversation, not merely dull repetition of the proper language, is expected of the dinner guest, and so it was also Rogers' goal as an architect. To him style *was* a language, and it was up to him not merely to speak in that language but to embrace it creatively. The act of composition was, in a sense, an act of conversation, an opportunity for eloquence, coherence, and charm. It was his obligation as an architect to put people at ease, to give them a physical surrounding that, like good conversation, left them both comforted and slightly intrigued.

If all of this suggests an approach to architecture as a trivial profession that pranced about lightly rather than attacked problems aggressively —as a profession that embraced good taste more than powerful ideas, we might say—that is not my intention. Rogers' architectural foundation was solid, and if he was no intellectual, he was no dilettante, either. He believed profoundly in the role of architecture as a civilizing presence, and his work demonstrated not only remarkable sophistication and technical mastery, but also a consistent faith in the ability of good architecture to shape a community. His social and political values were conservative ones, but that is less relevant than his belief that architecture could represent values, that it could be as much a route to the civic ideal as it is an aesthetic presence.

These ideas were not Rogers' alone, of course; he shared his willingness to move easily from style to style with numerous traditional architects of his time, of whom John Russell Pope, Whitney Warren, Cass Gilbert, Thomas Hastings, and William Adams Delano were perhaps the best known, while his commitment to *civitas* is entirely consistent with the values of the City Beautiful movement and the cadre of Beaux-Arts–trained architects in America of which he was a part.

Yet there was something different in Rogers' way of making buildings, something unique to his style of architectural conversation, so to speak. There was a particular lightness, almost grace, to his best work, especially those buildings finished before 1930, and a delicacy of scale that together distinguish Rogers' buildings from those of nearly all his competitors. They are understated, never overbearing; while no one could call Rogers' work modest, it is quiet and restrained beside the buildings of many of his contemporaries. There is no better demonstration of this than the comparison between the tight, firm house Rogers designed for his great patron Edward S. Harkness at No. 1 East 75th Street in Manhattan and the sumptuous mansion that Horace Trumbauer produced for James B. Duke three blocks north at No. 1 East 78th Street. The Rogers building is dense and urban and part of a larger whole; though it reads somewhat as a solid mass from the corner, it is primarily a pair of facades addressing themselves to the street, and it welcomes other buildings beside it. The Duke House, now the New York University Institute of Fine Arts, is somewhat larger, but Trumbauer's immense scale makes it appear bigger still. It is a great French Neo-Classical palace, standing free, set back slightly from the street and from its neighbors; instead of giving off a sense of comfortable, discreet accommodation to the realities of the New York streetscape, it seems to cry out to be alone amid acres of landscape.

Rogers did not indulge in such fantasy—even so dazzling a work as the Harkness Quadrangle, now Branford and Saybrook colleges at Yale, has a kind of grounding in reality. The quadrangle, like virtually all of Rogers' major work, is magnificently, even brilliantly, detailed, but it possesses a modesty of scale that exudes a sense of deference and good manners. It honors the streets of New Haven, even as it turns away from them to offer up its most lavish architectural pleasures to private inner courtyards, and everywhere in this complex, as in all of Rogers' great Yale work, there is a sense of the design reaching out to its neighbors to form a larger whole.

These are the values of urbanism—to respect the street, to design with cognizance of context, to reach toward a greater whole—and while Rogers never articulated them, his natural expression of this value system in his work may have been his greatest contribution. (His impulses toward what a later generation would come to call "urban design" also yielded what was surely his strangest design, the south wing of Davenport College at Yale, which is Gothic on one side to echo the style of Rogers' own Memorial Quadrangle across the street, and Colonial on the other side for compatibility with a Colonial courtyard. Here, the laudable instinct toward integration reached a level of parody.)

Paradoxically, it is in the values of urbanism rather than in any of the stylistic choices he made that Rogers separated himself most emphatically from Modernism. The Modernists flaunted their rejection of context, and saw the city more as a podium for abstract forms than as an assemblage of elements that cried out for some expression of continuity. Rogers sought the very continuity in the cityscape that Modernism disdained, and his determined pursuit of urbanism, even more than his dislike of the glass box, marks him as a figure who stood apart from the Modernist revolution.

Here, perhaps most of all, we can feel a comradeship with Rogers across the generations. If the new traditionalists who reached prominence in the 1980s have only occasionally, if at all, produced work as convincing as Rogers' was, they, along with others, have helped bring about a sea of change in attitudes toward urbanism. The values of the city—more to the point, the values of the street—are ones shared by nearly all architects right now, including many who design very different kinds of buildings. This is a more profound change in architectural values than any stylistic shift, and it is clearly going to remain with us, even as the fascination of the 1980s with historical form and detail begins to fade.

Rogers' architecture was, and is, vibrant; its picturesque qualities exist firmly in three dimensions, and his buildings are meant to be walked through, their spaces experienced in sequential unfolding. This is architecture as procession, not architecture as a series of elevations and details. It is sensual, not cerebral; though Rogers appears not to have been a particularly emotional man, his architecture celebrates feeling. It is a feeling, first of all, for the various Western traditions, but even more so for architecture's basics—for scale and proportion and space and texture, for the joy of space and the physical beauty of elegant form. Whether the forms are Gothic or Classical or Colonial or whatever should matter as little to us as it appears to have mattered to Rogers himself—it is in the feeling of it all that this architecture gives us its greatest gift.

Introduction

James Gamble Rogers was a Chicagoan, an interpreter of traditional forms applied to modern functions, a businessman/organizer, a romantic composer of forms, a man with a good sense of humor, an architect, and a gentleman. These were the qualities that defined James Gamble Rogers and allowed him to become one of the most successful designers of institutions of higher learning in America. Beyond the success of his buildings, Rogers' work can today also be seen as the perfect embodiment of the integration into elite East Coast culture of the methods and values of a Midwestern-bred culture of middle-class professionalism.

Rogers' architecture is the architecture of pragmatism, in both the general and the specific senses of that word. Most of his major buildings are tied, either directly or indirectly, to institutions that were closely allied with the American Pragmatist movement. His work can be seen as an architectural translation of the values of John Dewey, William James, and their followers. In a broader sense, his work is functional, sensible, made of compromises, and it thus can be opposed to the more self-consciously grand work of his peers as well as to either populist or avant-garde countercurrents.

James Gamble Rogers' work cannot be understood as that of a genius creator existing outside of his milieu. In fact, the problem one encounters in looking at Rogers' work is that it appears to be so much of its time and place that we cannot easily define what makes it succeed so much better than that of his contemporaries. Similarly, Rogers' personality often disappears into the self-deprecating image of a gentleman designer, leading one to assume that he was no more than the ringmaster directing and exploiting the talents of his employees. Nothing could be farther from the truth, but it is from his self-image that one must start.

"All of his clients were his friends," says the son of one client who was at the same time a friend and family member. The statement can be read either way: his clients became his friends, or he worked only for clients who were, or could become, his friends.[1] He was the image of a perfect gentleman of the 1920s. He dressed well, was cultured but not pedantic, and above all had an infectious sense of humor. He was the perfect companion for card games, golf, and trips to Europe. He moved easily among some of the richest families in the East, several of whom he was related to by marriage, as well as among workmen and institutional clients. He wandered around his large drafting rooms in the mornings, directing the production of complicated buildings, and met with clients in the afternoons. He lived on the Upper East

Side of New York, wintered in a "club" he had designed near Charleston, South Carolina, and summered either in another such compound in Black Point, Connecticut, or with his wife's family in Lake Forest, Illinois. He often made fun of his own architecture, but he amassed a serious fortune by designing buildings for some of the most prestigious universities in the United States. He produced in eminently professional fashion a gentlemanly architecture at a time when the very notion of the gentleman was changing into that of a cultured professional.

Rogers was part and parcel of that change. Of a good Kentucky family, he grew up in the northern boomtown of Chicago after the fire of 1871 and then went on to Yale. This education determined the two sides of architecture he so successfully combined: on the one hand, he was a member of a group of aggressive businessmen and professionals who were converting the immense agricultural, mineral, and human wealth of the Midwest into the concentrated metropolitan culture of Chicago, developing a philosophy along the way that stressed the primacy of work, the immediacy of experience, and a pragmatic realism. By working for designers and developers of large commercial structures and residential subdivisions Rogers learned how to make practical buildings. At Yale, on the other hand, he became a member, along with several other pioneering "Western men," of an elite network—a small group of men, related by blood, marriage, or business interests, who shared similar backgrounds, tastes, and values—that sought to coordinate and control this explosion of wealth.

By subsequently leaving an already thriving practice to study at the Ecole des Beaux-Arts in Paris, he learned how to place these buildings within a tradition that would allow them, through their iconography and composition, to further the aims of the exclusive institutions they housed. By 1900, he knew how to make efficient buildings that were elegantly formed. He then synthesized this background in the design of residences and civic buildings that were both academically correct and efficiently rational. If he had done no more than this, he would be a designer of only secondary importance.

But James Gamble Rogers had the good luck to find himself connected with a group of men who had developed a way of translating the realism of the Midwest into the language of moral and civic leadership. From the moment he designed the School of Education at the University of Chicago, his work was allied with two important forces. The first was the Chicago School: the group of philosophers, psychiatric thinkers, education specialists, and protosociologists grouped around John Dewey and George Herbert Mead. These thinkers adapted the work of Boston Brahmins like William James to the practical exigencies of modernization as it was evidenced in the industrialization and urbanization in Chicago. That city became a conscious laboratory for seeing how one might give an appropriate shape to an emerging mass culture.[2] James Gamble Rogers designed their first experimental headquarters, the School of Education, and then went on to design his most important buildings for James Rowland Angell, Dewey's young associate and later president of Yale University. His other major client, President Walter Dill Scott of Northwestern University, was also a student of Dewey's. Many of the institutions for which Rogers worked, including the Colgate-Rochester Theological Seminary and the Columbia-Presbyterian Medical Center, were embodiments of the philosophy of the Chicago School.

It is from this condition that Rogers developed what Paul Goldberger has called his "romantic pragmatism."[3] The phrase recalls the roots of Rogers' work in romantic styles of architecture, but also connects his work with the Pragmatist thinkers who provided its theoretical underpinnings. William James, who gave Pragmatism its name, preached the primacy of perception and practical knowledge in a world whose only stable reference point is experience. James did not refuse to accept any ideal or validating principle for knowledge, but he observed that nothing could be known or said of that ideal.[4] We should, he said, live our lives according to common sense, or what he called the knowledge of our ancestors.

The emphasis that James, George Herbert Mead, John Dewey, and their followers placed on experience, practicality, and simple, logical, or "commonsensical" reactions to situations created a theory for a country that was continually in the process of inventing itself. It spoke to a class of men who sought to liberate themselves from dependence on religion and inherited morality. They hoped instead to embrace the constantly changing aspects of modernization while anchoring themselves in an inherited capability to know, organize, and order those processes of modernization. The Pragmatists and their allies in politics, education, and the arts accepted the appearance of chaos, flux, and change that characterized the modern world, and sought to erect a culture that could, by the fact that it was itself nothing else than a process, a way of knowing and acting, order the disorder they saw around them.[5]

Education was central in this process, and therefore Rogers' role as a designer of those institutions taken over by Pragmatist thinkers was crucial:

> Education became the secular religion of twentieth-century American society. To progressives and their successors, institutions of higher education would train and socialize the expert leaders needed to guide society in such disparate fields as business, teaching, and government. . . . Education was viewed increasingly as the salvation of progress and democracy. The urban university was our largest cathedral: there Americans paid homage to the culture of aspiration.[6]

On a larger scale, Pragmatist education was part of what Burton Bledstein has called "the culture of professionalism," the process by which the
middle class found, in institutions of higher learning, a training ground for
their version of a national elite.[7] Professionalism adapted traditional Christian
values to a more rational moralism and integrated scientific, social, and cultural models of understanding into a coherent course of study for future professional leaders. James Gamble Rogers was part of this process and, in his
institutional work, codified its values in stone and steel.

This is not just a story of abstract ideas, though. Rogers' mature
career was guided largely by his friendship with one man who embodied
many of these developments: Edward S. Harkness. From the moment Rogers
designed Harkness's house in New York City, to his last buildings for the
Harkness-financed Commonwealth Fund, designed just before he died, the
bulk of this architect's designs were financed directly by one man.

Harkness could give with such largesse because he was the heir to a
large chunk of the Rockefeller fortune, his father having been John D. Rockefeller's lawyer and partner in Cleveland. In 1916, he set up the Commonwealth Fund to "do something for the welfare of mankind."[8] The focus of this
fund and of Harkness's private donations was on reforms in education and
health care, as well as on progressive religious institutions. His was not a
hands-off form of largesse: he forced the institutions he endowed to transform themselves into more efficient, businesslike entities appropriating the
methods of science and the corporate ethos in their organization and peda-
gogy. At the same time, he supported the artificial re-creation of an image of
confident and closed communities built for an effective elite, and he encouraged the emergence of bastions of self-definition that convinced users of the
reality of a place through an appeal to their senses. Harkness's work may
therefore be interpreted as the rationalization of charity into the task of an
elite that did not remove itself from the realities of modernization, but sought
to guide them and incorporate them into its own methodology. It was James
Gamble Rogers who gave shape to these institutions.

Rogers' clientele thus represents the integration of the Midwestern
elite into the East Coast establishment. In a larger sense, it represents the
reinvigoration of the effective elite of this country through specific philosophical and pedagogical programs and through the adoption of vast
amounts of new wealth. The brilliance of the architecture of James Gamble
Rogers is that it managed to make this process look almost effortless. Root-
ing his buildings securely in the past and choosing models that exemplified
an ideal acceptable to both newcomers and entrenched elites—the models
were far enough away to be vague and specific enough to serve as clear
exemplars—he created sensuous, picturesque buildings constructed additive-
ly, as if they were responding to a logical accumulation of needs. The build-

ings are full of feints and twists and turns, but are always organized rationally. This is the very embodiment in architecture of the integration of romantic notions of empathy into the logic of modernization, a development T. J. Jackson Lears has traced in literature:

> Sentimentalizing emotional spontaneity and instinctual vitality, much antimodernism . . . melded with new-style theories of abundance and some versions of corporate liberal social engineering. All these responses to cultural crisis . . . helped ease the transition to secular and corporate modes of modern culture—new forms of evasiveness for a new social world.[9]

Rogers was a master at creating buildings whose interiors obeyed the strict laws of business and their underlying economic realities: organized around double-loaded corridors and built around repetitive cells, they were tightly planned and constructed out of the most up-to-date materials. Over these steel skeletons and institutional corridors Rogers would then throw a skin that alluded to England or France in the fourteenth century, Italy in the sixteenth century, America in the eighteenth century, or even some mythological, vaguely Mayan kingdom.

Yet the goals of the allusions were still quite specific. Rogers' own favorite style referred one particular privileged group to its roots: he chose the American Colonial forms employed "by a group of men who represented older values threatened by the rise of the city, who were Protestant in religion and English or Northern European in ancestry," to recall this group to its former strength and control over the country.[10] His Gothic forms, meanwhile, traced those roots even farther back.[11] The so-called Collegiate Gothic style developed by Rogers, which evoked the world of Oxford and Cambridge, elevated these references to the most elite status possible, as did his predilection for the aristocratic Georgian forms and imagery of the Southern plantation.

Yet Rogers' architecture went beyond this closed model for American cultural elitism and toward the integration of this model into its context by means of three architectural strategies: first, in what I would call the pavilionization of major program elements and the reliance on open space or courtyards; second, in the uses of Gothic and Georgian styles instead of Academic Classicism in his mature work; third, in the full exploitation of "picturing," which is to say, a visually organized, unstable, and experientially composed architecture. This resulted in buildings that wore their traditions lightly, not as a corpus of set rules, but as the accretion of the experience of the ages—what William James called "common sense"—that could be relived every day through experience. Modern methods of construction and planning were used, and, like historical styles, they were neither denied nor allowed to dominate, but instead were appropriated. Rather than alienating and grand, Rogers' architecture is convincing, sensuous, and richly enveloping.

The success of these designs was extraordinary. They still stand as some of the best institutional designs in America. Yet that success was circumscribed by the conditions under which they were built and by the logic of the design process itself. Rogers' work summarized the historical and functional appropriation that marked American architecture from the second half of the nineteenth century onward, and turned it from an eclectic agglomeration into a coherent structure exactly because it was embodying a philosophy of integration. It is under the shadow of Rogers' best work, not under the austere and pompous dome of Richard Morris Hunt's Classical architecture, that one can see "American thought tending towards unity."[12]

It was, however, an isolated unity, one reserved only for the effective elite of America. After 1910, Rogers' clients were few and choice, and part of what makes his buildings so successful is that they *are* closed bastions, cities set upon hills that serve as models for a future world lived in today only by the chosen few. By the time Rogers had built such confident statements, they were already dangerously overconfident. The emergence of new social groups entering into the effective elite, and the changed status of that elite itself, made the institutions look for forms that were more self-deprecating. James Gamble Rogers did not design the architecture of the bureaucratic populism of the Roosevelt era, nor did he share the utopian optimism that began to pervade cultural production in the 1930s. He was not Ralph Adams Cram nor Howard Roark nor Walter Gropius: he did not believe that architecture could save society, and never saw his forms existing outside of the typological constraints in which he worked. He was a pragmatist, not an idealist.

As a result, Rogers' work came under attack for being exactly what it was: elitist (even in its sensuous, accommodating way) and an attempt to discipline modernization by using existing styles and structures. As the times changed, his architecture adapted, appropriating the forms of Modernism as if they were just another part of the historical continuum. Unfortunately, Modernism was, as several critics have pointed out, the cloak of invisibility behind which elite institutions now sought to hide themselves. What happened in office buildings earlier in the century finally occurred in the last bastions of self-confident elitism: they disappeared into fragmented and translucent reflections of technological forces, and were in the end held together only by a contradictory notion of their own static monumentality. There was less and less need for the kind of architectural ideology Rogers provided so well. The final justification for the architecture of James Gamble Rogers became solipsistic: it was an educated and didactic architecture reserved for those who were predisposed to understand it. It was all a matter of taste: "For the introspective conscience of Puritanism, ['genteel' critics] substituted moral taste. The man who possessed this faculty would by definition be a gentleman. . . . It was true that gentlemen would no longer be born gentlemen, but that is where culture came in—it would train them up in the ways of moral taste."[13] Such questions of taste were easily replaced by the high ground of modernism, and even the populist eclecticism of Postmodernism could not serve to resuscitate Rogers' reputation.

Yet Rogers' vision survives today in institutions like Yale, where almost all of his designs still function as they originally were supposed to: they provide a physical setting for the rational acculturation of diverse entrants into the effective elite. That vision still holds a strong attraction. I was educated at Yale, I lived in the Harkness Memorial Quadrangle, and I learned about architecture surrounded by that of James Gamble Rogers. I absorbed this architecture's practical lessons—its choreography of spaces, its collaged compositions, its sensitivity to light and weather, at the same time as I learned the rules of etiquette, the modes of expression, and the workings of the Old Boy Network through which it is assumed that every Yale man will become a member of the nation's elite. I learned about the connection between architecture and appropriation of knowledge achieved through the tactile, immediate qualities of architectural artifacts, and this lesson is still more appealing than any grand, autonomous, and blank monument to mute and unchanging power.

1. James Gamble Rogers.

CHAPTER ONE

Foundations

James Gamble Rogers grew up in a middle-class subdivision on the north side of Chicago. His father, Joseph Martin Rogers, had moved to Chicago from Bryant's Station, Kentucky, during Reconstruction. It was in the Southern hamlet of Bryant's Station, situated in the middle of what is now the horse country outside of Lexington, that James Gamble was born in 1867 (Fig. 1). In his Yale Class Book, James Gamble said that he "was born in Bryant's Station, Ky, March 3, 1867. Traces his ancestry to Noah, but before that nothing is Noahn. His father is in the insurance business."[1] In fact, his family was well known around Kentucky. His great-grandfather, Joseph Rogers, had bought the two thousand acres on which Bryant's Station was founded in 1780 and had moved there in 1784 from Virginia. By the time he died in 1832, he was one of the largest land and slave owners in the area.[2]

Joseph's grandson, Joseph Martin Rogers, married Katherine Gamble, daughter of an Irish family who had been in Kentucky since the early 1700s. Moreover, the two were distantly related by marriage and counted among their in-laws such luminaries as William Clark of Lewis and Clark Expedition fame and pioneer George Rogers Clark.[3] Apparently Bryant's Station was either too small or too devastated after the Civil War to support Joseph Rogers and his new family, and shortly after James Gamble's birth the family moved to Chicago.

Joseph Martin Rogers soon made enough money selling insurance to buy a house in the new Buena Park subdivision on the Northside and to support a family made up of Katherine (apparently a strong presence), and sons James Gamble, Bernard Fowler, and John Arthur. Both James Gamble and John Arthur became architects, while Bernard followed his father into the insurance business.

The home in which James Gamble Rogers grew up was fortunately situated. Buena Park was one of many subdivisions constructed to house the explosive growth in population that Chicago experienced during the last quarter of the nineteenth century.[4] This particular development was on land owned by the occupants of "Buena House," J. B. Waller and family. Several doors down from the Rogers' family residence, #74, was the home of architect William Bryce Mundie, of the office of William LeBaron Jenney, where James Gamble Rogers obtained his first employment in architecture. J. B. Waller was born in Maysville, Kentucky, and counted among his friends a number of families in Versailles, twenty miles outside of Lexington, who were later to become clients of James Gamble Rogers. Waller made his fortune not only by dealing in real estate and building apartment buildings, but also by selling fire and general insurance.[5] He presided over a prosperous community with a strong Southern flavor and a coherence fondly recalled by residents, including James Gamble, forty years later.[6]

Rogers attended Division High School, a nearby public school, and graduated in 1885. For him, unlike his brothers, graduation did not mark the end of his formal training: he received a scholarship to attend Yale College. James Gamble Rogers was the first member of his family to attend an Ivy League college, and his four years in New Haven brought him into altogether different circles from those in which he had grown up. Whereas in Buena Park his family and friends were mostly white Christian Americans from the South engaged in one of the clerical professions, Rogers' classmates and friends at Yale included scions of wealthy New York clans, descendants of old New England families, Jews, and self-made "boys" such as himself from all parts of America.

James Gamble, or Gamble, as he was known at Yale, quickly made a mark in this condensed world of high-class culture: when a classmate from Atlanta was asked to list his "favorite amusement" for the 1889 Class Book, he singled out "listening to Gimble [sic] Rogers' jokes."[7] Education of the classical sort does not appear to have been central in Gamble's Yale experience, as he himself would note toward the end of his life, when he wrote: "I think that the funniest is that anyone with such a college scholastic record as mine should later in life become so interested in education."[8] For Gamble, Yale was the place where he was introduced to a particular culture. His world was made up of shared amusements, sports, and a tradition acquired and continually renewed in the collective and ritualized activities of a group of young men just starting to define their lives. It was this "Yale spirit" that Gamble, his classmates, and colleagues later spent ten years of their lives trying to define, rescue, and reconstitute in a viable form, and Gamble himself was the first to acknowledge the primacy of social values in this spirit.[9]

At Yale, Gamble became one of the editors of the undergraduate magazine *Pot Pourri*. He was also a member—and in his senior year the manager—of the baseball team. In the meantime, during his freshman year he managed to receive some of the lowest grades in his class and during his sophomore year earned reprimands for his poor academic performance. By the end of his junior year, however, he received one of the most important forms of recognition the college had to offer: he was "tapped" or elected to the Scroll & Key secret society, one of the three most exclusive and powerful senior organizations in the college. His election to this group, made up of sixteen men whose predecessors in the senior class had supposedly identified them as leaders in the various important aspects of Yale society, marked his arrival in the inner circle of social respectability at Yale.[10]

In the summer after his graduation, Gamble traveled to Europe for the first time. He managed to receive this "grand tour" not as a graduation present, as did many of his classmates, but as part of the tour of an exhibition baseball team organized by A. J. Spalding to introduce Europeans to this latest American invention. Gamble never discussed this tour, nor his choice of career, but when he returned to Chicago in the summer of 1889, he went to work in the office of William LeBaron Jenney, where his neighbor, William Bryce Mundie, was a rising star.

Rogers at this point had, as far as can be ascertained, no formal architectural training at all. Certainly Yale did not offer courses in a profession only just receiving respectability.[11] Yet the first firm for which he worked was one of the most fertile breeding grounds of successful architects in Chicago. In an often quoted remark, Siegfried Giedion pointed out that "William LeBaron Jenney played much the same role in the younger generation of Chicago architects that Peter Behrens did in Germany around 1910, or Auguste Perret in France. He gave young architects the preparation they needed to tackle the new problems for which the schools could offer no solutions."[12] Among Rogers' fellow alumni of this alternative to an architecture school were Louis Sullivan, both William Holabird and Martin Roche, and Daniel Burnham.

Whereas Rogers had learned about baseball, culture, and social graces at Yale, in Jenney's office he was exposed to the business of architecture. "Major Jenney," as he preferred to be called, had been a chief engineer in the Civil War, and had been trained not at the Ecole des Beaux-Arts but at the Ecole Centrale des Arts et Manufactures. After he moved to Chicago in 1867, he began an office and capitalized on the building boom in downtown Chicago. He designed efficient office buildings with a coherent image by employing a method of construction based on utilizing the strength and repetitive nature of steel in combination with a thin and malleable skin of fireproof terra-cotta and glass. Whether or not Jenney's 1885 Home Insurance Building is the first skyscraper, his method of making architecture set the tone for downtown Chicago construction until he was eclipsed by his pupils in the 1890s.[13]

To Jenney and his "Chicago School" followers, *business* was not a dirty word: the business of architecture was to compose and erect the structures of business. If architects were taught, according to the precepts of the Ecole des Beaux-Arts, that their primary responsibility was the designing of appropriate focal points and monuments to the central institutions of society, then American architects could look to the corporations that were transforming the American social, economic, and physical landscape as their natural field of action.[14] To Louis Sullivan, such a course of action was almost a religion, in which the logical economic "action and interaction" that created the "modern office building" had created a structure in which "a new grouping of social conditions has found a habitation and a name," whose construction will lead to the perfection of "a natural and satisfying art, and architecture that will soon become a fine art in the true, the best sense of the word. . . ."[15]

To those less imbued with Sullivan's romantic sense of purpose, the nascent Chicago School, which defined itself during the 1890s through the foundation of the Western Association of Architects and through the voice of Robert Craik McLean in the magazine *Inland Architect*, was made up of architects who specialized in creating buildings for business, in opposition to their East Coast colleagues, who still saw the center of their profession as lying in the creation of cultural institutions and monumental residences. The hardheaded Chicago approach was one that used imported styles as a way of giving coherence to what was seen by many as essentially an engineering achievement. [16]

Jenney's greatest success—though it was not a unique one—may be said to have lain in his ability to transform an eclectic amalgamation of romantic styles (Neo-Gothic, Neo-Romanesque) and academic orders into a coherent cladding for a construction whose low cost and technical perfection made the production of the image possible. Whether his sources were vernacular[17] or based on French examples, the result was, in his eyes, still art: he called his office an "atelier" and believed all architecture students should speak French—even if his own command of that language was atrocious.[18] His business was the basis for a life of bonhomie and social exuberance, and he became the prototype of the architect as a hard-nosed businessman in the American tradition whose task it was to clad himself, his buildings, and his clients with the cultural signification that articulated the purposes for which they all worked. It was a model that James Gamble Rogers was to follow effectively.

In Rogers' own evaluation, his first architectural position was crucial not only for his own development, but also for that of the firm:

> . . .all during my career I have been greatly benefited by the many good things that I learned in his office. Such things as I learned there made such a deep impression on my mind that I do not believe it possible ever to forget them. . . . The custom of that time was for any man starting in the office to work for six months without pay. . . . It is pleasing to have this opportunity to testify to the fact that Jenney taught well the men in his office, always insisting on sensible methods and good, sound construction and it is greatly to his credit that he had such a good idea of construction. Yes, Jenney had a great reputation, but nevertheless, Mundie was the architect of the office and its dominating force. . . . Through one or two friends I was able to bring a certain amount of work into the office. When I was able to do this in connection with a man who was to erect the largest building that had come into the office, I asked my

friend to make one of the conditions that Mr. Mundie should be a partner. It succeeded and so the name of the office was changed from W. LeB. Jenney to Jenney & Mundie, Architects.[19]

2. Jenney & Mundie. Manhattan Building, Chicago, Illinois, 1889–91.

Rogers' assertions, that Mundie was the central designer in the office and that Rogers was responsible for the change in the firm's structure, cannot be confirmed, though Rogers did not usually engage in self-aggrandizement.[20] The largest building to come in to the office during this period was the Manhattan Building, finished in 1891, but there is no reason to link Rogers with its builders (Fig. 2). The story does illustrate the freewheeling, go-getting atmosphere that appears to have prevailed in the architectural world of Chicago during this period. It is not inconceivable, given the achievements of some of his contemporaries (Frank Lloyd Wright, designing major houses and running Sullivan's office at the same age, comes to mind), that the twenty-three-year-old young man with strong local ties and newfound social connections could play a strong role in the development of a major downtown building. One has only to note, for instance, that John Wellborn Root, the leader of the next generation of architects after men like Jenney and Sullivan, was not yet forty years old at the time.[21]

To James Gamble Rogers, his "apprenticeship" was a valuable but not all-encompassing learning experience:

> I have always felt that I was most fortunate in not having had enough money to enable me, after college, to go to Boston Tech [M.I.T—*author*] or Columbia, which stood very high as an architectural school at the time, but instead had to work in an office. I learned so much more from both Mr. Jenney and Mr. Mundie that I have always had the greatest feeling of appreciation of my good luck in having gotten my fundamentals in such an office. I never was able to do the pen and ink work in spite of such an opportunity. I believe now that of all the learners, Elmer C. Jensen was so much more proficient that we others did not like to show our inferior work so I missed the golden opportunity to learn to be a good pen and ink artist which would have stood me in good stead when I was earning my living in Paris making perspectives.[22]

This rambling reminiscence, typical of Rogers' writing style, defines the role Jenney's office played in introducing the young Yale graduate to the world of making buildings out of real materials in response to the needs of real clients—"the fundamentals." It also shows Rogers marking himself early on as an eager young man who concentrated on business (bringing clients in) over art, and used art only as a tool in his career. Whether or not such a self-portrayal is accurate, it certainly points out where James Gamble Rogers placed his priorities.

After less than two years, Rogers left the Jenney & Mundie office to join the fast-growing practice of Burnham & Root. His position there was a lofty one: he was Superintendent of Building for the Ashland Block (1892), the largest building then in that office and an important addition to downtown Chicago during the boom years right before the 1893 depression (Fig. 3). Given the fluidity of the profession at the time, it is possible that Rogers was indeed the most qualified man, in terms of architectural and managerial skills, for this position. But the Ashland Block was owned (at least publicly) by Robert A. Waller, brother of the Buena Avenue neighbor J. B. Waller, and Lucas Broadhead of Versailles, Kentucky, a friend of the Wallers' and later a client of James Gamble Rogers.[23]

3. Burnham & Root. Ashland Block, Chicago, Illinois, 1891–92.

Rogers did not stay at the Burnham office for very long, though he seems to have left on good terms: Daniel Burnham was instrumental in obtaining for Rogers one of the latter's first major civic commissions,[24] and James Gamble's brother John Arthur later designed a thirteen-story addition to the Ashland Block.[25] Certainly Rogers' experience working for a firm that was the prototype of the large, commercially oriented type of firm that was later to dominate American architecture must have been valuable. Rogers had managed, in two years, to work for the two firms that stood at the core of the development of the Chicago School.[26] By 1891, however, the two brothers had struck out on their own.

On October 24, 1891, the Chicago newspaper *The Economist* announced that the project for the corner of Madison and Fifth streets, "which has been under consideration for some time now," was to go ahead on January 1, 1892, ". . . and the plans will be prepared by James Gamble Rogers, who is now superintending the construction of the Ashland Block. . . . The building will be first class in every particular, only the best materials being used. The interior will be superbly furnished."[27] There is no record of any other architect being involved with the design of the structure. The building as constructed cost $325,000 and did indeed "present a substantial appearance" to contemporary viewers.[28] The agent for the owner of the building—the latter was a Mrs. S. P. Lees of New York—was William Waller, another member of the clan that was so helpful to Rogers' early career.[29]

The Lees Building was constructed on a fireproofed steel frame and clad with pressed brick and terra-cotta (Fig. 4). The Rand McNally Company, in its compendium of downtown Chicago buildings, called it "the best lighted office building in the city."[30] Unfortunately the Lees Building was torn down in 1969. This first building for which James Gamble Rogers was substantially responsible was an essay in business design squarely in the traditions of what has been dubbed retroactively the Chicago School. The front of the building was divided into five bays defined by brick piers rising from a two-story base. The only decoration on the building was concentrated in the

4. James Gamble Rogers. Lees Building, Chicago, Illinois, 1891–93.

brick and terra-cotta sills, lintels, and cornices. The base appeared massive because of the lack of vertical elements, the deep window openings on the second floor, and the large arched door. The Lees Building was a thoroughly businesslike, well-composed building, displaying no surfeit of decoration or articulation other than what was necessary to make the building recognizable and representative of its kind.[31]

Rogers thus seemed well on his way to becoming a successful practitioner who could use his family, his neighborhood, and his Yale connections to convert his practical experience with Jenney & Mundie and Burnham & Root into buildings for Chicago's business community. Yet less than a year after receiving the Lees commission, in the summer of 1892, James Gamble Rogers left Chicago to study architecture and construction at the Ecole des Beaux-Arts in Paris. One can only speculate why he would leave a city in the midst of its most sustained economic expansion ever—a city, moreover, that was about to stage its own coming out party in the form of the World's Columbian Exposition, whose design was in the hands of the firm for whom Rogers was working. Perhaps Rogers had no direct prospects for further work, or perhaps the Lees commission gave him the funds he had lacked after graduating from Yale to pursue an architectural education. It is probable that Rogers recognized that an academic training was increasingly a prerequisite for receiving important civic and residential commissions. The design of the "White City" at the 1893 Exposition only confirmed this development, though many of Rogers' contemporaries continued to thrive as architects after only a practical education. Rogers' report to his Yale classmates in 1896 was short, commenting only that he:

. . . has been engaged in the study of architecture ever since graduation. He was first in the office of W.L.B. Jenney, Chicago, Illinois, and then became superintendent of the construction of the Ashland block. . . . He opened his office as a practical architect, but finally decided to interrupt his practice by taking a course in designing in Paris. He passed the February, 1894, examinations for the Ecole des Beaux-Arts, and is now an enrolled student. . . [32]

Rogers was by no means the only American at the Ecole during his stay. In the ateliers of his professors, Louis Henry Georges Scellier de Gisors and Paul Blondel, Rogers was joined during this period by his later friend Donn Barber, Philadelphia, architect and campus designer C. C. Zantzinger, Ernest Flagg, and Grosvenor Atterbury. His future partner, Herbert D. Hale, had entered three years previously.[33] Moreover, he was following the lead of contemporaries such as Howard Van Doren Shaw who were at the time leaving their native Chicago to gain an education in Europe or the East Coast and who would later, like Rogers, return as cultured designers for an increasingly cultured clientele.[34]

Rogers lived at various addresses in the Latin Quarter and in the autumn of 1898 culminated his education by receiving a "maximum note" for his thesis design, "A House for the United States Embassy at Paris," while receiving a diploma and "medals" in both design and construction.[35]

What Rogers learned at the Ecole was a deliberate and rather abstract way of making buildings. By the 1890s, the teaching of the Ecole had become fairly unified across all of the ateliers, having assimilated a series of revolutions and contradictory movements, the last of which had been the "néo-Grec" revolt of thirty years before. Though tensions remained between various theoretical positions, such as those between Auguste Choisy and Julien Guadet, the most consistent debate within the Ecole was that of how to use evolving modern technology and how to design for such new types as office buildings, departments stores, and railroad stations. By the turn of the century, the teachers at the Ecole, included among them Scelliers de Gisors, had proved that it was indeed possible to use steel and glass in combination with stone and other traditional building methods. What remained unchanged were the two organizational principles for composing buildings, the "parti" and the use of the orders.

The parti, or overall layout of the building, was seen as the primary organizational principle for any building. One determined the most important space in the building, placed it at the focal point of the site, developed a major axis to serve this function, then developed cross axes to serve the progressively less important spaces. The whole design was composed through the use of a rigid geometry first developed in the eighteenth century, with

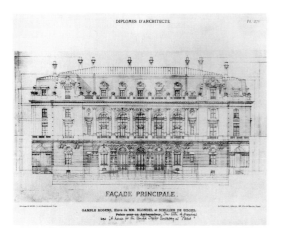

5. James Gamble Rogers. "A House for the United States Embassy in Paris." Diploma project, Ecole des Beaux-Arts, Paris, 1898. Front elevation.

6. James Gamble Rogers. "A House for the United States Embassy in Paris." Diploma project, Ecole des Beaux-Arts, Paris, 1898. Garden elevation.

structure and subsidiary spaces used (as "poches") to allow the major spaces to obtain their formal purity.

The second constant of the teachings of the Ecole was the correct use of "the orders," including not just columns, pediments, and bases, but also the elaborate proportioning systems and ornamental language developed at the Ecole and continually fine-tuned to meet the demands of changing materials and iconographies. Taken as a whole, this method of designing produced an architecture that has been described as Academic Classicism. One of its greatest virtues was that, as a system, it was eminently transportable, and Rogers was just one of many "colonials" who imported their knowledge from Paris.[36]

The work Rogers did at the Ecole, if his thesis project is any indication, is not especially remarkable, and the execution of the drawings does seem inferior to the work of some of his contemporaries (Figs. 5, 6).[37] The American Embassy design is a dry essay in that strange mixture of palatial residential elements and institutional scale that did so much to damn the efforts of the pupils of the Ecole in later years. A solid, six-story building, it presents a garden facade and a "principal" or street frontage distinguishable only by the presence of portes cochères and two-story arched windows above the heavily striated base on the front. One can recognize such motifs as the disengaged flat lintels posed over the third-story windows, the complete suppression of a central focus, and the rather dramatic striations that occur in later Rogers buildings, but these elements are here placed in a composition that is as much an integral part of its architectural context as the Lees Building's brick arches and structural expression were part of the Chicago School.[38]

Rogers' achievement at the Ecole, however, stands in marked contrast to his lackluster academic record at Yale. If Yale had served to make him into a young gentleman, a high-living and convivial member of a class of people who saw themselves as living out the role of a social, economic, and cultural elite, then the Ecole gave him the aesthetic rules through which he was able to define and discipline such a vague purpose. The Ecole des Beaux-Arts taught its students to compose buildings according to a method validated by a social and economic order that their buildings were, in turn, to celebrate and ratify. The classicizing monuments produced by Beaux-Arts–trained architects thus fixed and made real a complex set of assumed social values and economic relationships. The ability to control the composition of this representation—whether as client, user, designer, or comprehending viewer and critic—marked one as a distinct and distinguishing member of an elite: if one could own, build, commission, design, or physically or mentally enter into the central institutions of our society, one had power.[39]

James Gamble Rogers' fellow students at Yale either had such power by birth or gained it through an education in one of the professions that rationalized, organized, and created a framework for power. Places such as Yale helped to pull together an effective elite out of an increasingly large and socially diverse society, and to provide that elite with a series of markers by which they might define themselves: a certain use of language, the ritual of sports, and shared literary, artistic, and political traditions.[40] The fluidity of the business world to which Rogers turned after his education gave him the chance to learn the constituent parts and parameters of the field of operation open to the members of that elite. At the Ecole, Rogers learned how he could organize these worlds into programs and representations that were coherent, functional, and clear in their ability to communicate to his chosen audience. He learned a trade.

Rogers' position upon his return to Chicago in 1898 was an enviable one. He was living in the most active and fast-growing metropolis in America. He understood and was part of the forces organizing that environment. He could bring to that metropolis the material by which it might assemble in concrete form a system of values that could serve as its built ideology or raison d'être. At the age of thirty-one, he was ready to use his charm, wit, talent, and ambition to take full advantage of that position. He was a member of a brash young group of designers, led by Frank Lloyd Wright and Dwight Perkins, who were just emerging as the first generation of native architects, designers who were to develop the Chicago School in the domestic and civic realms as the Prairie School.[41]

When Rogers returned from Paris, he went into business with his brother, John Arthur, who had maintained an office in the Ashland Block all during Gamble's absence and had designed an annex to the Ashland Block during that period.[42] There is no record of John Arthur having received any formal training, and he did not practice fully independently until he left Chicago fifteen years later. It is therefore difficult to assess Gamble's relationship with his brother, though it is clear that the former took the lead in the office both before and after his stay at the Ecole.[43]

The office James Gamble Rogers headed in Chicago between 1898 and 1905 was an active and diverse one. Starting immediately upon his return, Rogers engaged in the design of a series of residential commissions that included grand mansions, town houses, apartment buildings, and developer housing. He also designed two important educational structures, a church, and a few commercial buildings. These buildings were programmatically, stylistically, and contextually diverse. In carrying them out, Rogers defined some of the organizing principles of his architecture. He also started to map out a career created out of a combination of social contacts and an expertise in the organization of educational institutions.

The residential work came first. Like his work before his departure to Paris, the earliest of these commissions were tied to the neighborhood in which he grew up. In July 1899, *The Economist* announced the planned construction, at a cost of $350,000, of a luxurious apartment building in the heart of Chicago's Gold Coast. The client was J. B. Waller.[44] The project was abandoned, however, and not resurrected until 1905, when Rogers designed a three-story building for a third of the original budget, remarkable chiefly for the ingenious manner in which the formal rooms of each apartment faced onto the street, while the service rooms snaked back-to-back down half of a middle wing along the axis of the diagonal corner entry.[45]

Rogers also worked for developers who were continuing the construction of neighborhoods like Buena Park farther north. In August 1901, Rogers designed two groups of speculative houses for the prolific builder Sam Brown, Jr.: eight houses on Dover Street and eleven on Winthrop Street (Figs. 7, 8).[46] All but three of the houses were to cost under $5,000, and all were of the kind of plaster-and-timber Tudor style that Rogers had probably learned as the construction manager for a group of extremely similar houses designed in Buena Park by Jenney & Mundie.[47] Within the confines of budget and standardized plans, Rogers produced a series of remarkably varied and dignified homes. "While they will be inexpensive," *The Economist* noted, "it will be the aim of the architect to make them very complete and to finish them in a style equal to that of many houses of a much higher grade and costing much more money. Some will be constructed of boulders and shingles and some of stone and plasters, while others will be frame."[48] Porches built up out of Richardsonian masses of boulders and treated as separate pavilions, roofs supported on articulated frames, and grids of half-timber that organized the functionally placed and scaled windows, all served to carry out this romantic domestic image.

7. James Gamble Rogers.
Houses on Dover Street,
Chicago, Illinois, 1901.

8. James Gamble Rogers.
House on Winthrop Street,
Chicago, Illinois, 1901.

9. James Gamble Rogers.
Vonnah Apartment Building,
Chicago, Illinois, 1901–2.

10. George W. Maher.
Seymour House, Chicago,
Illinois, 1913.

That same fall, Rogers designed a large apartment building along Sheridan Avenue, the main thoroughfare connecting these subdivisions. The Vonnah, as the building was named (after its builder), is a three-story block completely filling its 130-by-160-foot lot and constructed "in the English style of architecture" (Fig. 9).[49] The abstraction of the entrance elements, the deep shadow of the attic, which allows the roof to appear to float above the block of the apartments, and the Arts and Crafts detailing of the brickwork make this apartment building reminiscent of the work of turn-of-the-century Chicago architects such as George Maher, whose work hovers sensibly and confidently between the dignity of a stripped-down Classicism and the exaggerated vernacular of the Prairie School.

In fact, there is a marked similarity during this period between the work of Rogers and that of Maher (Fig. 10). Rogers, in buildings like The Vonnah, followed Maher in adopting the cleaner lines, more prominent roofs, and abstracted geometries Maher started to affect around the turn of the century. Rogers was the same age as Maher, Frank Lloyd Wright, and many other members of what was to become the Prairie School, and for a while he seemed to be following his peers in their adaptation of the influences of European architects like Joseph Maria Olbrich and C.F.A. Voysey. But while Wright, Purcell & Elmslie, and Maher continued these investigations as ways of turning the Chicago School emphasis on structure into both decoration and geometric abstraction by stripping their buildings down to concatenations of spaces and sparse walls, Rogers followed this movement only briefly, returning, like Van Doren Shaw, to the use of more literal historical styles shortly thereafter.[50]

Perhaps his choice of architectural approaches was influenced by a change in his clientele. While hard at work in his old neighborhood, Rogers was also expanding his social and, as a result, his professional horizons. Many of the larger homes he designed during this period were for clients who were friends or family of the woman James Gamble Rogers married on October 12, 1901.[51] Anne Day was one of the five daughters of Albert Morgan Day, the second president of the Chicago Stock Exchange, president of the Presbyterian Hospital, and a pillar of Chicago society who could trace his ancestry back to the *Mayflower*.[52] Mr. Day was related through his wife to the McCormick family, owners of the McCormick Reaper works.

Even more important for Rogers' future career, Anne's older sister was married to Francis C. Farwell, who belonged to one of the oldest families in Chicago. John V. Farwell, the patriarch of the clan, had first started a store with Marshall Field, and then gone into dry-goods wholesaling; by the turn of the century he was one of the largest property owners in Chicago. Francis's brother Arthur was married to Katherine Isham, daughter and sister of two prominent physicians and downtown property owners, while another brother, John V. Farwell, Jr., later became president of the Yale Corporation, chairman of its Corporation Committee on the Campus Plan, an active participant in James Gamble Rogers' career, and a close friend of the Rogers family.[53] James Gamble Rogers' marriage was apparently an extremely happy one, but it also changed his sphere of operation and allowed him to achieve many of his ambitions. Within a few years after the marriage, he had abandoned his Baptist upbringing for the Presbyterian church and had moved from Buena Park, by way of downtown Chicago, to the most exclusive Chicago suburb, Lake Forest.[54]

The first and grandest of the mansions James Gamble Rogers designed for this group of friends and families was a residence for Dr. George Isham, Katherine Isham's brother, on State Street in the Gold Coast area of Chicago (Fig. 11).[55] Dr. George Isham (1859–1926) possessed a considerable fortune and played an active role in the economic and social life of the city.[56] Isham himself was also a Yale man, having "come down from New Haven" in 1884, and it is not inconceivable that the tightly knit circle of graduates from that faraway fairytale land welcomed Rogers into this circle after he had put the finishing touches on his cultural and professional character in Paris.

The Isham commission was large ($50,000, according to *The Economist*'s projections).[57] Moreover, it was situated in one of the most prestigious neighborhoods in the city. Announced in June 1899, it was occupied by the

11. James Gamble Rogers.
Isham House, Chicago, Illinois,
1899–1903.

Ishams by the end of the following year.[58] The house is an imposing and solid-seeming block of brick adorned with limestone trim. Its simple and forthright appearance is marred only by the addition of the doctor's office entrance wing projecting to the south. The main entrance is a modest door in the middle of the front elevation. The facade displays a mixture of simple classicizing window surrounds, porches, and pedimented gables, with detailing carried out in pressed brick in the "English Style" of Norman Shaw then popular in Chicago. Inside, a cramped, marble-clad hallway and vestibule lead one to the middle of the house, where a light court blocks one's direct passage.

Though countless restorations and alterations make it difficult to differentiate clearly the various original rooms and spatial sequences—the building became notorious during the 1960s when it was the home of *Playboy* publisher Hugh Hefner, who installed colored lights in the ballroom, a kitchen in the light well, and a grotto swimming pool in the basement—the house does present some of the strengths and odd mannerisms James Gamble Rogers was to exhibit more fully in later houses. The reserved quality of a house whose scale and importance in the community might have led another architect toward a more exuberant manipulation of either mass or detailing serves to create a dignified, confident presence for the house. The suppressed entrance sequence denies the primacy of ceremonial paths in favor of filling the volume of the construction with as many usable rooms as possible. The unresolved secondary doctor's entrance and service wing strengthen the primacy of functional considerations in the massing of the house, while the sparing yet fully correct detailing and proportioning of the facade place the building firmly within the realm of cultured, self-confident architecture and social life.

Rogers also worked in his new neighborhood of Lake Forest. The Farwells, the Days, and some of the McCormicks together had a compound or colony there, whose entrance was a Rogers-designed stone gate in the boulder-and-timber manner of his developer houses.[59] During 1902, Rogers designed a series of structures for the staff. These were small houses clad with stucco and timber and marked by clearly expressed roof rafters and entrance elements. He also created a few small pergolas and garden structures. He renovated a ten-year-old house on the site for his father-in-law (Figs. 12, 13), and built a new mansion for Arthur Farwell (Fig. 14). The latter was a two-

12. James Gamble Rogers. A. M. Day House, Lake Forest, Illinois, 1905.

13. James Gamble Rogers. A. M. Day House, Lake Forest, Illinois, 1905. Interior.

14. James Gamble Rogers. Arthur Farwell House, Lake Forest, Illinois, 1902.

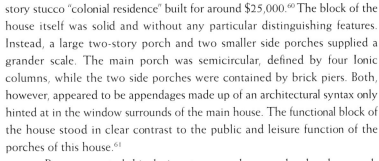

15. James Gamble Rogers.
H. S. Robbins House, Lake
Forest, Illinois, 1903.

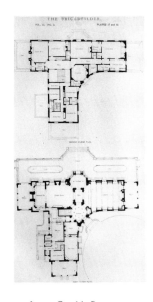

16. James Gamble Rogers.
A. B. Dick House, Lake Forest,
Illinois, 1902. Plan.

story stucco "colonial residence" built for around $25,000.[60] The block of the
house itself was solid and without any particular distinguishing features.
Instead, a large two-story porch and two smaller side porches supplied a
grander scale. The main porch was semicircular, defined by four Ionic
columns, while the two side porches were contained by brick piers. Both,
however, appeared to be appendages made up of an architectural syntax only
hinted at in the window surrounds of the main house. The functional block of
the house stood in clear contrast to the public and leisure function of the
porches of this house.[61]

Rogers repeated this device at an even larger scale when he remodeled a house down the street from the Farwell compound for H. S. Robbins
(Fig. 15; see also Fig. 19). Here Rogers moved and enlarged a white Colo-
nial-style structure clad in wood, thus changing a small cottage into "a thorough colonial house enhanced by an appropriate setting," facing Sheridan
Road with a six-columned, two-story portico and a long pergola that partially hid the confusion of windows on the long facade. "In this house," the
reviewer writing in *Architectural Record* commented, "the architect has secured
dignity by adding an effective but not very utilitarian feature on colossal
columns."[62] Indeed, neither the Farwell nor the Robbins porch served as anything else than an entrance element. In this manner, the porches stood in for
the central focus, grand entry sequence, and central axis that were completely lacking from the houses themselves. Thus, architecture as a stylistic manipulation of autonomous elements that allow the "character" or social function
of the structure to be articulated clearly was consciously added on to a structure defined by function, rather than arising out of the design process itself.

By far the largest house James Gamble Rogers designed during this
period was the now-demolished A. B. Dick Residence (Fig. 16). It presented a
strange collection of formal elements in an el-shaped building sited in the middle of an extensive estate.[63] Rogers designed at least two other smaller houses
in the Lake Forest area during this period, as well as one in Hyde Park, the

17. James Gamble Rogers.
F. H. Page House, Highland
Park, Illinois, 1902.

18. James Gamble Rogers.
C. Edward Pope House, Lake
Forest, Illinois, 1902.

fashionable neighborhood just north of the University of Chicago. The F .H.
Page House of 1902, in Highland Park, was a stucco volume covered with a
grid of expressed timber and sheltered by a shingle roof (Fig. 17).[64]

The C. Edward Pope House, built in Lake Forest in the same year,
was a much more radical statement of Rogers' design strategy of the period
(Fig. 18). As a contemporary reviewer remarked: "This interesting house is the
result of practically disregarding any attempt at architectural treatment. It was
planned, the walls were built and plastered, the windows punched through
wherever they were needed."[65] The plaster of the house was deliberately
roughened, and the magazine noted the absence of a cornice or other consistent architectural detailing. Instead, a long porch covered the entrance area
with a slanting roof, while smaller versions of similar shingled roofs were suspended over the master bedroom window and a side porch. Inside, trim once
again was lacking, and the rooms on both floors were arranged on either side
of a narrow corridor that ran parallel to the gable (and perpendicular to the
entrance axis). The rough and self-assured functionality of the house give it
the image of a Swiss cottage. It is a rustic, artful, and simple retreat away from
the city.[66] One can sense the influence of the Arts and Crafts movement in

19. James Gamble Rogers. H. S. Robbins House, Lake Forest, Illinois, 1904–5. Living room.

20. James Gamble Rogers. F. H. Finch House, Chicago, Illinois, 1903.

21. James Gamble Rogers. F. H. Finch House, Chicago, Illinois, 1903. Plan.

these humble but elaborate details and in the concentration on pattern over the delineation of formal spaces. The same can be said for the H. S. Robbins House, built 1904–5 (Fig. 19; see also Fig. 15).

In Rogers' other large in-town house of the period he took abstraction of form and experimentation with arrangement of rooms a step farther. The F. H. Finch House, built in 1903, is a cruciform two-story brick structure (Figs. 20, 21). The clarity of this geometry, more reminiscent of Frank Lloyd Wright than of the formal homes around it, is masked by several porches. The house actually displays a strange mix of detailing: a French door with a curved transom interrupted by a rondel—a door design that became a favorite motif in Rogers' work—is lifted a foot off the ground and screened off from the street by a diminutive stone balustrade. Above, a bedroom window, framed by Colonial shutters, sports a simple slab as a sort of detached sill echoing its French classicizing counterpart below.

The inside is even more convoluted. A wall forces one to turn 90 degrees inside a small vestibule, then one must turn again to avoid a closet, before entering a central hall defined by four columns. A "parlor" acts as a side room to this central space, while the living and dining rooms rotate around the four-square heart. Solids and voids pivot in a Wrightian manner, while retaining a more familiar formality.[67] Though Rogers was obviously working in architectural idioms that were familiar to his clients, he was displaying a certain amount of inventiveness based on functionality and a more

22. James Gamble Rogers.
Laurel Court (Peter Thomson
House), Cincinnati, Ohio,
1904–8.

playful compositional sense. The Finch and Pope houses were, however, the
last time Rogers was to engage in this kind of overt experimentation. Once
again, one assumes that his subsequent channeling of his personal experi-
mentations with architectural form into more sedate formats was dictated by
a clientele that was increasingly upper crust and increasingly concerned with
defining itself as part of a nationwide elite, rather than as a group of self-
made men and women.

In 1904, James Gamble Rogers worked on an extensive remodeling
for Mrs. Emmons Blaine, his client on a much larger institutional project during the same period,[68] and received his first major commission outside of the
Chicago area. Once again, the commission came through a family connection. His aunt, Laura Gamble Thomson, had left Kentucky to marry, against
the opposition of her family, a young clerk in Cincinnati. That clerk, Peter
Gibson Thomson, converted his job at a bookstore into the ownership of the
Champion Paper Company. In 1904, by now one of the richest men in Ohio,
he commissioned his wife's cousin to design Laurel Court, a grand residence
on the outskirts of Cincinnati.[69]

Working at a large scale on an ample site, Rogers displayed both his
command of Academic Classicism and his ability to deviate from its strictures (Figs. 22, 23). When Montgomery Schuyler came to see the completed
building four years later, he remarked that Laurel Court was the only palatial residence in Cincinnati, "a 'villa' in the Italian sense as well as in the Italian
style. . . . This is much more in the regular way of the most modern of our
palatial country seats."[70] The grand house was in fact modeled rather directly,

23. James Gamble Rogers.
Laurel Court (Peter Thomson
House), Cincinnati, Ohio,
1904–8. Detail, facade.

at least as far as the facade went, after Richard Morris Hunt's Marble House in Newport, Rhode Island. Schuyler thought that Rogers had actually improved on the Hunt model. "Given the classic scheme," Schuyler concluded, "the architect of the Cincinnati house is to be congratulated on the scholarly and exemplary execution of the same."[71]

The outside of Laurel Court indeed reveals the full control of Classical elements of which Rogers was capable. This detailing is heightened by the rather deep incisions with which Rogers marked the moldings and the blocks of granite. The latter serve to ground the Classical elements solidly in a rich and clear materiality, substantiating the scholarly articulation through the emphasis on the basic building blocks out of which the orders are constructed. On the outside, only the long pergola connecting a detached side porch—itself a more lavish stone version of such elements in the Day and Finch houses—with the elaborate gardens, and a brick stable and service structure which is almost a direct replica of the one on the A. B. Dick Estate, remind one of the more relaxed residential structures Rogers had designed around Chicago.

On the inside, however, the palatial formality of the house is once again mitigated by the use of a long cross corridor as the primary circulation element leading off in either direction from a small but richly decorated vestibule (Fig. 24). The main public rooms are placed at either end of this corridor and fill the solid wings of the building, while service spaces create a corresponding U around the back of the house. What is left over is a small courtyard, clad in brick and filled with lush vegetation. The heart of this solid and solemn apparition of Classicism is thus revealed as a romantic, nondirectional, and completely protected retreat. Given the fact that Laura Gamble Thomson felt uncomfortable with the grand style to which her husband's success had accustomed her, it is this courtyard that is perhaps the true Laurel Court of the residence.[72] Together with the long string of bedrooms inter-

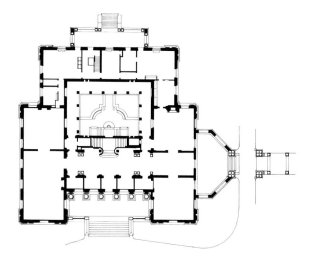

24. James Gamble Rogers.
Laurel Court (Peter Thomson
House), Cincinnati, Ohio,
1904–8. Plan.

spaced with dressing rooms and bathrooms, opening up with wood slat doors
that respond to the often hot and humid summer weather of Cincinnati, the
inside of the Thomson house creates a place of comfort and domestic scale,
while presenting its formal, cultured face to the public and the landscape.[73]

During the same year that James Gamble Rogers designed what was
the most expensive and lavish house in Cincinnati, he designed two other
residences for wealthy members of that city's business community. Both the
E. P. Harrison and the Hofer houses were located on property adjacent to
that city's first golf club.[74] While the grander Harrison House is an eclectic
mixture of Tudor stucco and timber, shingles and brick, the Hofer House is a
more coherent exercise in Dutch brick Colonial design. Both houses share
understated entrances and rambling internal organization.[75]

The interiors of all of the houses described above, whether large or
small, new or remodeled, city or country, display a marked similarity in certain design elements. The denial of axial penetration into the formal rooms is
highlighted by placing wood columns, usually Doric, around narrow, pinched
vestibules. In the Day House, pairs of columns are placed directly in front of
the main door, so that one is forced to move diagonally into the main hall
(see Fig. 13). The broad corridors are terminated by porches and give on to
large public rooms through an asymmetrical succession of doors. All of the
halls, and most of the formal rooms as well, have ceilings defined by heavy,
square, and usually dark-stained wood beams. The interiors pose these
homes as carefully crafted havens of culture and comfort within a still unset-
tled land, while the exteriors seem much more comfortable with the possibility of importing an Eastern and generically Western European set of
traditions to the edge of the prairie.

In 1905, however, James Gamble Rogers moved his office from Chicago to New York. On May 13, 1905, *The Economist* announced: "James Gamble Rogers has entered into a partnership with Herbert D. Hale of New York, and will hereafter divide his time between Chicago and New York. He will continue an office in Chicago, in charge of Charles A. Philips."[76] In fact, by the following year the Rogers family had moved from Chicago to New York. It is not entirely clear why Rogers decided to make such a large jump. He was thirty-eight years old, had a thriving practice in Chicago, and seemed well on his way to obtaining a central position in that city's architectural community. At the same time, he was starting to receive commissions outside of his hometown (see Chapter 3), and many of his friends from his days at Yale lived in and around New York. James Gamble was no doubt ambitious, and the prospect of larger commissions may have lured him into his new partnership.

The building that allowed him to make his mark on New York, however, was a house. It was commissioned by the one client who was to define the rest of his career, Edward S. Harkness. Together with his brothers and his mother, Harkness paid more than $80,000 in fees to James Gamble Rogers between 1907 and 1912,[77] and it was the work on these private commissions that led to Rogers' most important public work.

Edward Harkness was the youngest son by a second marriage of Cleveland businessman Stephen V. Harkness. In 1867, the elder Harkness invested between $70,000 and $90,000 in the fledgling enterprise of the young John D. Rockefeller, in exchange for which Stephen Harkness eventually received roughly 15 percent of the shares of the Standard Oil Company. The Harknesses remained faithful to the Rockefellers for fifty years, reinvesting their money in the various remnants of the Standard Oil trust and marrying into the same families as the Rockefellers. By the time Stephen Harkness's widow died in 1926, her wealth could be measured by the fact that her son had to pay the highest estate tax ever assessed to date in the United States.[78]

After Stephen Harkness died in 1889, the family estate was managed for twenty-seven years by his eldest son, Charles William Harkness, who greatly increased the fortune through investments in railroads, banks, and insurance companies. His young half-brother, Edward Stephen, showed little interest in the estate, however. A shy and retiring boy, he went to Saint Paul's School in New Hampshire and then to Yale, where he graduated in the Class of 1897. Harkness loved theatricals and Christian charities, and later was to see Yale as the one place where he had felt completely at home.[79]

He was not a businessman and was never actively involved himself in any of his or his family's investments. He was not interested in leading a social life, and did all he could to keep his name out of the newspapers. He married Mary Stillman, a millionaire in her own right. The couple led opulent but reserved lives in three mansions but rarely entertained on a large scale. By the time he died in 1940, Edward Harkness's main achievement had been to give away $129 million in amounts over $5,000, and much more in smaller gifts. He used that money to help construct major buildings for many educational and religious institutions—Yale, Harvard, Columbia, and Atlanta universities, Columbia-Presbyterian Medical Center, Colgate-Rochester Divinity School, the Taft and Saint Paul's schools—as well as for pioneering regional health centers all across rural America. James Gamble Rogers designed the great majority of these buildings, and the development of Harkness's interests in charities defined Rogers' career from 1916 until his death.[80]

Edward Harkness formalized his overriding interest in charity in 1918, when, together with his mother, he founded the Commonwealth Fund, whose only charter was "to do something for the welfare of mankind."[81] To organize this institution, he called on his longtime friend and financial advisor, Sam Fisher. Fisher was a lawyer practicing in New Haven who shared Harkness's interest in the activities of the Y.M.C.A. He was also a Yale graduate, Class of 1889, where he had been a member of Scroll & Key and a friend of James Gamble Rogers'. Whether or not Fisher was the one to introduce Rogers to his benefactor, the three became close friends, taking frequent trips together.[82]

The first major commission Harkness gave James Gamble Rogers, a Chicago architect newly arrived in New York with a young wife and some faraway designs to his credit, was the design of a home for himself and his wife on the corner of Fifth Avenue and 75th Street. The design of a Fifth Avenue mansion was a major step up for Rogers, as its completion would put his work visibly at the center of New York's social world. At the same time, Harkness, like many of his generation, wanted to avoid the ostentatiousness and grandiosity of some of his future neighbors. Though he had no desire to deny his wealth and seemed to have little insecurity about his position in society, he wanted a house that would not flaunt or exhibit such power as he had gained only by inheritance.

The design James Gamble Rogers produced between 1907 and 1908 satisfied both his client and the major architecture critics of the city (Fig. 25). Though it appears to be only four stories, it rises to the equivalent of seven stories on a lot 35 feet by 100 feet; two mechanical and service floors are hidden underground, and the servants' quarters disappear into an attic shielded from view by a balustrade. The main block is sheathed in a smoothly cut Tennessee marble that is, for the most part, left alone: "The ornament has been reduced to the lowest possible terms, and has been applied with a proper understanding of where it is desirable and necessary," while the open-

25. James Gamble Rogers.
Edward Harkness House, New
York, New York, 1907–8.
Elevation.

ings are not enough to deny "the kind of dignity which can be derived from a certain amount of plain wall surface."[83] The most often noted evidence of this desire to suppress architectural ornamentation while acknowledging the necessity for its presence both as a signal of the position of the house in its context and as a part of the design's compositional language is the presence of a line of pilaster bases and capitals in the rusticated first floor. The actual pilasters are only implied by the placement of the stones between the base and capital. These markers of a grander order float in the manner of the lintels Rogers more often detached from the windows with which they were associated (Fig. 26).

The Harkness House resolutely turns its back on Fifth Avenue and on any pretensions of being anything more than the appropriate container for the life of one of the richest men in America. Its tripartite composition is marked only by the use of rustication at the base, by a simple set of string-courses and cornices separating the three parts, and by a delicate balustrade crowning the structure. There is no modulation of the block, and the focus of the palazzo-like 75th Street composition is a low doorway marked only by two Doric columns and a slightly richer window surround above. The whole strongly recalls Rogers' final project at the Ecole des Beaux-Arts. The Embassy design here has been pared down, drawn together and shorn of its line of columns, large mansard roof, and highly embellished attic windows. No friezes, swags, or inscriptions catch the eye, and at the same time the pro-portioning and execution of the facade elements are so self-assuredly correct as to become almost invisible:

> In other words, the frank costliness of the effect of the house never even suggests mere ostentation. An intelligent and conscientious architectural purpose has given coherent form to every detail of the house and its decoration, so that the effect of mere costliness has become subordinat-ed to a more dominant effect of architectural balance and integrity.[84]

The main axis of the house, perpendicular to Fifth Avenue and the entrance axis, runs through the back half of the stark but richly colored and detailed lobby (Fig. 27). The whole ground floor is made up of a series of disconnected formal, nearly functionless rooms, each in a slightly different French or Italianate mode, and all drawn together at different points by a

26. James Gamble Rogers. Edward Harkness House, New York, New York, 1907–8. Detail.

double-loaded corridor. The use of rich woods, marble pilasters, elaborately worked ceilings, and, in the dining room, windows designed by Kenyon Cox, gives this ground floor a generalized sense of opulence but no insistent order.

The second floor is even simpler: it contains the staircase—a floating stone oval rising up slightly separate from the back wall—a library, a music room, and a gallery. This is the realm of art, lifted up above the level of the urban noise and the rituals of reception and entertaining below. One observer noted that the architect "has given a feeling of dignity to the interior without in any way sacrificing the elements of domestic comfort."[85]

The author who reviewed the house in *Architectural Record* went even further, noting that the interiors "cannot be classified as belonging to any specific period, but [are] rather an example of that free adaptation of elements derived from various sources, which is becoming increasingly characteristic of American interior design." What Rogers had done was to create a home in which "everything is as compact and convenient as possible" and thus "Mr. James Gamble Rogers . . . has used every device which modern taste and ingenuity has suggested to make the house a safe, convenient and luxurious and beautiful habitation."[86]

While the New York mansion was still under construction, both Edward Harkness and his brother Charles asked Rogers to renovate their respective country estates. The Charles William Harkness Estate in Madison, New Jersey, was designed by James Gamble Rogers at a cost of approximately $500,000.[87] In 1913, Rogers contracted with William S. Harkness to build a home in Glen Cove, Long Island.[88] This is probably the home that later came to be known as Weekend and served as Edward Harkness's out-of-town residence during the seasons when he was in New York. In the only remaining photographs of this estate, it appears to have been a slightly rambling wood structure, closed to the back and opening up with a series of porches and stepped gardens to Long Island Sound.[89]

The estate Edward Harkness purchased for himself outside New London, Connecticut, and which he called Eolia, was even larger than the Charles Harkness spread in New Jersey, but, unlike his elder half-brother, Edward Harkness decided to keep the existing brick mansion. He asked Rogers to help him remodel the interiors. Very little of these renovations

27. James Gamble Rogers. Edward Harkness House, New York, New York, 1907–8. Plans.

remains, though the expenses were considerable and helped the James Gamble Rogers office through some lean months. Rogers also added a series of porches and pergolas that extend the closed mass of the house out to Long Island Sound.[90] Apparently Rogers had the help of the famous landscape gardener Beatrix Farrand in the design of a formal garden to the side of the main house. This garden was framed at its back by a stone teahouse and pergola whose delicacy and formality stand in strong contrast to the unassuming size and design of the main house.[91] (Farrand was a frequent collaborator with Rogers in later years. She created the landscaping for two houses and five Yale residential colleges designed by Rogers.)

A clear mark of the close relationship developing between Rogers and his client may be seen in his decision, made sometime in 1910, to start a summer colony to which both he and some of his friends and clients could retreat from the heat of New York. The Rogers family frequently visited Harkness and his wife while they were in residence in Connecticut, and Rogers and Harkness played golf at the latter's golf course regularly. According to family lore, however, Rogers was actually sent out by some of his businessmen friends "to find the coolest spot between New York and Boston."[92] He found a small peninsula only a few miles from Eolia called Black Point. Together with his friends, he bought the whole area, razed or moved most of the existing cottages, and founded a club. Today, Black Point is still controlled by the association he founded, and his daughter and a granddaughter-in-law still live there during the summer. The homes James Gamble Rogers designed here repeat the themes of formal comfort in a lower key. His own house was based on an existing cottage, and consists of two end pavilions held by cross gables and connected by a front porch.

Rogers attracted to his enclave such classmates as lawyer A. Henry Mosle and other well-to-do, but not rich, young men with promising careers. The three remaining houses Rogers designed for Black Point are all placed along long axes running parallel to the water to catch the views and the breezes, and are covered in local materials (Fig. 28). They infuse a well-worn vernacular with the more statically organized spaces of formal entertainment, and strike a balance between shaded openness and flowing propriety. They make no statements, and yet do not disappear into their context completely. Their architecture organizes the world in the manner with which Rogers felt most comfortable. Rogers spent a great deal of time at Black Point, often commuting up from New York on Friday evenings and making the two-and-a-half-hour trip again Sunday.[93]

More than a decade later, Rogers created a Southern cousin to Black Point. Beginning in 1924, Rogers designed a series of homes and club buildings for Yeamans Hall, a winter colony outside Charleston, South Carolina. The colony was founded by Rogers himself with several of his early clients

28. James Gamble Rogers.
Frank Rogers House, Black
Point, Connecticut, 1914[?].

and friends from the New York and Chicago areas, including Edward S.
Harkness.[94] After Olmsted & Olmsted had laid out the grounds for a golf
course, a clubhouse, and a series of private residences, Rogers proceeded to
design the clubhouse, service buildings, and at least thirteen "cottages,"
including one for himself and his family.[95]

The structures at Yeamans Hall are simple wood buildings, painted
white and extended into the landscape through the extensive use of porches
and telescoping side wings. The clubhouse bears a passing resemblance in
its massing to some of the houses Rogers designed for the country around
New York, and many of the cottages resemble Rogers' own home in Black
Point (Fig. 29). Yet the horizontality of their composition, the light, two-
story porches, the brick chimneys tacked on to the end elevations, and the
setting apart of the service elements mark the buildings as part of the landscape, climate, and traditions that surround them.

Rogers designed a series of modest country homes outside of New
York, most of them of the scale of his earlier work in Lake Forest and Highland Park. By far the largest of these homes was the one he designed in 1912
for Richard C. Colt, son of the inventor of the Colt revolver and a graduate
of Yale. Situated on a mountaintop near Garrison, New York, the structure
can be seen for miles down the Hudson River (Fig. 30).[96] The view from the
river shows two large, pedimented white pavilions, defined as two stories of
open porches framed by wood columns. A long pergola stretches between

29. James Gamble Rogers.
Yeamans Hall, Charleston,
South Carolina, 1927.

30. James Gamble Rogers.
Colt House, Garrison, New
York, 1912.

these two temples to summer living and hides the plain stucco expanse of the
main house. The actual house itself is almost lost, as were the Harkness
homes, between the blank face to the outside world and the architectural elements added to mediate the sweeping scale of the landscape.[97]

The most visible commission Rogers completed during the years after
his design of the Fifth Avenue Harkness Mansion, however, was that for the
Jonathan Bulkley Residence at 600 Park Avenue, which was completed in
1910 (Fig. 31).[98] Bulkley was a a graduate of Yale and a wealthy paper merchant. The house is similar to the Harkness House, but it is much clearer in
its ceremonial and public function. The Bulkley House, which now houses
the Swedish Embassy, is also a four-story palazzo clad in stone, with a strongly rusticated base and a roof that disappears behind a low balustrade. Rogers
used the same restraint in allowing the solidity of the wall and the deep insets
of the windows to state the scale and importance of the building.

The Bulkley House may not be the largest or the most lavishly
designed of James Gamble Rogers' palatial residences, but it exhibits the
architectural strategy the designer brought to these commissions in a form
that caught the eye of the critic Montgomery Schuyler when he set out to
review the new structures of the fast-developing East Side (see Fig. 31).[99] Schuyler

31. James Gamble Rogers.
Jonathan Bulkley House, New
York, New York, 1909–10.

asked the question of whether the needs of individual expression and domestic comfort could be met in an architecture controlled by the need for a large scale. He did not question the notion that the order of such an architecture should be academically Classical in its application of typological models and details. Like Rogers, he sought an architectural solution in the refinement of such a system in order to bring out, first of all, the inherent logic of the structure:

> . . . it is never left in doubt that what you are looking at is a pierced wall and not a sash frame with the minimum of masonry border that will, even precariously, hold it together. The moldings, alike of the string course over the basement and of the main cornice, by their moderation and delicacy, promote this total impression, which is again promoted by the refinement and the delicacy of the decorative detail, whether in carved stone or wrought metal. In the same interest is the attenuation much beyond the classical minimum of the columns which carry the pediments. The execution is worthy of the design, insomuch that even the "dish-towel ornament," which the designer could not prevent himself from hanging under the windows of the third story above the pediments, become inoffensive for once.[100]

The result, according to Schuyler, is a "palazzetto" that, instead of seeming larger and more important than its program warrants, refuses the Beaux-Arts call for grandiosity in favor of, on the interior, domestic comfort and, on the exterior, contextual sensitivity.[101] As such, the Bulkley House held out the hope to Schuyler of the creation of an "Anglo-Saxon" response, in terms of individualization and adaptability, to the grandiose importations of Beaux-Arts methodology.[102] It turned out that James Gamble Rogers, for better or for worse, could provide exactly such an architecture, whether for domestic programs inserted into an urban environment or for institutional programs that redefined their context.

CHAPTER TWO

The Architecture of Pragmatism

By the time James Gamble Rogers moved to New York, the outlines of his architecture were becoming clear. His work distinguished itself from that of his contemporaries not because it presented a markedly different appearance, but because it appropriated historical types and transformed them into lucid representations of the new institutions they housed. The achievement of James Gamble Rogers can best be understood by exploring his application of existing styles, his manipulation and breaking of their rules, and especially his pragmatic manner of organizing buildings. The rest of this book will trace the development of these themes in the buildings themselves, yet it is here worth noting their principal sources, outlines, and characteristics in a general sense.

I have used the word *pragmatic* to describe the work of James Gamble Rogers. I use this term first of all in a technical sense, because his work housed many of the institutions responsible for integrating Pragmatist philosophy into American culture. I also use it as a way of describing an architecture that was marked by its acceptance of inherited formal languages, a commonsensical organization, antihierarchical tendencies, a reliance on the revelation of materiality, didacticism, and collage-like sensibilities. These characteristics I would describe as pragmatic because they accepted inherited traditions (one of William James's criteria for truth) and embraced the realities of building practices while seeking to express a free, scientifically oriented, and democratic state of mind.[1] James Gamble Rogers used his training in Academic Classicism and business-oriented practice to create an approach toward architecture that was both fully recognizable by and functional for his clientele. Out of the blending of these two influences came buildings that are recognizable as having been designed by Rogers. I would argue that the blending of business and "high art" under the influence of Pragmatist programs was accomplished by an empathetic, picturesque, and episodic or collage-based architectural composition that defines these buildings.

The deformations of plan and type evident in Rogers' best designs certainly created what Robert Venturi might call "the difficult whole."[2] This kind of organically connected looseness is at least partially a result of the transitory nature of Rogers' architecture, occurring as it does in the period when the classicistic rules were breaking down and new types such as metropolitan hospital complexes and modern universities were emerging. Rogers responded to this situation by reaching out in his architecture to embrace and control change, thus reflecting the attitudes of his clientele. For these very reasons, Rogers never developed a fixed style or ideology. Perhaps the success of his work merely proves that architecture is more interesting in transition than when fixed in a style. Certainly the sheer skill of the craft of design comes out in such situations.

To trace the outlines of James Gamble Rogers' architecture, one must answer questions of components, characteristics, and style. By looking at how Rogers defined his own work and what appearance he chose to give to his buildings, I hope to outline a context within which the specific nature of his design achievement can be placed. If we are to understand Rogers as more than "just" a revivalist architect, we have to look carefully at the styles he chose to revive and the formats he gave them.

Rogers' buildings were organized rationally, but they refused grand axes (Figs. 32 a–i). Double-loaded corridors, placed at a right angle to the entrance, stood in the place of expository axes. The development of this parti seems to have been guided by a strong concern for comfort, but also by a desire to create a varied visual experience. This Rogers achieved by layering his buildings from front to back, and then deliberately interrupting the path one would take through a set of layers defined by their own scale, light, and materials. The building developed as a path winding its way through and past a series of screens placed in front of or between separate pavilions dedicated to the different parts of the program. This choreographic composition often was organized around open courtyards, places that were not so much the formal heart of the building as the leftover spaces from which the various functions of the building, though they were often hidden on the outside, could be identified by those who had been allowed inside.

The final appearance of the building was dictated by the demands of whatever style Rogers adopted, and rarely expressed the interior organization. The style was never allowed to overwhelm the building, however, and was usually more implied than stated: colonnades and pedimented porches were posed in front of the building as separate items added on to a functional box. Pilasters were present only in capitals and bases, the shaft having been subsumed into the structure of the building. Instead, the building was often covered with an elaborate iconography that explicitly stated the purpose, history, and values of the building.

This was not a particularly self-conscious kind of design approach. Rogers' first explanation of his architecture—and one of the few he committed to paper—can be found in a description he wrote in 1903 of his first major institutional design, the School of Education at the University of Chicago.[3] It was a straightforward explanation, and not particularly innovative. The building he was discussing was the direct result of a memorial gift (see Chapter 3). Rogers therefore felt that the "character" of the building should be "monumental." But such a character was to be added on only after

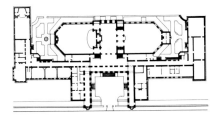

32. *a*. James Gamble Rogers. The Chicago Institute (project), Chicago, Illinois, 1899. Plan, first scheme, 1899.

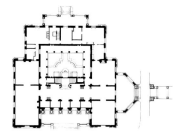

b. James Gamble Rogers. Laurel Court (Peter Thomson House), Cincinnati, Ohio, 1904–8. Plan.

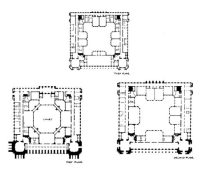

c. James Gamble Rogers. Shelby County Courthouse, Memphis, Tennessee, 1905–9. Plan.

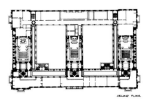

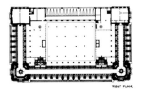

d. James Gamble Rogers. New Orleans Post Office and Courthouse, New Orleans, Louisiana, 1908–15. Plan.

e. James Gamble Rogers. Harkness Memorial Quadrangle, Yale University, New Haven, Connecticut, 1917–21. Plan.

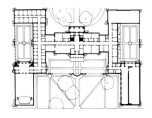

f. James Gamble Rogers. Norton Hall, Southern Baptist Theological Seminary, Louisville, Kentucky, 1925–28. Plan.

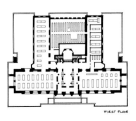

g. James Gamble Rogers. Deering Library, Northwestern University, Evanston, Illinois, 1929–32. Plan.

h. James Gamble Rogers. Davenport and Pierson colleges, Yale University, New Haven, Connecticut, 1930–33. Plan.

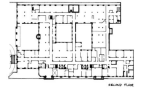

i. James Gamble Rogers. Memorial Sloan-Kettering Hospital, New York, New York, 1937–39. Plan.

the plan had been efficiently organized and the character specific to the building's use firmly established:

> In making the plans—I say "plans" because the best plan is capable of giving the best elevation, and the plan carries with it all the elements of true architecture—in making plans the first duty of the architect is to learn the requirements and their relative importance. These requirements may be divided . . . into local requirements, generally easy to determine because they are direct and definite, though sometimes requiring keen judgment; and inherent requirements, arising from the particular kind of building and from the individual use of such a building.[4]

In the case of the School of Education, the local requirements included the need for fireproofing, which led to the use of Bedford stone for the walls and red tile for the roof, as well as the need to work in a style that harmonized with the rest of the campus. That style had been mandated by the University of Chicago as being "Gothic," and this was the first time Rogers was confronted with the necessity of using Neo-Gothic elements.

A functional plan, appropriate materials, and a contextual assemblage set the framework for the design. Elevations, constituting the formal presentation of the building, were of only secondary importance. The "inherent" requirements were those given by the client in terms of program size and required adjacencies. These requirements made the general considerations of size, site, and program more specific. What was left for the architect was the need to transform all of these givens first into an abstract organization and then into a coherent presentation:

> . . . it should be possible to ascertain simply by a glance at the building what are its uses. A home should look like a home, a city hall should differ from a post office, an engine house should not possibly be mistaken for a church, a seat of learning should be distinguished from a factory or restaurant. Moreover, in expressing its character, a building must express the spirit of its times and the place in which it is built.[5]

Thus, after fulfilling the internal requirements, the architect had to make the building look like something recognizable, both typologically and contextually. In addition, Rogers felt that the building had to possess "dignity, repose, grace and bearing, and . . . at the same time be cheerful and attractive and have a well-defined retired character."[6] In order for it to be a natural part of its culture, the building had to bear itself with the same good taste and distinction as marked the gentlemen and gentlewomen who designed, paid for, and used the building. Business and art merged into an appropriate, pragmatic, and elegant whole that appealed to (refined) senses.

The approach Rogers took to achieve this result was based, in the manner he was no doubt taught at the Ecole des Beaux-Arts, on precedents: a clear understanding of the appropriate sources for any building. The "character" of a building summed up much of how the Ecole defined its work. Despite often violent disagreements about such a definition during the first half of the nineteenth century, by the period after the Second Empire a consensus had been reached out of a synthesis of the ideas of Antoine Quatremère-de-Quincy, J.N.L. Durand, and later theoreticians. The result was a tenuous compromise between the acceptance of the building's site in time and place, and the need to discipline new materials, functions, and places with an inherited body of knowledge about architecture. The character of a building was thus the result of a pseudoscientific analysis of all its components, transformed by the particular vision of the architect into a coherent summation of the qualities of the institution to be housed.[7]

At the same time, German and English theoreticians were developing similar notions about the appropriateness of certain forms and styles. Though the French arguments about style and type were focused on providing a correct working method for the architect, the English, German, and American versions took a more philosophical tack by veering off toward a belief in the revelatory possibilities inherent in architectural form. This kind of organic argument cut across stylistic boundaries, emphasizing instead the need to allow structure, material, and function to dictate the final result. It also emphasized the need for didactic ornament and picturesque organization of spaces, because architecture was a form of education that would work directly through the creation of easily seen models to help build a more beautiful and just society. Culminating (at least in the United States) in the writings of Claude Bragdon and Louis Sullivan, this Organic School of architecture laid the groundwork for the work of Frank Lloyd Wright, but it also served as the theory for the Chicago School and fit into that strain of American architecture that was informed by Emersonian theories of natural self-sufficiency. Rogers' pragmatism was the direct result of this kind of thinking, but shorn of its mysticism.[8]

In general, there is thus nothing particularly innovative about Rogers' credo, but it does explain his emphasis on the overall coherence of the building over its stylistic or typological correctness. Of course, what Rogers did not discuss was his actual contribution to the design process, that which actually made his buildings so sensuous:

> The proportion of the windows, the band courses, the relation of the moldings, and the general composition, are questions of architectural imagination and technique that would demand a development beyond the limits of the present article.[9]

What determined many of these proportions, compositions, and techniques was of course the actual architectural style chosen for, or rather imposed on, the building. Its elaboration was the realm of the artist, the skillful composer of forms, the gentleman designer who could learn from the sources of antiquity and use them to mold new materials and functions into harmonious forms. Rogers was quite skilled in these matters, and he knew how to attract fellow workers who were equally adept, but it was a skill that he never discussed—it was, after all, art, something that could not be explained logically. Perhaps Rogers' avoidance of a discussion of these terms, however, had more to do with the fact that art was a repository for qualities of taste and judgment specific to—and thus unspoken between—Rogers and his clients. Style and taste were enshrined in these schools and colleges as marks of a deserving and vital elite.

This method of working has little in common with the present-day image of the architect as individual, as genius creator in the mold of Frank Lloyd Wright. Rather, it presents the image of an architect who managed to combine his function as businessman with that of an artist by seeing his task as the translation of complicated functions into appropriate form. The result was that Rogers was able to complete a number of large commissions at the same time. To do this, he had to collaborate with many other architects, consultants, and craftsmen, both within and outside of his office. He often acted more as a chief executive officer than as a hands-on designer, with the result that talented project architects in his office, such as Otto Faelten, are often given credit for much of his work. Yet it was Rogers who had the particular talent to organize both the plans and the people working for him into a coherent whole. One might even say that Rogers' office is an exemplar of the transformation of the American architectural office from an atelier into a corporate office. It was a smooth operation. The characteristics of a Rogers building remained constant through forty years of work, no matter who in the office acted as the principal executor of his designs. Others may have drawn and designed pieces, but James Gamble Rogers gave the whole his own understated but unmistakable style.

What is remarkable is the manner in which James Gamble Rogers managed to channel such a talent through a variety of styles, the foremost of which, the Neo-Gothic, he had little or no experience with by the time he came to the University of Chicago commission. Luckily for Rogers, the Ecole des Beaux-Arts was, by the time of his education there, no longer inimical to the uses of Gothic motifs and had created its own rather formalist version of Neo-Gothicism, which Rogers may have seen in Paris in the work of Viollet-le-Duc and his followers.[10] It was also very much in evidence (in a rather reduced form) at the University of Chicago by the time Rogers came to build there. The university had been laid out in 1891 by Henry Ives Cobb using what he called "Gothic" architecture. This term was a loose one for Cobb and his successors at the university, as it grew to encompass a great deal of ornament, plan elements, and compositional motifs derived from models ranging from ninth-century churches in Spain to late-fifteenth-century English colleges.

In fact, neither Cobb nor any of the other architects who executed buildings on the campus were rigorous, archaeological, or doctrinaire Neo-Gothicists in the manner of Henry Vaughan or Ralph Adams Cram. It appears that to Cobb "Gothic architecture was seen as providing adaptability and variety with a controlled plan."[11] In the case of the University of Chicago, Gothic ornament was used to soften the outlines of large, functional institutional buildings with fanciful flourishes of stone carving, while the picturesque interpretation of the accrectionary composition of medieval buildings, seen as growing less out of predetermined forms and more out of the changing necessities of function, softened the impact of new monuments paid for by "merchant princes" and containing self-consciously elitist institutions (Fig. 33). To Thorstein Veblen, writing about the university's campus, the new academic pragmatism that embraced industry expressed itself as "decorative real-estate, spectacular pageantry, bureaucratic magnificence, elusive statistics, vocational training, genteel solemnities, and sweatshop instruction . . . advertising art."[12]

The "Gothic," used in this sense, was a way of creating an artificial history and sense of reality for a newly invented institution in a new city, paid

33. Shepley, Rutan & Coolidge. Ida Noyes Hall, University of Chicago, Chicago, Illinois, 1916.

for by self-made men. The buildings of the campus, organized as rationally as any office building, were presented in forms that layered on allusions to a past so far out of reach that the structures neither carried much specific (religious) baggage, nor had to refer to any specific models to achieve their ends. What was important to architect and client alike was that vague association, which university president William Rainey Harper interpreted a bit differently than Veblen: "Classic buildings were financed by merchant princes. Gothic buildings arose through the combined efforts of humble workmen. . . . Classicism stood for the burgeoning materialism of the Renaissance, Gothic for timeless religious values."[13] It did not seem to bother Harper that the University of Chicago was in fact paid for by merchant princes, and that the university was a proud symbol of the new riches and sophistication of Chicago. What mattered to these men was the conversion or presentation of this condition in an appearance that would effectively deny the reality it served, creating instead the image of a "democracy" of working people together, experimenting on the city and rebuilding it in a more scientific but also more moral way—a vision promulgated above all by the new university's most famous teacher, John Dewey, and his fellow Pragmatists.[14]

Perhaps because of the underlying contradictions, the "Gothic" skin on the School of Education was not particularly convincing: the building is symmetrical, tall and formal, and its ornaments in most cases are more reminiscent of Loire Valley châteaux or nineteenth-century English manor houses than of any medieval sources. James Gamble Rogers was adopting himself to the context, but he was not sold on Gothicism. He continued to change styles with almost every house and building he designed during the next fifteen years. His institutional buildings predominantly followed the strictures of Academic Classicism. His houses ranged in their references from sixteenth-century American homes to Italian villas and Tudor farms. His eclecticism during these years was matched by few of his contemporaries.

In each of the designs, however, he defined the architecture with the same combination of functional compactness and responsiveness to the given site, program, and client that he had outlined in his 1903 credo. In the hot weather of Memphis, for instance, the colonnaded front of the Shelby County Courthouse was both a correct face for a public institution and a kind of giant veranda (Fig. 34). Furthermore, while the outside of this building represented civic monumentality in an accepted, Academic Classicist manner, the interior courtyard was a rambling, functional affair carried out in brick. It is in fact in the distortions of the Classical precedents that Rogers' particular contribution can be read.

One has only to compare his Classical work with that of a contemporary like John Russell Pope, who refined his models and attempted to adapt them seamlessly to new types and landscapes, as one can see in his

34. James Gamble Rogers. Shelby County Courthouse, Memphis, Tennessee, 1905–9.

35. John Russell Pope. National Gallery, Washington, D.C., 1936–41.

extensive and eclectic work at the Marshall Field Estate on Long Island, for instance, or in his many museum buildings, culminating in the National Gallery of 1937–41, to see the alternatives (Fig. 35).[15] Rogers reveled in the adaptation and forthright confrontation of different building elements, while Pope covered them up. Nor was Rogers interested in creating unified formal envelopes in the manner of Ernest Flagg or Daniel Burnham. Instead, he seemed to enjoy the disjunctions inherent in modern programs and urban sites, since they allowed him more compositional freedom. Perhaps this was because these challenges offered him the chance to articulate more of the pieces of the building, thus allowing the viewer or user to understand more clearly the underlying relationships that made up the building.[16]

Academic Classicism, with its heavily codified rules, may have been a bit of a straitjacket for Rogers, whose buildings seem unsophisticated when judged by someone looking for nothing more than correct interpretations. Rogers was much more comfortable with a kind of Southern variant on the Neo-Georgian and Neo-Colonial styles then gaining popularity because they recalled Americans to their supposed roots.[17] For Rogers, who designed his own homes in variations on these styles, this Colonial offshoot of a British version of an Italian or French style may just have offered a more flexible though still socially acceptable appearance.

36. Russell Sturgis, Jr., Lawrance Hall, Yale University, New Haven, Connecticut, 1885–86.

But in 1916 he was forced once again to confront the issue of the use of Gothic architecture in a way that was to make it the style for which he became famous. In that year, he was asked to design another educational building at least partially intended as a memorial. The Harkness Memorial Quadrangle was a continuation, originally planned in 1911, of the existing campus of Yale College. Though the administration apparently had no clear strategy for the design or funding of the new dormitory quadrangle, a decision was made that the appearance of the building would be "collegiate gothic."[18]

This decision was itself the result of a movement away from the original Colonial style of the first buildings at Yale and toward a series of successive Gothicisms, each more self-consciously evocative than the one before it. Whereas the Henry Austin–designed Yale Library of 1843 had been part and parcel of a wave of Neo-Gothic designs tied to both the religious revivals of the period and to the moralizing architecture propounded by John Ruskin and his American followers,[19] the Victorian Gothic that the architect Russell Sturgis employed for the dormitories of the post–Civil War period was both vaguer and more consistent in its purpose (Fig. 36). Rather than recalling specific ecclesiastical and therefore religious prototypes, Sturgis sought to give Yale a general sense of a past and a consistent appearance flexible enough to be carried out in different materials for various building types. The dormitories he designed, including Farnam, Durfee, and Lawrance halls, were the equivalent of tall apartment blocks with small entrances, gabled roofs, and carved stone rosettes—but also with Ionic columns.

Yale continued to try both Academic Classicism and Neo-Gothicism in its effort to create a unified and traditional image for a school that had to bring together an increasingly large and diverse student body. The Bicentennial Group of 1902 by Carrère & Hastings, for instance, organized a major corner of the university as a colonnaded courtyard (Fig. 37), but Osborne Hall of 1913, designed by Charles Haight, was a rambling assem-

blage of brick decorated with an eclectic mix of medieval ornament.[20]

By 1910 the school had, according to critic Montgomery Schuyler, "fixed as 'Gothic' the style of Yale."[21] The choice of Neo-Gothic had, said Schuyler, at least three distinct advantages. First, "monotony is avoided" by the vertical variations and much richer ornamental possibilities of the style. Second, a Gothic building could be impressive without being monumental and could set itself off as an object of significance without alienating itself from its neighbors. Finally, the use of a Gothic model for the making of "quadrangles manqués" recalled not just a certain type or time of building, but one powerful model: "How enviable the man who has availed himself of the opportunity to recall, in bustling New Haven, the charm of 'that sweet city with her dreaming spires' of Oxford. . . ."[22] The models for Yale were to be the universities of Oxford and Cambridge, the latter to a lesser degree because its more bucolic setting mirrored less well the industrial context of New Haven. One might speculate that such a choice coincided with the Pragmatist emancipation of American intellectual life from both French and especially German influences, bringing the university back in touch with its roots in Puritan philosophy.

While Schuyler's writing, the constant advocacy of such propagandists of Gothicism as Ralph Adams Cram, and the choices of individual architects may all have influenced the decision to mandate the use of a Neo-Gothic style for the new campus, the most powerful model for the largest planned expansion of the school was undoubtedly the recently completed complex of buildings at Princeton University, designed by the Philadelphia firm of Day & Klauder (Fig. 38). Princeton had been much more aggressive than its Ivy League counterparts in expanding its campus, and had in 1906 entrusted the planning of the new campus to Cram. As was the case at Yale, Princeton already had many Neo-Gothic (and some differently

38. Day & Klauder. Freshman Dormitories, Princeton University, Princeton, New Jersey, 1910–16.

styled) buildings on its campus, and Cram proposed formalizing its development into a plan that turned them from isolated objects of use or veneration into integral parts of a complex of enclosed and connected quadrangles controlled by a Beaux-Arts plan made invisible beneath the picturesque massing of the actual buildings (Fig. 39).[23] Princeton itself was not the first college to adopt a Gothic style, it should be noted. Seminaries across the country were often Neo-Gothic in appearance, but campuses like the University of Pennsylvania had also experimented with the Oxbridge model during the 1870s and 1880s, having done so for all the reasons Schuyler outlined in his survey of American colleges in 1909 and 1910.[24]

The first major part of the Princeton plan was realized in 1909 with the erection of the freshman dormitories according to a design by Frank Miles Day, who had earlier worked on the University of Pennsylvania campus. The design used local stone and a sparing application of limestone Gothic motifs to house repetitive blocks of housing. Classically derived axes composed the whole and created openings and vistas in the blocks, while Gothic elements such as towers, turrets, bays and piers activated and punctuated the quadrangle. The result was a building that mitigated the foreign nature of its style by responding, in organization and material, to its site. The buildings also served to formalize, order, and place the heterogeneous assemblage of styles and the accretions of architectural decisions and traditions into a ready-made environment designed by professionals who could abstract history and function into a plan and project a coherent image. Business and art found themselves successfully married in a beautiful and functional new setting.[25]

Finally, according to Schuyler in another installment of his multipart

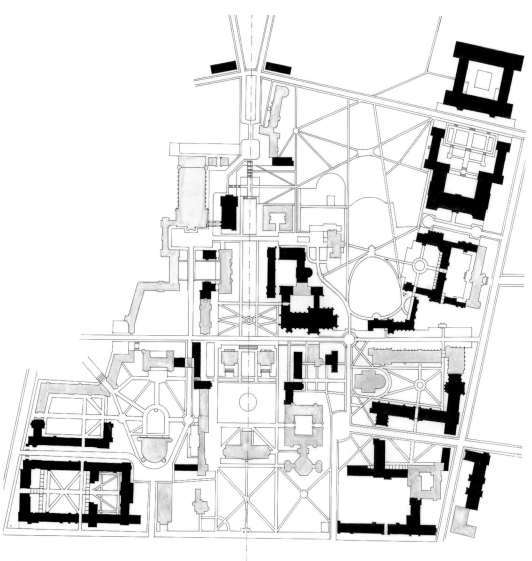

39. Ralph Adams Cram.
Princeton University General
Plan, Princeton, New Jersey,
1907.

survey, "The Architecture of American Colleges," this method of designing produced, "perfectly that blend of the monastic and the domestic which makes the 'collegiate character'. . . ."[26] Apartment types that had developed in the nineteenth century were combined with design strategies aimed at the protection and sanctification of a small group in monastic courtyards and were organized as if they were part of larger urban constructs. The result was then given the validation of history and compositional coherence by a specialized variant of the chosen style: Collegiate Gothic. The program and typological response developed for institutions of higher learning around the turn of the century was well established when Rogers was asked to design the Memorial Quadrangle.

It is important to note that this was a slightly different form of Neo-Gothicism than the closed, overtly romantic version championed by Bertram Goodhue, Henry Vaughan, and, most of all, by Goodhue's onetime partner, Ralph Adams Cram. Cram himself defined his collegiate architecture as one that would "tie the anarchy of the past to the order of the present":

> . . .a citadel of learning and culture and scholarship, at the same time inclusive and exclusive, containing within itself all necessary influences towards the making of character, repelling all those that work against the same; a walled city against materialism and all its works . . . the ultimate unity should result from a congeries of subordinate units, individual buildings being connected up with each other, in many cases forming "quads" . . . which should form the various nuclei of residence; that the whole setting should not reveal itself at once and from any spot, but gradually, through narrowed and intensified vistas, the unforeseen openings out of unanticipated paths and quadrangles, the surprise of retirement, the revelation of the unexpected.[27]

Cram thus laid out many of the principles of Collegiate Gothic architecture, but pushed its exclusionary, reactionary character much farther. Working in the tradition of Pugin and the English Neo-Gothicists who had been the architects for the political and religious reform movements of the mid-nineteenth century, Cram called for a consciously archaeological architecture, one that refused any mark of modern technology and would act as the seed for the destruction of the bureaucratic, capitalist state. This was a visionary, wholly romantic form of Neo-Gothicism that was popular in certain sections of the architectural community, if not among many clients outside of the ecclesiastical sphere.[28]

Cram's romanticism can be contrasted with those theories of Neo-Gothicism that saw the style as a more rational mode of design. Charles Herbert Moore, who was also the apologist for such classicist architects as Daniel Burnham and was the teacher of George Howe, saw the Gothic as being both constructive—that is to say, not organized around symmetrical and pre-planned walls and spaces, but dedicated to the revelation of structural forces—and concerned with the sublimation of nature and "everyday life" into conventionalized forms. This process was—and here Moore follows John Ruskin's moralistic version of Gothicism quite closely—dictated by the nature of the materials out of which the representation was made and by their architectural composition. In the end, this design methodology would bring back to the modern world an organic and natural order based on the community of makers.[29] Working in a long tradition of rational theoreticians of the Gothic,[30] Moore stressed its essential appropriateness to the modern act of construction.

Moore also posited the role of architecture in creating a coherent language out of the forms of life, rather than imposing forms and spaces on that life.[31] It is in these arguments that one can see a continuity between Neo-Gothicism and Pragmatist thinking, since both emphasize the necessity for a clear understanding of the physical world based on a tradition of direct, empirical experience codified into truths that are not absolute but relative to social conditions—a relationship made explicit by Claude Bragdon, who contrasted "the Gothic architecture, so called, which is pre-eminently a striving towards a free organic expression of plan and construction, with Renaissance architecture, wherein predetermined canons of abstract beauty are imposed," and which was raised to the level of philosophy in John Dewey's *Art As Experience.*[32]

As noted above, the result was an architectural practice that connected the rational strains inherent in both Neo-Gothicism and Classicism with the picturesque tendencies also present in both, while rejecting both hierarchies, symmetries, and systems of preplanned order, and mystical ideas about the inherent rightness of organic form. Though the work of Goodhue and others may be analyzed in terms of such a pragmatic Neo-Gothicism, it is only James Gamble Rogers who, probably because he emerged from the same milieu that created the Chicago School of Pragmatism (and architecture), fulfilled its tenets in a series of remarkable structures beginning with the Memorial Quadrangle at Yale.

Rogers came to Neo-Gothicism reluctantly, perhaps because of his experience at the University of Chicago. "At the time," he commented in a series of notes for a lecture to alumni and school officials, "I felt Yale had made a mistake choosing Gothic. Colonial best for size of Old Campus. Too institutional and dreary. Too inflexible for large windows . . . best for large institutions, gothic sprinkling of Georgian, colonial, some renaissance properly placed."[33] Yet he set to work to fulfill his mandate, and he did so in a manner that combined rational methods with a reliance on the long history of Neo-Gothicism, thus drawing on its strengths as a time-worn condensation of practical and structural concerns.

Faced with a style in which he was generally unaccustomed to working, Rogers immediately set about outfitting his design with eclectically chosen and scientifically arranged details by collecting an album full of postcards of generally medieval buildings in France, England, and Italy.[34] Most of the postcards were from the Musée de Sculpture Comparée in Paris and thus reflected an academic gathering of isolated motifs classified by year of production and region of origin. The album is organized into two parts. The first section contains postcards and views of Gothic and Romanesque churches. The second section isolates building elements such as statues in niches, capitals, rosettes, grotesques, tracery panels, and shields. In this section, Renaissance stucco work and even urns from the palace at Versailles are mixed with elements taken from churches as far afield as Spain and southern Italy that illustrate similar functions: screens and balustrades, whether for choirs or royal balconies, for instance, are grouped together.

The volume is a rich and eclectic compilation of details, many of which can be recognized in the Memorial Quadrangle buildings. But each of the elements is cut loose from its spatial and temporal context, and is treated only as part of a composition. The style thus assembled is neither strictly Gothic nor Romanesque. It is itself an invention based on an investigation on how one connects differently scaled objects, rather than giving each an echoing order; how one combines the structural and ergonomic or ritualistic elements of a building, rather than isolating them; and how one applies a narrative decoration so that it transforms the forms to which it is added, rather than merely being inscribed on top of them. In general, this style is a collection of techniques that run counter both to the logical exposition taught at the Ecole des Beaux-Arts and to purely rational building processes. It is a collage-like form of design. One might say that it shows a pragmatic way of working, and one that Rogers was to pursue for the rest of his career. The impulse to assemble the scrapbook was akin to that of a businessman or scientist cataloguing his field of operation. It formed an encyclopedia or handbook by which Rogers could transform his two architectural educations (the Chicago and the Paris ones) into a more lively, picturesque style, a Collegiate Gothic that sought to blur the differences between function, structure, and image. It is hard to imagine a form of Neo-Gothicism that could be more modern (if not to say Modernist) in its genesis.

After Rogers had thus scientifically collected the building blocks of his style, he needed to fuse them into a coherent appearance. For this, he hired an expert: E. Donald Robb, a designer who had worked for Cram and Goodhue. Robb specialized in renderings, creating the kind of moody drawings that converted the stones of a building into an evocative image (Fig. 40). His presence in Rogers' offices, though it was not of long duration, seems to have been necessary for the development of the kind of Collegiate

40. E. Donald Robb (Brazer & Robb). Reformed Dutch Church, Poughkeepsie, New York. Rendering, 1913[?].

Gothic Rogers had in mind (see Chapter 4).

The peculiarities of the style evidenced themselves in the most noticeable elements of the buildings—the skin and the eye-catching details—and then, so to speak, seeped through the rest of the structure. In a letter to the client, Edward Harkness, Rogers pointed out his struggle to rid the complex of any symmetry, which, like the "factory-made appearance," would make one aware of the existence of the mythology of Yale.[35] Rogers understood that Neo-Gothicism depended on a romantic suspension of disbelief, however rationally constructed. He further enhanced this image by blurring the edges of his forms, setting gateways slightly off axis, layering screens, adding bay windows and entrance porticoes, and generally softening the rational plan of the complex with numerous picturesque touches. The result was a successful molding of this large dormitory and memorial into a coherent carrier of meaning.

The nature of this romantic cloak actually became an issue during the design of the Memorial Quadrangle. During the construction process, a dispute between university secretary Anson Phelps Stokes and the architect forced Rogers to define his architectural strategy as not one of imitation in order to literally re-create Oxford or Cambridge, but as the invention of a Collegiate Gothic that used modern means to create a new Yale. Stokes had complained about the fact that Rogers was using a synthetic tile, or "imitation slate," as roofing material. The secretary had gone so far as to contact the great arbiter of Neo-Gothicism, Ralph Adams Cram himself, to obtain a concurrence. Rogers thereupon wrote Stokes a long and rambling letter in which he denigrated Cram, defended his own years of practical experience, and pointed out that only his new material would instantly reproduce the many centuries of dirt that had given the English colleges their patina. He was not a copyist, Rogers claimed, and was not caught up in traditions for their own sake:

> As far as traditions go, I hope that the only traditions governing us will be Yale traditions and our country's traditions. Architecturally we will, I know, keep our effects as essential and not the traditions. Of course we will have to have architectural traditions because in most cases there is no other way of getting the desired effect except by employing the traditions which we use only because in those cases they are necessary to get the effect. It does seem awfully hollow and servilely cringing to use a tradition that means nothing to us.[36]

Here one can see Rogers clearly rejecting both Cram's brand of archaeological Neo-Gothicism and any notion of unfamiliar Modernism in favor of a more experientially based and pragmatic approach. This strategy became the hallmark of his Collegiate Gothic buildings, which are still wonderful chimeras of Neo-Gothic villages of forms strewn together with ornamental narratives along revelatory paths and constructed on steel skeletons with double-loaded corridors.

As James Gamble Rogers became more successful, this method of designing undoubtedly became a style, a signature for his work, and therefore a major reason why he was hired. This fact became evident in a conflict between Rogers and one of his clients, John J. Wigmore, dean of the School of Law at Northwestern University. When the design for the new school severely strained the budget allocated for construction in the summer of 1925, and Rogers argued for cutting back on the program while preserving the architectural detail of the design, Wigmore launched a vigorous attack. He accused Rogers of having become, first of all, an East Coast architect who put "outward presentation" over internal necessity, thus forgetting his training in Chicago, and, second, "an artist" who applied a preexisting aesthetic judgment to his work. The very success that had come to James Gamble Rogers in New York, and had brought him back to the place where he was introduced to the making of architecture, had turned him into an alien. Wigmore went on to criticize Rogers, saying:

> You, yourself, have been among the few fortunate artists in this world that has at last been able to carry out your ideals in scores of buildings without regard to limitation of expense. Therefore, the ideal as you form it for a particular building is always an ideal which has no initial relation to money at all; and any later proposal to economize on the money cost of this ideal seems to you naturally an artistic sacrilege.[37]

James Gamble Rogers had found a style, and was in danger of becoming an architect in the high-art sense of a fabricator of cultural artifacts that added imagery to functional structures. One might speculate that this development was paralleled by the rising dominance of Pragmatism in institutions of higher learning, as well as by the transformation of the progressive movement into a movement dedicated to supporting a white middle-class elite.[38]

That is exactly what many of Rogers' clients during the 1920s were looking for. When in 1930 he proposed a simple Neo-Georgian design as the new home for the main library of Northwestern University, the building committee rejected his proposal. Rogers then did an about-face and redesigned the whole project as a Gothic building. He explained his design to university secretary William Dyche in a letter later incorporated into the Minutes of the Meetings of the Northwestern board of trustees:

Since going out to Evanston and having another point of view and reconsidering the whole, I believe that your best venture would be to develop the Evanston campus in a very modern Gothic without tracery in the windows. Then when it comes to the secondary buildings, we could make them in Gothic that was of the same type but still more economical. . . . When I think of the number of buildings that the Evanston Campus will eventually hold, I am quite sure in spite of my first impressions, that the Georgian will not be as capable of variety as the Gothic, which presents more freedom and picturesque composition and does not demand the symmetry that Georgian has to have.[39]

Rogers was here dealing with a college president who wanted recognizable monuments, not frugal buildings (see Chapter 6), but he justified his backpedaling toward the style for which he had by then become known by pointing out that Neo-Gothic architecture did two things: it allowed for more incremental and responsive planning by utilizing a picturesque organizational scheme to give unity to functionally arranged buildings, thus permitting Rogers to create what he considered a more responsive and thus more "modern" architecture, and it projected an image of grandeur and spirituality that could attract donors to Northwestern:

There are two things that appeal to me in this partial change of mind on my part—the first is the chance to make a distinctive style of elastic Gothic architecture that will be 'Northwestern Gothic' and the other is, that it will be so much more impressive that I am confident that you will find it easier to raise a 110% cost building in this style than you will be able to secure funds for a 100% cost building in the Colonial style.[40]

Thus Rogers presents the Collegiate Gothic as the perfect marriage of pragmatic concerns about organization and image. This merger would allow for growth, the construction of a clear image, and the creation of a coherent institution. In the end, Rogers managed to manipulate the whole situation to his advantage by freeing more funds for his buildings. The change from Georgian to Gothic turned out to be remarkably simple: the building remained exactly the same, including its internal and external symmetry, but the full range of Gothic elements replaced their Georgian counterparts. One rendering of the main circulation room and stair hall shows a light-filled room in which domes and rounded arches project a kind of Soanian grandeur. Another rendering, done several months later from the same vantage point, shows exactly the same room, but now cast in a darkness shot through by shafts of light coming from windows with pointed arches.[41]

The whole episode highlights the specificity of the manner in which Rogers used the Collegiate Gothic. Especially in the design of separate buildings, which lacked the necessity for picturesque planning that allowed him to inflect the programmatic forms of larger complexes, Rogers managed to develop his method to the point where the Collegiate Gothic elements were completely separate from the rationally planned interior. They were used instead to make the whole comfortable and natural-seeming and then to package, style, and sell the program visually, as a composed picture, to the client and viewer. The integrated idealism of the Harkness Quadrangle had by now been standardized into an architectural package. Rogers' pragmatism had hardened into a working method, a way of manipulating historical styles that turned out not to be tied to the organic nature of Neo-Gothicism.

Throughout the 1920s and 1930s, Rogers refined and adapted his Collegiate Gothic style to different programs and changing architectural fashions. In defending the design of Yale's Sterling Memorial Library in 1928, he said:

> The style of Sterling Memorial Library . . . is as near to modern Gothic as we dared to make it. We kept, however, sufficiently close to the sound principles and tried traditions of old Gothic to be certain that there would be no sense of freakishness and no danger of becoming, in the passing of time, a little out of style . . . an architecture that would be imposing but not too austere, picturesque but not too trivial, with something of grace but with enough strength to be as enduring as the old, tried, styles that have stood the test of time.[42]

That style was nonetheless Gothic, because of its power to convince. As one observer noted: "If . . . a university can bring [the student] within its influence, not the least of its opportunities unique with it, unique for him, will be to invest him with the visible responses to state and mood. And in architecture none responds as does the Gothic."[43] The architectural resolution of Sterling Memorial Library thus was engendered by an allusive approach to the transformation of a value-laden past in a productive present while creating a monument decomposed into picturesque pieces and yet permanent in its organization. The modernity of Collegiate Gothic, which is to say its functionality, collage-ness, and scientific flexibility, was both its strength and its literal undoing.

Indeed, the very success of this attempt made the Sterling Library building the object of the most extreme and virulent attack to which James Gamble Rogers' architecture was ever exposed. The attack came from within the Yale community itself in the form of an article written by an undergraduate, William Harlan Hale, in the second issue of a remarkable magazine called *The Harkness Hoot*.[44] To Hale, Sterling was the pinnacle of un-American imitation, an archaeological dig at what should have been the summit of the campus. Hale not only reversed the reading of the physical shape of the

IT MIGHT HAVE BEEN

From the Yale Alumni Weekly

The Book Tower of Sterling Memorial Library as it was while under construction. It might have been made into a monumental modern building—with the structural and decorative ideas evolved by American skyscraper designers newly adapted to a splendid and living institutional structure. On the opposite page is the Library as it appears today.

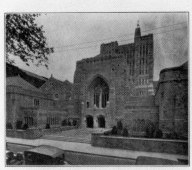

From the Yale Alumni Weekly

You shall no longer take things at second or third hand, nor look through the eyes of the dead, nor feed on the spectres in books.
—WALT WHITMAN

There, because hee doth know
That shee was there a thousand years agoe,
He loves her ragges. . .
—JOHN DONNE

41. Harlan Hale. "It Might Have Been," illustration in *The Harkness Hoot*, November 15, 1930.

building, he also reversed the implications of its "modern gothic" compromise as well. It was not a reaching toward something but instead, he claimed, was "safely constructed—alas! for the ages. Few works can equal it as a monument of lifelessness and decadence; none can surpass its extravagance and falsity."[45] Hale saw monumentality and tradition as deadly rather than conducive to college life, while the decorative richness was a falling back toward ignorance. Sterling, said Hale, was built out of an "ideal of academic isolation, of escape from the present, of flight from fact. . . . It erects dead buildings to inhabit, and proclaims a dead ideal to follow."[46] As an illustration to his point, Hale offered the scaffolding placed around the old library when the books were moved to the new building as a negative model for the Sterling Library (Fig. 41). Here was a model for the antiarchitectural stripping away of the myth of Yale as it was embodied in its new, James Gamble Rogers–designed buildings. Though the impulse for this critique may have been formal, its final justification came, in a quotation from Thorstein Veblen, out of an accurate reading of the Sterling Library as a highly successful monument to the ability of American capitalism to commute its wealth into places of flexible control, or highly designed bastions for its effective elite:

An appreciable store of the funds given by wealthy donors to public institutions is present in the construction of an edifice faced with some aesthetically objectionable but expensive stone, covered with grotesque and incongruous details, and designed, in its battlemented walls and turrets and its massive portals and strategic approaches, to suggest certain barbaric methods of warfare. The interior of the structure shows the same pervasive guidance of conspicuous waste and predatory exploit.[47]

Frank Lloyd Wright is said to have had the article read out in the drafting room of his self-imposed economic and stylistic exile in Spring Green, Wisconsin, and it was reprinted with acclaim by newspapers and Modernist-oriented magazines around the country.[48] This indeed was the final application of Rogers' pragmatic architecture: more than the isolated work of John Russell Pope or the grand schemes of Burnham, it had become the very emblem and realization of the institutional power of the effective elite of America. Pragmatism had by this time become the ideology of the ruling elite, and its architecture, just at the point when it was becoming the most idealized expression of its tenets, had solidified into a beautiful monument to what was supposed to be a lively and experimental approach to education and knowledge in general.

Throughout James Gamble Rogers' career, he relied on a counterpoint to the Collegiate Gothic. The last three colleges or dormitories he designed for Yale University combined elements reminiscent of buildings constructed in America and England in the seventeenth and eighteenth centuries, thus producing what might be called a "Collegiate Georgian." Rogers seems to have been comfortable with this style, if one can judge from his behavior in the design of the Northwestern University library or from the fact that he lived in homes that harked back directly in their design to Colonial precedents. Rogers never felt the need to hire stylistic specialists in his office to produce such an architecture, as he had for the design of the Memorial Quadrangle, nor did he assemble a book of snapshots with Georgian details.

This was a simpler style, to be sure, made up of brick walls accented by white-painted wood trim using a much more limited repertoire of ornaments, including pedimented gables, Ionic, Doric, and Corinthian columns or pilasters, oriels, a few swags, and casement windows.[49] The Collegiate Georgian institutional buildings, however, shared with the Collegiate Gothic designs the ability to convey a picturesque image of days gone by, adapted to modern needs. They also shared many compositional traits, though Rogers in this case developed a design strategy that combined ecclesiastical, industrial, institutional, and domestic precedents. As such, the Collegiate Georgian answered more explicitly the question of how the emerging large-scale institutions of the modern state (especially hospitals and universities) could liter-

42. James Gamble Rogers.
Norton Hall, Southern Baptist
Theological Seminary,
Louisville, Kentucky, 1926.

43. James Gamble Rogers.
Norton Hall, Southern Baptist
Theological Seminary,
Louisville, Kentucky, 1926.
Detail of entry.

ally be domesticated, be made to seem part of a familiar, smaller-scale tradition. The Collegiate Georgian style was both more modern in appearance—because it was stripped down and made up of large geometric solids—and more traditional, containing as it did fewer of the innovative characteristics that marked Rogers' Collegiate Gothic buildings.

The composition of the Collegiate Georgian can be read clearly in Rogers' design of 1926 for Norton Hall at the Southern Baptist Theological Seminary in Louisville, Kentucky (Figs. 42, 43). Consistency in this picturesque composition of Neo-Georgian elements is provided by the overlapping of three different typological precedents. The largest and most formal type is that of the New England church. Its bell tower, colonnaded front, and large Classical ornaments placed over simple forms provide the central imagery for all of the buildings at the seminary. These pediments, columns, and towers are then reflected in a smaller scale at the secondary entrances and at the crossing points in the composition. Thus, the central religious character and ceremonial scale of the campus are fixed. The actual texture or mass of the functional elements is then treated in an almost industrial vernacular of plain, robust brick walls whose windows are organized into simple grids. Since the ecclesiastical elements give shape to the overall composition or collection of these functional volumes, these separate pieces are connected without the kind of complicated transitional massing Rogers used in his Collegiate Gothic buildings. Finally, the institutional mass of the whole building is scaled down to the user through the use of domestic doorways, windows, and other decorative motifs, which appear to have been deliberately tacked on to the building for this purpose.

Why then did Rogers in one case create a seamless image and in another case layer on various scales and references? In most cases the solution was dictated more by the contingencies of the commission than by any stylistic preference: the architecture had to answer the seminary's call for "conformity to the general type of architecture known as Colonial, and seen in a very attractive form in the buildings of the University of Virginia."[50] Such was the case also in the design of the three Collegiate Georgian colleges at Yale. Only in a few cases was the choice between Gothic and Georgian an explicitly ideological one. When Rogers was asked to design a new Schoolhouse (classroom building) at Saint Paul's Academy in 1933, its rector, S. S. Drury, argued strenuously for the adaptation of "the Colonial" style:

> And need such a building be Gothic in its style? Though the Gothic has been chosen as our norm, I plead for the ample, square-windowed Georgian style when we come to the teaching scene. There is something exotic in a completely Gothic equipment for American youth. The Gothic is suitable for churches, and adaptable for domiciles or dining halls; but for the give-and-take of learning let us consider the dignified Colonial, with welcoming wings and gilded cupola—something with which the countrymen of George Washington might feel comfortable.[51]

To Drury, the Collegiate Gothic implied an imported ideology and a certain ceremonializing of everyday life. The "Colonial," on the other hand, implied real work by young men fulfilling an organic tradition—the real architecture of Pragmatism. One can imagine that Rogers might be sympathetic to such an outlook, but Drury was finally overruled by his board and possibly by donor Edward Harkness, who all felt that the Schoolhouse should be Gothic "so as to harmonize with the [nearby, Henry Vaughan–designed] Chapel, but being made of different material and trim, [which] will permit the Chapel, as is fitting and proper, to maintain its dignity, charm and individuality."[52] Rogers performed a detailed cost analysis on the differences between the two styles, in which he fleshed out his claim, stated earlier at Northwestern, that a Gothic building would cost 6 percent more by noting such constructional details as the fact that doors with arches cost 50 to 60 percent more than their square counterparts, that stone fireplaces cost 100 percent more than those in "simple Georgian brick," and that stone cornices cost a full 300 percent more than the same detail carried out in wood.[53] The Collegiate Georgian would thus seem to be a more appropriate style in a time of rationalization of the economics of building. In the end, however, the weight of tradition and context was heavier than either the preferences of the modernizing rector or the economic analyses of construction, and a "Tudor Gothic" design (as Harkness described it) was presented to the board of the academy in 1934 (Fig. 44).[54]

44. James Gamble Rogers. New Schoolhouse, St. Paul's Academy, Concord, New Hampshire, 1934–37.

What speaks most clearly from this sort of situation is Rogers' flexibility and the clear role Collegiate Gothic played in providing an image. Perhaps catching the winds of the times, Rogers continually argued for Collegiate Georgian as a more rational approach to building, while his clients wanted the more evocative, romantic, and expensive Gothic detailing added to their institutions. In the end, one could argue that the Collegiate Gothic style, though it fulfilled many of the Pragmatist ideals, became an inflexible impediment to the rationalization of such institutions, and thus contradicted many of the tenets of flexibility, responsiveness, and organic revelation central to pragmatic architecture. Perhaps it is for this reason that the later buildings at Yale were designed in Collegiate Georgian, though this style represented more of a retreat from the creation of a complex and inclusive architecture than an expression of Modernist reductivism.

There is, however, another side to this argument. Just as Neo-Colonial styles came to be preferred by business in the 1930s, so Colonial homes gained wider and wider acceptance during this period. Rogers and his clientele were retreating from the confident and didactic forms of Neo-Gothicism toward a style that more directly reflected their cultural roots. The increased use of Collegiate Georgian can thus also be seen as a mark of the increased elitism and isolation of the institutions for which Rogers worked. The reaction against this process came, starting with Walter Gropius's work on the Graduate School at Harvard University, in the form of Modernism—a style with which Rogers was sympathetic, but which he never fully embraced.

Rogers ultimately justified his work only in terms of professionalism and that undefinable mark of a gentleman, good taste. His architecture must thus finally be put in the context of attempts in the 1920s and 1930s to define architecture as part of an upper-class, business-oriented form of art that was essentially autonomous in its directions and definitions. Pragmatic architecture ultimately was both successful and superseded because it confided itself to this narrow realm. Two developments of the early 1920s affirm Rogers' position in this regard. In 1924 Rogers incorporated his office, thus fixing its production as part of a rational, corporate endeavor, and he became chairman of the board of the highly successful new architecture magazine *The Architect*, which was founded in the spring of 1923. While the reorganization allowed him, as he said, to "get into a position where my time will have to be given to only architectural questions which enable me to give to my clients more of the service for which I am employed,"[55] the editorials and articles published in *The Architect* defined the nature of such an architecture. One might say that in this magazine Rogers found a voice for his aspirations.

The voice of the magazine was George S. Chappell, an often witty and irreverent embodiment of the kind of urbane, well-read architectural culture that suffused the practice in New York during these boom years. Chappell had also been a fellow student of Rogers' at the Ecole des Beaux-Arts in the 1890s. The magazine prided itself on presenting only a few carefully chosen and photographed projects in each issue. This "best work being produced in America," as they put it, showed the correct and creative adaptation of historical styles.[56] Almost half of the projects were residences for the wealthy. Chappell sprinkled the editorial pages with chatty discussions of the day-to-day travails of the busy architect as he confronted demanding clients and sought insurance policies.[57] His irreverence encompassed his primary audience as well: he authored a series of parodies, based on Greek comedy, of the manner in which architects managed to give clients not what they wanted, but what suited the designer.[58] One can compare Chappell's writing with the drier, more trenchant prose of Malcolm Cowley of *The New Republic* or of Lewis Mumford in *The New Yorker.* Against these writers' calls for social relevance and analyses that took buildings to task for their functional and economic inadequacies, Chappell's prose and arguments cannot but seem overwrought.[59]

The Architect also served as a vehicle for the self-promotion of its board members and friends, including as it did elaborate displays of Rogers' work and that of such architects as Electus D. Litchfield, Donn Barber, and Aymar Embury. [60] The "Editorial Comment" in each issue offered a justification for the kind of architecture these men produced. "Our architecture is rapidly passing into a new chapter," asserted the editor in "To Our Public" in one of the first issues of the magazine,

> . . . which clearly reveals a saner play of mind, a more controlled imagination, and a higher grasp and use of interpretative and suitable forms. . . . There is more style, more grace, a better taste in handling constantly appearing in the solution of our many and varied problems of planning and design. It is the function of architecture to clothe utility with beauty and commensurate fitness in lasting materials.[61]

The question of architecture to Chappell was thus not one of relevance, but of translation. The criteria for judging this kind of architecture were embedded in this kind of interpretative activity. Control, taste, suitability, the thoughtful ordering of building materials, and the considered response to context according to the discipline of a historically formed craft: all these qualities were combined in buildings of sound-seeming construction. Thus architecture fixed values without recourse to political or literary ideologies. Beaux-Arts notions of character had become questions of cultured taste.

Such a "recipe for successful building" defined what Chappell thought the designer added and the client paid for in excess of housing the program: ". . . architecture puts into it logic plus imagination. . . . Beauty will be the inevitable result. It is a mistake to think of beauty as a thing apart."[62] While logic may be learned, and imagination may be the province of the creative artist, the meaning of the combination of the two could not, thought Chappell, be extracted from the actual built result or from the character of the institution as it was realized in the architecture: "The designing of a complete and harmonious whole, the composing of detail, fenestration, and ornament in a pleasing relation to the mass of the building involved, this is the architectural problem in its larger aspect."[63] Thus the core of design, as Chappell defined it, was exactly that about which Rogers refused to speak. All one could comment on beyond such matters would be certain "tendencies of modern design," which would "appear to be away from the conventional classic. . . . A more romantic note is creeping into architecture. It is more inspired, more vital, more native." Yet at the same time one had to understand that "the beauties of the past and those of the future are but links in the chain of continuity."[64] This was essentially a conservative architecture:

> Because of the innate conservatism on the part of the public and the high cost of experimentation, architecture remains the most perfect record that we have of man's efforts since the beginning of civilization. . . . While painters are wallowing in the throes of confusion and poets are seeking an easy form by the cross-cuts of *vers libre*, architecture goes its own way, displaying, in spite of isolated examples of eccentricity, a serene continuity, an immunity to fadism, a respect for tradition, and a steadfastness to beauty which fully accounts for her preeminence in the world of idealistic impression.[65]

Obviously, the Neo-Colonial architecture that filled the pages of *The Architect* was more appropriate to the goals of these arbiters of good taste.

Thus one can trace the outlines of James Gamble Rogers' architecture, no matter what its appearance: the assimilation of new techniques of production and new technologies into a built reality; the spatial and temporal contextualizing of that building; the embodiment in architecture of the ordering power of culture; the confident representation of this process in a series of coherent compositions; an organic idealism thrown over all of these pragmatic concerns. Yet pragmatism had become a style well adapted to its increasingly limited clientele. Just as he felt more comfortable in an architecture that was old-fashioned and humble in its appearance, and thus chose to build Neo-Georgian structures for himself and his family, so he felt most at home in a milieu where it was all a matter of taste. From the reuse of accepted styles adapted to modern functions, to the sophisticated articulation of a Pragmatist program for understanding, organizing, and reforming the world, to delicate matters of taste and a vague representation of the nature of the times—this is the trajectory of Rogers' work. It achieved its fullest clarity and beauty in his Collegiate Gothic work and descended, toward the end of his life, more and more into the polite and tasteful adaptation of modern programs.

CHAPTER THREE

Civic Architecture

James Gamble Rogers had the opportunity to define his public architecture very early in his career. He did so in the design of a series of schools, post offices, and courthouses constructed in the first decade of the twentieth century. These projects were stylistically similar and appeared little different from similar types of buildings being produced at that time by other architects. It is only in the organizational responses and in the manipulation of some of the iconography and detailing of these buildings that one can find a clear indication of the pragmatic and picturesque response Rogers was to develop in his later designs.

Rogers received his first public commission in 1899, when he was thirty-two years old and only just back from the Ecole des Beaux-Arts. On August 5, 1899, *The Economist* announced that Mrs. Anita McCormick Blaine had, in the largest real estate transaction of that year in metropolitan Chicago, bought a large tract of land in the Near Northside of Chicago. She intended to erect a school on this lot, one that would compete with the new museums and libraries of Chicago as one of the city's major public monuments. Remarkably, this civic project was to be designed by an unknown young architect:

> . . . the school will be one of the beauty spots of Chicago, and the architecture will be as much of a credit to the city as that of the Newberry Library, the Public Library, or the Art Institute. . . . James Gamble Rogers' designs have been accepted for the buildings which will comprise the institution. He has been at work on them for some time, and it is understood that others have also submitted plans, but Mr. Rogers was the successful competitor. It will be recalled that Mr. Rogers is the young Chicago architect who graduated this year from the Ecole des Beaux-Arts in Paris and was awarded a diploma by the French Government and was the recipient of medals for proficiency in art and construction. He has designed several fine residences for the city—one for Dr. George S. Isham and one for Robert H. Allerton. . . .[1]

The client was the daughter of Cyrus McCormick, inventor, founder of the McCormick Reaper works, and industrialist. She was the young widow of Emmons Blaine, a lawyer and son of a Secretary of State under President Harrison. Mrs. Blaine was also related through marriage to the Day family, who were Rogers' in-laws. After the untimely death of her husband, who had been a rising star in progressive political circles, she was left with a large fortune and one son. She devoted the next several decades of her life to the education of her son in particular, and to the cause of progressive education in general.[2]

Her advisor in these matters was Francis Wayland Parker. Colonel Parker, as he was known, was the head of the Cook County Normal School with a reputation as an educational innovator. His philosophy was to have his students participate directly with the real world and its objects through work and play. Instead of teachers inculcating abstract dicta into unformed minds, Parker wanted open classrooms that would resemble laboratories or workshops. He saw them as experimental and scaled-down versions of American society: "That which children learn from each other in play or work, though the work be drudgery, is the highest that is ever learned. The mingling and fusing and blending of each with all, gives personal power, and makes the public school a tremendous force in the upbuilding of democracy."[3] His school buildings were experimental versions of the real world idealized into the common pursuit of individual goals.

When Colonel Parker lost his position with the Cook County school system, Mrs. Blaine offered him the opportunity to begin an institution wholly on his principles for the education of her son and the children of like-minded parents. She pledged to pay the cost of the construction of the new institution out of her family fortune. Together with her fellow trustees she selected both the site and the architect.

It is unclear how James Gamble Rogers was finally chosen.[4] On July 12, 1899, he submitted a program and cost estimate to Mrs. Blaine for a building to house six hundred students and to include a kindergarten, an elementary school, a grammar school, a high school, and a teachers' training college. Facilities, in addition to ample, well-lighted, and fireproof classrooms, were to include a gymnasium, two swimming pools, a fifteen-hundred-seat auditorium, and a library for sixteen thousand volumes. Yet Rogers promised that this behemoth would be designed in a manner "expressing repose and scholarly bearing. Simplicity, solidity, durability and 'intime' character should be sought for, rather than a monumental impressiveness."[5] Perhaps his businesslike clarity and promised lack of pretension won the day both with a woman known for the forceful presentation of her (not always conventional) ideas in polite society, and with the hard-nosed trustees of the McCormick Estate.[6]

During the winter of 1899, Rogers visited schools in the East, and in February 1900 he presented a plan for a three-story building 442 feet long, clad in Bedford granite and brick, and grouped around a central dome (Fig. 45). The building was large, but not at all coherent or contained in the manner one would expect from a recent graduate of the Ecole des Beaux-Arts. Two wings extended from the long main building to enclose a courtyard

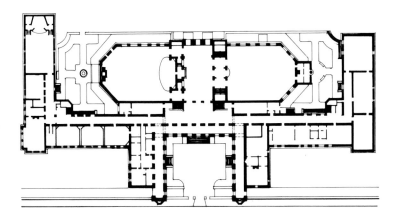

45. James Gamble Rogers. The Chicago Institute (project), Chicago, Illinois, 1899. First plan.

screened by a cloister and containing miscellaneous offices and classrooms. The rotunda occurred not at the center, but behind the stretched-out main axis of the building, which itself was perpendicular to the actual direction of entrance. This rotunda was flanked by a gymnasium and an assembly hall treated as symmetrical rooms ending in semihexagonal apses. This body of large and formal spaces was connected only tenuously with the main mass of the building by an elongated line of toilets and wardrobe rooms. Asymmetrical side wings, containing classrooms and various workspaces, abruptly ended the whole composition to either side.[7] In general, the building bore little resemblance to the compact containers of classrooms that were then the norm for high schools in Chicago.[8]

This strange amalgamation of disparate shapes and functions was rejected by Mrs. McCormick and her fellow trustees, and Rogers presented a revised design by May of the same year, deleting the stone, the gymnasium, and the assembly hall.[9] Apparently still not satisfied, the trustees asked Rogers to associate with the large and experienced firm of Holabird & Roche. After initially refusing, Rogers agreed in June to design a building in association with the firm.[10] This second design, of which only plans remain, was to have been a more conventional T-shaped building, in which a central wing containing a small auditorium and gymnasium (omitted during the redesign process) pierced the long cross axis of offices and classroom spaces were arrayed on either side of a corridor that terminated in two short-end pavilions (Fig. 46).

Though neither plan was constructed, this first civic commission already illustrates Rogers' distaste for central axes and his preference for stretching functional spaces along hallways running perpendicular to the entrance sequence. The almost casual assemblage of disparate shapes around this central axis evokes the absence of a clear central organizing space or idea. Rather than imposing a formal space or spatial sequence in order to rep-

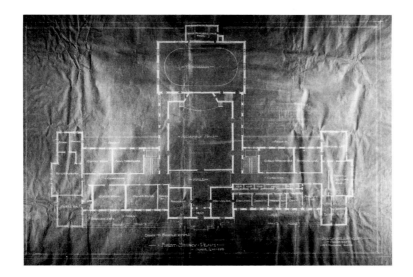

46. James Gamble Rogers. The Chicago Institute (project), Chicago, Illinois, 1900. Second plan.

resent the meaning or role of the institution, Rogers chose to let the large scale, the materials, and the functional organization dictate the forms of the institution. In a sense, Rogers was allowing his practical training to govern the organization of the building, while using the lessons of the Beaux-Arts only to construct a thin and malleable image, often fragmented into no more than isolated motifs or decorative focal points.

In his first architectural essays after his stay at the Ecole des Beaux-Arts, Rogers thus already displayed an attitude toward his work that differed fundamentally from that of many of his fellow American Ecole students. He did not seem to be interested in creating integrated and imposing master-pieces that would subsume all functions and meanings into themselves, but sought rather to break up his buildings into functional and articulated objects. It is interesting to note that in August 1900, Rogers held Jefferson's pavilionized University of Virginia up to Mrs. McCormick as an example of "the sentiment of architecture that a seat of learning should have."[11]

The exact form of "the Chicago Institute," as the school was to be known, became a moot issue by the spring of 1901. Possibly under pressure from her fellow trustees, Mrs. McCormick during the winter of 1900–1901 abandoned her attempt to start her own comprehensive institute, and instead agreed to donate a building at the University of Chicago to house a new School of Education. The school was to be headed by Parker and by the philosopher John Dewey.[12] Dewey had given a series of lectures in Mrs. Blaine's living room in 1899 entitled "The School and Society,"[13] and by then was the leading exponent of progressive education in the country. His emphasis on the importance of practical experience, his championing of prag-matic policies in both morality and politics, and his insistence on the importance of the acquisition of knowledge as the central factor determining the success or failure of American society echoed Parker's methods, but in a larger and more far-reaching sphere.[14] The School of Education was to be the formal representation of Dewey's central role at the University of Chicago, and later problems related to its administration would lead to his departure for Columbia University.[15] Through the commission for the School of Education, Rogers thus had the chance to build not merely a civic building, but one of the most fully developed monuments to progressive liberal thinking in the country.

The change in venue for the commission also served to confront Rogers for the first time with American Neo-Gothic architecture. The plan of the University of Chicago had been laid out in 1891 by Henry Ives Cobb because "Gothic architecture was seen as providing adaptability and variety within a controlled plan."[16] The Gothic of Cobb and his successors was, however, a thin veneer of medieval motifs gathered mainly from England and France and applied to massive and compact buildings that had been placed as solitary objects within the grid of city blocks. Only with the arrival of a younger generation of architects around the turn of the century, including Dwight Perkins and the firm of Holabird & Roche, did the campus start to achieve a more picturesque and varied massing, assembling itself into a series of semi-enclosed quadrangles reminiscent of monastic cloisters or English colleges. At the same time, the detailing and landscaping of the buildings became more Classical, thus reversing the original order; Gothicism became a way of making more picturesque the many orders and rules of Academic Classicism.

James Gamble Rogers was brought along as the architect of this latest version of Mrs. McCormick's dream. He carried with him the bricks that were to have been used for the construction of "the Chicago Institute," and, until John D. Rockefeller donated an extra $50,000 to clad the new school in the same stone as was used on the rest of the campus, the building was to have had stone as trim only.

Emmons Blaine Hall was completed in 1903, at the rather substantial cost of over $1 million,[17] and was quickly joined by Belfield Hall, an addition that housed workshops for the manual-training division of the school. A planned gymnasium was never built on the site, although Rogers designed a temporary facility nearby. The school was organized in response to climate and sunlight, stepping down from a four-story street frontage on the Midway (the grand civic space at its southern edge) to two three-story wings. Rogers called the overall parti "monumental," but noted that he had created "enough movement in the roof line to prevent too great severity in its appearance."[18]

The building faces the expanse of the Midway with two wings whose gables run parallel to the street and with middle pavilions whose gable ends

47. James Gamble Rogers.
School of Education,
University of Chicago,
Chicago, Illinois, 1901–4.

48. James Gamble Rogers.
School of Education,
University of Chicago,
Chicago, Illinois, 1901–4.
Detail.

49. James Gamble Rogers.
School of Education,
University of Chicago,
Chicago, Illinois, 1901–4.
Interior.

face the street (Figs. 47–49). The latter offer a visual counterpoint picked up
in the three gable ends that surmount each wing. Finials and turrets seem to
sprout everywhere from the moldings, yet the overall impression of a large
and relatively unmodulated wall cannot be avoided. The moldings seem
applied at the last moment, barely pulling the large expanses of glass into a
proportional composition. With its symmetry of all elements, from the wings
to the skylights, and its lack of any mass or color, the design avoids monumentality but seems to offer only bulk in return.

To the sides, the scale of the building declines; originally it gave way
to an open cloister connecting Blaine with the smaller, more agitated forms of

50. James Gamble Rogers.
Belfield Hall, School of
Education, University of
Chicago, Chicago, Illinois,
1901–4.

Belfield Hall (Fig. 50). The latter is remarkable because Rogers left both its Gothicism and its industrial or commercial precedents more clearly present on the facade. Here the pointed arches actually define the areas of glass, whereas on the more polite, urbane front facade the transom below the arches is treated only as a blank panel, or the arch is applied only with the kind of detached molding already familiar from Rogers' Beaux-Arts project. At the back, the sawtoothed roofs of the workshops march across the length of the block, rising out of a stripped-down stone box.

The whole complex was supposed to have formed a series of detached buildings, each one housing and expressing a different part of the School of Education,[19] with a series of cloisters connecting the separate units in an articulation of the bureaucracy or communality of purpose that ruled the institution. The school would thus have been a built analogy to "the real world" in the same way the educational system was supposed to mimic the world beyond the confines of the school. Unfortunately, lack of funds and a brutally insensitive post–Second World War addition have made it impossible to judge whether such a compound would have had the desired effect.

At the same time that James Gamble Rogers was designing this large home for the School of Education, he was also building a small school on the original site of the proposed Chicago Institute. It was in this more modest school, later to be known as the Francis W. Parker School, that Mrs. Blaine's son, and the children of many of her Near Northside neighbors, friends, and admirers, were to be educated (Fig. 51). Mrs. Blaine paid $45,000 of the $55,000 to $60,000 cost of this modest structure, which was built in four months after Rogers' design and estimate were approved on May 20, 1901.[20] The two-story building housed 180 pupils and contained classrooms, "laboratories" or workshops, a kindergarten, a gymnasium, and an assembly hall with seating for three hundred people.

Whereas the School of Education was a formal, monumental project whose compromise of industrial, classicizing, and Neo-Gothic architecture

51. James Gamble Rogers.
Francis W. Parker School,
Chicago, Illinois, 1902.

bespoke both its generic importance and the education of future citizens, the Parker School was more an extension of the type of domestic environment in which, according to the conventional wisdom of the time, children were to be nurtured in their early years. There were fireplaces in the classrooms, rather than one formal set piece in the vestibule, as was the case at the School of Education; the corridors were scaled and designed as playrooms, and the architecture of the building was described in the prospectus as being "in the English style,"[21] similar to many of the Tudor houses then rising up in the new developments of the North Shore.

A Tudor treatment of the second floor in rough yellow plaster and timber rose out of a first floor clad in Flemish bond brick, while the roof over the asymmetrical mass was steeply pitched and shingled. Rogers' original design did call for a symmetrical building, but the slightly rambling and confused mass of the final design pleased client and students alike, and the much-used buildings served as the unified home for a steadily growing combination of kindergarten, grade school, and high school until it was replaced by a large modern campus after the Second World War.[22]

52. James Gamble Rogers.
Winton Block, Chicago,
Illinois, 1904.

The work James Gamble Rogers did on the School of Education and the Francis Parker School led to only one other educational commission during this period: the design of the Gorton School in Lake Forest, Illinois,[23] since remodeled beyond recognition. Rogers' office still seemed to focus on the production of houses and apartment buildings,[24] of which he produced a regular stream, though he also designed several small commercial structures[25] and one three-story commercial building, the Winton Block, which gained notoriety for its early use of reinforced-concrete structure (Fig. 52).[26]

Rogers also designed one church, the Hyde Park Baptist Church, just a few blocks north of his School of Education building (President William Rainey Harper of the University of Chicago was a congregation member) (Fig. 53). The building as completed is less remarkable than a 1901 rendering produced for fund-raising purposes. This perspective shows a composition dominated by a tall, openwork tower rising from a square base adjacent to the nave and continuing through a series of flying buttresses to a polygonal crown. The tower strongly resembles some of the early versions of the Harkness Memorial Tower that Rogers was to design at Yale fifteen years later, and the treatment of the buttresses as independent but interlocking elements stands in strong contrast to the planar Gothic of the School of Education.[27]

The most interesting structure Rogers designed during this period was a clubhouse for the McCormick Reaper Works of the International Harvester Company (Figs. 54, 55). It appears that the relatively luxurious clubhouse was part of the McCormicks' benevolent social policy of the period, as the Reaper Works proclaimed that it was "the aim of the company to make it

53. James Gamble Rogers.
Hyde Park Baptist Church,
Chicago, Illinois, 1906.

a model institution of its kind."[28] The building was connected by a tunnel to
the factory across the street and contained an auditorium for seven hundred
people, a library and reading room, various club rooms and classrooms, and a
bowling alley in the basement.

After the worker had showered and changed in an area adjacent to
the tunnel, he rose into a world of culture and camaraderie. The large garden
adjacent to the building extended both the educational and the social functions of the building with a bandstand, a small "technical college" where
young men could learn skills that might allow them to advance in the company, and a model cottage where their wives might learn the basics of good
housekeeping.[29] The building thus served to translate the world of the
McCormick Works into a cultural home, an addition made possible by the
profits from the industrial plant across the street and dedicated to the propo-
sition that such a surplus might be converted by both employer and employees into a defined set of values focused around learning, social graces, and
play. In a sense, the McCormick Club was the Francis Parker School extended into the real world and married to the model of an English club.

The building was almost completely split between the large mass of
the auditorium, which doubled as a cafeteria, and the house-like two-and-a-
half-story block containing the other club rooms. The club rooms were clad in
dark oak and in several cases were elaborately painted above the wood wain-
scot. Monumental fireplaces, each one slightly different, were the focus of the
main rooms, which were themselves arranged around a small vestibule and
stair hall. The monumental and axial space of the auditorium found its coun-

54. James Gamble Rogers.
McCormick Club, Chicago,
Illinois, 1904.

55. James Gamble Rogers.
McCormick Club, Chicago,
Illinois, 1904.
Club rooms.

terpart in the informal arrangement of these rooms, tied together with only two small hallways. Elaborate carvings and colored tile mosaics continued some of the Arts and Crafts–influenced motifs of Rogers' houses of the period.

The exterior of the building expressed these two different parts clearly. Though the whole building was clad in brick with limestone trim, the auditorium was expressed as a low, almost factory-like shed, while the club rooms were placed in a gabled and dormered house that met the street with an asymmetrically placed two-story bay beneath a pedimented cross gable. Windows were grouped in bands in a manner that recalled both Rogers' educational work and, however slightly, English Neo-Gothic buildings such as those Richard Norman Shaw designed in the late nineteenth century. The joint between the two halves was not masked. Instead, it celebrated the complex program of the clubhouse by becoming the location of the main entrance, which was marked by two stone columns supporting an arched pediment. By allowing the functional requirements and minimal, almost abstract architectural compositional elements to play off of each other, rather than either laying a unified architecture over them or expressing one or the other, Rogers created a strategy, here carried out in simple and economical materials, that would be of great use to him in a career later focused on such types of buildings.[30]

By 1905 James Gamble Rogers was moving outside of Chicago and the realm of his family, friends, and new relatives to work on larger civic commissions. In fact, by the following year Rogers had moved from Chicago to New York to form the office of Hale & Rogers.[31] It is not entirely clear why Rogers chose to associate with Herbert D. Hale: his daughter claims that he always regretted his decision.[32] Rogers, who was by now exploiting his contacts with fellow Yale graduates on the East Coast, may have felt the need to associate with a firm whose experience and expertise could supplement his own background in residential work, office buildings, and small civic institutions. His association with Hale may well have added the degree of professionalism to Rogers' firm that persuaded several clients, as we shall see, of the ability of Hale & Rogers to handle large commissions.

Herbert Hale himself had been working out of New York for only a few years, but was already in the process of designing a major department store, a prestigious midtown club building, and numerous suburban schools. Hale, who was eight years older than Rogers, was the son of the eminent minister and ideologue of Boston Brahmindom, Edward Everett Hale. He had graduated from Harvard in 1888, and his background was thus entirely different from that of the public schools, scholarships, and middle-class urbanized Southern family that had formed James Gamble Rogers. In 1889, Hale entered Blondel's atelier at the Ecole des Beaux-Arts, and it is entirely possible that he met Rogers there when the latter appeared four years later. Upon Hale's return to his native Boston, he set up a small architectural practice that, after several false starts and many competition entries, evolved into a firm specializing in the design of high schools. His South Boston High School of 1902 and his Winchester High School of the following year are brick behemoths sparsely decorated with limestone trim. Their formality, rigorous symmetry, and clear focal points, both on the interior and the exterior, stand in strong contrast to Rogers' School of Education of the same period (see Figs. 47–50).[33]

Hale, and later Hale & Rogers, continued to produce high schools and grammar schools in such towns as Plainfield, Montclair, and Paterson,

56. Herbert D. Hale.
Engineering Society Building,
New York, New York, 1904.

57. Hale & Rogers. Delaware,
Lackawanna & Western.
Railroad Station, Scranton,
Pennsylvania, 1906.
Competition entry, elevation.

New Jersey; Bridgeport, Connecticut; and Philadelphia all through the first decade of the twentieth century, thus providing a steady income for a relatively small office and building up a strong expertise in educational design among the members of the firm.[34] It was the opening of the New York office in 1905, however, that broadened the scope of Hale's business, mainly through the addition of two major Manhattan commissions.

The Engineering Society Building on West 39th Street was the national headquarters for that organization, and its twelve stories contained an auditorium, club rooms, a library, and offices (Fig. 56). Resplendent with cartouches and colonnades, it is an Academic Classicist version of a somewhat ceremonial office building.[35] The McCreery Building, a ten-story department store, was more remarkable for its simplicity and for the speed of its construction. The gray-granite-clad steel building was constructed in eight months in 1906 and was, according to one reviewer, "designed along strictly practical lines, yet reminiscent of French Renaissance in the architecture of its ornamentation."[36]

Aside from an office building for the Baltimore & Ohio Railroad in Baltimore, however, four commissions—the Engineering Society, the McCreery store, and two schools—appear to have been the only work that Hale brought into a barely solvent office.[37] The firm was asked to enter several competitions, including those for the Soldiers' Memorial in Pittsburgh[38] and a railroad station in Scranton, Pennsylvania, for the Delaware, Lackawanna & Western Railroad (Fig. 57).[39] It appears that both Rogers and Hale worked on these two competitions, and their designs evidence a blending of the former's tendency to closely align the elements of a composition with separate functional elements and the latter's facility in molding all the parts into a more traditionally symmetrical, hierarchical Beaux-Arts composition. Herbert Hale's health was failing, however. He retired from the firm sometime in 1907 and died at the age of forty-three in 1909.[40]

By then, James Gamble Rogers had made the office into a viable concern, both through the work given to him by Edward Harkness and through commissions for three major civic structures. Each of these three projects was tied directly to local progressive political initiatives that were part of the nationwide City Beautiful movement.

Around the turn of the century the dominant philosophy for coping with the pressures of increased population, overloaded transportation systems, and sanitary and visual chaos was a combination of rational planning (new sewer systems, straightened roads) and the creation of unified building blocks arranged around orthogonal and diagonal avenues, squares, and thoroughfares. This vision of the city, promulgated by a coalition of architects, progressive politicians, and other members of the rising professional class, presented the ideal metropolitan scene as a rational, sanitary infrastructure that would service future industrialization while presenting the image of a controlled, clearly legible world.[41] As such, it was a further development of Pragmatist thought, and in the figure of Henry Adams one can easily find the transition from the delight in a critical understanding of the world to a desire to clean up the politics and the visual chaos of the city, and finally to dreams of perfect research institutes—whether called universities, museums, or hospitals—for the rationalization of daily life.[42]

This vision was instrumental not only in the creation of specific city plans, but also in the emergence of architectural competitions for civic focal points.[43] The movement was legitimized in 1893 by the passage of the Tarnsey Act, which aimed to replace the haphazard and corrupt process of commissioning Federal buildings with a mechanism that supposedly would give the design of the building to the most professional architect. The writers of the act envisioned highly trained managers producing functional masterpieces whose appearance would give an academically correct representation of the civic function the buildings housed. After the turn of the century, these competitions, and in fact much of the Federal building boom, subsided, to be replaced by a phenomenal growth in private civic monuments: downtown skyscrapers and private universities and hospitals, and James Gamble Rogers' commissions, as we shall see, followed this trend.[44]

With the move into the private realm, the rational functionalization of these civic buildings and their architectural representation became increasingly split, allowing each client and each architect a much greater latitude to express the nature of their institution. Right before the Great Depression of the 1930s, civic reform had isolated itself into elite institutions such as Ivy League colleges or religious structures serving the progressive section of the Protestant elite. Office buildings and apartment buildings appropriated the language of civic reform to validate their activities. This development finally reversed itself in the 1930s with the advent of both Modernism and large public-works projects, which together tended to strip stylistic expressions down to points of emphasis more closely integrated with functional mass. Rogers again participated in this development toward the end of his life.[45]

The first of the civic commissions Rogers received was that for the Shelby County Courthouse in Memphis, Tennessee.[46] The construction of this lavish courthouse was the result of a ten-year-long crusade by a "good government" movement, headed by local bank president N. C. Perkins. The movement had earlier engineered the amalgamation of the City of Memphis and Shelby County, and had helped to clean up the town's laissez-faire style of government. Perkins wanted the new courthouse to be a symbol of a new South governed by rational methods derived from the business world, and in 1904 he set off for Chicago with a committee of city elders to find the architect for the new courthouse.[47] He stopped in the office of Daniel H. Burnham, the guiding spirit of the City Beautiful movement and the most successful designer in corporate America. Burnham recommended the young Southern architect who had worked for him ten years ago, James Gamble Rogers.[48]

Rogers' second major institutional building was thus also directly associated with the rationalization and incorporation of many aspects of American culture and politics in the years around the turn of the century. Furthermore, the justification used by the Memphis building committee for hiring him highlights the fact that, though the facade and ideology of such movements as progressive education, the City Beautiful, and Beaux-Arts architecture were formal, logical, and suffused with an aura of moral, economic, and aesthetic inevitability, their inner workings were more often marked by a clubby and informal associationism. Although the commission found the young architect, with only one other public building to his credit, "specially qualified for designing buildings of a monumental character" because of his "education and technical training, supplemented by study and experience abroad," the real reason for hiring Rogers in a noncompetitive process turned out to be the fact that the members of the committee felt that James Gamble Rogers shared their system of values; they could work with him:

> . . . the Commission felt that Mr. Rogers could and would not only share its inspiration as to the character of the building desired, but be able to embody its ideas and wishes into an actual satisfactory reality. Furthermore, it believed that, aside from professional capacity which was unquestioned, the disposition and character of both Mr. Hale and Mr. Rogers were such as to insure harmonious relations during what promised to be a lengthy and intimate personal association.[49]

They were pleased to note that this feeling turned out to be well founded. The building that Rogers designed, working with the office he had by then set up with Herbert D. Hale in New York, fulfilled all of the committee's

expectations. The Shelby County Courthouse became a grand white palace of justice, whose lavish design in the end cost more than $1.5 million, 50 percent more than the original estimate.[50]

The building was raised and set back on its site, so that, according to one reviewer, "it has the effect of allowing the entire building to present itself as a complete, harmonious unit to the observer approaching from any direction" (Fig. 58, see Fig. 34).[51] The building is a handsome but formidable box, anchored at its corners by pedimented entrance pavilions on a grandiose scale. Its main facade is hidden behind fourteen colossal Ionic columns, while its sides rise up from behind a moat in a forbidding march of square pilasters and overscaled windows. Only the back facade allows for a central entrance, and there only in the rusticated base through three doors that seem overwhelmed by another pedimented portico. The Bedford limestone facade has a slightly gray color, and the detailing is simple and severe.

59. James Gamble Rogers.
Shelby County Courthouse,
Memphis, Tennessee, 1905–9.
Detail.

The grandest space inside the courthouse is the hallway that lies sheltered behind the front colonnade. Covered with marble and granite, this lofty space displays its richness in a juxtaposition of different materials and textures that reaches its climax in a series of marble panels, each a different color and grain, and each quarried in a different part of the nation. The corridor opens up through tall mahogany doors onto the shaded portico formed by those columns, so that civic grandeur and Southern living are combined in what is essentially a gathering space left over between the flanking entrance pavilions.

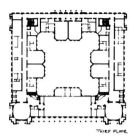

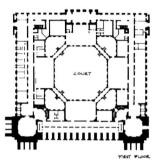

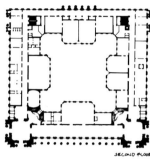

THIRD FLOOR

COURT

FIRST FLOOR

SECOND FLOOR

60. James Gamble Rogers.
Shelby County Courthouse,
Memphis, Tennessee, 1905–9.
Plans.

61. James Gamble Rogers.
Shelby County Courthouse,
Memphis, Tennessee, 1905–9.
Courtyard.

The courtrooms themselves are on all three floors, located in the middle of each side of the structure and flanked by a series of waiting and robing rooms (Fig. 60). They are on the inside of the building, away from the street noise and isolated from the formal and civic spaces and the scale of the entrances, stair halls, and front portico. Lofty and light, they rise up to beamed and stuccoed ceilings from a setting of mahogany benches, wainscoting, and trim. The whole building in turn is organized around an internal courtyard, clad in brick and isolated from the city. There, the octagonal bays of the courtrooms activate and complicate an otherwise simple means of allowing light and air to enter the rooms on the interior of the building (Fig. 61). The civic grandeur of the outside and the public spaces inside, the quiet, elegant courts, and the commonsensical yet serene courtyard at the heart of the building are gathered together into one coherent block, but are also effectively isolated from each other by placement, material, and scale.

Contemporary commentators remarked that the building was "up-to-date" and "the most pretentious public building south of the Ohio River,"[52] and that such gestures as the portico compromised—as in the Robbins House (see Fig. 15)—the integrity and architectural coherence of the building.[53] James Rogers had made a civic building that was both grand and relaxed, both dramatically defined by a coherent architectural system and gathered together out of functional parts without a superfluity of expository spaces. The collection of the parts into a cohesive building and their rationalization by, first, aesthetic rhythms, second, connecting, rather than divisive circulation, and, third, a functional, context- and climate-sensitive arrangement was enough for Rogers and his clients, even if the results sometimes offended those looking for greater formal consistency.

In 1908, the firm of Hale & Rogers won the competition for the design of a new Post Office and Court House in New Orleans, Louisiana (Figs. 62–65). At a cost of $2 million, the New Orleans building was a much larger version of the same program and set of ambitions as that which had created

62. James Gamble Rogers. New Orleans Post Office and Court House, New Orleans, Louisiana, 1908–15.

63. James Gamble Rogers. New Orleans Post Office and Court House, New Orleans, Louisiana, 1908–15.

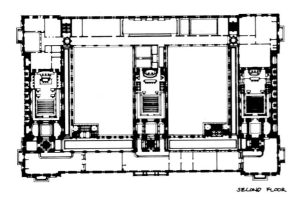

SECOND FLOOR

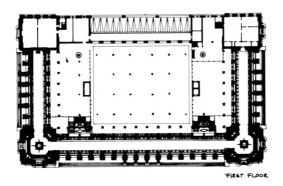

FIRST FLOOR

64. James Gamble Rogers.
New Orleans Post Office and
Court House, New Orleans,
Louisiana, 1908–15. Plans.

65. James Gamble Rogers.
New Orleans Post Office
and Court House, New
Orleans, Louisiana, 1908–15.
Courtroom.

the Shelby County Courthouse, except that the structure was also to contain a post office.[54] Rogers produced a design whose basic strategy was the same as that of the Memphis building: a three-story box held by strong corner pavilions opened on to the street with a long corridor or vestibule, while the courts were placed on the inside middle of the block looking into a courtyard. Here, however, the west facade contained a matching corridor that served as the post office lobby and was in turn mirrored by a loading dock on the east facade. All the courtrooms were thus on the second floor, and the largest of these spaces is placed as a bar in the middle of the courtyards, splitting them in two. The two resulting courtyards were then filled in on the ground floor and used as the main, skylit workspace for the post office.

When Russell F. Whitehead reviewed the architecture of the South in 1911, he called the New Orleans Court House and Post Office "the most important public building of the New South." [55] Whitehead caught the essence of Rogers' architectural strategy in his review of the drawings:

> The development and emphasis of this [front facade] dimension may be said to be the nature of this architecture. . . . [It is an] Italian "palazzo," powerfully reinforced by massive and solid pavilions at the end, but without the dominating pavilion you would expect at the center. The absence of this central feature, however, of course accentuates the length . . . and the detail, as far as can be judged, is academically correct and refined.[56]

The New Orleans structure is much more lavish and more richly detailed than its counterpart in Memphis. A coalition of local businessmen managed to persuade the Federal government to pay for the substitution of white marble for limestone as the cladding material, and Rogers cut the Cherokee, Georgia, stone more deeply and repeatedly than he had in Memphis. The whole base is striated, and window moldings and stringcourses are often tripled or quadrupled. The effect of this detailing and of the whole mass is reserved, compact, and opulent.[57]

James Gamble Rogers designed one other courthouse and post office building under the Tarnsey Act, though in this building the hierarchical importance of the two elements was reversed. The New Haven Post Office, which, in addition to its main (ground floor) function, houses a courtroom and miscellaneous Federal offices, was the result of agitation by that city's good-government movement, in this case spearheaded by lawyer George Seymour. Simultaneous with the erection of the Public Library on the downtown Green in 1911, the Civic Improvement Committee managed to convince the Federal government that its post office and other agency offices in New Haven were unsanitary and inefficient, and a competition was announced.[58]

66. James Gamble Rogers.
Post Office, New Haven,
Connecticut, 1912–16.

67. James Gamble Rogers.
Post Office, New Haven,
Connecticut, 1912–16. View to
New Haven Green.

James Gamble Rogers beat out such competitors as George B. Post with a scheme that presented to the Green a temple front of ten columns and placed all of the functions in a unified block behind that front (Figs. 66, 67). By keeping the height of the building modest and blending in "colonial motives" with the Classical severity and grandeur of the building, Rogers sought, according to his New Haven associate, George Nichols, to "harmonize with the Colonial churches which face it, without sacrificing the monumental character to be desired in an important government structure."[59]

The scale of the portico, which is lifted off of the street by a flight of stairs, is indeed grand, and yet the portico is contained by the functional building it serves, which aligns with the other public buildings around the Green. The portico is echoed in wood and stone in the churches and the courthouse (Fig. 67). While the Post Office thus has a clear and rather grand presence in the heart of the city, it does not appear as a mere container for a massive bureaucracy. The detailing of the facade further modulates the large

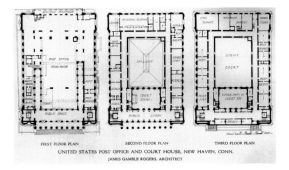

FIRST FLOOR PLAN   SECOND FLOOR PLAN   THIRD FLOOR PLAN

UNITED STATES POST OFFICE AND COURT HOUSE, NEW HAVEN, CONN.

JAMES GAMBLE ROGERS, ARCHITECT

68. James Gamble Rogers. Post Office, New Haven, Connecticut, 1912–16. Plans.

scale of the structure. The modulation of the base as a series of very low geo-metric blocks meeting the sidewalk, the niches carved into the front facade, and the metal doorways applied to the sides all serve to bring the scale down to pedestrian level. Only the attic, necessary to frame the portico and to house the third floor of offices, seems, as in Memphis and New Orleans, not fully integrated into the composition.

One senses Rogers' desire to pack and control tightly all the elements of the composition, adding a separate architectural element—the portico—as a conscious face to the city, then pulling the order of that face through the rest of the facade in the spare architectural ornamentation, and finally carving into the walls, compressing the base, and hiding the attic to bring the whole down to human scale in a single pavilion. The translation of both the grand character and the functional requirements into a sensuous object is height-ened by the careful placement and carving of the Tennessee marble, articu-lated glows and contrasts its veins in different planes.

The self-imposed reserve of the building is in line with Rogers' initial statements on the role of architecture in the making of civic buildings, made when he designed the School of Education in Chicago. According to his associate, George Nichols:

> The building as a whole justifies the belief of its architect in the effec-tiveness of restrained design well executed in fine material. It is single and practical in plan and has clear architectural expression of the func-tion and importance of its parts. The studied simplicity of many of its features insures permanency of style and continued harmony with its surroundings.[60]

Oak and marble, grand porticoes and Corinthian capitals thus have a func-tion as clear as corridors and offices: to express the character of a building which does no more than crystallize and realize the requirements that create it. The architect effaces himself, disappearing into the compression and mod-ulation of the elements, controlling the whole behind the scenes as tightly

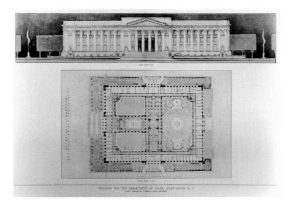

69. James Gamble Rogers.
Department of State,
Washington, D.C., 1906.
Competition entry.

as any businessman orders his productions, and producing an object that is utilitarian, sensuously consumable, and yet—by the very dense logic of its efficiency—monumental, permanent, and assertive about its role in society.[61]

Each of the three major civic buildings that James Gamble Rogers designed between 1905 and 1912 was a focal point for its community. Each cost between $1 million and $2 million. The buildings were at least partially the result of progressive political movements and were combinations of bureaucratic institutions and honorific spaces. Rogers had found a niche for which, by the time he came to design the New Haven structure, he had developed a clear design strategy. Yet these three buildings were only part of a much more ambitious strategy by which this modest and reserved composer of civic elements apparently hoped to become the architect for some of the most important civic monuments in the country.

During these years, Rogers entered many different competitions, winning only the New Orleans and New Haven commissions but gaining honors and recognition in several cases (Fig. 69). [62] He consistently proposed his version of the civic monument. It was an efficient container incorporating closed courtyards of escape and corridors of connection. Its character was added like a thin mask. Its meaning was hidden in delicately buffered and richly detailed formal relations, and its unity was defined by the reality of its materials rather than any abstract ordering system. Rogers never spelled this attitude out in words, nor is his method visible except by analysis of the buildings. Instead, the architecture of James Gamble Rogers disappears into buildings in which scenography and functional representation are superimposed with a skill that seeks to make them indistinguishable. Civic architecture disappears into unstated values.

Such grand structures were by no means the only buildings in Rogers' office during the period after the death of Herbert Hale, however. While James Gamble Rogers did less and less residential work, he took on a number of larger urban structures. These included an office building in Memphis, a museum in the same city, a small school and a chapter house in New York, a high school in Bridgeport, Connecticut, the programmatically hybrid Yale Club of New York, headquarters buildings for the Connecticut General Life Insurance Company and the Aetna Life Insurance Company in Hartford, Connecticut, and an exhibition pavilion for the Crane Company in Atlantic City.

In 1909, the same year that the Shelby County Courthouse was finished, N. C. Perkins, the man responsible for finding its architect in Chicago, commissioned Rogers to design a new building for the Central Bank and Trust, of which he was president (Fig. 70). When the building was finished it took its place, at eighteen stories, as the tallest structure in Memphis. The building is chiefly remarkable in that it was the largest office structure Rogers had designed since the Lees Building (see Fig. 4).[63] Sited four blocks away from the courthouse in the center of Memphis's building district, the Central Bank and Trust building rises from its corner lots as a simple tripartite shaft, three bays by five bays. Proportionally static, and confused in its mixture of materials, the building seems bare and uninspired compared with the courthouse.

James Gamble Rogers made one other contribution to Memphis, a design for its art museum (Fig. 71). The Brooks Museum of Art was built with money donated by the widow of one of Perkins' business partners, Samuel Hamilton Brooks. After some hesitation on the part of the client, Rogers was asked to design a small exhibition pavilion in Overton Park a year after Brooks' death in 1912.[64] The tiny and delicate pavilion sits as "a veritable jewelbox," as one contemporary reviewer noted, of cream-colored marble on top of a hill in a city park. It is a reserved and sensuous container for elements from cultures far away in time and place from Memphis, Tennessee.[65] It is

70. James Gamble Rogers. Central Bank and Trust Building, Memphis, Tennessee, 1911–12.

71. James Gamble Rogers. Brooks Museum of Art, Memphis, Tennessee, 1912–16.

the only museum building Rogers ever designed, and its simplicity and the delicacy of its detailing stand in marked contrast to the more forceful civic structures he was designing during this period.[66]

Though Rogers does not appear to have pursued the expertise in secondary schools that Herbert Hale had brought in to the Hale & Rogers office, he did design one major high school after Hale's death. In 1913, the City of Bridgeport commissioned James Gamble Rogers to design a central high school on a hilltop overlooking downtown (Fig. 72).[67] Rogers' three-story solution is typical of his institutional mode of the period: the building is essentially an extremely long bar placed along the ridge of the hill, and terminated by two symmetrical pavilions.[68] It is a confident, solid-looking building but does not offer much in terms of a sensitive response to its urban setting, its program, or its nature as an institution. It is, however, large enough that it is now used as the city hall.

Between 1911 and 1913, Rogers renovated several brownstones in the Upper East Side neighborhood of Manhattan where he and his family had moved.[69] All of these alterations added only the most delicate and understated classicizing touches to buildings that were completely gutted to make them conform to more modern and convenient forms of living.[70] This neighborhood work culminated several years later in 1919 when Rogers renovated a row of brownstones to house the Mannes College of Music. Rogers' daughter attended the school, and when the institution faced extinction because of a loss of its lease, Rogers found the school a new home and produced a set of drawings. His style of organizing the whole project epitomizes his no-nonsense approach to the importance of culture. According to David Mannes, the school's director, Rogers asked:

> "What sort of building do you want?" We told him the absolute necessary requirements. "And now the facade." [I wanted] a combination of the old Colony Club and an ancient Boston private dwelling; something typically American and simple without the slightest trace in outline of the average educational type of architecture—those

73. James Gamble Rogers. Mannes College of Music, New York, New York, 1919. Elevation.

heavy, formal buildings usually associated with educational purposes. . . . Rogers sent the sketches within two weeks.[71]

The sketches show a white facade whose front is screened by a delicate colonnade that casts the central door in shadow, while overhead only a cartouche and an arched window surround add a hint of formality to the building (Fig. 73). David Mannes's desire for an educational building in which a confluence of domestic, American historical, and educational associations worked themselves out in a minimal and antiformal architectural language is as close to Rogers' philosophy as the school was to the architect's home. There is a strong Southern flavor in the houses Rogers designed in New York and Black Point: wrought-iron trellises, detached porches, and the plantation-like compaction of disparate shapes under an overarching roof show Rogers adapting forms possibly familiar to him from his youth in Kentucky or from visits to his family.

Three blocks away, Rogers designed his largest building in his own neighborhood, the eight-story parish house for the Madison Avenue Presbyterian Church, of which he was a member (Fig. 74). The brick structure is composed as a tripartite block whose divisions are marked with limestone cornices and trim. The parish house is remarkable chiefly for the variety of spaces contained in its simple shaft: a swimming pool in the basement, a two-story auditorium, a school, church offices, and apartments for several church officials are all fitted together on successive floors. Here Rogers condensed the program of such buildings as the McCormick Club and discarded the double-loaded corridor in favor of its vertical equivalent, the elevator. As such, the building points the way to his largest commission in New York City, the Yale Club of New York.[72]

74. James Gamble Rogers. Madison Avenue Presbyterian Church Parish House, New York, New York, 1916.

The Yale Club commission, which he received in 1912, was the first job Rogers executed that had a direct relationship with his alma mater, Yale University. The building was erected at a cost of $500,000 on the newly developed land over the tracks of Grand Central Terminal at Vanderbilt Avenue and 44th Street. The plans called for a clubhouse for the activities of the rapidly growing group of more than three thousand fellow alumni, as well as accommodations for out-of-town visitors and an elaborate set of dining and entertainment rooms.[73] The size and scope of the building was unprecedented for this kind of club in New York, and was a reflection of the rapid transformation of a small association of elite gentlemen recalling their youth into a forceful civic group dedicated both to raising the money their alma mater needed to become a modern institution and to solidifying their position as a tightly knit group of men in leading positions.[74] The call was therefore for a "hub of activity in the city" that would have "the characteristics of a somewhat homelike centre of Yale graduate activity and influence."[75]

The Yale Club fills out its block according to the regulations set by the Grand Central Corporation, which included the mandate of a cornice at 81 feet. Within the structural web and given volume, Rogers decided to divide the considerable bulk of the program into three distinct parts: a base of six floors of reception rooms, lounges, a library, and a gym; "Thereafter, a plain brick apartment house reaching skyward for eleven stories,"[76] containing 140 bedrooms; and a crown containing three floors of dining rooms and an outdoor terrace, framed with three-story stone columns and clad in terracotta (Figs. 75, 76).

The social base of the club, carried out to resemble the Palazzo Massimi, presents a solid, historically referenced appearance weighing down on its place in the city grid with all the force of tradition. Inside, the rooms resemble those of English city clubs or even country estates (Fig. 77). They are elaborate and yet restrained, ranging from a wood-paneled library to the airy expanse of the white-painted main lounge.

The exterior of the building is little more than an extension of the three aspects of the club, formed to fit the context of the site and the sky-scraper/block tradition: ". . . there has been no hesitation about changing rules or sacrificing any details or regulation prescribed in the nineteenth century's servile and unreflecting employment of classical architecture," noted one critic.[77] The plain Doric pilasters that stretch between the third and the six floors define an extended *piano nobile* above a tall base, though the latter is in reality the place of the largest and most formal lounge. The stretched proportions of this palazzo display motifs that are, according to the same critic, "of a simple and dignified neo-classical design, decidedly Italian in spirit, with colonial modifications."[78] In other words, they are a collection of elements that convey a vague but clearly ordered sense of tradition that cannot be tied

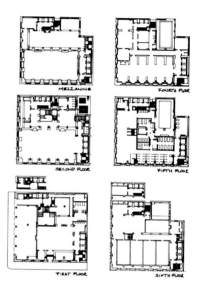

75. James Gamble Rogers.
Yale Club of New York (center
building), New York City.
1912–15.

76. James Gamble Rogers. Yale
Club of New York, New York
City. 1912–15. Plans.

77. James Gamble Rogers. Yale
Club of New York, New York
City. 1912–15. Main lounge.

down to one specific source or ideology. It thus realizes the past, in both personal terms and in terms of values, that Yale represented and represents to its alumni. The brick apartment building suspended above this base, and the terra-cotta and stone exuberance of the crown of dining rooms at the top, responds to and interiorizes the skyline. The whole is not a masterpiece of architectural integration, either on the outside or the inside, but it is a skillful composition that asserts the place of the Yale Club in the city.

The two largest commercial structures James Gamble Rogers started to design during this period were not finished until the late 1920s, but the roots for their design and their commissioning go back to the years before Rogers had made his name as the architect of Yale and Northwestern universities. The commission to design the Connecticut General Life Insurance Company Home Office in Hartford, Connecticut, dated back to 1918, when company president Robert Huntington convinced the other members of the building committee to ask James Gamble Rogers to design their latest entry in the competition in which each Hartford insurance company was trying to erect a taller building.[79] Huntington knew Rogers personally, since they had not only graduated from Yale in the same class, but had both been members of the Scroll & Key secret society.[80] On the back of the letter Rogers sent Huntington in reply, he sketched the plans for an H-shaped building,[81] which he later developed into an elongated brick shaft with vaguely Tudor detailing. The cost of this building was estimated at $1,350,000, considerably more than was originally contemplated by the company's building committee.[82] In the meantime, the company was hard hit by claims as a result of the Spanish influenza epidemic (which also delayed the realization of Rogers' designs for Sophie Newcomb College in New Orleans), and it shelved its new home office for five years.[83]

In 1925, Rogers once again was asked to design a home office for the Connecticut General Life Insurance Company. This time, the emphasis was on size, monumentality, and functionality, rather than on height. The resulting design, which was constructed by the summer of 1926, was a curved, six-story Italian palazzo at the corner of a row of insurance company buildings facing Bushnell Park along a street leading up to the Connecticut State Capitol (Figs. 78, 79). The building has over 100,000 square feet of office space, more than three times the planned total of the original building, housed in two wings 140 feet long by 70 feet wide, and in a glazed-yellow-brick four-story building set at the back of the site. The formality of the front stone palace forms a strong contrast to the industrial appearance of a building containing printing and service functions at the rear, less public, side of the site.[84]

The model for the main building is a cross between several Italian Renaissance palaces, while the building also echoes some of the details of the Phoenix Insurance Company Building farther up the street.[85] The most direct

FIRST MEZZANINE FLOOR

FIRST FLOOR

78. James Gamble Rogers. Connecticut General Life Insurance Company, Hartford, Connecticut, 1925–26.

79. James Gamble Rogers. Connecticut General Life Insurance Company, Hartford, Connecticut, 1925–26. Plans.

precedent, however, is Michelozzo's Medici Palace, here bent to adapt to its curving site in the manner of Peruzzi's Palazzo Massimo (see Fig. 79). By not articulating the separate wings and placing the entrance at the corner, facing a large traffic circle, "instead of two elevations the building presents a massive facade."[86] That facade is divided vertically into three parts, each of which is defined by an increasing smoothness of the granite blocks out of which it is composed. The stone itself came from Stony Creek, Connecticut, and its slight pink hue evidences the richness of the granite around Rogers' summer home near there.[87] The base is composed of large blocks of this stone incised a full 6 inches, so that they seem to bulge out of their courses (Fig. 80). The clarity and reserved quality of the building belies its size, while allowing the building to achieve a monumental presence. A contemporary

80. James Gamble Rogers.
Connecticut General Life
Insurance Company, Hartford,
Connecticut, 1925–26. Detail.

observer noted, "The whole effect is one of tremendous strength," adding that the tactile quality of the stone base, the pink tinge of the material, and the generosity of the arches gave the building "a warmth of appearance often lacking in large buildings."[88]

Though Rogers did not have to worry about a central axis in this building, since he brought the visitor in at a 45-degree angle to all functions, he still went to great lengths to state the (for him) necessary diffusion of the formal entrance into its functional cross axes. The entrance lobby is a two-story space modeled after the temple of Apollo at Bassae, here carried out in semidetached marble columns supporting a polychrome coffered ceiling. Directly facing visitors as they enter this rich environment is a black marble Ionic column hewn from a single block. One must pass to either side of this colossus to reach the apsidal elevator lobby beyond, or one can step up a half-floor to reach the public functions on the *piano nobile*.[89]

The commission for the new home of the Aetna Life Insurance Company had as long a history as that for the Connecticut General Life Insurance Company. The two companies were related, Connecticut General having been founded out of a section of the Aetna. During the 1920s the two shared a number of directors, which may account for the fact that the Aetna's board asked James Gamble Rogers in 1923 to design a new headquarters for the company. It had bought a large tract of land on fashionable Farmington Avenue, outside of the traditional downtown of Hartford, and it had an ambitious new president, Morgan B. Brainard. On November 19, 1923, Rogers presented his design to the board in the form of a model and sketches.[90]

The board was a bit taken aback by what they saw. They were expecting the latest entry in the tower wars of Hartford, a building that would be taller than the then current record holder, the seventeen-story

Traveller's Building. Yet they approved the low, spread-out scheme proposed by James Gamble Rogers, and Brainard expressed his amazement "that such an unusual scheme would appeal to so many of different views."[91] That scheme was undoubtedly the one presented in the April 1924 issue of *The Architect* as "The New Home of the Aetna, Hartford, Conn." (Fig. 81). It was identified as a plan "suggestive of the type of architecture one would expect to find in a large university or college group," carried out in an architecture defined as "New England Colonial, reminiscent of some of the eighteenth-century brick churches and public buildings so appropriate to the locality."[92]

The Aetna was to have a home that defined it as an institution, a conglomeration of civic and ecclesiastical structures housing and ennobling clerical activities. The design may indeed have been inspired by the Colonial architecture of the area and by the semi-suburban, semi-urban nature of this specific site, as Rogers himself claimed.[93] Yet the impulse to break the building into pavilions clearly came out of Rogers' twenty-year experience with institutional buildings, as did his decision then to place those pavilions in a tradition that would compose them into a whole capable of invoking an image inherent in, but not necessarily clearly defined by, function. While the plan, especially in its exploration of how simple bar buildings can be combined to form multiple courtyards, is reminiscent of the Southern Baptist Theological Seminary (see Chapter 6, Figs. 147–154), the design as a whole most clearly resembles a design of more than a decade earlier, Rogers' competition entry for the Loomis Institute.[94]

With this design, Rogers was proposing that the Aetna was more than just a business. In its ability to encompass a large space between and beyond its buildings, and to further a tradition of civic architecture, it was contributing to the overall definition of American culture. He claimed that the inspiration for the design was a statement made to him by William Dean Howells, chronicler of the mutually defining role of American business and culture in such novels as *A Hazard of New Fortunes* and *The Rise of Silas Lapham,* to the effect that "the businessmen of this country are the idealists."[95] In this manner, Rogers was responding to a redefinition of the role of American business during this period, and his campus solution became a model for other insurance companies and headquarters across the country.[96]

The specific design for the Aetna called for a generally U-shaped complex fronting on Farmington Avenue and opening up down the hill toward downtown. The design emphasized its connection with the University of Virginia in the design of the central pavilion, originally organized around a central rotunda and fronting both street and courtyard with a two-story temple front above a stone plinth. The simple shapes of the remaining buildings, each the home for a different division or section of the company, were similarly to be given scale and significance by the addition of pedi-

81. James Gamble Rogers. Aetna Life Insurance Company, Hartford, Connecticut, 1923–30. First plan.

82. James Gamble Rogers.
Aetna Life Insurance Company, Hartford, Connecticut, 1923–30. Final plan.

83. James Gamble Rogers.
Aetna Life Insurance Company, Hartford, Connecticut, 1923–30. Final elevations.

ments, pilasters, Palladian windows, Georgian doorways, arched openings, and sandstone bases.

The complex not only formed one large courtyard, it was also broken up to provide no fewer than thirteen internal courts. None of the buildings was to be more than three stories high, allowing the ceremonial central entrance and administration building to rise up above the campus with its tall attic and elaborate openwork turret. Inside, some of the floors were to have been 14 feet high to emphasize their ceremonial nature, while the system of interlocking double-loaded corridors that coursed through the complex would have provided maximum flexibility.

The scheme may have been too radical even for the progressive Aetna company, or the company's needs and resources may not have matched Rogers' vision, for after the unveiling of the first design the project was put on hold for five years. Rogers was authorized to proceed in the beginning of 1929, and the building was finished two years later.[97] The final design was more compact, higher, and larger: it contained 769,000 square feet in a range of buildings 660 feet long, reaching up to a nine-story central section topped by a four-story tower (Figs. 82, 83).[98] The colossal size of the building was controlled by its composition, which made full use of the ample

84. James Gamble Rogers.
Aetna Life Insurance Company,
Hartford, Connecticut,
1923–30.

site, and by the articulation—with the full range of "Neo-Colonial" elements at Rogers' disposal—of entrances, focal points, and public spaces.

The design remained organized around a central pavilion, which was now placed on top of what amounted to a stunted skyscraper (Fig. 84). The building steps back in a series of notches above the sixth floor to allow a small pedimented temple, designed in white-painted wood and containing the board rooms, to emerge on the Farmington Avenue side. A further series of setbacks forms the transition to a square wood tower, whose gold-domed steeple echoes that of the Connecticut State Capitol a mile away. Though there are certainly other examples of the placement of a self-sufficient New England church on top of a brick skyscraper, the success of the Aetna owes much to this frankly emblematic placement of the honorific board-room temple on top of the central administration wing, and to that element's integration into the overall composition, both by the manipulation of the mass of the tower and by the echoing of its forms at crucial points on the facade.

The six-story wings, whose top floors are set back and hidden behind a low balustrade, are simple brick expanses. Their tall windows are grouped into bands of three, and their base is formed by a continuous stone colonnade, pulled forward from the rest of the mass and denoting the public functions of the company. The crossing of the wings is marked by slightly higher hipped-roof pavilions, visible only at a distance. The overall effect of the massing is thus one of a series of cubical volumes that set back toward local and overall symmetries near the top of the building. They appear to grow out of a common base, while remaining unified by the repeated use of pediments, colonnades, and balustrades (Fig. 85). This compositional strategy allows a monumental grouping to be composed out of a functional assemblage of simple spaces. The exceptional and public spaces are then pushed to the point where they address the outside world most efficiently at base and top.

The huge program contained within this complex is arranged around one central double-loaded corridor, which extends the length of the principal

85. James Gamble Rogers.
Aetna Life Insurance Company,
Hartford, Connecticut,
1923–30.

facade on each floor, and around two cross corridors that run through the side wings (see Fig. 82). The main corridor is one-eighth of a mile long and, on the ground floor (the basement as seen from Farmington Avenue), it contains stores, a gymnasium, a post office, community rooms, and the employee cafeteria (since relocated). The corridor is treated in stone and stucco and its large breadth and height make it the internalized Main Street of the complex.

The Aetna home office succeeded admirably in masking what was upon its completion the largest office building of its kind in a gentle, historic image that was meant to make the building seem a natural outgrowth of its setting. According to one journalist:

> The architecture is distinctly in sympathy with the atmosphere of Aetna's own historical background and with those romantic traditions that cling so insistently to the tract itself . . . seldom, if ever, has a modern office building of such proportions been endowed with a truer spirit of Colonial days. To get a glimpse of its details through the trees of the drive . . . is to feel the spell of early Connecticut and New England "when the farmers tilled their fields the lively day."[99]

Rogers thus succeeded—at least in the eyes of one observer, and probably in the eyes of the many imitators of the Aetna building—in making this large corporate structure disappear behind a veil of historic allusion. He thus created a corporate version of the Collegiate Georgian. Rogers never pursued further work in this direction, and the Aetna building remains his only essay in large-scale Neo-Georgian commercial architecture.

The most unusual structure James Gamble Rogers designed for a profit-making client was the Crane Company Exhibition Building, erected on the Boardwalk of Atlantic City in 1925 for a company whose bathroom fixtures he specified frequently.[100] The program of the building called for "a resort with showrooms," an ephemeral showplace for "displaying specified articles, not in themselves beautiful."[101] The larger aim, or so Rogers claimed, was to design, in the service of a company whose products he used continually, and which he considered "indicative of the highest efficiency and economy," a building that would "stimulate emulation in the smaller industries and the smaller business houses, and to cultivate the taste of the observant American people generally."[102] Even this modest two-story building made real a vague but validating myth, in this case about the relationship between fixtures and the elegant life of the consumer.

Unlike Rogers' larger institutional buildings, the Crane showroom was determined completely by a central axis, which one entered under a deep archway taller than the mass of the building itself (Figs. 86, 87). One passed below a 7-foot-high gate valve ("use Crane valves," a sign admonished above this monumental door) into a two-story exhibition space and foyer whose columns were covered in blue-green hexagonal tile, and whose arched ceilings, simple walls, and smooth floor were treated in a mixture of marble, Alundum tiles, and Zenitherm covered with gold leaf. This exotic mixture of man-made and natural materials created a series of smooth yet sensuous surfaces that heightened the mixture of hygiene and sexuality associated with the fixtures displayed in small alcoves off the main axis.

Marrion Wilcox, Rogers' champion at *Architectural Record* (he was responsible for the immensely favorable reviews of most of Rogers' large institutional buildings), saw much more in the Crane Building than would be expected from its size. Claiming that it anticipated the innovations of the Exposition Internationale des Arts Décoratifs held in Paris that same year, he asserted that "the tendency of the time has been perceived," and that "rationalism" was preparing itself in this building to lead architecture to a new set of ideals. That *Zeitgeist* was not an alien importation from Europe, nor was it a strange concoction of new elements. Rather, "no traditional style was quite appropriate, but the element of novelty might be translated, as it were, into a well-proportioned old form with extreme propriety of detail."[103]

The Crane Building was a paradigm of one of James Gamble Rogers' design strategies. His methodology here consisted of using architectural elements to discipline new materials, types, and scales according to modern and rational methods in order to create a representational and sensuous reality. In the design, he used a visual strategy that imposed a coherent architectural style on the program. This style realized, but did not define, the character of the institution—whatever that institution might be. In the end, this malleability moved Rogers ever more into a kind of self-effacement, especially in his noninstitutional buildings. After the Crane Building, that architectural style became more and more reduced under the twin pressures of rationalization, namely the increasingly technical and functional demands made on large buildings and the stylistic preference for streamlining and reductive abstraction.

86. James Gamble Rogers. Crane Company Exhibition Building, Atlantic City, New Jersey, 1925.

87. James Gamble Rogers. Crane Company Exhibition Building, Atlantic City, New Jersey, 1925. Interior.

CHAPTER FOUR

Building the New Yale

On May 1, 1916, Charles William Harkness, the much older half-brother of Edward S. Harkness, died of pneumonia. This event left Edward Harkness as the sole heir and director of the family fortune.[1] His first major act as such was to offer, in the name of his mother, to build for Yale University "as a memorial to my brother. . .a series of dormitories in the form of a quadrangle."[2] The dormitory was to house at least six hundred men and, if the "plans prepared by an Architect to be chosen by the Donor and satisfactory to the University" were accepted, Mrs. Harkness would donate $1.8 million "or more" for its construction.[3] When James Gamble Rogers was selected for this commission, his career took on a new character. The moderately successful designer of mansions, schools, and courthouses became one of the leading designers of institutions of higher education in America. He also developed his own variant on Neo-Gothicism, or, as Montgomery Schuyler called it, the Collegiate Gothic, and thus offered a coherent and concrete image of the ideals of the cultural elite of America between the two World Wars.

Yale University was well prepared for the Harkness gift, and may indeed have been soliciting the family for some time. The overcrowding of the dormitory rooms on the so-called Old Campus, the city block where the college had been founded, had reached acute proportions during the years preceding the First World War, and President Arthur Hadley had made the alleviation of this condition a strong priority of the latter part of his administration.[4]

Yale was no longer what it had been throughout most of the eighteenth and nineteenth centuries: a small assemblage of young men from similar backgrounds temporarily encamped in a series of buildings on two blocks of New Haven. The very process that had brought to it middle-class students from the far reaches of the "Northwest" (such as James Gamble Rogers) had profoundly changed the character of the institution. By 1916, Yale had more than a thousand students and was spreading somewhat haphazardly over the surrounding city blocks. Most of the new buildings, including the monumental Bicentennial Building group of 1902, were dedicated to classrooms, laboratories, and the other functions that allowed the university to operate.

The residential core of Yale, however, remained completely defined by the original campus. A series of freestanding buildings placed in various relationships to the street were replaced gradually after the Civil War with a row of five- to six-story buildings used exclusively as dormitories (Fig. 88). These structures surrounded the open heart of the Old Campus with a solid

88. Bruce Price. Welch Hall, Yale University, New Haven, Connecticut, 1891.

wall. With the erection of Farnam (1870), Durfee (1871), and Lawrance (1886) halls, Yale created a bastion of brick to defend the private enclave of the students from the outside world. The university was no longer an integral part of the urban life of New Haven. It had become an alien being, a place inhabited by sons of the privileged from all across the country.

It had also redefined its character: no longer a loosely defined gathering of young men to be disciplined by theology, it was now a place that sought to translate the world into more and more rational pieces of knowledge. The discipline of learning gave these young men the power to control the outside world both by the abstraction of learning and by the architecture of the school, while a more and more complex and intense set of myths about Yale validated and defined a sylvan, arcadian never-never land contained within the dormitory walls. This cloister became the setting for social bonding and a place of origin to be remembered by alumni as the common and culturally significant source of their positions. The Old Campus became a quadrangle defining the institutionalization of knowledge and socialization.[5]

More than that, it became the site for the Yale myth: the combination of rituals, folklore, and real accomplishments that made Yale into more than just a place of learning. By the turn of the century, the Yale Man, fixed in the popular imagination by the Dink Stover books, became a recognizable type: an athletic, moral, not too scholarly young man who could use Yale to enter into a network of social and business relations that would ensure his success in the world beyond school. Though every college and university in America has worked to create a mystique to bind its alumni to it, arguably only Harvard has been as successful as Yale in presenting so clear an image of its students. The Yale myth combined this image with a reputation for high academic standards and great institutional wealth, but also with a sense that it was a place with a more closed, coherent, and sometimes perverse culture. Rather than fraternities, for instance, Yale collected its supposedly best and brightest into secret societies, mysterious places that were reputed to indulge in strange rituals while bonding their members for future success. By the 1930s, the songs of Cole Porter and stories in popular magazines had elaborated the image of the Yale Man and the myth of the place that created him. It was, I would argue, the place itself that helped define that image so clearly in the first decades of this century.

The impetus for the development of such a place was, however, purely practical. By 1911, Yale realized that it needed to rationalize its own development not only in terms of the definition of its curriculum and its student body, but also in the physical realization of that development. Hadley and his powerful secretary, Anson Phelps Stokes, engaged in years of delicate negotiations with the various parts of the University in the hope of transforming the city block to the west of the Old Campus into a duplicate of the original by clearing the various laboratories, museums, and privately owned buildings on the site.

In 1913, Yale appointed Frank Miles Day as Supervising Architect of the university, largely on the strength of his recently completed dormitories for Princeton University, and asked him to prepare plans for the new dormitory quadrangle.[6] Unfortunately, Day died in 1916, before he could complete plans for the quadrangle, but also before the announcement of the Harkness gift. His firm, Day & Klauder, continued with the commission, but Edward Harkness wanted to use his own architect. Though he initially suggested a competition for the Harkness Memorial Quadrangle, by February 1917 he had commissioned James Gamble Rogers to do "a series of dormitories in the form of a quadrangle (with tower or other memorial feature) . . . for the use of the students of Yale College as a memorial to . . . Charles W. Harkness."[7] Harkness thus put in place a personal friend who had already completed at least four commissions for him, but who had little experience in or obvious inclination toward "Collegiate Gothic." Theirs was a personal relationship, formalized in a contract between the two in which Yale was the subject or beneficiary, not a partner, and developed over the five-year building period during which the officials of the university could only comment on and react to decisions already made. This relationship and the final building were based on the almost unlimited funds at Harkness's disposal and on Rogers' ability to subjugate his tastes and personal motifs, developed over twenty years of practice, to a vision of the function and character of the building as defined by his client and by the institutional, historical, and physical context.[8]

Though little remains of Day's plans for Yale, one can imagine that he would have adapted the architecture of Holder, Hamilton, and Madison halls at Princeton (1910–16), with their long rows of gabled forms arranged on multiple courtyards (Fig. 89). There is in fact a marked similarity between this arrangement and Rogers' work at Yale, though Day's architecture itself borrows heavily from the work of Cope & Stewardson at the University of Pennsylvania and Washington University (Fig. 90). The Collegiate Gothic

was a well-established method of housing academic buildings. All that James Gamble Rogers had to do was refine this tradition.[9]

But though this was also not James Gamble Rogers' first building for his alma mater,[10] it was a commission of a completely different sort than anything he had designed previously. In order to familiarize himself with the Collegiate Gothic and to help him design the project, Rogers turned to three men: E. Donald Robb, a designer from the office of Cram, Goodhue & Ferguson, the firm responsible for the master plan of Princeton of 1911, as well as of its Hall of Graduate Studies of 1910; Otto Faelten, a Beaux-Arts–trained architect; and George Nichols, the New Haven associate with whom Rogers had just completed the New Haven Post Office.[11]

Faelten, a German émigré who had progressed as a student from New York public schools to the Massachusetts Institute of Technology and then to the Ecole des Beaux-Arts, was to stay with Rogers until the latter's death in 1945. Faelten apparently functioned as the chief designer for most of the Yale commissions in the Rogers office. Some observers have claimed that he was in fact the form-giver of these buildings, and that James Gamble Rogers was only the businessman who ran the operation and met with clients. Faelten's reputation as a major designer was greatly enhanced by his teaching career at Yale, where he was the chief architectural instructor in the School of Fine Arts between 1922 and 1936, when he departed for the University of Pennsylvania.[12] The view of Faelten as the true designer in the Rogers office may, however, have more to do with Rogers' self-deprecating, often ironic attitude toward whatever it was that his professional services added to the translation of program and building material into architecture. Since the buildings on which Faelten worked can be compared with designs executed by Rogers and his office without the former's participation, but cannot be compared with any work Faelten did on his own, it is far easier to see the consistency of concerns and compositional modulations throughout the work of James Gamble Rogers. [13]

While Nichols clearly was brought in to manage the Harkness Quadrangle commission, the role of E. Donald Robb, who stayed with Rogers for only about a year, was probably much more clearly aesthetic. Robb was during this period primarily a renderer, though he was later to become a successful designer of ecclesiastical buildings. He had been with

89. Day & Klauder, Holder and Hamilton halls, Princeton University, Princeton, New Jersey, 1910–16.

90. Cope & Stewardson, University Quadrangle, Washington University, St. Louis, Missouri, 1904.

the office of Cram, Goodhue & Ferguson since 1903, and when the firm split he followed the romantic theoretician Cram to Boston, rather than staying with the more pragmatic Goodhue.[14] He practiced briefly by himself, but the reputation he developed even as an architect was due largely to his moody, extremely dark renderings, taken from low vantage points and emphasizing the contrast between light and dark. The solemnity and mysteriousness of the buildings he drew—the "misty" buildings on rainy days—were impressionistic qualities, "showing," as one contemporary put it, "little of Mr. Goodhue's influence."[15] Robb's was a vision of an architecture already worn by time and created as if by a force of nature or an undefined communal will. This was a conviction that the pragmatic, incisive, and reserved James Gamble Rogers no doubt felt was entirely appropriate for the building of a memorial designed for a wealthy client who wished both to impress and to remain somewhat mysterious.

For his part, Edward Harkness appears never to have expressed a preference for any particular style of architecture, despite Yale legend that he preferred the Gothic and his wife insisted on Georgian. His reticence was legendary, and yet he insisted on having his own way with all of the numerous commissions he funded, thus creating very large and coherent monuments that bore his personal stamp.

The first presentation James Gamble Rogers made of his design for the Harkness Memorial Quadrangle illustrates his apparent strategy of combining the well-developed pragmatic organizational skills he had developed in Chicago with something purposefully vague and mystifying that he picked up from looking at the work of architects like Cram or the early Goodhue.[16] Instead of a complete set of plans, sections, and elevations, a series of perspectives, or an articulated model, Rogers presented only two items: a plan of a single suite of rooms and a clay massing model (Fig. 91).[17] The plan showed how two student bedrooms could be grouped around a living room in suites that could be stacked up around common entryways, stairs, and bathrooms. The entryways could then be grouped around courtyards, and the courtyards formed into a large walled compound. Aside from a few public spaces and the memorial tower, the whole of Harkness Quadrangle was composed out of variations on this single plan. A simple plan devised with careful attention to the pragmatic requirements of student living, and based on Rogers' own experience designing apartment buildings, was turned into the basis for the overall layout of the building by playing out the complexities inherent to its organization.

The method by which this transformation was effected, however, was dictated by the needs of the site, the style, and the character of the building. The clay model showed a regularization of the Old Campus model of an enclosed world guarded by turreted entryways and filling out the maxi-

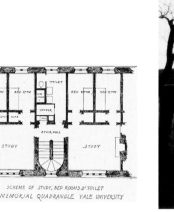

SCHEME OF STUDY, BED ROOMS & TOILET
MEMORIAL QUADRANGLE, YALE UNIVERSITY

91. James Gamble Rogers. Harkness Memorial Quadrangle, Yale University, New Haven, Connecticut, 1917–21. "Scheme of Study, Bed Rooms & Toilet," 1917.

92. James Gamble Rogers. Harkness Memorial Quadrangle, Yale University, New Haven, Connecticut, 1917–21.

mum expanse of the site. This strategy opened up a private Yale inside the courtyards, which were light courts and monastic retreats at the same time. A memorial tower announced the monumental function of the grouping to the outside. The courtyards themselves actually were formed by a series of dominant bars running east-west, connected by generally lower north-south elements. The building became lower toward the south and taller toward the north, thus allowing the maximum amount of sunlight to penetrate the complex. At the same time, the quadrangle became more closed toward the north and the west, the sides of the site facing commercial New Haven, while the tower was placed in the middle of the east facade facing the Old Campus, thus signaling the heart of the newly extended Yale campus (Fig. 92). This site-sensitive modulation and the tight scale and closed character of the campus contrast strongly with the more expansive groupings that Day & Klauder or Cram prepared for Princeton, and with the more repetitive blocks that were then filling up other colleges around the country.[18]

The comparison with Cram, Goodhue & Ferguson's Graduate College at Princeton is especially apt. Like the plans for the Memorial Quadrangle, the plan of the Graduate College is dominated by a large courtyard and tower (Fig. 93). A similar organization of entryways is used, and the counterpoint of smaller turrets at the intersections of the ranges of gabled dormitories also serves to mark the corner entrances. Yet the Cram, Goodhue & Ferguson plan is simpler in organization and less rich in its variations. There is only one secondary courtyard, and both the height and texture of the buildings remain relatively uniform. The variety is due to the greater complexity of the program, which included academic facilities. The tower, meanwhile, is an extruded shaft. The Graduate College is vastly more sophisticated in its massing and composition than the work of Cope & Stewardson or of Day & Klauder, but it is also less richly varied and detailed than the Memorial Quadrangle.[19]

The whole Memorial Quadrangle complex is dominated by its central courtyard, a wide expanse of space that seems to echo the scale of the

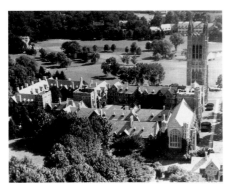

93. Cram, Goodhue &
Ferguson. Graduate College,
Princeton University,
Princeton, New Jersey,
1910–12.

94. James Gamble Rogers.
Harkness Memorial
Quadrangle, Yale University,
New Haven, Connecticut,
1917–21.

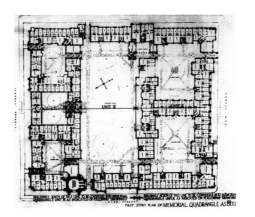

95. James Gamble Rogers.
Harkness Memorial
Quadrangle, Yale University,
New Haven, Connecticut,
1917–21. Plan.

tower (Figs. 94, 95). It is not entered axially, and a series of towers provide
subsidiary focal points around its periphery, thus giving the space the feeling of a void between building masses, rather than a planned and formalized
core. In fact, the whole building represents an extreme example of Rogers'
fondness for parallel cross axes slipping by each other. When seen in plan,
the building is defined by two of these that run from turreted gates on Elm
Street through the main courtyard, only to end in two of three smaller courtyards on the Library Street side of the quadrangle. Because these axes develop
through a succession of courtyards and gates, never acting as central axes and
never terminating, neither they nor a third, implied axis running down the

96. James Gamble Rogers. Harkness Memorial Quadrangle, Yale University, New Haven, Connecticut, 1917–21. Entrance.

middle of the complex forces a singular understanding of the building on the viewer. What one is left with is a series of alternative routes that uncover the experience of the six courtyards—five small and one large—surrounded by ranges of buildings that are similar but varied enough in height and decorative treatment to give the quadrangle the sense of a slightly rambling succession of spaces grown up over the years. The towers, turrets, and cross gables then act as focal points, giving a rhythm to this whole complex. The gateways act as frames from which each courtyard can be viewed, but, since they are not lined up, each experience remains connected, but singular and episodic (Fig. 96).

The actual design of the pieces of this complex was based on Rogers' study of the Collegiate Gothic. He had learned well from previous examples and—given the ample resources at his command—was able to create a more perfect example of this style. Once the organization of the complex was set, the next task was the development of the architectural envelope. The Collegiate Gothic that gave form to the Memorial Quadrangle was made up, as described earlier, out of direct quotations melded together by Robb's atmospheric sense of composition, composed by Otto Faelten, and finally synthesized by James Gamble Rogers.

One of the remarkable aspects of the design was its elaborate iconography. The application of the architectural elements was governed by two separate programs: a contextual response to the urban environment and a multilevel program of direct quotations. As George Nichols pointed out in his article on the Memorial Quadrangle, the detailing is at its finest and most Gothic where it faces the intimacy of Library Street to the south. Here the buildings are low, and bays and buttresses frequently push out of planar facades. The plasticity of the volumes and the level of articulation of every change in level or direction of the mass decrease around the corners, and these details are more nearly subsumed into the wall. On the east side, facing the Old Campus, large Gothic windows on the lower floor give way, after the wall has been interrupted by the base of Harkness Tower, to a taller wall

97. James Gamble Rogers.
Harkness Memorial
Quadrangle, Yale University,
New Haven, Connecticut,
1917–21. Wrexham Tower.

with Renaissance-style openings. Finally, Nichols writes, "on Elm Street the highest and most rugged characteristics obtain. Later Gothic details and early Renaissance touches are interwoven."[20]

While the detailing serves to differentiate the several parts of the group, the identification of its parts creates an internal narrative about the buildings. Each courtyard was named for a different place where Yale had been located, and for such early institutions as the Linonia & Brothers club. Each entryway fills in the places of Yale tradition with the names of famous Yale graduates. Then each archway, doorway, and transition point between outdoor spaces is surmounted by an inscription that exemplifies the values of Yale and its graduates: the sayings are admonitions to study, to temperance, to high morals, and to other vague standards of good behavior. The whole is tied together with finely crafted, if somewhat conventional, floriate motifs and stylized animals that dance around the stringcourses or punctuate the dropped sills.

The decorative program sets up a syntax of Yale-dom by revealing its location, its heroes, and its principles in a narrative legend in which the places of gathering are tied to origins and movement in both a temporal and a spatial sequence. That movement is controlled by a mixture of academic, Puritan, and commonsensical inscriptions, but it is all internal. Harkness Tower then announces Yale's achievements to the outside world as well as to the students. The tower is itself balanced by a duplicate of the church at Wrexham in Wales where Elihu Yale lies buried (Fig. 97). Wrexham Tower was added as an afterthought at the suggestion of Secretary Anson Phelps Stokes,[21] and its white stone forms sit rather incongruously on top of the crossing of two gabled forms, though Rogers tried to mask its alien form by refusing to rely on measured drawings and instead building a free interpretation of the original.[22] Here is the most concrete symbol of the ontology of Yale turned into a building without any specific function other than to comment on the day-to-day experience of current Yale and to recall it to its mythic self-justification. Against the confident assertion of Harkness Tower, it stands for the validating roots of the institution.

Rising from a base containing stone portraits of the donors, architect, and builders of the Memorial Quadrangle, and from a chapel dedicated to William Harkness, Harkness Tower first supports the likenesses of great Yale men of the past, including Elihu Yale, James Fenimore Cooper, and Samuel F. B. Morse (Fig. 98). It then presents statues of figures deemed to be the founders of Western learning: Phidias, Homer, Aristotle, and Euclid. As the tower rises, the figures become larger and more abstract in form and content, representing freedom, courage, war, death, peace, and martial figures. Finally the statues disappear into gargoyles and masks and into a web of finials and arches barely containing the carillon housed in the upper section of the tower, which itself becomes more and more abstract as it meets the sky, thus, according to Marrion Wilcox, "visualizing art-tendencies of the past and present, and in its turn [affecting] those of the future."[23]

The ornamental program of the complex starts out by applying specific names and concrete facts to the functional buildings and creates a map of the spatial and historical path Yale has taken in order to establish its place (the building) and its values (the inscriptions). The student is thus given a concrete context within which to place himself. He is then reminded, as he lifts his eye, of the source of the institution—the English church in which its first donor is buried—so that he may place himself in line with that tradition. Finally, the tower pronounces the great dynasty of Yale men to the world and places them in a progression going from today's builders, through yesterday's heroes, to the pantheon of our culture. As these figures become more and more abstract, the patient observer can literally read into them (by reading the works of the authors portrayed) or place himself among them (the gargoyles represent students), while the architecture falls away into more and more open abstraction.

This ideology defines a path for Yale men. The reality of that path and of the building is then carried out through a careful attention to the sensuousness of the complex. Rogers made a number of decisions that allow the student to feel as if the story must be true, because it is told in an ancient form that has been there for centuries, and because its forms, textures, and colors are seductive. Rogers chose the stone, whose Ohio origin seemed to him appropriate because of the Harkness family's connections with that state,[24] "not for sentimental reasons, but purely to secure an effect of beauty;

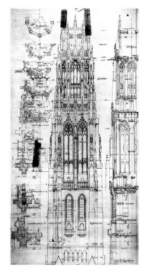

98. James Gamble Rogers. Harkness Memorial Quadrangle, Yale University, New Haven, Connecticut, 1917–21. Elevation, Harkness Tower.

I determined at the start to endeavor to make the walls like the stone of some of the little islands between Saybrook and New London as they look in the afternoon when the sun shines on them."[25] The warmth of the stone is increased at the base, as is its size, and the coloration contrasts with the cold monumentality of the smooth-cut granite Rogers had used on his earlier buildings. This sense of ancient and comfortable well-being was enhanced by setting up a random-seeming pattern in the laying of the stone, which was in fact fully set out in a series of measured drawings.[26] The flagstone walks were artificially worn down, and, in the most blatant effort to deny the contemporariness of the buildings, a specification was written to break one pane in each of the glass-in-lead windows and then to repair the broken panes rather than waiting for baseballs or student fights to do that work.[27] "There are numerous refinements," commented Rogers, "that prevent a factory-made appearance."[28]

The end result was a sensuous, rambling, and wholly convincing picturesque composition. In a letter to Harkness, Rogers pointed out his struggle to rid the complex of any symmetry which, like the "factory-made appearance," would make one aware of the existence of any crack in the mythology of Yale.[29] As Rogers' good friend, the architect Donn Barber, asked rhetorically upon completion of the building:

> For with "nothing new under the sun," and the past to choose from, does not a convincing, understanding choice of suitable and appropriate elements and forms, and the intelligent assembling and blending of these into a scholarly composition which adequately clothes the scientifically and practically planned structure, come close in determining whether the building is great architecture or not?[30]

When the building opened in 1921, it was hailed as a masterpiece of Neo-Gothicism, and *Architectural Record* devoted a whole issue to the building.[31] Its popularity in the Yale community also instantly identified James Gamble Rogers with his alma mater.

For the success of this building he was awarded an Honorary Doctorate of the Arts at the graduation ceremonies in 1921.[32] In that same year, he was named to a post which he may have long sought, and which was to determine the rest of his career: he was appointed Consulting Architect to Yale University, specifically charged with guiding the physical growth of the university.[33] Yale had received a major gift from John Sterling three years earlier. Sterling was an extremely successful lawyer who had led an ascetic life. At his death in 1918 he left $5 million to his sister as well as $15 million to Yale "for the erection of at least one enduring, useful and architecturally beautiful edifice, which will constitute a fitting memorial of my gratitude to and affection for my Alma Mater"[34] This classic act of alumni loyalty, which instantly transformed a lifetime of hard work in business into a nostalgic monument, was administered by a group of conscientious businessmen, including representatives of the Rockefeller family that had made much of Sterling's wealth possible, and whose stewardship of the estate proved so astute that eventually the original bequest resulted in the erection of more than twenty-nine-million-dollars' worth of buildings.[35]

In addition to the opportunities offered by these funds, the newly appointed president, James Rowland Angell, made one of his most important goals the raising of millions of dollars to improve the physical plant of the university. Rogers was to have the task of overseeing the phenomenal growth that led observers during the late 1920s to see their quiet college turned into a continual construction site. From this planning position, he could and would also move to take control of the actual design of the majority of the buildings making up the plan.

For Rogers, the path toward such a powerful position had been long and not always easy. It was the success of the Memorial Quadrangle and a strong family connection that brought his name to the forefront. In 1911, John Villiers Farwell of Chicago was appointed an alumni member of the Yale Corporation. He was the first "Western" member of that body, and represented the arrival of a more business-oriented attitude in the government of this educational institution. A successful businessman himself, for twenty years Farwell advocated the steady growth and rationalization of Yale. Especially through his influence on the physical plan and by his crucial role in selecting a new president in 1921, Farwell was instrumental in transforming Yale into a modern corporate entity reflecting the kind of structure and values for which it educated its graduates. In fact, the appointment of Angell marked the integration of "Western" schools of thought into the Eastern elite, since Angell had been one of John Dewey's most loyal associates.[36] John Farwell, meanwhile, was also related to James Gamble Rogers: his brother Frank had married the sister of Anne Day, Rogers' wife. James Gamble Rogers' daughter remembers fondly the warm and frequent visits of "Uncle Frank" and "Uncle John Farwell."[37]

This close connection became a matter of mutual benefit when John Farwell accepted as his first assignment on the Corporation a post on the Committee on the Architectural Plan, a committee he would chair until 1930.[38] In accepting his appointment, Farwell noted that he was "delighted to see that Yale is adopting the Collegiate Gothic, as there is certainly something about it, with its perpendicular lines, instead of horizontal lines, to point the mind upward." The relationship between an undefinable spiritual uplift and concrete forms would lead to an "unconscious influence of good architecture on young people."[39] An expert was needed to add that architectural spirit to the plans of the university, just as experts were needed in every aspect of an operation, and Farwell in 1912 went to visit James Gamble Rogers in New York to see how much such an expert would cost, and whether Rogers would accept such a "consulting architect" position. Farwell was delighted to report that Rogers thought that "a good man" would cost no more than fifty dollars a day, and the businessman suggested to university secretary Anson Phelps Stokes that Rogers himself might be the right consultant, especially since "he has a great many friends among pretty wealthy graduates and it might be that such acquaintances would be of help. He also spoke confidentially of something which I think may later on be of great benefit to the University."[40] In the very first contacts among Rogers, Farwell, and Yale, the intertwining of personal and professional motives and relationships—and the shadow of Edward Harkness—already defined the role each was to play.

James Gamble Rogers, however, turned down the offer. Either he felt he was too busy to accept such a low-paying job or, as is more likely in the light of later developments, he foresaw being excluded from the design of specific buildings because of his consulting role. Instead, the corporation appointed Frank Miles Day, the architect of the Princeton Freshman Quadrangle, to the post in June 1913.[41] In this manner, the corporation was getting not the most famous designer of Neo-Gothic colleges, but a prolific builder in that mode. If Rogers had hoped for the appointment of an impartial consultant, however, he was disillusioned in 1916, when Day was asked to prepare the preliminary plans for the Harkness Quadrangle. It was only when Day died later that year that Rogers received the commission.

Meanwhile, a group of trustees under the leadership of John P. Garvin authorized John Russell Pope to produce a plan for the future development of the campus. The scheme Pope produced in 1919 (which acknowledged the presence of the Memorial Quadrangle, then just starting construction) foresaw a lightly gothicized Yale organized around a series of grand axes: often a sprinkling of Gothic elements clothed symmetrical and repetitive buildings of a large scale (Figs. 99, 100). The plan produced much controversy. Though its sweep and vision were greeted with acclaim, it was also criticized for its relentlessness and the monotony of its forms. In the fall of 1920, the corporation turned to James Gamble Rogers to fulfill the vision of the plan in a manner more sensitive to the needs of the community.[42]

After lengthy negotiations during the fall of 1920, Rogers finally was invested with sweeping powers by the corporation on November 15, when the committee agreed with his proposal that he would "formulate the requirements for a general plan for the systematic development of the University holdings in New Haven," that he would have "authority to decide the location of new buildings," and that he should "outline a programme of requirements" for all new buildings, including their style and massing. In a letter to Harkness advisor

99. John Russell Pope. "Yale University. General Plan for Its Future Buildings." Perspective view, 1919.

100. John Russell Pope. "Yale University. General Plan for Its Future Buildings." Plan, 1919.

and future corporation member Sam Fisher, Rogers promised to make "the plan more open, [with] more vistas and more distance," including some "intime colleges"—all with the help of Edward S. Harkness.[43]

The one power he did not ask for was the one he evidently wanted most: "During the term of my office I shall not be chosen by the Corporation as architect for any building at Yale University except where it might happen that it is the express wish of the donor that I be the architect."[44] Perhaps Rogers was operating according to a hidden agenda, for during this whole period he was corresponding actively with his client, Edward Harkness, finally explaining that he had accepted the position against Harkness's advice because "it would help to unify Yale's interest if I did accept. You would be surprised to see how well pleased the Yale men are with your group and also surprised at the number of them who have voluntarily expressed their indignation at my being left out in the distribution of the building plans."[45] Harkness was already involved with giving a new classroom building at Yale, and would be active in planning the campus.

At the same time, Bertram Goodhue had been hired at the instigation of the trustees of the Sterling Estate to build the new library, and was therefore in line to design the other buildings to be made possible by this large bequest. The architectural development of the plan threatened to be

101. James Gamble Rogers. "Sketch Plan for the Future Development of Yale University and Environs," 1921.

split between the interests of its two largest donors, Sterling and Harkness, and in the Consulting Architect position Rogers could define the development of the whole while still being available as Harkness's favored architect. The whole episode illustrates the degree to which personal relationships, political maneuvering, and a genuine vision of the role of a unifying—but not imposed—architectural strategy conspired to make James Gamble Rogers a successful architect.

Work on the new General Plan was made public a year later. It was the Pope plan "brought down to various limitations" and produced in consultation with Pope himself (Fig. 101).[46] During the spring of 1922 Rogers and George Nichols met with civic leaders of New Haven and started to prepare the public for the advent of a "$20 million plan" of construction. The plan itself was, according to the local newspaper, "after the French idea: [Rogers] does not take a plan of a building and say it 'goes there.' Rather he outlines vistas and a comprehensive outlook and marking spots says 'a building should go there of a certain type.'" Two principles guided his revision of the Pope plan: "The vistas and views must come first" and Yale should look toward an "English plan by which the student body is segregated as much as possible."[47] James Gamble Rogers' vision of Yale was dictated by a combination of a belief in picturesque site planning (no doubt influenced by the City Beautiful movement), organized around the perceptual placement of the most important structures of the institution and a desire to continue the enclosing tradition of the Old Campus and the Memorial Quadrangle.

Because the plan was essentially an infill project, it has little of the grandeur that comes through in such plans as Cram's 1911 vision of Princeton, which sought to align the campus along a major axis defined by large building masses. But the plan is also more spread out and dotted with open space than some other of the urban campuses, such as that of Columbia University, the University of Chicago, or Trinity College in Hartford. Rogers also did not have recourse to the invention of fountains, statues, or memorial plazas to impose order on the campus, as was proposed by Paul Cret at the University of Wisconsin, Madison, for instance. Finally, Rogers' plan seems most of a kind with Olmsted's 1888 plan for Stanford or Cram's 1910 plan for Rice: a knitting together of courtyard buildings around a series of partial axes.

But while the Stanford campus was conceived of essentially as one building, and the Rice campus was formed as a series of detached buildings implying much larger spaces, Rogers' plan proposed isolated moments of coherence, defined by courtyard buildings and building masses, and strung together through the regularization of existing axes.[48] It is almost as if circumstances gave Rogers as a condition what he pursued as a matter of course in his individual building designs: the lack of a major axis, and the consequent distribution of major elements along a cross axis that is more introduced and interrupted than dominated by the major ceremonial space, in this case the Cross Campus green. Here, however, the design is completely episodic: the three main areas of the plan (the Old Campus, the Science Quad on Whitney Avenue, and the proposed new academic heart of the campus) are disconnected entities strung together by axes that reach toward each other but never quite line up.

Rogers left the actual appearance of the buildings open: "Although most of the buildings now planned will be in Gothic architecture, Mr. Rogers said that he would not recommend this as a universal style for the university."[49] Rogers knew that he would be able to control whatever was built, and in fact between 1921 and 1925 he actively criticized and changed the appearance and location of almost every building planned for construction on the campus.[50]

For all of his work and advice, Rogers received no Yale commissions between 1921 and 1923. All he could do was to work with Delano & Aldrich, who built several classroom and laboratory buildings, and with Goodhue. The latter promised to make his library harmonize with the Memorial Quadrangle,[51] and Rogers and Farwell worked with the Sterling trustees to expand the library site to include a dormitory building. In this manner, the university obtained a further commitment from the trustees, who were reluctant to commission a separate building not connected with their original mandate to give Yale a library. At the same time, the Goodhue design was consolidated in one position.[52] Rogers had to resign, wait for Goodhue to die in 1924, and then work behind the scenes with Farwell until he finally was given an expanded mandate and a large set of new commissions by the university.[53]

Through the influence of Rogers, Farwell, and the Yale Corporation, the library became part of a much larger complex, which was to transform the heart of the campus into a research center clad in Gothic splendor and including dormitories, a law school, and a graduate school, all paid for by the same donor and all planned and designed by James Gamble Rogers, thus constituting Rogers' major design achievement.[54] Yet the basic layout and image of the library were not conceived by James Gamble Rogers or his office.[55] The original conception was that of Rogers' arch rival for the design work at Yale University, Bertram Grosvenor Goodhue.[56]

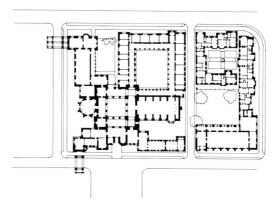

102. Bertram Grosvenor Good-
hue. Sterling Memorial Library,
Yale University, New Haven,
Connecticut. "Plan 6," 1923[?].

Goodhue had been appointed by the Sterling trustees because of his fame and good name with these businessmen, and because of his reputation (at that point far in advance of Rogers) as a designer of major Gothic institutional buildings.[57] Relations between Goodhue and Yale University were strained, however, and Rogers and Goodhue appear to have at times been openly feuding.[58] The design Goodhue proposed in 1923 was ambitious in its scope (Fig. 102). A sixteen-story fortress of bookstacks was to rise from a low base of reading rooms, completely filling the vista from the new lawn created where Pope had envisioned a great axis. The boldness of the design was accentuated by the treatment of the fenestration, as if the building was a solid block with narrow slits through which one can imagine scholars shooting arrows of knowledge at the infidel undergraduates.

Yet the stripped-down gothicism of the proposed building, its scale buttressed by picturesque contextual elements and its ceremonial spaces suppressed in favor of private places of reflection and functional circulatory nodes, was closer to the work of James Gamble Rogers than to some of Goodhue's other work during the period.[59] Perhaps Goodhue had understood the needs and self-image of Yale as well as Rogers did, or perhaps he had gained, despite his bluster, from his consultations with the Consulting Architect: Goodhue argued with John Farwell about the design all during 1923, and when he showed Rogers his design, the latter was not impressed. Eventually, Rogers worked through a mutual friend, with the result that Goodhue did change the design presented to the Corporation Commitee on the Architectural Plan.[60] Whatever developments might have occurred after this conversation between two of the most successful builders of institutions and manipulators of Gothic styles in a modern mode were cut off by Goodhue's untimely death in April 1924.

The speed with which James Gamble Rogers then obtained the commission for himself vindicated Goodhue's suspicions as to Rogers' intentions and outraged Goodhue's office. The replacement of Goodhue by James Gamble Rogers was, as the treasurer of the university unashamedly noted, based on the fact that the university was concerned with "the personal equation."[61] The members of the Goodhue office who had been barred from presenting their proposal to continue the work claimed that Goodhue had warned them before his death of "Mr. Rogers' opposition to the employment of other than Yale graduates as architects for work at Yale University."[62] Though this charge was denied vigorously by Farwell and members of the Yale administration, Farwell himself had, six months earlier, written that "as far as possible it is the desire of the Architectural Plan Committee to recommend to the Corporation architects who are Yale graduates."[63] With the appointment of James Gamble Rogers as both principal architect of the Sterling group and as overall planner of the campus—two developments closely tied to each other[64]— the tight network of Yale graduates was in fact drawn even closer around a small group of men related by marriage, common background, and intellectual outlook. Even the two principal donors to the university shared a connection, since their wealth in each case derived from the Rockefeller fortune. The result was, for better or worse, an extremely coherent architecture.

It remained now for James Gamble Rogers to form Goodhue's initial design, which had already been made public, and the complicated and vast program proposed by university librarian Andrew Keogh, into a building. The site itself caused problems. It was hemmed in between a swimming pool to the south and a holdout house on the north. The building had to address an axis suggested by the Pope plan and carried out by Rogers as "Cross Campus," which was a set of lawns running through what was envisioned as the new heart of the campus. The program called not only for the capacity to house three to five million books, but also for an unusually large amount of study and research facilities.[65]

Rogers presented his preliminary sketches to a meeting convened by Keogh in February 1925 and attended not only by administration officials but also by the Librarian of Congress and by the heads of the libraries of such institutions as Harvard and Princeton and of large public libraries in New York and the Midwest. Rogers used the meeting to convince the university of the soundness of his strategy, which revolved around a vertical organization of the bookstacks on top of a ground floor containing virtually all of the public spaces. Though the assembled experts were at first a little startled by this unusual arrangement, they were quickly convinced by Rogers' argument that "in most buildings, factories, etc., it is cheaper to have vertical than horizontal" circulation, and that such a pattern could be applied to the scholarly program of a library, confining the public rooms to the ground floor where they could be integrated into the life of the campus. There was to be no *piano nobile*, no imposing order lifted up and out of the campus and spreading out in its own realm. Instead, the program was to be squeezed in and up, with the help of the latest in elevators and pneumatic tubes. This form of organization appears to have been a rare case where Rogers actually experimented with a basic building type, and the design parallels Charles Z. Klauder's 1926 conception of the "Cathedral of Learning" at the University of Pittsburgh of 1934 (Fig. 103), and may have influenced such later structures as the library at the University of Texas at Austin. Certainly the design marked a logical exten-

103. Charles Klauder. "Cathedral of Learning" (Library), University of Pittsburgh, Pittsburgh, Pennsylvania, 1926.

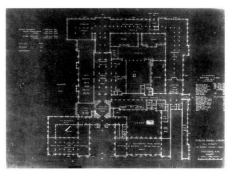

104. James Gamble Rogers. Sterling Memorial Library, Yale University, New Haven, Connecticut, 1926–31. Perspective view, preliminary scheme, 1925[?].

105. James Gamble Rogers. Sterling Memorial Library, Yale University, New Haven, Connecticut, 1926–31. Scheme "M," first floor, 1927[?].

sion of the increased compaction of the stacks, which during this period were seen as less and less dependent on the reading rooms and more subject to the logic of their own functional requirements.[66]

The design of the Sterling Library was defined by inward efficiency and an outward blending in with and summation of the activities of the campus (Figs. 104, 105). In announcing the design the following year, Rogers emphasized the fact that "in outward appearance, the new library will harmonize with the Harkness Tower and the Memorial Quadrangle," while at the same time forming "the dominating architectural feature" of the new Cross Campus. The program called for "far-seeing vision and fine idealism, made practical by plenty of good sense," and as a result, claimed Keogh, "the architect's solution will give us a building as efficient as an up-to-date factory and as beautiful as a cathedral."[67]

The only factor not easily accommodated by Rogers' design proved to be the budget. Once Rogers had specified the grand spaces and soaring tower of the library in seam-faced granite, roofed with variegated slate and furnished with oak cabinetry,[68] had commissioned Lee Lawrie, who had done the sculptures at the Memorial Quadrangle as well as on Goodhue's Nebraska State Capitol, to do the outside stone models,[69] and had asked his longtime associate René Chambellan to execute the hundreds of decorative models for the interior, the total cost of the building started to approach $12 million.[70]

Rogers set about to rationalize the plans and simplify the massing, without losing any of the decorative details. In the end, the Sterling trustees and the Yale administration, despite all of their lip service to Keogh's "factory of learning," preferred to take out six tiers of bookstacks, reducing the height of the tower by 50 feet, rather than compromise on the level of detail and the monumental quality of the library.[71] After all, one of the trustees had already pointed out, the building was meant to be a memorial first of all,[72] while Farwell pointed out the importance of enhancing and focusing the whole campus.[73] The functions of the library would be housed efficiently, but they were not the reason for the building. When the drop in the height of the tower exposed the mechanical equipment on the roof to view from the campus, money was quickly found to house these unsightly technological components by covering them with a lead-coated copper Gothic village.[74] In the end, the building was so grand that Keogh wanted to carve an inscription on the front that would read: "This is NOT the Yale Library. That is inside."[75]

James Gamble Rogers finally was authorized to prepare construction documents in October 1927, and the building was dedicated in April 1931, eleven years after the first contract for its design was signed.[76] The building was massive and elaborate: more than three hundred sculptural models were used; 900 cubic yards of crushed stone filled in the base; 142 tons of steel made up the skeleton; 85,000 cubic feet of stone, 105,000 square feet of granite, 170,000 square feet of terra-cotta, and 6.5 million common bricks made up the skin. [77]

The final design was made somewhat easier by the fact that the university finally managed to buy up the holdout property in 1928, but the layout of the building still reflects a desire to create both an internal and an external clarity about the functions and character of the complex. In order to achieve this clear organization, Rogers retained one essential aspect of the Goodhue design: a central axis running south from the front of the building all the way to a circulation desk in the middle of the complex, directly below the stack tower. The ceremonial importance of this axis was enhanced both by the gathering of all of the main public spaces around it, and by the displacement of the tower to the back of the site, where it was left to loom in its full functional height over the noncampus world to the west.

Just as Rogers had appropriated monastic and collegiate models for the Memorial Quadrangle group, so he here turned the main nave of his cathedral into an expository axis, a place dedicated to helping one find one's way around the concrete facts of knowledge. It was also the spine of the building: the central nave of Sterling is both its main corridor and its card catalogue. It terminates at the circulation desk, where one is guided through the rest of the building or through the acquisition of knowledge under the

106. James Gamble Rogers.
Sterling Memorial Library, Yale
University, New Haven,
Connecticut, 1926–31.
Courtyard.

watchful gaze of a painting of Alma Mater and her attendants—in other words, in the manner visualized by Yale. Knowledge itself—the bulk of the building and its main content—displaces the tower of the cathedral to the back (service) side of the complex, where it addresses the outside world with its size and force. Meanwhile the human-scale entrance portal, carved with letters from all the alphabets of the world, makes knowledge available. The tower is further deformed into a slab, especially when seen from the north or south, so that it is cast in the mold of an office block, defining it as part of the "factory," a modern and up-to-date part of the building equation.

The two characters of the library meet at the crossing in front of the circulation desk, where bundled piers hint at the weight of the books stored above. They reach up into fan vaults that open up the grand space where the axis of the campus is diverted into the landscape of reading rooms. Adjacent to the nave is a courtyard, a place of respite dominated by the looming book-stacks and the more fanciful collage of forms that make up the library offices (Fig. 106). It is treated as a monastic courtyard, surrounded on three sides by arched openings and focused on a small fountain. This is the place where one can see all the main elements of the library, and where one can contemplate the quiet world opened up within this complex.

After one enters and is exposed to the whole building at a glance, but before one embarks on the journey toward Alma Mater, one can turn and enter two rooms hidden away behind several turns of vaulted transitionary spaces. The easiest to reach and the plainest in design is the open under-graduate reading room. This space was meant to be easily accessible and was relatively unadorned. It is balanced on the other side of the axis by the Lino-nia & Brothers Reading Room, which houses the collections of an undergrad-uate organization that was assimilated into the library. It is the room most defined by tradition and quiet repose: leather easy chairs are strewn around the two-story space. There is a large stone fireplace and a carved oak musicians' gallery over the entrance, while low, book-lined alcoves provide even more isolated areas for reading and reflection. The democratic box for goal-oriented acquisition of knowledge is thus contrasted with the leisurely and traditional world of a private library: Sterling Library grows out of the combination of both along the long axis of its collections.

The main reading room is located at the end of this axis, to the south of the circulation desk. It is a tall and long space given over to the march of endless flat tables. Though the bookcases that line the base of this room are capped with Gothic ornament, it is the stone walls rising up behind them, the tall windows with their occasional stained-glass emblems, and the placement of a screen of large columns rising up to fan vaults at either end of this relatively narrow room that make the room the monumental and practical equivalent of the stack tower above.

The transition to the spaces of the main bulk of the program—the stack tower—is abrupt. One reaches these rooms mainly through an elevator, given its own tall lobby next to the circulation desk, and thus the rooms are cut off from the processional of the ground floor. Though there are public collections and seminar rooms on upper floors, all spaces are treated as residual to the main stack tower, and their materials and decoration are sparse. The stacks heighten the denial of spatial clarity because there are two levels of them to every floor, forming a metal cage set within the stone mass of the tower. Reading carrels ring the perimeter, allowing scholars to hover between the mass of books and the drop to the outside world. The storage of knowledge is thus controlled by functional concerns, while its use is defined by a choreography of acculturation dominated by religious, moral, and social models and decoration.

The whole east front of the building, facing the campus, is broken down into the components that compose that narrative, stated as a series of pavilions: each reading room is its own box with a hipped roof and rhythms of windows and buttresses, pulled away from its neighbor and from transitional elements (Fig. 107). The entrance portico itself stands in for the main mass of the bookstack tower, while hiding the processional that subjugates the elements to overall comprehensibility. This village of forms then tightens itself toward the north (the south was hidden behind the gymnasium, and is revealed only from the courtyard of a later residential college building), where the manuscript and archive room is a larger, more dominating block placed on the corner. After a secondary entrance in the middle of the north facade, the building rises to a six-story administration wing. Though this form is also articulated as a separate element, its size overwhelms the delicacy of connections so evident in the front facade. Here, closely spaced piers define a tight, massive wall into which the windows are deeply set.

107. James Gamble Rogers.
Sterling Memorial Library,
Yale University, New Haven,
Connecticut, 1926–31. View
from Cross Campus.

There is a deliberate tension in the architecture of Sterling Library between the massing of the forms and the language of their decoration. The overall composition of the elements places the building in its urban context as the summation of the campus. Its cloistered, horizontal masses and spaces become a solid vertical block. This vertical orientation is counteracted by the spreading out from the stacks of the expository and functional arrangement of the places for gathering, managing, storing, and dispersing knowledge. There is a continual tension between the closing in and massing upward of the building and the penetration by the viewer and user into this body of books. That tension is released in the airy simplicity of the spaces of learning, whether they be the boxes of the reading rooms or the hidden courtyard.

The ornamentation and articulation of this organization then provide both an overt and an implied ideology for this resolution (Figs. 108, 109). If the massing of Sterling Library states the idea of the gathering of books and scholars to convert facts and values into knowledge, the decorative scheme illustrates how the library itself is the primary tool in such a process. Rogers made an explicit comparison between the decorative scheme of the Memorial Quadrangle, which illustrated "the history of Yale," and that of the library, which was "studied to symbolize the great or interesting facts connected with libraries, bibliographies, books, etc."[78] In the Memorial Quadrangle, the extension of personal life into a historical past and its mimetic conversion into

concrete models was of primary importance. In Sterling the extension of this specific library by the recollection of other places of knowledge and the making concrete of knowledge itself through the recollection of the processes of printing, storing, and reading books became the focus of the decorative explanation.

René Chambellan, the sculptor with whom Rogers collaborated beginning with the Memorial Quadrangle, prepared models for the wood carving, stained-glass inserts, and internal stone sculptures and decorative friezes. These models were based on an extensive research process directed by Anson Phelps Stokes, who had also defined the decorative scheme of the Memorial Quadrangle. Now retired from the university administration, Stokes acted as the conscience of Yale.[79] With the help of Keogh, Stokes assembled several books of images illustrating printing processes, bookshops, famous figures in book collecting, the calligraphy and book designs of cultures around the world, and inscriptions exhorting students to read and learn. Chambellan then converted these images into three-dimensional models, "gothicizing" them in the process.[80] The images range from those carved on the front, where alphabets from all over the world surround the entrance into this world of learning, to the painting of Alma Mater, in which knowledge is shown to have been put to use in the building of Yale as an institution and a myth.[81] Stained-glass windows in between show everything from medieval illumination workshops to modern printing presses, and quotations gleaned from sources as diverse as Shakespeare and the Bible define the value of the images.[82] Sterling Library thus became the validating heart of the Yale campus. It had this position because of its function and site, but it was the architectural organization, forms, and iconography that realized the character of this building in a highly successful way. But James Gamble Rogers did not stop at the library. The Sterling funds provided money for two large adjacent buildings—a law school and a graduate school—and Rogers received the commissions for both of these buildings in 1926.

The commission for the Law School involved an often acrimonious debate between President Angell, who wanted to make the graduate programs into autonomous places of research, separate from the traditions of Yale College, and most of the trustees, the Sterling Estate, and James Gamble Rogers, all of whom argued strenuously for the importance of continuing the traditions of the university in the placement and design of the new graduate facilities. It is the clearest instance of a conflict arising between the pragmatic, pseudoscientific impulses of Angell and Yale's more tradition-bound ways of doing things. In one of his few major defeats, Angell was forced to give in, and the Law School and the Hall of Graduate Studies were designed as Collegiate Gothic extensions of the library.[83]

Their organizations were based on that of the Memorial Quadrangle, and they thus resembled the residential complexes of Yale College, which Rogers was planning at the same time. Yet they layered on to this residential plan a series of monumental forms—a library for the Law School, a tower for the Hall of Graduate Studies—that brought them into the scale and character of the Sterling Library. These elements also started to open up the stylistic hallmarks of Rogers' Collegiate Gothic to more modern and—not coincidentally—more economical forms. The presence of offices and classrooms in both of the graduate buildings then served as the architectural and programmatic glue that bound the traditions of Yale College and its more modern elements together. Rogers envisioned this as the "University Center," an integral part of "a group of fine Gothic buildings" that eventually would include not only the graduate buildings and dormitories made possible by the Sterling gift, but also a post office, health center, dining hall, chapel, and administration building. The whole complex represented the emergence of a more scientific, centralized, bureaucratic version of Yale.[84]

The program for the Law School was in itself innovative. The historical model for the complex was the London Inns of Court, where a medieval elaboration of a multitude of functions revolved around both the dispensing of justice and the learning of the law, but at Yale this model was transformed into an integrated machine for the production of future lawyers. A 1925 program envisioned not only seminar rooms, lecture halls, a moot hall, and a very large auditorium, but also a library, administrative offices, and dormitory rooms for 225 students.[85] Though some adjustments were made to this program, the final design of 1927 closely follows this vision (Figs. 110, 111).[86]

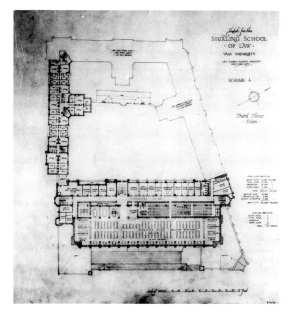

110. James Gamble Rogers. Sterling Law School, Yale University, New Haven, Connecticut, 1927–31. Section.

111. James Gamble Rogers. Sterling Law School, Yale University, New Haven, Connecticut, 1927–31. Plan.

The complex program of the Law School and its somewhat awkward site make for a rambling agglomeration of forms held together only by Rogers' decision to keep rigorously to the streetline. The result is that on three of its public facades, the Law School appears, much like the Memorial Quadrangle and later dormitory buildings, as ranges of four-to-five-story gabled facades punctuated at the corners by slightly protruding crosspieces. Only on the east facade does the more monumental side of the building become apparent, as the buttressed housing for the classrooms and offices supports a reading room rising up to openwork piers and large expanses of glass (Fig. 112).

This modulation is expressed also in the choice of materials. The Law School faces the Sterling Library with a facade of stone, but around the corners more and more bricks become interspersed with the stone, so that the rear, or north facade, of the library, where it faces the urban thoroughfare of Grove Street, is predominantly made up of this material. Similarly, the main mass of the Law School's library, which rises behind the main entrance, is clad in brick, as are all the forms in the courtyards. Stone is reintroduced only where these forms meet the sky and attract the eye, and as accents at essential points where the forms of the facade change direction, scale, or use (Fig. 113). The utilitarian boxes are sheathed in a thin veneer of monumentality, draped around them not according to some preexisting system, but according to the manner in which the architecture will be seen.

On the interior of the block, however, another world opens up. There the different scales and geometries of use are allowed to present them-

112. James Gamble Rogers.
Sterling Law School,
Yale University, New Haven,
Connecticut, 1927–31. View
from Wall Street.

113. James Gamble Rogers.
Sterling Law School,
Yale University, New Haven,
Connecticut, 1927–31. Side
entrance.

selves and are in fact emphasized by changes in level, the placement of rooms in towers, and the addition of a cloistered walk, so that the whole becomes a picturesque, continually unfolding world of romantic shapes. The large expanse of the main lawn, which faces the dining room, contrasts with intimate and rambling spaces that lead one through the dormitory spaces. Close and far vistas are composed to succeed each other in layers that unfold as one travels through the many parts of the building.

Holding the internal and external composition of the Law School together is the large mass of its library. This is the functional and spiritual heart of the institution, the place where precedent is converted into current use. The model for the library was clear and singular: it is based directly on the Chapel of King's College at Cambridge University. As such, the form resembles the original Pope design for a University Library, here scaled down and carried out mainly in brick with stone accents (Fig. 114). Its large shape is carefully embedded in the overall fabric of the composition. The form is held back from the street at all sides and surrounded by two-to-three-story buildings. While the library anchors the angular confrontation of geometries at the back with its clear rectangular shape, at the front it provides an off-center focus from the main entrance, whose low gateway tower stands slightly to the west of the southeastern corner of the complex. As such, it denotes the main axis of the Law School and stands to the side of that axis; thus it forms a perpendicular coun-

terpoint to the Sterling Library stack tower, provides a sense of closure to the monumental composition on its eastern edge, and is more visible from the Cross Campus lawn to the southeast.

The original schemes for the Law School had been simpler and more uniform. [87] The final scheme articulates and melds the parts together to a much greater degree. The dining hall and lounge, for instance, continue the use of the auditorium as transitional elements to blend together the residential and instructional sections of the program. Just as the dining hall had formed the contrapuntal focus for the courtyard of the Memorial Quadrangle, so here a sequence is established that moves one from the long succession of formal classrooms at the main entrance, to the gathering of the community of law students in the auditorium, to the informal mixing of social and academic life in an oversized lounge, to the daily sit-down ceremony of the dining hall, to the privacy of the bedroom suites. The courtyards—one of which is large and animated by elements at a larger scale, while two smaller, wholly residential outdoor spaces are intimate and completely enclosed—are surrounded by a rich variety of elements whose arched windows and turrets are festooned with stone carving and tracery. The exterior elevations, however, are simple and pinned down not just by the overlapping of their gables, but also by the regular appearance of two-to-three-story ranges of bay windows that demarcate the presence of living rooms on the inside of the residential bars.

While the compositional strategy appears to have been quite rational, the final arrangement of forms increased the sense of the building having grown over the years. The northwest corner of the courtyard, for instance, is made up of a lower screen of large glass windows between low buttresses that seem to have been added on to the four-story residential bar above. The screen is interrupted by a slightly higher block that provides entry; this block is marked above by a triangular gable end that then produces another, larger gable end directly to its east, at the intersection with the classroom building. A slightly angled screening element at the base, which also accepts a cloistered walk added on to the classroom wing, completes the layered composition of brick elements, accentuated with a few seemingly randomly placed stone stringcourses, and builds up to a confusion of forms that turns the awkward intersection into a rich architectural picture.

Such additive strategies abound throughout the building, and they are most successful when the complexity is carried through in the patterning of stone and brick. There seem to be few hard and fast rules as to the uses of specific forms or materials: while the semioctagonal bays are often surrounded with carved limestone trim, at other times the windows are inserted directly into the field of brick. In general, however, almost all edges are quoined and all cornices are picked out in stone. Certain elements are then given an exaggerated importance by turning them into stone blocks. This mix of materials, forms, and geometries serves to focus one's attention on the most honorific elements of the complex, while at the same time punctuating large stretches of the building in order to break up their mass. The echoing of these punctuations—from side to side and from element to element—creates a general visual field that gives the sense of a whole, without revealing the order and hierarchy of that whole at any given point. The monumental point of the Law School remains buried and carefully couched in multiple forms, in the manner of the Sterling Library. Only at the points where the monument is actually penetrated by use (entrances) or light (windows and bays) is its formal nature stated.

The forms of the building and the architectural styles in which they were carried out fulfilled a specific program. First of all, in its overall form, its response to the site, and the scale of its courtyard, the building was meant to authenticate a tradition carrying back even beyond Yale to English precedents:

> The men will live together and frequently, if not always, dine together. Thus will be developed, we hope, an intimate sense of solidarity and interest in legal problems. . . . The Inns of Court idea is best adopted for use in a small school of highly selected men.[88]

Second, the building size would in fact dictate the new selectivity of the Law School, mandated by both Angell and Law School dean Robert Hutchins, which would re-create a small body of socially connected students. That selection itself would be a rationalization of the Yale strategy of converting the disparate group of the best and the brightest into a coherent elite through the Law School's innovative curriculum and strongly composed physical organization. Finally, once inside and imbued with the cloistered values of the Law School, the student would be confronted with the latest teaching methods and "new buildings [that] will give us exactly the kind of facilities which the work requires."[89] Between the rambling courtyards and the doubled rows of functional classrooms, between the dining hall and the library grounding this world in knowledge, the students would find the modern applicability of tradition.

James Gamble Rogers left it to the decorative scheme of the building to make overt points. Though the building ran over budget by at least $500,000, or 15 percent, the trustees discussed removing only squash courts and other amenities, and refused to touch the plans for decorative friezes, carved mottoes, and stained-glass panels, which are scattered densely throughout the Law School.[90] The direct historical allusions made by the use of Gothic forms—culminating in the crowning of the building with a replica of King's College Chapel—are carried through in the use of carved gargoyles, rosettes, and stylized floriate patterns, sometimes directly copied from such sources as fifteenth-century choir stalls in the College of San Orso in Aosta, Italy, which are transformed into the flat panels that line the main corridor.[91] But these elements are here deformed both by the change in use and material and by their extension into other styles and modern modes:

> The design of the Sterling Law Buildings follows what is generally known as Collegiate Gothic. In this instance, however, it has been interpreted quite freely to include Norman, various periods of Gothic, early Renaissance, and modern Gothic motifs, carried out with limestone trim, part seam-faced granite, and part special size brick field, steel casements and leaded glass windows, textured slate and copper roofs.[92]

The full weight of tradition is carried through from stone figures of Old Testament judges and prophets and the obligatory statue of Justice and her scales to portraits of some of the old judges of Connecticut, a Puritan, an Indian making peace, unidentified but vaguely modern judges, and even a figure of Sherlock Holmes. The most remarkable figures are those that tell the outside world toward what all of those internal traditions (most of the above-mentioned figures appear either in the courtyard or at the back of the building) are leading the students. Above the main entrance, a teacher lectures to a sleeping class, while next to him a sleeping teacher allows the pandemonium of his class to sweep over him (Fig. 115). René Chambellan's gallery of rogues here includes robbers, both at work and in chains, cops chasing them, and a drunken man. The most stunning figure is a weighty capitalist who sits atop a buttress at the southwest corner of the building, chained both to the Collegiate Gothic architecture and to his moneybags.

The buildings of the Law School, themselves too complex to be coherent and frankly stylistically inconsistent, present themselves with a great irony about their function and even their donor, thus disarming and accepting the very challenges that a coherent monument to the legalistic validation of capitalist power in an institutional setting might attract.[93]

The decorative scheme of the Law School thus seems to progress beyond those of the Memorial Quadrangle and the Sterling Library. In the first, the Yale myth was authenticated, and in the second the building blocks of that myth, the acquisition and use of knowledge, were used to create a bastion of elite power. In the Law School, the subject is the process by which knowledge and power are manipulated directly in the everyday world, and Rogers and Chambellan show the Yale lawyers grappling with the confusions of the everyday world. The architecture thus responds to the complexities of the modern world. In that response, Rogers carries his forms into richer areas of contradiction, overlap, picturesque amalgamation, and ironic self-commentary, decomposing the sureties of Collegiate Gothic into more and more parts rather than abstracting them into almost Modernist gestures.

The apotheosis of the decorative scheme can be found on the interior of the library, just as the library culminates the whole composition. Hutchins' and Angell's calls for an involvement with the modern world and thus a breakdown of the monolithic traditions of the Law School are symbolized in the transparent images in stained glass, which "typify some of the phases of modern life with which the law deals": a reaper, a dynamo, a typewriter, a grain elevator, a skyscraper, and numerous other icons of a nonarchitectural and nonlegal world point the student and the building toward another world beyond the Inns of Court.[94]

The last of the three major building projects made possible by the 1918 Sterling gift was the Hall of Graduate Studies.[95] The construction of this complex in 1932 marked the new power of Angell's cherished graduate school. By 1926, Angell had centralized all financial and administrative offices, and new classroom buildings had started to pull students away from the traditional homes of the various departments spread throughout (and outside of) the campus. The erection of a new Hall of Graduate Studies would at this point finalize and justify these administrative actions.[96]

Rogers received the commission in December of 1926, but expressed severe reservations about the size of the site and the size of the program.[97] These conditions necessitated a dense range of buildings culminating in a tower meant to house the students. The final design, presented the following year, however, added an extra programmatic element, which does not appear to have been envisioned by graduate school dean Wilbur Cross: a large dining hall and lounge was to form the horizontal counterpart to a tower . The latter was to rise, like Harkness Tower and the Sterling Library tower, out of

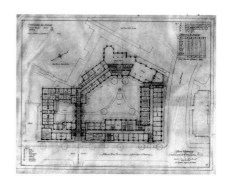

116. James Gamble Rogers. Graduate School, Yale University, New Haven, Connecticut, 1926–32. Plan, 1927.

117. James Gamble Rogers. Graduate School, Yale University, New Haven, Connecticut, 1926–32. Perspective view from Wall Street, 1927.

an enclosed courtyard,[98] on axis with Wall Street and to the rear of the site, up a full fourteen floors (Figs. 116, 117).

The tower rivals the Sterling Library stack in height, if not in bulk: against the massive slab of the library, the graduate school tower appears as a slender skyscraper, housing three to five students per floor and culminating in a steeply pitched pyramidal spire (Fig. 118). Rogers here extrudes his rambling, low-slung Collegiate Gothic architecture up into an office-like courtyard building whose tower is, for once, both the focal point of a major axis and a fully inhabited structure. As such, the massing of the graduate school recalls the more vertical, dense Collegiate Gothic of urban campuses that rose during this period in cities like New York and Chicago.[99]

Both John Farwell and Wilbur Cross had emphasized the division in the program of the Hall of Graduate Studies between its residential and bureaucratic functions and challenged the architecture to bridge that division. On the one hand, the Hall was to be an office building, and Farwell always seemed to have in mind double-loaded corridors with offices to either side, stacked up and connected by elevators. On the other hand, dormitory rooms for two hundred to two hundred and fifty students were to be provided, supposedly in the entryway system Rogers had used at the Memorial Quadrangle, which also organized the Law School dormitories.[100]

Cross wished to emphasize the connection between these two disparate elements, and Rogers' solution was to be found in the overall composition of the building. The offices were indeed grouped around long, double-loaded corridors that ran parallel to York Street and provided a simple but monumental presence on the street facing the other buildings of the Sterling group. The dormitories formed an irregularly snaking U around the other three sides of the site, each change in angle or height marked by a transitional element that appeared to deform the building, but in reality housed only more dormitory rooms.

Farwell had dreamed of a "long corridor" that would connect these two elements,[101] and Rogers provided just that: the office building is pulled open where it faces Wall Street to allow entrance into a covered arched walkway (Fig. 119). This walkway continues the axis of Wall Street and ends at the base of the tower, which is the symbolic and visual heart of the Hall of Graduate Studies as well as a dormitory building. One passes underneath the tower, shifts to follow the contours of the courtyard, and finally ends one's journey at the dining hall, where one enters through a centrally placed door into a nave-like space that looks out on the back of the site through tall windows. It is in the procession from function to function and from one end of

119. James Gamble Rogers.
Graduate School,
Yale University, New Haven,
Connecticut, 1926–32. Detail,
entrance.

the site to the other—from formal and symmetrical entrance to romantic and relaxed elements along a path defined and deformed by buildings as walls, tower, and courtyard—that the unified program of the Hall of Graduate Studies is revealed.

The layering of forms, held in place by elaborative decorative devices, which Rogers had employed so successfully in the Sterling Library and the Law School, is here both more intrinsic to the actual mass of the building and more delicate in its composition (Fig. 120). The architectural ordering of the main office building, moreover, is simpler, more abstracted, and less Gothic: the arches are less pointed, there are very few protrusions from the plane of the wall and fewer expressionistic elements such as buttresses or cross gables to measure the progression of the facade down the street. And while the materials and the design of the entrance closely mirror those of the Sterling Library, to the point where the northernmost entrance tower looks like a miniature of the stack tower across the street, the seam-faced granite quickly gives way to brick in the manner of the Law School.

The design of the courtyards continues the formal implosion that seems to be driving the design of the later Sterling buildings, and the nervous thinness of the ornamentation seems to respond to the taut skin of Collegiate Gothic elements thrown over the meeting of different forms and functions in a courtyard of contemplation. The transition between different geometries is marked not with elaborate towers or entrance pieces, but with slot-windowed bays stuck on to the reentrant angle. The back of the office building in particular appears as a flattened collage of planes and grids of windows held together with only the thinnest of limestone outline.

The dominant feature of the complex remains the fourteen-story tower. In contrast to the delicate and wholly symbolic structure of Harkness Tower, the Hall of Graduate Studies Tower is a solid, functional mass made

120. James Gamble Rogers.
Graduate School,
Yale University, New Haven,
Connecticut, 1926–32.
Courtyard.

up of brick piers rising with only minimal setbacks to a crown of patterned brick and limestone. A few finials and stretched windowframes suggest the elaborate Gothic language of the surrounding buildings. The most extravagant part of the tower is the pyramidal lead-coated copper roof, which President Angell derided as a "candle-snuffer."[102] Though James Gamble Rogers felt this element was necessary to finalize the silhouette, its presence points to the otherwise unadorned quality of the whole building.

The tower is placed off-center to the whole complex, but sits right on axis with Wall Street, thus creating a focal point that signaled to the urban environment the new world of professionalism, in the way that Harkness Tower represented the dormitories. The warm brick color of the Hall tower is not mediated or hidden in any way. The tower is functional and urban, with few of the symbolic overtones of the libraries and memorials that organized the other complexes designed by Rogers at Yale. In fact, Angell and the other members of the administration were never quite pleased with the design, though the fact that it was completed under budget, for less than $3 million, met with their approval.[103]

The Hall of Graduate Studies complex thus contains all of the elements that made Rogers' buildings such successful realizations of the Yale myth, but at the same time it turns the corner toward a less expressive, more reductivist architecture. The sheer size and straightforward placement of the elements becomes the point of the construction. The ornamental scheme does not even add a message to this composition—though a few owls are carved into the stone as metaphors for the wise, nocturnal graduate students. Instead, Chambellan's models show endless variations on the methods in which a repetitive floriate motif can be turned, twisted, and elaborated in order to provide visual articulation of the facade. Much of that patterning is achieved in the brick itself, which was specified to be "laid in pattern as will be detailed," rather than being added on as expensive cut stone.[104] The pattern often consisted of Dean Wilbur Cross's monogram, or simple geometric shapes forming a Y for Yale. The clearest precedents for the stone carving were Celtic, an exotic departure from the mainstream English and French traditions.[105]

The Hall of Graduate Studies is a place for serious studies, not a place for the elaboration of the Yale myth, the making available of knowledge, or even the application of the power of the institution to the outside world. In fact, the only references made in the decorative scheme are to those responsible for the construction of the building itself: portraits of Rogers and his draftsmen, as well as of Dean Cross and President Angell, refer the student entering the Hall not to some large body of knowledge, but only to the immediate presence of the building and its makers, and perhaps to the work of the graduate student.

The stylistic elaboration of the building can be ascribed to the increased popularity at the end of the 1920s of such arcane cultural sources as Middle America or Ireland, or to the fact that Rogers' associate, John Donald Tuttle, and not the more romantic and picturesque Otto Faelten, was the project architect of the complex.[106] But the different function of the complex, and the increased sense that Yale had to integrate itself into the modern world, may have been equally responsible for the shift toward a simpler, flatter, and more abstract functionality that incorporated some of the energy and nervous patterning of the urban environment.[107]

CHAPTER FIVE

Bright College Years

121. Unsigned cartoon, *The Yale Record*, February 12, 1930.

James Gamble Rogers was not content with designing the academic heart of Yale. He spent the years between 1926 and 1930, while he was occupied with the design of the Sterling buildings, collaborating with his friends and clients to transform the residential heart of Yale College as well (Fig. 121). What he created was a residential ideal, a model community set aside from the realities of the fast-changing urban environment. Based on the Memorial Quadrangle, the colleges he designed at Yale were sanctuaries for the traditions of that institution transformed into both efficient apartment buildings and ideal communities grouped in quasi-utopian, yet nostalgic, monasteries.

The creation of the new home of the Yale Man took a great deal of maneuvering and the extraordinary generosity of one donor. During the summer of 1927, four of the principal architects of the new Yale that was taking shape under Angell's presidency traveled together to England on a secret mission. President James Rowland Angell, architect James Gamble Rogers, Yale Corporation member Sam Fisher, and donor Edward Harkness visited Oxford, Cambridge, Saint Andrew's, and several other colleges and schools. At each stop, the visitors were received by dons and dignitaries eager to explain the advantages of their hallowed traditions to the Americans. The Yale men were on an exploratory voyage to discover what had made the "Oxbridge" tradition so attractive. The colleges of England had been the model for the most successful new building at Yale, the Harkness Quadrangle, and this model had set Samuel Fisher, who had acted as a liaison between the architect, James Gamble Rogers, and the donor, Edward Harkness, thinking. Yale was growing rapidly and needed new dormitory space. Why not adopt the college plan for Yale as a whole, and create smaller, more congenial residential units in the process? President Angell's and the Sterling trustees' ambitious building programs were establishing a new Yale. How could alumni such as Harkness, Fisher, and Rogers maintain the flavor of the old Yale of which they were so fond?

The impulse may have been nostalgic, but it also appealed to the most progressive ideals held by President Angell. Along with many other college presidents of the period, Angell was concerned that the large jump in enrollment after the First World War and the expansion of the curriculum to include ever more diverse areas of study would make for a confusing situation at Yale. Students would not be efficiently served by a curriculum and residential structure held over from smaller and more innocent days, and a mere streamlining of this structure would make Yale indistinguishable from the large state schools. The new Yale needed a new organization, and Angell was certainly willing to listen to the suggestions of one of the school's richest alumni and his two advisors.[1]

What is more, Angell had come out of the Chicago School, which held education to be at the center of the creation of a better democracy. Two important hallmarks of any educational experience, Dewey and others had argued, were the creation of a sense of community that mimicked the real social spheres of neighborhood and family, and the ability to give individual attention to each pupil. As Angell created a larger and more rational Yale, thus fulfilling those parts of the Pragmatist agenda that emphasized the necessity for the professionalization and rationalization of our understanding of the world, he was in danger of losing that sense of close-knit community that he held dear for reasons as idealistic, if perhaps less romantic, than those of many alumni.[2]

The idea of looking at the Oxbridge tradition as a model for Yale that might answer to the various agendas of the more powerful leaders of Yale had been Sam Fisher's, though he was probably inspired by the Memorial Quadrangle.[3] He easily convinced Harkness, who had been miserable at Yale until he found a congenial living situation (with life-long friend Henry Sloane Coffin) and a manageable social circle dedicated to such extracurricular pursuits as theater. Rogers himself was not easily convinced, according to his own later account, though he foresaw substantial commissions if Harkness were to fund a residential break-up of the college. According to Yale historian George W. Pierson, who pieced together the lengthy process by which the reorganization of Yale College was finally achieved,

> . . . suddenly in the late spring of 1926 Rogers had an accidental shock. He found that a Freshman of his acquaintance didn't know the men on the Freshmen crew or even who they were. Also this young man seemed in poor physical shape—which turned out to be nothing more than improper feeding, from eating around town in coffee shops and the like. So Rogers's enthusiasm was enlisted for better housing, homelike atmosphere, and good food. Rogers became the fourth key figure in the planning.[4]

Rogers was also interested in the creation of a new atmosphere, which he saw as a re-creation of his own experiences at Yale. It is not insignificant that this freshman "of his acquaintance" was probably his own son, Frank. Rogers had a direct interest in creating a home at an institutional scale, where correct living and correct values would be sheltered. Fisher shared such views, and had a specific model: the English colleges. Harkness was interested in both the atmosphere and the prospect of the reorganization of Yale more in accordance with his own moral views. He wished to create places where rich and poor alike could be educated into high moral thinking and action, isolated from the pressures of the modern world (though surrounded by its advantages) in congenial, small-scale surroundings. Angell wished to rationalize and humanize that part of his rapidly growing empire most rife with strife, tension, and tradition. The English colleges seemed the perfect model to all four of these gentleman, and so, without telling the Yale Corporation, they set off on their visit.

All three were impressed by what they saw, though they also had their doubts about the actual living conditions they encountered. In the end, however, they agreed that Yale should adopt the college model. Rogers would have a chance to build a new residential world at Yale and the model answered to the Anglophiliac tendencies of Edward Harkness:[5] "Sam, I'll do it," the rich alumnus reportedly said to Sam Fisher.[6]

Rogers wrote his own report to back up the president, in which he gave more practical reasons and a more definite vision to the plan. The advantages of small colleges, he said, were not unlike those to be found in the small towns of the Midwest: he and his friends had found men from such places better trained and more committed than those who had received their practical and moral education in the confusion of the city or at state institutions. In an accompanying letter, he lauded the ambitions fostered by small towns. He recommended the foundation of small, self-contained communities of no more than two hundred men. Yale College could be broken up into fifteen such groupings. In this manner, the Old Boy Network, of which he had been a prime beneficiary, could be formalized and preserved—in the form of allegiance to one's residential college—in a world in which it was becoming harder and harder for "good men" to know each other.[7] In a memorandum entitled "The Future of Yale College," Rogers wrote an argument for bringing back and making real his memories of old Yale in a new construct:

> In our minds Yale College represented not merely a gracious association, but a great spirit, a spirit of fellowship, forbearance, sympathy and that highest of education, the culture that comes from close friction of those students who are not of our kind by the usual selection. . . . Possibly and most probably, the loss of these cherished advantages may be the penalty that we have to pay for the great expansion in the size of our classes of the last few years.[8]

Yale had not to ask itself whether it must "become just another university," or whether it did not have something unique to offer to American society. Rogers felt it did:

> Is not Yale's greatest contribution to the country to continue in its avowed policy of training men for church and civil state, and to maintain only so much of a university as will accomplish this end, with the

object of making that part of a university she may have the very best of its kind. . . ? The undergraduate division should be some system which will maintain any advantages in scholarship that we have gained, and also retain all the advantages of the old traditions which made life at Yale an inspiration for after life. More and more of us, I believe, are now becoming of the opinion that the latter can be secured only by some kind of division into smaller units.[9]

The project for the subdivision of Yale College was thus an explicitly social one: it sought to reestablish the small and sheltered academy where men had been educated into shared social and moral values so that they might eventually give leadership to the outside world. The graduate schools would be the laboratories for trying out new ideas and advancing scholarship, but Yale College would be the physical embodiment of that Old Boy Network that was able to make full use of such advances. The architecture of the quadrangles would allow this reactive and romantic image to be fulfilled in the modern world.

Unfortunately, the Yale faculty, as it turned out, had different ideas about the nature of modern education at Yale, and it took several years, a temporary defection of Harkness to Yale's rival Harvard, and the good offices of Rogers himself to finalize the plan.[10] The President's Committee on Undergraduate Housing finally produced a draft plan by April 1929, and then Rogers closeted himself with Harkness and the latter's assistant, Malcolm Aldrich, at Harkness's country estate, Eolia. The distinguished president of Yale and his fellow corporation members were left cooling their heels. Harkness and Rogers requested changes, the administration replied, with Rogers' advice. Finally, in September, news of an agreement started to filter back to New Haven: "Honorable James Gamble Rogers appeared incognito yesterday in the range of vision of Dr. Thomas W. Farham of the Graduates Club," Angell wrote sarcastically to Charles Seymour.

The latter laid instant and violent hand on him. . . . In the course of the expedition, he extracted from said Rogers the information that Mr. Harkness was in a very good state of mind and was desirous of having the question which he had proposed answered with appropriate deliberation and consideration. . . . P.S. I was unaware of the presence of said Rogers until he had escaped.[11]

Finally, on October 4, 1929, the corporation approved the final draft of the committee's report. The committee proposed a "House system" which would "provide definite social values which have disappeared from Yale. In this sense it implies the introduction of important educational factors, assuming that at Yale social elements play a significant role in education." In the house, upper classmen of all three classes would live together, breaking through the traditional class allegiances. In this manner, younger men would pick up the values of those about to graduate. Men without previous connections would more easily be able to participate in the extracurricular activities that often formed the real education offered at Yale. A master for each house would provide administrative but also, and what was more important, moral leadership. Nothing was said about a change in the curriculum, or indeed about how the new system could improve the academic situation at Yale. The change was only meant to preserve and update the central section of the Yale myth.[12]

That act was formalized the following January, when the Yale Corporation accepted Rogers' development of the houses into quadrangles, to be called "colleges," on the English model, each of which was to house between 150 and 250 students. Each college was to have a dining hall, lounges, a library, and a luxurious master's house. Harkness also insisted that college facilities be run with the help of students on a "work-study" program: instead of serving their richer friends in the dining hall, scholarship students would work as researchers, library assistants, or organizers of social events, and thus they would be pulled into the life of the college. For this massive project of social engineering, Edward Harkness was prepared to spend $15,725,884.96. It was his largest donation, and the largest one ever received by Yale University. Yale accepted with gratitude.[13]

The new plan, said Angell, "will permit us to build in accordance with an extremely flexible plan and permit us to experiment with small residential quadrangles around which we believe a wholesome and significant social life will develop."[14] "The changing attitudes of students towards education," he told *The New York Times,*

> the increasing distractions of modern life, both within and without the College, and the gradual disintegration of the class spirit, have all created serious problems. . .[these] methods. . .promise to restore *esprit de corps*. . .[with] the social advantages of the small Yale College of the earlier generation amid the intellectual advantages of the great modern university.[15]

Edward Harkness presented his project as one of giving "good health and good education" in a manner that would foster social equality through the very structure of the colleges.[16] Angell saw the colleges as places where individuals could change themselves, their social relationships, and their relationship to American society. They were to be places where

> [the student is] being stimulated to do independent reading and study that will broaden and deepen his culture: where the ideas that are stirring in the modern world may be constantly under discussion. . .training

[students] to use their native intelligence, widening their range of ideas, helping them to advance as rapidly as they have the power to do in their acquisition of knowledge, showing them how to correlate all the things they learn and to knit them together into something like a coherent philosophy with which to meet the problems of a complicated modern world.[17]

The residential colleges were to make sense out of the modern world, and that is exactly what James Gamble Rogers' architecture was designed to do.

On a more immediate level, James Gamble Rogers was finally given the chance to knit the monumental buildings designed for the Sterling Trust into the overall fabric of the university and thus to complete the decade-old vision of the Pope plan. His own plan, produced as part of the Harkness proposal, foresaw building seven new residential units, the breakup of the Memorial Quadrangle into two colleges, and the merging and extension of two dormitories he had completed in 1928 to form a tenth unit. One of the dormitories would actually be part of the Sterling group and would be paid for by that bequest's trustees, while two of the units would be associated with the Sheffield Scientific School.[18]

All of the colleges shared a set of formal characteristics. They were organized around one central and one to three subsidiary courtyards. The dining hall was to be the major focal point for the major courtyards. On either side of it, Rogers placed a series of common rooms, and one usually entered the dining hall through these rooms. A tower was placed either over or adjacent to the entrance. The master's house was treated as a separate structure with its own entrance, though tied to the fabric of the dormitory rooms that made up the bulk of the colleges. The buildings formed closed walls to the outside world, though the height and setbacks of these walls were varied according to the direction of the sun and the intensity of the urban life and traffic.

Though one might enter the major courtyard on axis, a slight splay in the entrance or an offset in the focal point one faced across the lawn denied the simple axiality of the complex. The walls of the dormitory rooms were punctuated by entrances, often marked by cross gables, pediments, or towers. Smaller honorific elements such as libraries and administrative offices further broke down the repetitive ranges of dormitories. Thus the whole rambled slightly, and Rogers and his design team seem to have delighted in opening up unexpected vistas terminating in carved ornamental details on chimney ends, entryways, or low walls. Although the ten original colleges vary in style and intensity—some are large and ample, some small and cramped—they all share these elements, which served to translate the Harkness and Angell program into unified physical entities.

The buildings that were to make up what became known as Jonathan Edwards College were the first to be completed. They had been commissioned as simple dormitory units in 1924. They were to face the Memorial Quadrangle and thus were meant to match these buildings in appearance, if not in the lavishness of their appointments. They housed 137 students in the same sort of entryway system as had been employed for the Memorial Quadrangle. In this case, the entryways were grouped in an L-shaped set of two buildings that held the southeast corner of Library and York streets. Rogers, in describing his original design, emphasized the picturesque composition of the building:

> For the general architectural improvement of an old university like Yale probably the most effective measure, and one of the easiest of accomplishment, is to make vistas of streets by coordinating the buildings on the two sides of the streets into a harmonious grouping. It is, however, not necessary to have the two sides of the street present a similar appearance. It makes for more charm to vary it somewhat, and even to a considerable degree, provided harmony is preserved. The greater simplicity of detail in this new building will contrast in such a way as to accentuate the richness of the ornament of the Memorial Quadrangle. . . . We hope in this way to make an interesting building of a more economical type.[19]

The dormitories defined a picturesque vista, measured by a series of cross gables, that ended at the new Yale Theater, which was later drawn into the picture by a Rogers-designed facade. The new structures were lower than the Memorial Quadrangle buildings along Library Street, thus continuing the stepping configuration of the complex. But the buildings of the future Jonathan Edwards College lacked some of the elaboration of detail that marked the Memorial Quadrangle: there were no bay windows in the cross-gabled pieces, and very little of the stone carving around changes in plane that caught the light and the eye in the original model. Rogers claimed that the basic qualities of the design could be extended over a greater field without having to replicate all the details, and his experiments on Library Street set the tone for the simpler and somewhat mass-produced forms of the later Collegiate Gothic colleges. In the organization of these elements into a building complex, however, Rogers had to confront the fact that he was embroidering on an already densely woven urban and campus fabric. The 1924 dormitories were simple masses placed along the streetline, organized around a row of central cores of fireplaces and mechanical equipment. Entry and its signification, in the form of cross gables and arched entryways, interrupted the linear flow of the buildings, and two covered entryways allowed passage from the streets into a courtyard dominated by a semicircular driveway.

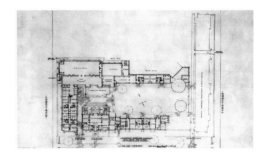

122. James Gamble Rogers.
Jonathan Edwards College,
Yale University, New Haven,
Connecticut, 1924–32. Plan.

123. James Gamble Rogers.
Jonathan Edwards College,
Yale University, New Haven,
Connecticut, 1924–32.
Courtyard.

By 1930, when the College Plan was approved, these dormitories had themselves become part of the context. When, in December of that year, the Corporation Committee on the Architectural Plan authorized the construction of the first new buildings to form Jonathan Edwards College, Rogers used the new program to extend the existing street wall of dormitories, enveloping a new courtyard for communal activities (Figs. 122, 123).[20] Ironically, the tightly constricted site and the existence of the dormitory buildings has made Jonathan Edwards one of the most intimate and sought-after residential colleges. Its entrance sequence, through an arched opening and a narrow passageway facing the common room, is full of picturesque discoveries. A series of turns continues this circuitous path all the way to the lofty dining room whose bulk is hidden at the back edge of the site, while the long, narrow main courtyard is further broken up into different levels.

The Corporation Committee also approved the division of the Rogers building that had started the movement toward residential colleges —the Memorial Quadrangle—into two new colleges, Branford and Saybrook

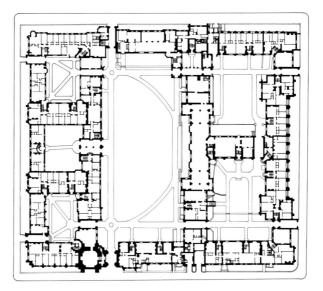

124. James Gamble Rogers. Branford and Saybrook colleges (renovation of Harkness Memorial Quadrangle), Yale University, New Haven, Connecticut, 1930–33. Plan.

(Fig. 124). A new dining hall was carved out of a series of rooms facing York Street, and the tall bay windows and large mass of this new space were almost seamlessly integrated into the existing fabric of the quadrangle. In fact, it may be said that Wrexham Tower finally gained an appropriate nave. On the other hand, the split of the complex into two colleges eventually served to cut the three cross axes, thus changing the picturesque reading of the many courts in relationship to one another.[21]

The fourth college created out of already planned buildings was Trumbull, a group of dormitories to the south of Sterling Library, whose construction was foreseen as part of the Sterling group (Figs. 125–128).[22] James Gamble Rogers hoped to extend the institutional mass of the Sterling group to the south, where it met his Memorial Quadrangle, while making its function and character more residential. The large new building would thus be integrated into the residential forms of Yale. His strategy was different from the more traditional sequence of spaces at Jonathan Edwards, however. While the York Street facade of Trumbull is a fairly straightforward wall of bedrooms, gabled and outfitted with bays in the manner of either the Memorial Quadrangle or the Sterling Law School dormitories farther up the street, the Elm Street facade is dominated by two pairs of forceful cross-gabled pieces that mirror—in a much more energetic way—the cross gables Rogers had placed symmetrically across the street (in the Elm Street facade of the Memorial Quadrangle) in anticipation of exactly such a building.[23] Most of the facade along this busy city thoroughfare is given over to an emphatic composition of streamlined Gothic forms that respond to the scale and pace of the street. Its walls are smooth, its sculptures crisp, and its organization effec-

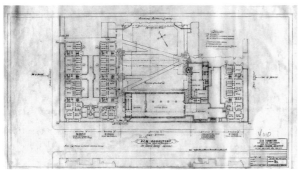

125. James Gamble Rogers.
Trumbull College, Yale
University, New Haven,
Connecticut, 1932–33.

126. James Gamble Rogers.
Trumbull College, Yale
University, New Haven,
Connecticut, 1932–33. Plan.

tively condensed by the cramped site. The scale of the Sterling Library serves to give Trumbull College a substitute communal focus for a dining hall (here kept to the street), and also makes the courtyard seem more of an isolated and protected haven at the base of a great castle of knowledge. Hovering between the monumental modernity of the Sterling Library and the evocative picturesqueness of the colleges, Trumbull was reportedly James Gamble Rogers' favorite college.[24]

Only one of the newly conceived colleges built under the Harkness plan and designed by Rogers was in the Collegiate Gothic style (John Russell Pope designed the Neo-Gothic–style Calhoun College). That college was split in half at the middle, revealing the brick used to fill out the walls where there was not enough money for stone, and was festooned with ornaments

127. James Gamble Rogers.
Trumbull College, Yale
University, New Haven,
Connecticut, 1932–33. View
from Elm Street.

128. James Gamble Rogers.
Trumbull College, Yale
University, New Haven,
Connecticut, 1932–33.
Perspective, courtyard, 1932[?].

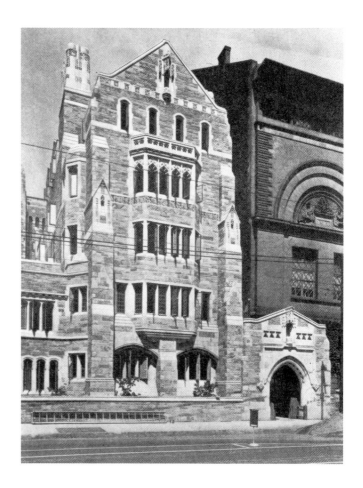

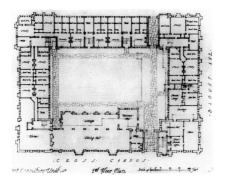

129. James Gamble Rogers.
Berkeley College,
Yale University, New Haven,
Connecticut, 1931–34. Plan.

more English Renaissance than medieval. Berkeley College reaches beyond Gothic in the same manner that it reaches beyond its original cramped site, which Rogers, in contrast to his usual accommodating attitude, evidenced at Trumbull, refused to accept.

Berkeley College started out as a proposed dormitory on the corner of Wall and High streets, whose back would face the new Cross Campus axis and be mirrored by an existing complex known as the Berkeley Divinity Oval. In the end, the new program dictated by the College Plan necessitated a building so large that it had to be placed on either side of the Cross Campus.[25] The argument for extending Berkeley across the oval was both functional and aesthetic, and led to a building (or two groups of buildings) that violated some of the most basic compositional rules of unity.

The Cross Campus axis had always been envisioned as a highly symmetrical centerpiece to a campus planned, as Rogers had explained in designing the 1924 dormitories, along vistas and allées bordered by mirroring buildings. The jumble of the Berkeley Oval, a group of buildings erected over almost half a decade, would not conform to this vision. The Sterling Library demanded a suitable base or introduction, and the axis a clear bilateral definition. Furthermore, the only way to accommodate the amount of bedrooms required for a new college was to build a five-to-six-story building. When Rogers presented these facts to Edward Harkness, the latter agreed that such an overwhelming building would create a lopsided and dark monolith, and agreed to pay for a college spread out on both sides of the axis.[26]

Rogers' first design, however, was rejected by Harkness, because he felt that the building was still too tall.[27] Rogers replanned the college as two U's whose open sides faced each other across the axis, keeping the tallest dormitory buildings to five-story forms placed along the northern and western edges. At the same time, he strenuously resisted attempts by the Yale Corporation to link the two colleges across the axis and thus make the whole more unified.[28] The cost continued to escalate, and President Angell complained that Rogers was dealing directly with the donor, leaving the universi-

150   James Gamble Rogers

130. James Gamble Rogers.
Berkeley College,
Yale University, New Haven,
Connecticut, 1931–34. Wall
Street unit.

131. James Gamble Rogers.
Berkeley College,
Yale University, New Haven,
Connecticut, 1931–34. Elm
Street Unit.

ty—which, after all, was the client—to find out about decisions affecting the central part of its campus after the fact.[29] Finally, Rogers agreed to cut the cost of the building somewhat by replacing some of the stone with brick and by simplifying its forms, thus bringing in a more stripped-down and modern mode by virtue of economy and function. The resulting building, whose design was approved in April of 1932, still cost more than $2.2 million, or at least $300,000 more than the original estimate.[30]

Berkeley College, as it was built in the subsequent two years, looks like a quadrangle building that has been pulled apart (Figs. 129, 130). The stretch marks of the energetic gabled pieces of Trumbull College where it confronts Elm Street are in fact duplicated not only on the Elm Street facade of Berkeley but also as the back ends of the bar buildings that end the composition to the east, so that the two halves seem to be have been pulled apart from each other, leaving the tall chimneypieces to fix them to the ground. Most of the communal functions are collected in the lower, southern section, of the college, but the master's house is placed on the northwest corner of the complex.

Berkeley College duplicates many of the elements of Trumbull College, and both buildings (whose design was overseen by Otto Faelten) share a more planar attitude toward the Gothic elements (Fig. 131). Groups of bedroom windows, carried out with their full complement of arches and tracery, are placed in fields of limestone floating in the granite field, and the field is extended even across the bays to undercut the seeming solidity of the stone. The tops of the walls of the dining hall drip with almost Romanesque friezes of detached arches, and diamond patterns of stone mark the center of some of the subsidiary volumes. The energetic articulation of all of these building

132. James Gamble Rogers.
Berkeley College,
Yale University, New Haven,
Connecticut, 1931–34. Detail,
Master's House.

masses stands in marked contrast to the thin, denuded forms of many contemporary Neo-Gothic college buildings.[31]

In Berkeley, one can see the unity of the Collegiate Gothic being
pulled apart at the seams. The utilitarian and functional demands on the one
hand and the picturesque composition of the earlier quadrangles on the other
here started to show their different sides. The actual connection that binds
this new community together is a tunnel, clad in the most modern and easy-
to-clean materials, that runs underneath the Cross Campus. While the dining
hall and common-room interiors are of a generic Gothic design, they go farther in displaying their underlying structure: giant oak trusses dominate the
space. The interiors of the bedrooms, meanwhile, were carried out with
almost no stone carving or wood wainscoting, "in a simple Georgian style,
adding greatly to that effect of space and light which is one of the most
delightful characteristics of these buildings."[32] Nobody was going to call
Berkeley "Darkness Hall," as the Memorial Quadrangle is sometimes still
known by its inhabitants. The master's house was, at the insistence of the
new master's wife, somewhat "French" in the 1920s, Elsie-de-Wolfe manner
(Fig. 132),[33] and above the dining hall a faculty lounge was made from a German medieval living room whose painted wood panels were imported for the
edification of Yale students.[34]

The need to save money, to house many students, and to respond to
the tastes of the inhabitants was starting to confront and alter the nostalgic
image of Yale College at the very time that it was being constructed at the
heart of the new campus. This change paralleled Rogers' own architectural
development, which was tending toward an abstraction, planarity, and structural exposition that differed substantially from the manner in which he had
composed previous commissions by using objects that mediated between
abstract requirements and the order of imagery and context.

This changing attitude toward the place of Berkeley College in the modern world was summed up in the iconography of the stone carvings and decorative panels. No myth of the founding of Yale, of the uses of knowledge, or of the morality of cultural leadership was outlined in these ornaments. Instead, all of the extracurricular and academic activities that had at one time or the other taken place on the site of the new college were memorialized: a bishop's hat hinted at divinity and Bishop Berkeley, but a bicycle represented the process of "heeling" (trying out) for the *Yale Daily News*, and a combination safe recalled the bursar's office on the site.[35] The eclecticism of the images represented the willingness of the architect and the client to allow the complexities of the modern world increasingly to dictate and define the architecture of the central buildings of the campus.

While these central dormitories were all designed in the Collegiate Gothic style that Rogers had first developed for the Memorial Quadrangle, it was not just the demands of economy and changing times (was Rogers stung by the vicious attacks in such journals as *The Harkness Hoot*, or did he merely feel a need to keep up with the times?) that caused these colleges to depart from the Collegiate Gothic model of the Memorial Quadrangle. Rogers had always stated that buildings not in proximity with either the Harkness Quadrangle or the Sterling group should be in a style other than Gothic,[36] and in 1924 he had become involved in controversy over his support for the construction of a nearly exact replica of Connecticut Hall, the oldest building on the Yale campus, next to the original on the Old Campus.[37] The final three colleges he designed at Yale (Davenport, Pierson, and Timothy Dwight) were all sophisticated stylistic translations of the same programmatic and ideological material; the Collegiate Gothic of the first five colleges became a more relaxed and domestic Collegiate Georgian style in the final three.

In the case of Davenport and Pierson colleges the choice of this latter style was justified in terms of the context of the new buildings. Yet that same context dictated a split in the design of the dormitories resulting in what has remained one of the most visible seams between the acceptable styles with which American institutions have clad themselves. The site for this seamed building was just to the west of the Harkness Quadrangle on land that Harkness had quietly acquired in the winter of 1929. John Farwell inspected the land in January 1930 and stated that "Colonial-Georgian would be very satisfactory for that location."[38] Rogers evidently agreed, and by April of that year he had presented to the Corporation Committee a plan for two new colleges on the site.[39]

The plan called for one college to be placed directly opposite the back of the Harkness Quadrangle, organized around a large courtyard, while a smaller courtyard continued the college toward Park Street in the rear (Fig. 133). The second college had to be shoehorned in, and since all

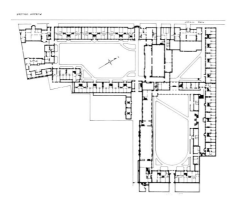

133. James Gamble Rogers.
Davenport and Pierson
colleges, Yale University, New
Haven, Connecticut, 1930–33.
Plan.

parties agreed that it was important that the front of the college face the
rest of the campus on York Street, a long walkway was created to the south
of the first college, leading back to a combination tower and gateway that
announced Pierson College. Two courtyards were then used to organize this
new range of dormitories, whose bulk actually faced Park Street.

Rogers felt it was important that this large new amount of building
should fit in with the existing residential character of the neighborhood he
was invading, while university treasurer George Parmly Day suggested that
the front of the college blend in with the commercial nature of York Street
and Broadway.[40] The softening of the fortress-like insularity of Yale on this
edge became the principal public justification for the adaptation of the Collegiate Georgian mode. Yet this style also had a function within the self-conscious attempt to give Yale an image that blended rationality and tradition.
Farwell explained

> . . . that the style of architecture in what might be called the University
> Center . . . should be what is called "Collegiate Gothic" . . . also that new
> buildings across the street from Harkness should conform to Harkness
> both in style of architecture and materials. This Collegiate Gothic is
> especially adapted to the Library, with its irregular requirements for
> rooms and the large and very high proposed stack room. . . . It has been
> felt, however, that there should be preserved somewhere at Yale the
> feeling of the Old Campus and of . . . Old New England. . . . Knowing
> also that the Colonial or Georgian style being built in brick was much
> less expensive than the Collegiate Gothic . . . [the Committee recom-
> mended that the two new Colleges] represent that Old New England
> feeling.[41]

The newest colleges thus recognized that the very building program
that proposed to restore the scale and social bonding function of the Old
Yale was destroying the actual forms in which those scales and functions had

flourished. The new colleges were to recall directly the founding condition of Yale, thus imbuing both the new Yale and the importation of English culture that constituted the old Yale with a simultaneous validation in their conscious duplication. That duplication was then justified in practical terms. First, it reconstituted in urban terms the relationship of the college, which was becoming more and more an alien utopia reserved for the privileged few, to the town and culture that it sought to imbue with knowledge and value. Second, it brought the building program back into the financial realities that were covered up by the lavish carvings of the Collegiate Gothic. In their new scale and twentieth-century appearance, the new colleges were to be functional, contextual barracks that sheltered the puritanical values of the college. Davenport and Pierson were to be both more modern and more ancient than the Collegiate Gothic buildings. Once again, Rogers had a long tradition of institutional buildings to look back toward, of which the then most recent examples were those designed by Coolidge, Shepley, Bulfinch & Abbott at Harvard, and once again his buildings at Yale refined and summed up this tradition.

The connection to the existing Yale was made on York Street, where a facade constructed out of the same stone as the Harkness Quadrangle, and designed at the same height and with the same compositional rhythms, made the new structures of Davenport College appear as a natural part of the central campus (Fig. 134).[42] The Collegiate Gothic style was continued in every detail, including such whimsical comments as the carving of a roast turkey over the kitchen service entry. Yet the facade elements here are thinner, less three-dimensionally molded than their counterparts across the street. They do not fade into brick toward the sky, thus changing the apparent hue and scale of the facade; nor, except in the center bay, do they turn corners in

135. James Gamble Rogers.
Davenport College,
Yale University, New Haven,
Connecticut, 1930–33.
Courtyard.

complicated turrets, cross gables, piers, and bays. The York Street Gothic face is just a facade, much in the manner of Rogers' first essay in clothing institutions in Gothic forms, the University of Chicago School of Education.

The thinness of this facade is revealed above the door, where a white-painted wood tower rises somewhat incongruously out of the slate roof, its four-square, telescoping form rising to a weathervane and its round-arched windows lighting an unseen space. The tower signals the world beyond the facade, encapsulated in both the library room, for which it served as a clerestory, and in the "large and beautiful Georgian Quadrangle" the student would "discover" after passing underneath the Gothic arch below (Fig. 135).[43]

The remainder of Davenport College is indeed a red brick community of forms, sometimes painted white and sometimes strung together with such Southern elements as wrought-iron balconies, brick colonnades, and "slave quarters" for the poorer students. The main courtyard is a large, flat lawn surrounded by ranges of dormitory bars on three sides, and by a dining hall and commons building to the south. The brick facades, punctuated by the regular grid of the vertical sash windows, form a unifying ground that is varied according to the directions of the site, onto which ceremonial elements are fixed. There is a grandeur and simplicity to Davenport that is lacking in Rogers' Collegiate Gothic work, but there is also a sense that the

136. James Gamble Rogers.
Pierson College, Yale
University, New Haven,
Connecticut, 1930–33.
Entrance from walkway to west
of Davenport College.

137. James Gamble Rogers.
Pierson College, Yale
University, New Haven,
Connecticut, 1930–33.
Courtyard.

138. James Gamble Rogers.
Pierson College,
Yale University, New Haven,
Connecticut, 1930–33. View
from Park Street.

complexity and sensuousness of that earlier work has been sacrificed.

Pierson College is more straightforward and even monumental in its design (Figs. 136–138, see also Fig. 133). The college has only one street facade and one full-fledged courtyard. The former is very much a back face made up of a four-story brick wall whose monotonous grid of windows is punctuated by two arched pediments at third points. Equally simple is the courtyard, which is even larger than the main courtyard of Davenport. It is unusually elongated in its proportions, due to the awkwardness of the site, and Rogers accentuated its length as seen from the entrance at the northeastern corner by closing the southern end with a one-story house-like graduate residence past which one can reach the small courtyard at the back of the master's house.

The function of the dining hall and common room as focal points is here further heightened by the repetitive nature of the rest of the architecture. The structures are made up of gambrel-roofed rectangular volumes clad in brick. Monotonous rows of white-trimmed windows are set at regular intervals into the walls. Only the slight difference in entryway doors, which catalogue domestic variations on civic Georgian modes, provides relief from this regular rhythm. The tour de force of the college remains the entrance axis, a long, stone-paved passageway leading to the Christopher Wren–like tower over the library. It is one of the grandest axes in Rogers' work, though it ends, typically, as a side axis to the main courtyard.

The final college that James Gamble Rogers designed at Yale, and the last building he completed on the campus,[44] was Timothy Dwight College. The site for this college had been earmarked for residential expansion since the mid-twenties, when Rogers had already foreseen a "colonial" dormitory for this "Temple group."[45] Rogers was authorized by the Yale Corporation in June 1930 to proceed with the design of a dormitory on the east side of Temple Street, "of brick and of colonial design, as approved in the preliminary sketches" of as early as 1928.[46] Working drawings were approved and construction was authorized in 1932, when all of the other work had just about been completed on the other Yale colleges.[47] As had been the case with at least three of the previous colleges, the project once again went over budget, and Rogers appealed directly to Harkness for extra funds. "I suspect we shall find ourselves in another of our frequent jams," sighed President Angell in a letter to his successor, College Plan–promoter George Seymour, "where the donor deals directly with the architect."[48]

Yet the result of this direct intervention was a college that was apparently the client's favorite. Its design evidences an organizational logic intrinsic to the Collegiate Georgian mode that Rogers might, if he had received similar commissions, have developed into a full-fledged architectural strategy for the creation of more economical and modern institutional buildings.[49]

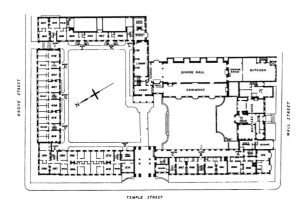

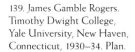

139. James Gamble Rogers.
Timothy Dwight College,
Yale University, New Haven,
Connecticut, 1930–34. Plan.

140. James Gamble Rogers.
Timothy Dwight College,
Yale University, New Haven,
Connecticut, 1930–35.
Entrance.

The basic fabric of Timothy Dwight is similar to that of Davenport and Pierson: simple brick building masses, white-painted wood windows divided into many-lighted vertical sashes, green shutters, square corner elements topped by polygonal wood turrets, slate gables, pediments dividing the expanses of the facades, and entryways marked by a changing array of Palladian windows, arched lights, columned porches, and brick reliefwork (Figs. 139, 140).[50] The focal point of the college is, as was the case at Pierson, a ten-story brick tower, here placed in the center of the Temple Street facade and rising up past a series of cones and pediments to a setback wood steeple.

On entering beneath this tower, one is confronted with a strangely split space. Slightly off-axis with the entrance is a four-columned pedimented building (Fig. 141). To the left of this "small white public building"[51] the main courtyard stretches off to the east. To the right, a much smaller, slightly raised courtyard leads back to the master's house. The latter is an unusually imposing three-story edifice, "a spacious model of a Colonial town residence."[52] The west side of both courtyards is surrounded by a covered brick arcade that rises, in the manner of the University of Virginia, with the main outdoor space. The Southern references are again reinforced by the introduction of wrought-iron porches and trellises.

The Collegiate Georgian here fuses Southern plantation style and Jeffersonian elegance with direct references to Connecticut Hall and other Yale buildings from the eighteenth century by assembling these references in a simple but rambling plan. The monumental and civic references, such as the tower and the little temple form, are put within a more residential framework by their picturesque composition, which is further emphasized by the sideways movement and offset placement of these elements. The avoidance of an overwhelming institutionality in planning thus allows the large bulk of the

program and its focal point to be married into a reinvented community. As a contemporary observer noted:

> Once inside the brownstone gateway, nearly every visitor who enters the College utters an exclamation. He finds himself unexpectedly standing on what seems to be the Green of a New England village. Facing him, at the end of a short walk, is some sort of small white public building, an old-fashioned New England Town Hall or church, almost fullsize. . . . The dining hall [beyond] is the heart of a club, of a monastery, of a garrison, and often of a home. It is certainly the heart of college life at Yale.[53]

The village green is the monastic courtyard and at the same time the parade ground of the army of students marching to conquer America with their newly acquired knowledge and social skills. The small town hall is in fact the lobby for the real place of civic activity of this renovated New England Puritan town. It leads either straight to the intellectual heart of the complex, the library, or, after a 90-degree turn, to the social center, the common room and dining hall (Fig. 142). The interiors of these spaces merge the simple clarity of the Collegiate Gothic architecture with the bowed wood trusses and wood paneling of the Georgian colleges in a seamless invention of a new type of institutional space.

Timothy Dwight College is a synthesis of many of Rogers' forms. From the courtyards that organize the ranges of dormitory rooms around the sheltered gathering space of new idealistic communities, to the towers that announce that world to the outside and beneath which the alternative world reveals itself to the visitor; from the anchoring square corner elements to the articulated entrances; from the fragments of a civic architecture inserted into this community to its series of simple places of social gathering where the

141. James Gamble Rogers. Timothy Dwight College, Yale University, New Haven, Connecticut, 1930–35. Courtyard.

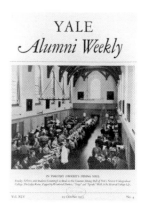

142. James Gamble Rogers. Timothy Dwight College, Yale University, New Haven, Connecticut, 1930–35. Dining room.

real work of the college can go on (since, as one administrator noted, "a dinner table is perhaps a better instrument of liberal education than a lecture
hall"),[54] Timothy Dwight sums up Rogers' achievement in creating a new
community at and out of Yale.[55]

The residential colleges can be seen as the clearest embodiments of
James Gamble Rogers' tendency to build bastions of composed coherence
that opened up a historical, visual, and spatial window through which the
modern world could see an idealized version of itself. As such, the residential colleges can, perhaps ironically, also be seen as some of the most completely realized utopias of modern architecture, standing halfway between
the romantic escape built into the very foundation of the Enlightenment and
the perfect rationalizations of architecture presented by Modernist designers.[56] The Yale colleges were to be small-scale realizations of ideal religious
settlements, as well as romantic re-creations of the original Puritan community, where all inhabitants shared the same values, sanctified by the elders
(upper classmen and the master) and symbolized by the body of the church
(dining hall) facing a common green (courtyard) and signaling the presence
of order with a steeple from an ordered world closed off from nature (the
city).[57] The delicate choreography of the pieces that composed this ideal
architecture summarized in a completely typical manner the state of the
architectural profession at the time of the Great Depression, integrating as it
did a plethora of stylistic and organizational techniques into a difficult whole
that stood as a built alternative to the uncomposed chaos and rapid change
taking place all around it. James Gamble Rogers here realized such tendencies
for once in a nearly ideal state.

The clarity of this program of course created resistance, though the
reaction to the plan was considerably more muted at Yale than it was at Harvard. There, the unilateral and sudden declaration of the plan by President
Abbott Lawrence Lowell had provoked the much more conservative students
to resist the equalizing tendencies of the plan: they were afraid that they
might lose the self-selecting intimacy of their eating clubs and be forced to
room with Jews, Italians, or other groups of what they thought were social
undesirables. To this Harvard community, their fear of progressive social
engineering became conflated, interestingly enough, with their apprehen-
sions about modern corporate capitalism, of which Harkness was seen as a
prime representative. The Harvard students dreamed instead of a smaller,
more intimate, and reactionary world completely divorced from the exigencies of modern life. As such, they rejected grand architectural plans of any
sort, preferring the adaptation of their existing environment. Purely out of
reaction, the Harvard students correctly identified social engineering, large-
scale capitalism, and the rationalized eclecticism of Rogers' didactically composed institutional architecture. What they wanted was the architecture of

Ralph Adams Cram. What they got were the bland boxes produced by the
firm of Coolidge, Shepley, Bulfinch & Abbott.[58]

Though some of the same rhetoric surfaced at Yale after the
announcement of the College Plan, the many years of preparation made it
much easier for students to accept the new plan. Furthermore, there was a
concrete and very popular model for the new colleges: the Memorial Quadrangle. *The Yale Record* did devote a special issue to the house plan, but the
criticism was directed more toward the increase in construction and toward
Harkness's aloof personality than toward the specifics of the plan.[59] *Fortune*
magazine, surveying the results several years later, noted that Sterling and
Harkness together had achieved not only a lasting memorial to their own
nostalgia, but also the transformation of Yale from a mere educational institution to a place dedicated to "the manufacture of cultivated gentlemen at the
precise moment when that product is least in demand"—though that model
proved more adaptable than the magazine imagined (Fig. 143).[60] "The new
Yale is a revolution," the authors noted, "but it is a revolution expressed in
chair seats, bedrooms and dining-room china."[61]

It was a revolution that was to define the character of the institution
for years to come. Montgomery Schuyler's vision of an Oxbridge mirage
transforming the grimy industrial town and the confused campus into a
utopia of educational and cultural assimilation was built into the modern
machines for graduate education and the romantic restorations of the effective elite of Yale, the Sterling group and the Harkness quadrangles. The size
and complexity of the campus made Yale appear almost otherworldly, a grand
Oz that still amazed visitors and arriving students many years later:

> I was stunned by the buildings. . . . Harkness Tower built by hand by
> imported European craftsmen. Standing below, staring up towards the
> gargoyles and the bells made me dizzy. . . . The flash got me, sure. One
> hundred and some thirty-five millions of Standard Oil silver certificates
> blown into Colleges and the library and the gymnasium and the tower,
> medieval Europe moved to New Haven, Early Establishment Oxford-
> land. We wanted to wear monks' robes and take vows.[62]

CHAPTER SIX

Cities Set Upon a Hill

Because of his successes at Yale, James Gamble Rogers had, by the middle of the 1920s, become publicly associated with the design of college, university, and preparatory school campuses. After he finished the design of the Harkness Memorial Quadrangle, Rogers went on to design a downtown campus, a library, dormitories, and several smaller buildings for Northwestern University; a campus for the Southern Baptist Theological Seminary in Louisville, Kentucky; the Colgate-Rochester Theological Seminary in Rochester, New York; the central buildings for Atlanta College; the central library at Columbia University in New York; the School of Education at New York University, and important buildings for the Taft and St. Paul's private schools.

In all these buildings Rogers continued to perfect both the Collegiate Gothic idiom he had worked in at the Memorial Quadrangle, and the Collegiate Georgian that defined the style of some of his later buildings at Yale. None of these commissions offered him quite the scope, budget, or challenging program that his alma mater had given him, but the buildings do show how the solutions developed for what was undoubtedly the set of commissions closest to Rogers' heart could be developed further and adapted to the myriad challenges of the modern city and its institutions. The result is a series of highly successful institutional buildings that respond to their programs with wit, grace, and sensuousness. While the preparatory schools show Rogers' techniques at their smallest scale, the larger institutional work for Northwestern and Colgate-Rochester starts to exhibit marked departures from the Collegiate Gothic, turning it into a more adventuresome but also internally less consistent style.

The first *campus*—as opposed to the more or less solitary building that housed the University of Chicago's School of Education—that Rogers designed actually predated the Memorial Quadrangle by several years. The commission for the Sophie Newcomb College for Women at Tulane University was also the last design Rogers obtained through a competition. This competition asked not for specific designs but for photos and plans that would indicate the skills and experience of the architect. The school also wanted to see drawings showing how the architect would respond to certain requirements: the need for a "harmonious . . . memorial," subtropical conditions, and the use of brick, the major building material as dictated by the budget. In making his presentation, Rogers won out over such invited luminaries as Cram, Goodhue & Ferguson, Day & Klauder, and Zantzinger, Borie

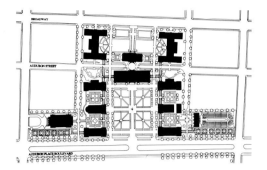

& Medary, but since the presentations do not survive, it is difficult to ascertain exactly how Rogers managed it.[1]

After Rogers was selected as the winner of the competition in
November 1911, he had to wait a full five years before he could start to build
the brick campus woven together with Spanish-style walkways and tile roofs,
and ordered by sparse Classical elements he had proposed. Problems with
the estate of the donor of the group, the outbreak of the war, and the subsequent yellow fever scare delayed construction until the summer of 1916.
Then only three buildings of the planned campus were constructed: a central administration building, sitting at the high point of the campus and dividing the new lawn of the campus, which faced one of New Orleans' gracious
boulevards, from the central lawn of Tulane to its back; a dormitory fronting
the new lawn; and an arts building facing the Tulane lawn. These three buildings together formed the beginning of an H, whose other leg was to have
faced the dormitory and arts buildings with a chapel and a music building
(Fig. 144).[2]

The complex is dominated by the four-story Administration Building
(Fig. 145). The plainness of this structure is emphasized by the use of brick
pilasters supporting a limestone course that defines the base. As in the Harkness House (see Figs. 25, 26), only the pilaster capital stands out in stone.
Small stone accents mark the centers of panels underneath the windows and
serve as keystones in flat brick lintels. The Administration Building faces the
boulevard with a pedimented portico of stone, and all attention is reserved
for gestures of entrance and for the administrative offices above the entrance
porticoes.

The most successful of the completed buildings is the Dormitory, a
strongly massed composition of two- and three-story wings grouped in a U
facing the main campus (Fig. 146). The building presents a series of symmetrical brick blocks and tiled gables whose simplicity becomes almost
domestic in its effect due to the attention Rogers paid to the entrances,
porches, and windows, while the whole building is made to seem more cultured by the sparing use of Classical ornamentation.[3]

145. James Gamble Rogers.
Sophie Newcomb College,
Tulane University, New
Orleans, Louisiana, 1916–18.
Administration Building.

146. James Gamble Rogers.
Sophie Newcomb College,
Tulane University, New
Orleans, Louisiana, 1916–18.
Dormitory.

In his next campus commission, that for the design of the Southern
Baptist Theological Seminary in Louisville, Kentucky, Rogers continued this
strategy of collecting functions into a few sprawling buildings composed out
of simple brick blocks and placed around a large lawn. He received the commission through his family connections in Kentucky and by emphasizing his
affinity with the South in general and his native state in particular.[4] The client
had a definite model for this campus: "The plans call for conformity to the
general type of architecture known as colonial, and seen in a very attractive
form in the buildings of the University of Virginia."[5] The Jeffersonian campus
was as obvious a model for an educational institution in the hilly landscape
and temperate climate of the not-so-deep South as Oxford and Cambridge
were for Yale.

The actual site selected for the new campus was a large hilltop outside of Louisville. In contrast to Yale, the Southern Baptist Theological Seminary was also dependent on contributions to the Baptist Church, not on those
of individual donors. It educated young men for a specific mission, not for a
life of cultured leadership. Its forms therefore had to be more Spartan and
functional. All of these factors led to the choice of an economical architecture

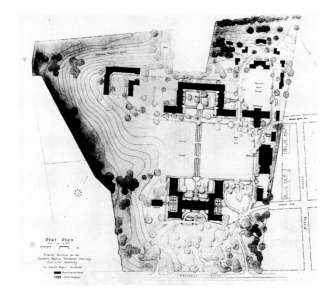

147. James Gamble Rogers.
Southern Baptist Theological
Seminary, Louisville, Kentucky,
1925–28. Preliminary plan,
1921.

that could be assembled without complicated technology to create a simple yet generically educational environment:

> Mr. Rogers has adopted the most economical plan for building materials—brick instead of stone, making pillars and small towers of wood, and leaving the interior walls of the class rooms with the rough surface of the brick unplastered.[6]

Despite such an economical and commonsensical strategy, it took four years between the time when James Gamble Rogers was appointed, apparently without competition, in 1921, and the groundbreaking for the first building of the campus in 1925. During that period, President E. Y. Mullins continually implored the Baptist Convocation for the $2 million needed for the construction of the campus, at one time consulting with architect and board members from his sickbed.[7]

The campus was constructed between 1925 and 1928 almost completely according to James Gamble Rogers' original drawings of 1921, and for $225,000 less than the original estimate.[8] The two principal components of the campus are Norton Hall and the new dormitories—later named Mullins Hall in honor of the president—which face each other across a 500-foot lawn cleared at the center of the property (Fig. 147). The complicated configuration of these two buildings allows them to incorporate disparate functions while at the same time creating courtyards that face not only each other but also the exterior of the campus.

The buildings are composed out of simple rectangular boxes—never more than four and usually two stories tall—whose repetitive rhythms of red brick and windows are punctuated only at the entrances and gable ends with porches, Palladian windows, and pediments in white-painted wood (Figs. 148, 149). Small towers over gable crossings and a more elaborate bell tower at the center of Norton Hall provide the vertical counterpoint to the horizontal sweep and containment of the campus. Mullins Hall is a relatively simple grouping reminiscent of Rogers' work at Sophie Newcomb College,

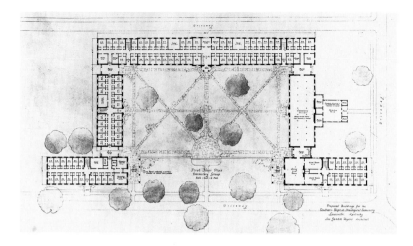

148. James Gamble Rogers. Mullins Hall, Southern Baptist Theological Seminary, Louisville, Kentucky, 1925–26. Plan, 1926.

149. James Gamble Rogers. Mullins Hall, Southern Baptist Theological Seminary, Louisville, Kentucky, 1925–26.

including the use of arcaded walkways and framed views through arches to tie together the otherwise rather plain masses of the building.

Norton Hall is more complex in its massing and articulation, since it serves a wider variety of activities (Figs. 150, 151). It is the administrative and ceremonial heart of the campus. The gable of the central mass facing the lawn is surmounted by a polygonal domed spire rising from a rectangular base. The double-loaded corridor at the heart of this building leads from a central stair hall directly to two cross-axial corridors that form the centers of the classroom and library wings. Each of these wings forms a U shape around a smaller courtyard where there are secondary entrances. Each wing is extended toward the campus front by a larger form containing the library and auditorium, respectively. On this southern side the ground slopes away steeply, and a detached temple front, crowned by the bell tower, emphasizes the importance of the seminary to the outside world. The north facade opens

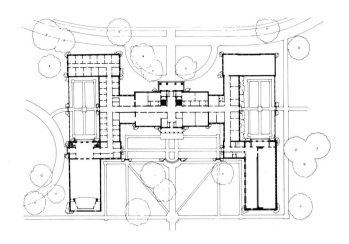

up into a courtyard mirroring that of the dormitory group but here raised a few steps from the level of the lawn, thus emphasizing its more ceremonial character.

    The complexities in scale and texture achieved for each of the many-faceted facades are resolved by the massing of the whole up the hill toward the center, and each change in level or in the direction of the gable serves to enrich this composition. Within this assemblage, the entrances and windows are placed as variations on a theme. Some are simple white doors flanked by white-painted wood Doric columns, while in other cases the pilasters support broken architraves into which blank decorative panels are inserted, while yet others extend to include Palladian windows (Figs. 152, 153). One can easily suspect the presence of a collection of postcards similar to the scrapbook Rogers used in designing the Memorial Quadrangle. In this case it would have been one filled with examples of Georgian doors, windows, balconies, gable ends, and colonnades.[9]

150. James Gamble Rogers. Norton Hall, Southern Baptist Theological Seminary, Louisville, Kentucky, 1925–26. Plan.

151. James Gamble Rogers. Norton Hall, Southern Baptist Theological Seminary, Louisville, Kentucky, 1925–26.

152. James Gamble Rogers.
Norton Hall, Southern Baptist
Theological Seminary,
Louisville, Kentucky, 1925–26.

153. James Gamble Rogers.
Norton Hall, Southern Baptist
Theological Seminary,
Louisville, Kentucky, 1925–26.
Detail.

In addition to Mullins and Norton halls, Rogers added a row of dormitories on the eastern edge of the campus, on newly acquired land within the city grid. The dormitories are higher than the buildings that face the lawn, and their whole appearance is both more urban and more utilitarian. They are simple five-story boxes with a few honorific elements, such as simple pediments graced with lunettes. The rectangular mass of the building is emphasized by the simple rooflines. Only one device serves to place these dormitory structures in relationship to the grander structures around the lawn: two vertical bands are created out of arched windows and doors facing the campus, and these are placed directly below the end of the pediment. In this manner, pilasters are implied without being built, and the motif is continued by the vertical grouping of the tall and narrow bathroom windows farther down the facade. The technique is reminiscent of both the implied pilasters of such houses as the Harkness House, and of the implied grandeur used in creating the heart of the Southern Baptist Theological Seminary itself.

The lawn of the campus is the design's grandest statement, the clearing from which all of the buildings can be seen and which most clearly exhibits the expanse of the institution (Fig. 154). Rogers emphasized the need of the architect, not the landscape designer, to define the virtually unplanted expanse of this space, and the result is a place that is both a parade ground and a village green, a ceremonial horizontal plane opened up in the hilly countryside.[10] Grandeur is thus achieved in much the same way Jefferson had created his Lawn at the University of Virginia: not by the erection of expensive buildings (Fig. 155), but by the creation of a void held between the dormitories and the academic functions. Here, however, the lawn is internalized by the placement of several subsidiary buildings at its edges: Rogers planned a

154. James Gamble Rogers. Southern Baptist Theological Seminary, Louisville, Kentucky, 1925–28. The Lawn.

gymnasium and a commons building on the eastern, higher, end of the lawn, and tennis courts on the western edge.[11] This composition was later altered, both because of the condition of the soil and because of changed functional requirements, to place the gymnasium closer to the lawn, facing a new library building (not designed by Rogers).[12] The power plant replaced the proposed commons building, and a small chapel also was added. Just as the courtyard of the Harkness Quadrangle had become the heart of that composition, so here the open space, rather than a solid object, became the focal point of the composition. Just as Rogers was silent about the meaning of his architecture, allowing functions and picturesque composition to imply a purpose, so his architecture increasingly turned toward implied voids for their organizing force: it is in the courtyards of James Gamble Rogers' educational structures that one sees the full complexity of his architecture and grasps its meaning.

155. Thomas Jefferson. The University of Virginia, Charlottesville, Virginia, 1817–25. The Lawn.

The buildings Rogers designed for the Taft and St. Paul's schools allowed him to create small institutional jewels with little of the grand aspirations of his larger institutional buildings, and here he seems to have concentrated on the craft and composition of the actual buildings. Popular myth has it that the buildings at Taft—in Watertown, Connecticut—were constructed by Yale workmen during the summer and off periods.[13] Though this story is apocryphal, the Yale connections were strong. Samuel Fisher, who together with Rogers and Harkness formed the triumvirate that dreamed up the Yale College Plan, was a member of the Taft board of trustees and chairman of the fund-raising campaign. The major gift that enabled the school to construct an infirmary, a servants' building, a school building, and an auditorium came from Edward S. Harkness. Robert French, one of the strongest proponents of the College Plan and the first master of Jonathan Edwards College, was also a trustee and advisor.[14] In a broader sense, the Taft School sent—and still sends—many of its graduates to Yale, and the founder of the school, Horace Dutton Taft, was a member of an extensive and influential Yale-educated family.[15]

156. James Gamble Rogers.
The Taft School, Watertown,
Connecticut, 1927–29.
"Proposed New Buildings," 1927.

Yet the Taft School under Horace Taft displayed none of the educational innovation for which the Yale of President Angell had become known. In fact, the school prided itself on old-fashioned values. According to the fund-raising booklet published by the school in 1928, "The headmaster of the Taft School has no modernistic illusions that education is possible without discipline. . . . The Taft School is founded on the conviction that education and mass production are incompatible terms."[16] The school provided conventional training for young gentlemen so that they might enter the Ivy League, and did so in a section of rural Connecticut where such future leaders still seem to outnumber the dairy cows. The buildings that housed the institution were a Neo-Gothic complex of gabled forms organized around a ceremonial tower.[17] When James Gamble Rogers was commissioned in 1927 to add an infirmary, a building for the "numerous servants of the School," classrooms, an auditorium, and a chapel, he continued this idiom (Figs. 156, 157).[18]

Rogers did not imitate the existing buildings completely, and themes from Yale and Northwestern can be found everywhere in the design. The entrance to the main school building is through an arched porch whose limestone trim merges at the base with a pair of lancet niches that reach up to hold the corners of the low, gabled brick shape of the porch roof (Fig. 158). The deft restatement of a pavilionized entrance porch, simple shapes, and Gothic ornament, which visually and tactilely defines this architectural element, sums up the treatment of most of the rest of the building. The walls of the main body of the school are built up out of large expanses of brick punctuated by windows grouped together within frames of Gothic stone trim, while the slate roof is marked by the regular march of dormer windows and cross gables.

As is the case at such Yale colleges as Berkeley and Davenport, as well as at the Colgate-Rochester Theological Seminary, library and lounge

157. James Gamble Rogers. The Taft School, Watertown, Connecticut, 1927–29. Chapel, Auditorium, and Classrooms, 1927.

158. James Gamble Rogers. The Taft School, Watertown, Connecticut, 1927–29.

spaces act as buffers or screens of public activity placed in front of the tightly packed three-and-a-half-story bulk of the building. This undulating screen of honorific elements disguises the main mass of the building, while creating a zone of accommodation to the outside world.

The interior organization of the building hinges on a complicated stair hall, with a series of landings, right inside the front door (Fig. 159). Steps lead up and slightly to the side of the entrance axis back into a long corridor, while other steps lead down to an auditorium to the east and the older buildings to the west. The slope of the ground at this point justifies the series of offset arches defining and holding axes that slide by each other, but rather than masking these transitions, Rogers has manipulated light, ornament, and materials to accentuate the compositional complexity of the area. In an extreme case of the architectural strategy he so often employed, Rogers confronts visitors with columns and screens so that they must maneuver past the architecture to reach their destination; thus they are made aware of the built reality of the building. The remainder of the classrooms, offices, and dormitory rooms that make up the main new school building are placed around a system of double-loaded corridors and are carried out in stone, stucco, and wood trim. The straightforward treatment of these spaces becomes the norm for all the architecture of the two ancillary buildings Rogers designed at Taft, the infirmary and the service building.[19]

The buildings at Taft are not particularly innovative, but they are not exercises in imposed architectural grandiosity either. The blunt expression of the fly space of the auditorium, the complexity of the stair hall, the careful modulation of the facades, and the site-specific inflection of the buildings all extend the functions and shapes of the Taft School into the landscape. In this manner Rogers fully exploited the expressive potential of the material of which the building is made. There is no larger discourse here, since Taft saw itself as no more than a place to handcraft students for future education. There is only the perfection of techniques developed elsewhere, such as the choreography of interior circulation or the marking of entrance pavilions. The one grand statement at Taft, the tall chimney of the Rogers-designed power plant, rises up behind the rear playing fields in a brick-and-limestone celebration of the power of Rogers' Collegiate Gothic architecture to shape and turn even the grittiest aspect of the program into a functional marker.

The St. Paul's Schoolhouse building, in Concord, New Hampshire, is a much smaller and later Rogers design for a school which did pride itself on educational innovation and experimentation. In the late 1920s, Rector S. S. Drury embarked on a renovation of the school's curriculum that was meant to achieve much the same ends as those aimed at by the College Plan at Yale. Drury wanted to accommodate growth and new teaching methods, while maintaining the intimacy and traditions of St. Paul's, a small institution that insisted on its lack of (internal) elitism and on its high academic standards. The solution was to break not the dormitories but the classes down into smaller groups or "conferences," with students and teachers seated at tables in groups of about a dozen. The democratic and more flexible way of teaching also allowed for the emancipation of the young gentlemen in a manner that would enhance their skills in debate and conversation. Within the protected environs of St. Paul's, Drury sought to create an idealized world of civilization and acculturation.[20]

This program necessitated a new building, which would house the conference rooms and at the same time help to refocus the expanding campus. Originally planned around a public street, St. Paul's had become an enclosed but fragmented campus spread out over a series of hills around a small lake. The New Schoolhouse, as Drury's projected building came to be called, was to mark the new center of this campus opposite the school's most famous landmark, Henry Vaughan's Chapel of St. Peter and St. Paul.[21] In 1931, Drury appealed to St. Paul's richest alumnus, Edward S. Harkness, to

159. James Gamble Rogers. The Taft School, Watertown, Connecticut, 1927–29. Interior stairs.

160. James Gamble Rogers.
New Schoolhouse, St. Paul's
School, Concord,
New Hampshire, 1934–37.

161. James Gamble Rogers.
New Schoolhouse, St. Paul's
School, Concord,
New Hampshire, 1934–37.

help pay for this building. Though Harkness was sympathetic, he declined because of the "general conditions" of the economy.[22] Though negotiations continued over the next several years, Harkness insisted that they be kept confidential, and he worked, as always, according to his own agenda and timetable, until he showed up incognito at St. Paul's in 1934 with James Gamble Rogers and gave the school both $1 million and a Rogers design for the New Schoolhouse.[23]

The New Schoolhouse contains twenty-seven classrooms, a library, and offices for the school administration (Figs. 160, 161). The building faces a large grass square on the crown of a hill, and thus takes the place of a meeting house facing a village green. It is organized around a square tower that anchors the center of the whole composition, holding the entrance and the crossing of the internal axes together against the sharp drop of the ground to the side and rear of the building. Completed in 1937, the building is still the focal point of St. Paul's.

The basic unit of the New Schoolhouse is the small study room or classroom, which Rogers designed as a low square box lighted by tall bay windows, paneled with oak bookcases, and equipped with large tables. The classrooms are arranged around broad corridors also paneled in oak (Fig. 162). The horizontal, grid-like quality of this paneling, which reaches up all the way to the cornice of the slightly arched stucco ceiling, contrasts with the vertically oriented Gothic design used on the outside of the building. One might say that the interior fulfills Drury's program—his office was on the second floor, was designed without a door, and overlooked both the whole campus and the center of the Schoolhouse—while the exterior inte-

grated this new way of teaching into the traditions and site of St. Paul's.

The building appears from the outside almost as if it were made up of a series of independent wings, each addressing a different part of the campus, each composed of intersecting gabled forms of brick punctuated by regular grids of windows and occasional bands of trim, and held together only by the tower that marks both the entrance and the rector's office.

The St. Paul's New Schoolhouse is simple and restrained, yet every detail and composition is specific to its site and function. The large expanses of glass that light the classrooms are divided into stone-trimmed groups, then set into expanses of brick. These planes are visually reinforced by buttresses ringed with multiple layers of stone stringcourses. Entrances are pushed out to meet the visitor coming down the paths from various parts of the campus, and low walls provide places to sit all around the building. The crossed gables define small courtyards, while the tower always provides orientation. The walls and roofs give an impression of self-assured containment, while allowing one to read functions and scales through the composition of the functional elements and the placement of ornament either at intersections of forms or at the most pronounced points of the structure.[24]

It was in the larger commissions that James Gamble Rogers was really able to experiment with the limits of both his organizational strategies and of the Collegiate Gothic, and his most important client for such work was Northwestern University. In 1921, when Northwestern, by then a well-established and expansion-minded university in Evanston, Illinois, was looking for an architect to direct its building program, its candidates included a long list of local architects and a short list of nationally known college designers: Bertram Goodhue, Cram & Ferguson, Paul Cret, and James Gamble Rogers. President Walter Dill Scott had assembled this list by writing to university presidents, paying special attention to the recommendations of the Ivy

League schools on which he wanted to model Northwestern.[25] The trustees wanted "an architect experienced in educational buildings and known for efficiency," and added that, since the architect had to "be of assistance in presenting the needs of the University to its constituency . . . refined publicity skills were of tantamount [sic] importance."[26]

President Scott, who had been appointed the previous year, was of the same breed of new university president as James Rowland Angell of Yale. Both shared a background in psychology and administration, but Scott had taken his research into the practical realm by becoming an expert on public relations.[27] In the same way, the unspoken needs of Yale became the conscious mandates of Northwestern: Scott needed to raise money and form a coherent image for a university that had had little of either, and he saw architecture as one of his most useful tools not only in educating young minds, but also in creating a coherent and salable image for Northwestern. The architect therefore had to "bring the advantages of a prepared and dignified approach to possible donors."[28]

James Gamble Rogers, who by this time, according to one university official, "was a consummate gentleman, finely dressed and projecting the image of one with a prominent place in New York's social life,"[29] fitted the bill. He came highly recommended from his clients and from such colleagues as the society architect Howard Van Doren Shaw, who noted, "He was a year ahead of me at college; I know him well and feel that he has made good."[30]

Riding in on this crest of personal recommendations, Rogers made a great show of his experience and his personal desire to return to the city where his career had started: "I am very anxious to make the Northwestern studies, partly, I think, because I lived in Chicago and would like to get up something great. I no longer run a large office because I have decided to take only such work as I can personally really keep guide of."[31] He claimed to be holding off on other jobs as he waited for word (he was at the time negotiating for his appointment at Yale), and thus overwhelmed by the personability, eagerness, and professional acumen of this native son, the trustees appointed him in August of 1921.[32]

Though Northwestern was based in a suburb of Chicago, the first focus of both Scott's and Rogers' attention was the establishment of a downtown campus, originally to be called the McKinlock Campus. By building a presence there, Scott hoped to service and draw upon the business community by representing the university as a modern professional institution. The campus was to house the schools of medicine, business, law, and journalism. It was not to be an isolated place for the inculcation of educational values; that function was reserved for the Evanston campus. Instead, it was to be a place where Chicago could rationalize and professionalize its authority in the areas of law, finance, and health. By splitting the two functions of the university, Scott avoided the conflicts of interest between the undergraduate college and the professional graduate schools that continually were to confront Angell at Yale.[33]

The site chosen for the McKinlock Campus was right in the middle of downtown, on land owned by none other than John V. and Arthur Farwell, of the influential family who were friends, in-laws, and clients of Rogers'. Negotiations for the site had gone on for several years before Rogers was appointed, but it is worth pointing out that Yale Treasurer George Parmly Day, when asked by Scott for a recommendation on Rogers, referred him to John Farwell as chairman of the Corporation Committee on the Architectural Plan for Yale.[34] Once Rogers' seemingly inevitable selection had taken place, he proceeded to plan the campus as a part of the natural landscape of downtown.

James Gamble Rogers must have realized that the explicit connection of the schools with the business community and their siting in downtown Chicago mandated a reversal of the protective stance of the buildings at Yale, Princeton, and the University of Chicago. His scheme stood in marked contrast to the original designs for the plot, produced a year before his appointment by the Chicago firm of Holabird & Roche (Fig. 163). Their drawings had shown a fortress of stripped-down Neo-Gothic buildings forming a series of quadrangles completely filling the long block running west from Lake Shore Drive along the south side of Chicago Avenue. A long bar of similar buildings directly to the south of this block continued the appearance of this rival to the University of Chicago across the city grid. Out of the middle of this low agglomeration of gabled buildings rose a memorial tower with no apparent function.[35]

Instead, Rogers proposed a series of tall blocks marching down Chicago Avenue, each housing one of the schools (Figs. 164, 165). The tallest of these structures, the medical school and hospital, was to be closest to downtown, and the group tapered off toward the lake. Thus the ensemble was to form a ridge mimicking the overall structure of the downtown of the 1920s as it rose from a grid in setback blocks to a peak of concentrated activity at the heart both of the city and of each building. The hospital itself was to be the very image of a modern skyscraper, an integrated machine for health layered vertically, justified by modern technology, and expressing in concrete form the energy and aspirations of its science. Over the next decade, this scheme was constructed almost exactly as proposed.

As to the style of the buildings, Rogers professed to have no strong sentiments, as long as the group would be unified in its appearance. He advised the board of trustees that they should "avoid mistakes that Northwestern and other universities have made in ill-considered types and loca-

163. Holabird & Roche. McKinlock Campus, Northwestern University, Chicago, Illinois. Perspective view, 1921.

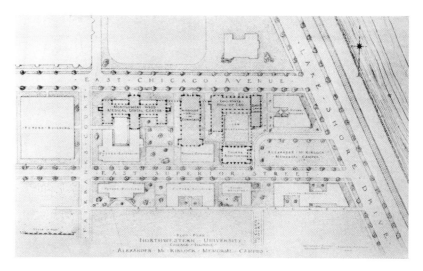

164. James Gamble Rogers. McKinlock Campus, Northwestern University, Chicago, Illinois, 1922–27. Site plan.

165. James Gamble Rogers. McKinlock Campus, Northwestern University, Chicago, Illinois, 1922–27.

tions of individual buildings (Yale, for example)" and should put him in charge of all buildings, thus avoiding the endless political maneuvering to which he had to devote so much of his time at Yale.[36] The politics of the situation and the appropriateness of the architecture were more important than their style, Rogers claimed:

> I do not know what style of architecture the group will be. The requirement of a building makes its architecture. If you try to force a style that is not a mature development of the group, you will have something exotic and not lasting. It takes some study, some knowledge, some experience, and some skill.[37]

166. James Gamble Rogers. Chicago Tribune Tower, Chicago, Illinois, 1922. Perspective view, competition entry.

Yet this site and this program inevitably led him to the use of a variation on the Neo-Gothic. In this case, his buildings appeared not as the Collegiate Gothic that Holabird & Roche originally had proposed, but rather in the guise of what may be termed Skyscraper Gothic, a style epitomized by Hood & Howells' Chicago Tribune Building, erected during the same period only a few blocks away from the downtown campus, and echoed, in a much more stripped-down form, in Rogers' own entry in the competition for that building, for which he received an honorable mention (Fig. 166).[38]

It was a style that used the perceived vertical emphasis of Gothic churches (as opposed to the monasteries and colleges favored as models by the makers of Collegiate Gothic buildings) as a natural way to translate the new scale and inherent direction of the skyscraper into a more or less recognizable form. Skyscraper Gothic architecture was thus inherently thinner and more attenuated than other forms of Neo-Gothicism, since it tended to function merely as an expressive cloak barely containing the demands of the tall office building. Skyscraper Gothic melded almost imperceptibly into various forms of Modernism, eventually (and despite Sullivan's despair over the outcome of the Tribune competition) fulfilling the logical reductivism of the Chicago School.[39] Rogers' own entry in that competition was, if anything, conservative. Seeking to emphasize the reduction of architectural style to an expression of the logic of both construction and business, Rogers found an idiom that helped him pursue the pragmatic reductivism of his early buildings in a more natural harmony with the iconography and picturesque strategies he had learned to adapt for his institutional work.

Just as Rogers counted on Otto Faelten and, however briefly, on E. Donald Robb, to help him realize his Collegiate Gothic vision for the Yale campus, so in Chicago he turned to two assistants—Samuel Baker and Ainslie Ballantyne—who could help him design highly complex tall buildings in a Skyscraper Gothic style. Of the two, Ballantyne was the designer. Born in New Zealand, he had come to Chicago in 1915 and worked for Holabird & Roche on several of their institutional projects. He then moved to New York, worked for James Gamble Rogers, and, when the Northwestern commission came in, went to England for four months to study "collegiate groups at Oxford, Cambridge, Winchester, etc., to get collegiate background from which to evolve a modern American college group."[40] If Faelten represented the picturesque attitude toward Neo-Gothic design, Ballantyne, who was to be Rogers' chief assistant on many of his larger hospital and college designs, represented a more rational approach. The work he was involved with is thinner, more attenuated, and often more varied in its materials, but it also has little of the exuberance in massing that marks the Yale buildings.

The Rogers office was also aided by the presence of Samuel Baker. An architect trained at the University of Pennsylvania, Baker had worked for John Russell Pope, but by 1922, when he entered the James Gamble Rogers office, his experience was mainly in providing the link between designers and engineers. He had worked for the construction firm of Marc Eidlitz & Sons, who built almost all of Rogers' buildings on the East Coast.[41]

Unlike the Yale campus, the downtown Northwestern campus was conceived and built as a single unit. The purchase of the land was made possible by a gift of Alexander McKinlock, for whom the campus was named until the donor's default during the Depression, and in short order President Scott, with the help of Rogers' drawings, persuaded Mrs. Montgomery Ward, widow of the store founder, to pay for the hospital and found donors for whom the buildings of the business school (Wieboldt Hall), law school (Levy Mayer Hall and Gary Law Library), and multipurpose auditorium (Thorne Auditorium) were named.[42]

The most important building of the new campus was the Montgomery Ward Building (Fig. 167). The structure rises to a nineteen-story tower out of a fifteen-story ridge, which sets back in a series of narrow steps from the street. The main ridge defines the overall organization of the building, which is made up of a collection of varied functional spaces stretched out along either side of a double-loaded corridor and stacked one on top of the other. The central block contains the most condensed functions of the hospital and school. Buttressing wings extend the building out toward the light and contain offices and hospital wards. Topped by solaria and molded to strengthen the overall composition of the Ward Building, they appear as a solid mass. Emerging out of this medical mountain, the tower is an expression of the vertical circulation and centralized mechanical systems rising up through the heart of the complex. Its corners grow as stair towers ascending all the way up from the base past a band of windows on the fifteenth floor. These mark the downtown offices of those who control the institution, including Walter Dill Scott. The tower continues as a bell tower transformed into a massive mechanical penthouse with a castellated flat top surmounted by a single flag. In the design of the Ward Building, the courtyard has been

167. James Gamble Rogers.
Montgomery Ward Building,
McKinlock Campus,
Northwestern University,
Chicago, Illinois, 1922–26.

condensed into an urban bar building, and the memorial tower has become a functional expression of the complicated technology enabling such condensation. Unfortunately, a recent addition has completely destroyed this massing while mimicking the style of the building in a rather crude manner.

The ornamentation of the Ward Building is concentrated around the doors and the large windows and in the ends of the buttresses, so that the overall mass of stone rising up in geometric blocks overwhelms any delicacy of stylistic delineation. This is not a didactic building. It is a medical institution, and the justification for the final choice of Gothic was its applicability to the steel-frame construction, the neighborhood of setback skyscrapers, and the monumental needs of the client. As one contemporary critic observed:

> The modernized Gothic lines are a blending of the massive modern skyscraper with the ethereal monuments meticulously worked out by the monks of the middle ages. A twentieth century workshop in reinforced concrete, with wide floor areas, central heating plant, elevator shafts, and equipped with the latest appliances, is done in the sculptured stone pinnacle style. . . . There is aspiration in those crags and spires and climbing buttresses of Bedford limestone, and there is practicality in the irresistible mass of monument itself. The combination is both worldly and celestial and is no cathedral and no ordinary office building.[43]

Wieboldt Hall, completed several months before the Ward Building to house the School of Commerce, is an even simpler block, yet its functional

requirements allowed for considerably more interior articulation (Figs. 168, 169). The eight-story building is a long rectangle running north-south directly to the east of the Ward Building, and in its height, as well as in the stripped-down Skyscraper Gothic style of its skin, it continues the mountainous massing of the latter building. Its main distinguishing feature is a short tower that rises over the mechanical core of the building in the middle of the block and whose multiple layers of pointed buttresses finally surround only the exhaust grilles. The crisp detailing of the finials and Tudor stringcourses emphasizes the simplicity and forthrightness of the mass of Wieboldt Hall.

Since the building is organized perpendicular to the street, the main corridor in this case does run back directly from the main entrance. One is brought up several steps into a small lobby and corridor, whose walls are covered with gridded wood wainscoting and whose low and broad proportions are emphasized by the shallow coves of the ceiling. A series of asymmetrical movements in the walls housing the reception function of the school immediately divert one up the elevators and stairs. The latter are wrapped around bathrooms and mechanical systems stacked in the aforementioned tower. This combination mechanical-and-circulation element forms a strange core to the building. It is pushed out from the main bar of Wieboldt Hall as the only expressive element rising from its functional mass.

The library and "club rooms" of Wieboldt Hall are both lavish and insistently organized around the actual structure of the building (Fig. 170). Facing the front of the Hall, their large spaces are interrupted by the grid of columns and exposed beams. The floors are covered with diamond patterns of white and black linoleum, and the wood wainscoting is kept simple. These

168. James Gamble Rogers. Wieboldt Hall, McKinlock Campus, Northwestern University, Chicago, Illinois, 1922–26.

169. James Gamble Rogers. Wieboldt Hall, McKinlock Campus, Northwestern University, Chicago, Illinois, 1922–26.

170. James Gamble Rogers. Wieboldt Hall, McKinlock Campus, Northwestern University, Chicago, Illinois, 1922–26. Library.

171. James Gamble Rogers. Levy Mayer Hall, McKinlock Campus, Northwestern University, Chicago, Illinois, 1922–27.

are no-nonsense rooms, whose main decoration comes in the form of brackets that articulate the joints between columns and beam. The library presents a vast expanse of undifferentiated space in which reading tables are evenly spaced, while the Commerce Club room fills its equally unmodulated space with half a dozen seating groups arranged below vaguely medieval chandeliers. Only the Women's Club Room is more delicate, being furnished with rattan furniture and clad with framed plaster panels on which paintings were hung. Wieboldt Hall thus represents a particular view of business in the early twentieth century. The outside is a reserved but cultured facade; the real work takes place in efficiently organized, bare-bone spaces, while at the heart of the building is a private and rather luxurious club.

The lowest, most gothicizing, and most elaborate of the original structures of the McKinlock Campus is the L-shaped building comprising the Levy Mayer Hall of Law and the Elbert H. Gary Library of Law (Fig. 171). There is little wasted space in this, the smallest building in the McKinlock group, and even such ceremonial spaces as the library are organized so tightly that circulation, stacks, and reading areas have been combined, while the nooks and crannies left by the larger classroom auditoria are utilized for stairs and offices. The ornament here is more delicate and the massing is more highly differentiated than is the case in either the Ward or the Wieboldt building. These details seem in keeping with the smaller scale of this complex, and with the more exalted position that law holds as the keeper of ethical and social values in our society. The *Northwestern University Alumni News* likened the law complex to

> ...new Inns of Court here in Chicago, the counterpoint of the historic home of the English bar...an environment of professional dignity and propriety was sought...to implant in the aspirant the ideals of a scholar and a gentleman.[44]

The Gary Hall of Law is neither a skyscraper whose modern technology makes possible the advanced fight against all that threatens our rational and conscious existence, nor is it a business block for the inculcation of the corporate rules that allow our society to operate according to its chosen economic and legal system. It is a place that must supposedly allow its students to learn how to interpret those rules, and it would seem appropriate that, within this ridge of urban buildings, Levy Mayer Hall and the Gary Library of Law would be the only structures to form an area separate from the street (they surround a small courtyard) and to be articulated by an architecture that more consciously recalls an otherwise vague and distant value system to the reality of an institution realized in steel and stone.[45]

This law school is a condensed version of the Yale School of Law (see Chapter 4), wihout either the sprawling site or the elaborate iconography that helped make this kind of message explicit in New Haven. The result is a much more practical-seeming and therefore less convincing structure, without any of the glorious spatial moments that distinguish the Yale buildings. Levy Mayer Hall and the Gary Library take their place confidently in the city, rather than reserving their riches inside, and help to complete the magnificent ridge of the McKinlock Campus.

The final element in the range of McKinlock Campus buildings was not completed until 1931; in 1980 it was torn down to make room for an extension of the law school. George Thorne Hall was a container for a multipurpose auditorium seating 850 people (Fig. 172). The simple form of the hall was surrounded by a one-story base and was bridged over by two gabled elements that came down to four corner stair towers. Thus bounded, Thorne Hall presented a bold facade to the street, consisting of three tall arched niches set between massive flat buttresses. A semioctagonal porch absorbed the crowds into the building, which contained not much more than the auditorium and a lobby. Its stripped-down appearance and modern accouterments were defined by its placement at the most exposed corner of the site,[46] as well as by its use for community events,[47] but it also represented a more self-confident reworking of gothicizing forms. That language seems here to have assimilated the massing and self-confident manipulation of building forms

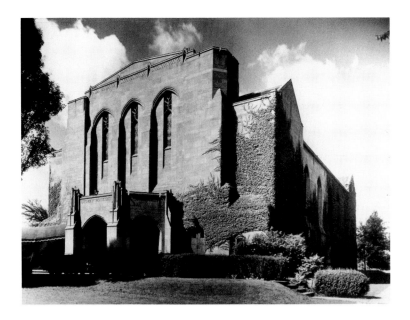

used by James Gamble Rogers in the large institutional commissions he completed between the design of the first group on the McKinlock Campus and the later addition of Thorne Hall.

Meanwhile, Rogers was also working on the planning of the main or Evanston campus of Northwestern. There had been several plans to reorganize and formalize that campus, but these successive plans had been implemented only in fragments.[48] Rogers continued this haphazard tradition: even though he was appointed as Campus Architect in 1922, he never produced a comprehensive plan for Northwestern. Instead, he designed a series of structures that incrementally changed the character of the campus. By the time he was replaced as Campus Architect in 1943,[49] he had designed the main library (Deering Library, 1931), the largest collection of residential buildings (Sorority Quadrangle, 1925–27), a recital hall (Lutkin Hall, 1940), and a university center (Scott Hall, 1939). He also designed the campus stadium, Dyche Stadium, about a mile from the main campus.

These buildings acted as focal points for the development of the campus, but Rogers failed to define completely the character and organization of Northwestern University. It is interesting to note that George Maher, the architect whose early houses had borne such similarity to those of James Gamble Rogers, had created the most complete plan for Northwestern, and had justified the design by claiming that its placement of isolated but related objects in a landscaped field was a representation of "democratic values," as opposed to the axes and formal groupings of the Ecole des Beaux-Arts–influenced campuses.[50] Certainly Rogers, whether consciously or not, continued this seemingly unplanned, more picturesque, and episodic tradition.[51]

Other than Dyche Stadium, which is remarkable more for its engineering than for its rather thin, De Chirico–like concrete arches and the way in which support functions are either lumped together into a bulky tower or uncomfortably tucked under the stands,[52] the first commission Rogers received on the Evanston campus of Northwestern University was for a series of dormitories collectively known as the Sorority Quadrangle (Figs. 173, 174). Unlike the schools of the Ivy League, Northwestern had a large female student population. In keeping with standards of propriety, however, the administration during the beginning of the "Roaring Twenties" felt a strong need to separate the two sexes on opposite ends of the campus. James Gamble Rogers was asked to develop a series of courtyard buildings on what was then the extreme southwestern edge of the campus. Again unlike Yale, and in keeping with President Scott's overriding concern for fund-raising, the group was not to be funded by either university money or the gift of one donor. Instead, Northwestern supplied the land and the plans, leaving it up to each of the existing sororities to raise the funds necessary to construct its own buildings.[53]

The design process was not an easy one. Each of the sororities wanted a building that would meet its perceived individual needs, while Rogers and Scott were concerned about preserving the integrity of the group and keeping expensive variations to a minimum. At a meeting in June 1924, Rogers managed to convince the sororities that sharing similar plans and party walls would not diminish their separate characters, and pointed out that the value of the grouping lay in the sheltered open space of the courtyards.[54] These courtyards were made possible exactly by the amalgamation of the buildings and the pooling of resources, and thus they added the value of community expressed in physical space. The implied significance of the courtyards in all of Rogers' work was here made explicit. Rogers emphasized the importance of this space by making the entrance into the middle of the block extremely narrow and circuitous: one enters down blind paths or between the firewalls of buildings, often changing level, and must usually turn a corner around a projecting chimney or porch to reach the interior world of the Sorority Quadrangle.

The courtyards, moreover, have none of the sweep of the main spaces of the Yale colleges. The Sorority Quadrangle is in fact broken up into two groupings, connected only by a narrow walkway. The courtyards are not surrounded by monolithic walls and focused on a bell tower or communal dining room. Instead, each sorority is differentiated as a separate building block, either U-shaped or L-shaped, with a raised outdoor porch opening up to the courtyard. While semioctagonal bays and dormer windows peek out of the mass of each sorority in the manner of other Rogers build-

173. James Gamble Rogers.
Sorority Quadrangle,
Northwestern University,
Evanston, Illinois, 1925–27.

174. James Gamble Rogers.
Sorority Quadrangle,
Northwestern University,
Evanston, Illinois, 1925–27.
Detail.

ings, the protuberances are here kept to a minimum: it is not a question of articulating, inflecting, and bringing to a human scale an institutional mass, but one of creating a rhythm of functional masses whose repetition and placement create an enclosed community. The porch, usually up several steps, serves to mediate between the shared space and the realm of each sorority. It is here that ornament, absent from the economical faces of the rest of the building, is concentrated, and an eclectic mixture of references to Georgian, Gothic, and Italian Renaissance styles allows one to recognize each building.[55]

The closed appearance of the grouping on the outside, the shared world of the courtyard, the variations on identical plans, and the elaborate set of indoor and outdoor public spaces, each more enclosed and monitored, each another step toward the private and modern world of the women students—all this reflected the roles assigned to women students at Northwestern. As modern women, they were there to learn social graces and to be courted. The sororities thus represented a more extreme version of the general function assigned to dormitories by Rogers and his clients. They are places of socialization into commonly shared values and traditions in order to be able to apply them to a controlled and controlling life in the modern world. At Northwestern, the mythological and architectural accouterments that surrounded this program at Yale have been stripped down, streamlined, and made more specific.[56]

Ceremonially the most important building Rogers designed at Northwestern was the Charles Deering Library. Charles Deering was heir to the farm implement company that (together with that of Cyrus McCormick) formed International Harvester, and he was an in-law of the McCormicks. On his death in 1929 a large part of his estate came to Northwestern, and Scott asked Rogers to proceed with designs for a central library to be named after its donor. A campus plan produced by the Chicago firm of Bennett, Parsons & Frost placed the library at the very heart of the campus, on top of a tall ridge overlooking and running parallel with the main city street, Sheridan Road.[57]

The very first design Rogers produced followed this siting, but also envisioned a Gothic collection of forms that even university librarian Theodore Koch thought was too close to the design of Sterling Memorial Library (Fig. 175). Koch responded with a detailed plan of what he considered the most efficient layout of the library, signed "Theo. Koch fake-it." He also circulated Rogers' preliminary plans to other university librarians for their comments.[58] Rogers then objected to the specificity demanded of him at this stage, and asked Koch what he thought the United States Congress would have done with the Gettysburg Address if Lincoln had submitted a draft of it to them for approval.[59]

175. James Gamble Rogers.
Deering Library, Northwestern
University, Evanston, Illinois,
1929–32. "Preliminary
Scheme," 1929.

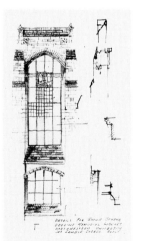

176. James Gamble Rogers.
Deering Library, Northwestern
University, Evanston, Illinois,
1929–32. Details, "Gothic
Scheme," 1930.

Rogers subsequently produced a Georgian scheme, consisting of a simple form with a central tower, and carried this design through several variations and refinements. He felt that such a design would blend in with the existing setting, which was eclectic in its display of different styles, without overwhelming the site. The building committee, led by the advertising expert President Scott, however, wanted a Neo-Gothic building of the sort Rogers had made famous (see Chapter 2), and the architect obliged (Fig. 176). While Scott thus obtained his Gothic monument, Koch managed to get a simplified design that in many ways resembled his own crude initial layout.

The Charles Deering Library possesses a simple parti that exploits the simplicity of the design to maximum effect (Figs. 177, 178). The building presents itself as a simple box placed on top of a ridge overlooking a lawn. The facade is divided into eleven equal bays by buttresses that start out as pronounced stone piers and at the top blend into the skin of the building. Each end elevation is organized around a single arched window, and the elaborately composed corners are held by piers topped by octagonal caps, which Rogers at one time had envisioned as towers.[60] These corners act as clamps rising from the base to hold in place the top two floors, which appear as if they were a single volume held in a cage of stone piers. There is a delicate balance between the rigid march of the bays, grounded by low arched windows and stone walls, and the ethereal quality of the reading room areas contained behind the glass windows, while the buttresses give one the sense that the whole box is riding the ridge.

The building then sets back a few times from the side elevation to contain what amounts to a second, rear, box whose facades are more closed and flat, since they contain little ornament or detail. This secondary set of shapes contain the bookstacks, expressed as a series of narrowly spaced stone sections facing what was then the rear of the campus, a marshy area next to Lake Michigan.[61]

177. James Gamble Rogers. Deering Library, Northwestern University, Evanston, Illinois, 1929–32.

178. James Gamble Rogers. Deering Library, Northwestern University, Evanston, Illinois, 1929–32.

179. James Gamble Rogers. Deering Library, Northwestern University, Evanston, Illinois, 1929–32. Section.

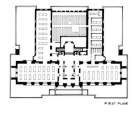

180. James Gamble Rogers. Deering Library, Northwestern University, Evanston, Illinois, 1929–32. First-floor plan.

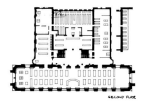

181. James Gamble Rogers. Deering Library, Northwestern University, Evanston, Illinois, 1929–32. Second-floor plan.

The front structure is in fact all that most visitors and users of the library inhabit, and within its shape a series of equally simple rectangular shapes are played off against a rich choreography meant, as at Yale, to slowly seduce one into the assimilation of knowledge through books (Figs. 179, 180). The visitor enters through one of three low arches—thus being confronted immediately with the structure of the building—thence into a loggia of vaulted spaces covered with stone, much like a dark medieval crypt. Open reserve reading rooms occupy the ground floor on either side of this space, so that the casual user can avoid the ceremony of enlightenment promised by the strong sunshine washing down from the staircases immediately ahead.

The central axis disappears completely on the second floor (Fig. 181). The building is here divided into a series of slots running at right angles to this axis and parallel to the ridge. The "front of the house" is taken up by a narrow "Stair Hall," which is nothing so much as a glorified double-loaded corridor through which one enters the two reading rooms on the sides and the main reading room in the center. The latter space is the main room of the building. It is an uninterrupted space of tall windows, long rows of desks, and a high, wood-paneled ceiling. Placed over the entrance and extending beyond the width of the other spaces, this room is the resting point at the end of the journey through the front part of the building. Along the way, hortatory inscriptions about the value of knowledge give one footnotes to the purpose of the journey, much in the way the decoration at Henri Labrouste's Bibliothèque Ste.-Geneviève illustrates a remarkably similar exposition of the parts of a reading library. "No elaborate guide to the building nor direction signs will be needed," explained librarian Theodore Koch; "There is no danger of a freshman getting lost in a labyrinth of dark corridors.[62]

James Gamble Rogers then set to work on plans for a theological seminary and a music school, but the economic depression frustrated Scott's energetic fund-raising efforts, and Rogers built only two small final buildings at Northwestern: Scott Hall, named after the president, in 1940, and Lutkin

Hall, a fragment of the music-school scheme, in 1941.[63] Scott Hall is the more complex of the two buildings (Fig. 182). Its program was novel: the building was meant to combine all those aspects of university life that served the social needs of the students: cafeteria, lounge, alumni center, auditorium, and offices for student organizations. A "women's building" had originally been intended for the site, and money raised for this social center helped make Scott Hall possible. The building is placed on the eastern edge of the Sorority Quadrangle and forms the community face that this residential area presents to the old campus and to the main university buildings on the other side of Sheridan Road.[64]

In the final design of Scott Hall, Rogers' Collegiate Gothic became much more stripped down and streamlined (Figs. 183, 184). Perhaps Ainslie Ballantyne, who worked on all of the Northwestern buildings, and whose buildings seem more restrained and streamlined than those of Faelten, had something to do with this. To the north, for instance, the building steps back not in a series of blocks organized into a picturesque composition, but in a series of screens that seem to undress the auditorium at the rear and side of the building. The top corner of the transitional element made up of these screens has been treated as a continual window framed in dark wood, giving the building a distinctly Prairie School appearance when viewed from the northeast. Such elements as the unadorned rear of the building (where one wall is even placed at a slight angle to accommodate the splay of the auditorium seating inside) and the original decoration of the interior enhance the Modernist appearance of the building. With Scott Hall, Rogers rejoined a Priarie School tradition he had abandoned at its very inception, and that had now effectively run its course.[65]

The Scott building was a multiuse structure in which the university finally gave a specific name and functional shape to the processes of socialization that had previously been housed in the library, the dining hall, the auditoria, and the other traditional elements of the campus. A new self-awareness of the mission of the university was here evidenced, as Scott himself declared: "The primary function of a college training, beyond that of imparting a certain amount of factual knowledge, is that of producing changes in the behavior and thinking of students."[66] At the dedication, the building was called "the student's laboratory for living, his machinery for learning by participation those skills which he instinctively knows he will need in adult society." Looking forward to the impending war with Nazi Germany, one speaker claimed that "the Hall must constitute itself a laboratory in democratic techniques and a testing ground for democratic values."[67]

Like Angell at Yale, Scott had been the first president of his institution to divide analytically the tasks of the university into a socializing college and a service-oriented graduate school, and had thus asked Rogers to

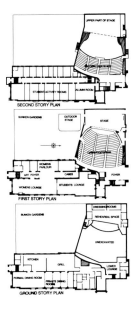

182. James Gamble Rogers. Scott Hall, Northwestern University, Evanston, Illinois, 1936–40. Plans.

183. James Gamble Rogers.
Scott Hall, Northwestern
University, Evanston, Illinois,
1936–40. Perspective sketch,
early scheme, 1936.

184. James Gamble Rogers.
Scott Hall, Northwestern
University, Evanston, Illinois,
1936–40.

make his buildings tools for fund-raising that would serve as functional symbols for advanced research and social assimilation. At the end of his career Scott asked Rogers to build a new university building type, a self-conscious machine that allowed the functions of social and ethical self-definition so central to the modern American college to shed the accreted and obfuscating skin of traditional functions and historicizing architecture. In this manner, he again did explicitly what Angell had called for or implied in his addresses during his tenure as president of Yale.[68]

The issue of the relationship between elite educational institutions and a quickly changing world is one that left its mark on all of Rogers' institutional buildings of the late 1920s and early 1930s. It was articulated most clearly during the design of the Colgate-Rochester Theological Seminary, a progressive institution that chose Rogers as its architect because it wanted to cloak itself in the traditions represented by the Collegiate Gothic.

The promulgation of a modern form of Christian religion was—and is—the goal of the Colgate-Rochester Theological Seminary. The seminary is the result of the marriage of the Colgate and the Rochester theological seminaries, two independent institutions that had requested funding from John D. Rockefeller in 1927. Rockefeller gave them $1.25 million in 1928, but only on the condition that they merge. Since the institutions were located near each other, and were alike dedicated to a liberal interpretation of theology (including a stress on social action and an acceptance of diverse interpretations of religious doctrine), the union took place that same year. Thus was born the Colgate-Rochester Theological Seminary, under the presidency of the Reverend Albert William Beaven.[69]

The site for the new school was at the edge of the city of Rochester, atop a high ridge overlooking the developing suburbs. The ridge stands almost alone in the landscape, and leads to the University of Rochester to the east. President Beaven was convinced that both the mission of the seminary and its location demanded an exemplary architecture for its new home:

> . . .[we desire] a building dignified and beautiful, as well as satisfactory from the practical point of view. We recognized that this hilltop, prepared centuries ago by the action of nature, would lift our buildings where they would be "a city set upon a hill, which could not be hid."[70]

Beaven was thus the only one of Rogers' clients to refer explicitly to Governor Winthrop's exhortation to the Puritans of Massachusetts, which could serve as the motto for all of Rogers' educational architecture.

The site implied a central tower, a beacon to the community and a symbol of religious aspiration. The program called for dormitories, classrooms, places of worship, a dining hall, an auditorium, a library, a residence for the president, and a home for returning missionaries. The choice of an architect was an obvious one to Beaven: "Partly because of our desire for a beautiful tower, but also more because of our feeling that the nature of our location and the traditions of ecclesiastical architecture involved some form of Gothic in our construction . . .," James Gamble Rogers, designer of Harkness Memorial Tower, was asked to be the architect for the new seminary.[71]

The client of this building thus seemed to have a clear idea of the kind of structure Rogers would give them. The major change in conception mentioned by both client and architect was the use of brick rather than stone for the majority of the walls. Rogers convinced the seminary that it could not afford stone without cutting into the amenities it needed. He also contended that brick would give the whole a warmer, more inviting character.[72]

Rogers appears to have given great latitude in the design of the seminary to Howard Moise, a designer who had entered his employ only a few years before.[73] It was Moise who was effusively thanked at the dedication of the building, and Moise who described the design process in the dedication booklet.[74] There he claimed that the terrain and the program suggested a "picturesque rather than a formal" grouping of buildings—though one cannot imagine another strategy being utilized by the James Gamble Rogers firm at this time. Yet neither this quality nor the reasons for selecting the firm predetermined the style of architecture chosen, according to Moise: "Geor-

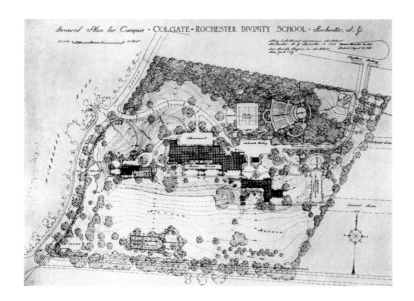

185. James Gamble Rogers. Colgate-Rochester Theological Seminary, Rochester, New York, 1930–32. Site plan.

186. James Gamble Rogers. Colgate-Rochester Theological Seminary, Rochester, New York, 1930–32. Aerial view.

gian/Colonial," "Collegiate Gothic," and "Modern" styles were all considered. The first was considered too formal and rigid, the third too fashionable and undignified, which left Gothic, a style that just happened to be eminently suited to both the site and the religious nature of the institution.[75]

Moise described a similar process for the organization of the building. The site was too narrow to allow for the kind of courtyard buildings that the firm knew how to design, and yet it was large enough to make the condensed Skyscraper Gothic of Northwestern's Chicago campus or Rogers' Columbia-Presbyterian Medical Center seem uncalled for. Finally, James Gamble Rogers, Inc., decided that "a number of the separate elements listed in the program should be tied together in one long closely-knit range of buildings crowning the ridge," while the rest of the functions were then "echeloned in depth" along the ridge (Figs. 185, 186).[76]

The result was a combination of the enclosed world of the Yale colleges and the vertically organized forms of the downtown buildings (Figs. 187–190). The inevitable double-loaded main circulation spine of the building runs along the top of the ridge, and the majority of classrooms and offices are placed in a three-story bar riding that height. The tower rises out of the

187. James Gamble Rogers.
Colgate-Rochester Theological
Seminary, Rochester, New
York, 1930–32.

188. James Gamble Rogers.
Colgate-Rochester Theological
Seminary, Rochester, New
York, 1930–32.

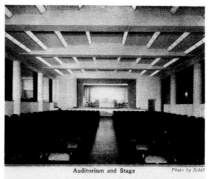

Auditorium and Stage   *Photo by Schiff*

Photo by Schiff

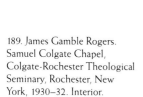

189. James Gamble Rogers.
Samuel Colgate Chapel,
Colgate-Rochester Theological
Seminary, Rochester, New
York, 1930–32. Interior.

190. James Gamble Rogers.
Colgate-Rochester Theological
Seminary, Rochester, New
York, 1930–32. Interiors,
Auditorium and Dining Hall.

western portion of this bar, its piers placed in front of the main wall of the
building in the manner of the Harkness Tower. The two main ceremonial
spaces of the school—the dining hall and the chapel—are placed to the front
or south of this composition and face each other across a broad terrace.[77]

The extensions of the building along the ridge are accomplished with
simple forms familiar from James Gamble Rogers' earlier work: a background
building containing tightly packed functions, cross gables, square towers at
intersections, slightly arched openings, roof dormers, and turrets, all covered
with brick, topped with slate roofs, and accented with limestone trim. What
is remarkable about the Colgate-Rochester scheme is its sheer picturesque
beauty, achieved through the compactness and the abstraction of the detailing, as well as through the clarity of its organization.

Moise discussed the allocation of ornament and the inflection of architectural style at length in his article. He saw no necessity in the design for

> . . . a spirit of cold archaeology or that any existing building or detail
> should be definitely copied. A historical style in general may be adopted
> for modern building because of the connotation it possesses—the halo
> of meaning which it has acquired through centuries of use [in Gothic
> architecture]. . . . Even potential disharmonies in the composition . . . can
> be changed into assets.[78]

The architecture was thus seen as a problem-solving skin that cloaked the building in meaning, and, to a larger extent than in earlier James Gamble Rogers buildings, the walls are expressed accordingly—as a stretched, almost separate, skin.

Moise pointed out that in fact only the tower and the entrance elements were designed in a "traditional" manner: as the building extends to encompass more mundane programmatic elements, he explained, "traditional detail has been modified and transmuted to meet the requirements of the design," giving the ends of the building a "contemporary" character. The meaning signaled from the hill is traditional, but it is literally buttressed by modern institutions.[79]

With these buildings, the Rogers firm seemed to be justifying its use of the Collegiate Gothic at a time when the style was subject to increasing fire, as it had been at Yale. The Colgate-Rochester buildings are first of all able, because of their multiscalar and multidimensional forms, to encompass a diverse program in a fashion that is both consistent and harmonious with the landscape. Secondly, the Collegiate Gothic idiom is stripped and stretched to the point where it can be seen as a layer of signification. It is here a separate system of architectural ornament and didactic formal structure, existing independently of the actual construction of the forms and allowed to become an object only where it is a purely ceremonial focal point. Moise extended this argument into the very way the building is made. He claimed that, wherever possible, the decoration came out of a resolution of the meeting of materials and shapes, and was used to punctuate and give scale to the large buildings, rather than being added on either according to some a priori schema or to give the building a decorated look.[80]

In dedicating these buildings, the client went to great length to emphasize both their religious nature and their contemporary modernity and functionality: "In a period of keen economic and moral depression," noted the spokesman for the alumni, "there rises upon a hilltop a religious structure that by virtue of its beauty and purpose proclaims anew the Christian message of faith and hope."[81] Professor Edgar Sheffield Brightman expanded on this theme in his address, "The Personality of God." Tracing the development of a native American train of thought that had been codified by John Dewey and George Santayana, Brightman called for a "finite theism," which, based on recent advances in physics and philosophy (he quotes Gestalt theory and Heisenberg), would recognize experience and the mutability of the physical universe as the two poles by which man might live in the modern world while understanding God as the very principle of uncertainty whereby there is no possibility of fixed knowledge: "his control of The Given is manifested in ever-changing forms on ever-changing levels."[82] This mixture of Pragmatism, science theory, and theology bears a marked similarity to the resolution of traditional meaning and modern functionality achieved in the shifting levels, picturesque compositions, experiential choreography, and cultured screens of James Gamble Rogers' architecture.[83] As such, the Colgate-Rochester Theological Seminary marks the culmination of Rogers' career as the designer of an architecture of pragmatism, and its transformation into something that was gesturing toward a more abstract, ethereal, and internally complex way of building.

Rogers designed several purely ecclesiastic structures during this period. While the Fifth Avenue Presbyterian Church addition of 1925 was a fairly dry essay in Neo-Gothicism squeezed into a narrow urban site (Fig. 191),[84] his chapel for the Connecticut College for Women of 1938 was something else altogether. While the New York church had been funded by Edward Harkness, the chapel was a gift of Harkness's wife.[85] The building is in many ways an oddity (Fig. 192). It stands at the edge of a sweeping lawn above a slight rise. It is a rectangular box with a gabled roof ending in a strong triangular pediment and topped by a polygonal tower. The execution of these elements manages at all times to emphasize the inherent characteristics of each form and material. The granite of the walls is massive, and the windows are incised into this wall with narrow, white-painted wood trim. They are drawn out the full length of the facade, so that they seem hewn out of the rock of the building.

The front and the rear portions of the rectangle are made to appear as if they are sliding out of the box through the use of slight reveals and setbacks. This device emphasizes the apsidal nature of the back and the temple-front composition of the main facade. On this latter facade, the triangular pediment is pulled out and etched out in the deeply incised stone tympanum. The wall supporting this aggressive pediment is an extension of the rough granite box that opens in the middle to reveal a slightly setback pair of giant Ionic columns, beyond which the main door is recessed even farther.

The Harkness Chapel facade combines elements from New England churches, Greek temples, factory buildings, and Georgian residences, which it subjects to a virtuoso combinatory effort, so that each element—walls, windows, supporting columns, tower—seems to have its own structural and iconographic logic. There is something familiar about the chapel, but the overall composition is wholly original. In a sense, Rogers manages here to sum up his strategy of compacting and combining precedents into multivalent images validated by a functional and structural logic visible in the overall composition.

After the tightly packed skin of the outside, the expanse of the chapel interior is astonishing (Fig. 193). The plain stone interior is free of columns or other subsidiary spaces. The tall, round-arched windows are set deeply into the wall, washing the box with a soft light. The ceiling is slightly

191. James Gamble Rogers. Chapel and Chapter House Addition, Fifth Avenue Presbyterian Church, New York, New York, 1925.

192. James Gamble Rogers. Harkness Chapel, Connecticut College (formerly Connecticut College for Women), New London, Connecticut, 1938.

193. James Gamble Rogers.
Harkness Chapel, Connecticut
College (formerly Connecticut
College for Women), New
London, Connecticut, 1938.
Interior.

bowed, rather than truly arched or gabled, and is supported by bow trusses
made of layers of oak beams lashed together so that they seem to be splitting
apart in the middle. The space is both completely static and filled with the
kind of tense details that mark the outside. These include the energetically
designed beams; the splayed corners of the window niches, which create an
ambivalent reading somewhere between wall and pilaster; and the drama of
the altar, set into the single secondary space of the chapel. That altar is
framed by what appears to be a vast arched opening, its corners defined by
stone bands set flush with the stucco of the end wall of the chapel. It sits in a
world of carved oak, surrounded by a polished organ and a stained-glass
rosette.[86]

    With the simple clarity of this space, the boldness of its scale and its
materials, and the delicacy and articulation with which it is formed, all of
James Gamble Rogers' craft is reduced to a set of finely honed devices of
material, composition, and detailing. Stripped of most ornament and functional inflection, it is as pure a statement of what he was capable of as can be
found in all of his work.

    The bulk of Rogers' work during this period remained more complex.
During the 1930s Rogers designed two large urban educational structures.
Neither of them is Collegiate Gothic, and they serve more as a coda to the
institutional work that had made his career than as the high point of his
achievements. The first of these, the School of Education for New York University, brought him back in many ways to his first educational project, the
School of Education for the University of Chicago, while the design for Butler Library at Columbia University was the only building after the early post
offices and courthouses in which Rogers made use of the Academic Classicism in which he had been trained in Paris.

    The School of Education, completed in 1930,[87] is a mixture of class-
rooms, laboratories, music rooms, studios, a gymnasium, and a five-hundred-
seat auditorium, all adding up to 120,000 square feet of space.[88] The school
originally housed three thousand students, and was meant to be the very
model of progressive education. The school not only trained teachers for
every grade from kindergarten through vocational school, but it was also one
of the first schools of its kind to engage in field research into the processes of
education.[89] In this sense, the New York University school was the final result

194. James Gamble Rogers.
School of Education, New
York University, New York,
New York, 1928–30.

of the rationalization of educational techniques championed by Dewey at the School of Education of the University of Chicago.

The two schools of education share both a stripped-down Gothic architecture in stone and an uncomfortable relationship to their respective—and very different—sites. The New York University building occupies the northwest corner of Fourth and Greene streets (Fig. 194). At its base it completely fills out its site, so that it takes its place among the older light-industrial, commercial, and office buildings that make up the streetscape to the east of New York University and Washington Square. There is little about the form of the building to denote its institutional character beyond a stone-clad base marked by tall, pointed-arch openings filled with assemblies of worked metal and glass. The whole is a functional, stripped-down assemblage of spaces forced into a singular form, and it recalls Rogers' commercial work on the Lees Building in Chicago or the Central Bank and Trust in Memphis (see Figs. 4, 70).

Education is treated here as a rational pursuit, almost stripped of the validation of tradition and lacking the kind of courtyard of understanding and contemplation or the tower of signification that had, in earlier Rogers-designed educational institutions, allowed architecture to give meaning to the work of education. Instead, whatever differentiation and ornamentation remains on the building serves to make the building part of the skyscraper idiom of New York. The required setbacks are marked with finials, crenellation, and telescoping buttresses, and a small mechanical tower tries to pull the composition away from its squat proportions.[90]

The failure of the New York University building can be measured against James Gamble Rogers' intentions for such a site and structure by contrasting this design with a proposal for another building for the same university, a twenty-story "Building for Wall Street Center," which was never constructed (Fig. 195).[91] This project—one of the few unbuilt designs in the Rogers office archives—was to have been similar to the School of Education in that it was a tripartite block in which closely spaced piers rose out of a Gothic-dressed stone base to end in a series of crenellated setback sections. In the unbuilt design, however, the central piers are clamped to the base and then rise beyond the setbacks to allow the much more elongated crown to grow naturally out of a series of giant carved figures that form their culmination. The space between the piers is filled with windows and what appears to be either terra-cotta or worked metal panels, thus allowing the mass of the building to shimmer behind these structurally expressive vertical devices. The building would have risen out of the city as one single expression, emerging from its solid and traditional base, climbing past a bustling cage of activity, and becoming narrower and more ornamented until its crown implied ever thinner and more delicate lines reaching up to the sky.[92]

195. James Gamble Rogers.
"Building for Wall Street
Center" (project), no date.

In the other large educational building that James Gamble Rogers
constructed in New York City, upward reach again was stymied by function
and by client wishes. The Butler Library at Columbia University remains a
problematic monument to the attempt to assemble large functional elements
through the use of a compromised representational and compositional strategy. The library was conceived as a building similar in function and symbolic
importance to Sterling Memorial Library. Deference to the McKim, Mead &
White campus plan and to Charles McKim's Low Library across the South
Lawn, deep cuts in the construction budget, and the failure of James Gamble
Rogers' architectural strategy led to the construction of a collage of brick and
stone screens masking the large rectangular bulk of stacks designed to house
almost three million books.

The library was given to Columbia University by Edward S. Harkness.
As early as 1926, Nicholas Murray Butler, president of Columbia, had asked
Harkness to expand his generosity to the university beyond the gift of the
Columbia-Presbyterian Medical Center (see Chapter 7).[93] Simultaneously, university librarian C. C. Williamson was actively campaigning for a building that
would draw the disparate libraries and collections of the university together in
one structure, capable of housing five million books; it would stand at the
southern edge of the South Lawn, the central space of the campus.[94]

The library was thus meant to fulfill the same kind of rationalizing
and centralizing function that had motivated the construction of Sterling
Memorial Library. It served not only to house books, but also to bring those
books and the activities related to them under the direct supervision of the
university administration. Once under that control, they could be handled
efficiently and the educational activities streamlined. These activities could

then be housed in a building that could further the self-definition of the campus by elaborating upon its symbolic language.[95]

Although Harkness originally wanted to give a "more useful" building to Columbia,[96] by the end of 1930 he had agreed to pay the entire cost of the new library.[97] Butler himself had proposed James Gamble Rogers as the architect, and by February 1931 Rogers had produced a preliminary design according to C. C. Williamson's specifications. Rogers went to great length to excuse the size of the eight-story building and its monumental appearance. "You will notice," he wrote in his cover letter to President Butler, "that the style of architecture is quite similar to the Low Library and in itself imposing . . . [but it] will not in any way detract from the dominance of the beautiful Low Building. Rather on the other hand, it will enhance the appearance of that masterpiece of beauty."[98] The building was to be designed with a columned limestone front and side wings of brick framed in limestone, in the manner of the surrounding McKim, Mead & White buildings. The stacks were to rise up behind this front as a brick and glass box. The costs for building this design were estimated at over $5 million, at least $2 million more than Harkness had contemplated giving to the university.[99]

Butler argued strenuously with Harkness about the importance of the building. He pointed out that the Yale library was to cost more than $8 million, and that the function of both buildings went beyond the mere housing of books:

> . . . it is the central workshop of every part of the University, thronged by students and professors both by day and by night. As projected by Mr. Rogers, this splendid plan would be quite worthy of the McKim masterpiece which it would face for generations to come, thus adding one more to the great monuments of the higher civilization which give distinction to the city of New York.[100]

The building was thus to reinforce three aspects of Columbia's institutional life: its communal activity, or day-to-day reason for existence; the continuity of its traditions as they were represented in the existing architecture; and its function as a builder of civilizing institutional structures. In all three ways, the Butler Library was to further the cause of education conceived of as the translation of the values of the past, through civilized and rational activity, into the fixed and built values of the future—a goal made explicit in the mural installed in the south hall of the completed building, which the artist said illustrated Columbia's ability "to inform, to impart traditions of thought and prepare youth for independent thinking and thus coordinate the past and present with the future."[101]

Edward Harkness insisted, however, that the building budget be brought more into line with the original estimate. He seems to have been affected by the economic depression, to the point where his assistant, Malcolm Aldrich, had to request a delay in payment of pledges during the construction of the library.[102] Rogers redesigned the library in a shorter, more compact version, with some of the ornament eliminated, and by April 1931 the client had approved a scheme housing 2,890,000 books and costing, by the time the building was completed in November 1934, $3,678,500.[103]

The Butler Library as constructed is a long mass 85 feet high, presenting its columned front to the South Lawn and masking fifteen tiers of stacks behind a screen of reading rooms and offices. The building is conservative and without a clear focal point, especially given its size. Even at the time of construction, critics, students, and faculty members voiced their disapproval of the building. As Professor Helmut Lehman-Haupt worded the widely felt criticism in a letter to Williamson:

> . . . the result appears to me a very dry and uninspired product of "academical" taste in the very bad sense of the word. . . it lacks heart and soul. . . . Is there not really a splendid chance for Columbia University to set an example of spiritual independence and courage in breaking away for the first time from an absolute custom?[104]

Lehman-Haupt received no reply, and Butler, Williamson, and Rogers appear to have ignored all criticism. They were not interested in setting an example or breaking new ground, only in reinforcing architectural and university authority.[105]

The principal problem in the composition of Butler Library stems from the fact that Rogers chose to express frankly the nondirectional layering of the building. It has none of the self-centered confidence of the Low Library it faces, having neither that building's setting nor its Greek-cross plan. It is a place for storing and using books, not the ceremonial heart of the campus, and it presaged the divorce of the ceremonial from the functional aspects of buildings that was to plague campus design in America after the Second World War.

As is the case with most of Rogers' other buildings, the main entrance axis of Butler is immediately diffused upon entering the building, here into a long crossing corridor opening on to offices on the ground floor and a staircase through which one reaches the reading rooms on the *piano nobile* (Figs. 196, 197). The main reading room stretches almost the entire length of the front facade, and the subsidiary reading rooms, catalogue rooms, and special-collection rooms then wrap around the two sides of the building. This leaves the bulk of the stacks in the middle of the structure. They are unseen, unsung, and stratified according to the logic of low, metal stack floors, which is to say, independent of a ceiling height scaled to human and social activities.

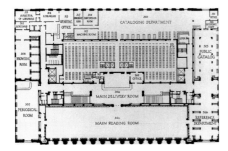

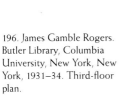

196. James Gamble Rogers. Butler Library, Columbia University, New York, New York, 1931–34. Third-floor plan.

197. James Gamble Rogers. Butler Library, Columbia University, New York, New York, 1931–34. Reading Room interior.

The main facade has no sense of hierarchy, and there is little to give it a human scale. Even more problematic is the treatment of the side wings and the rear, where a limestone base and corner pilasters give way to a brick facade into which stone-trimmed windows of various sizes are placed and which is held together by a system of stringcourses, cornices, and cartouches. The side wings neither reinforce the major pavilion, nor do they elaborate upon its shape (Fig. 198). To the rear, the building becomes a virtually unadorned brick wall rising straight up from a city street. The attic of the building, barely visible beyond the main facades and wings, is marked by a stone cornice whose acanthus leaves and vaguely Mediterranean ornaments give a frilly ending to the otherwise solid-looking building. To appreciate the awkwardness of this design, one has only to compare it with Horace Trumbauer's roughly contemporary Widener Library at Harvard, whose architecture, though not much more elaborate than that of Butler, manages to give an impressive coherence to the whole monumental structure.[106]

The not-so-splendid isolation of Butler Library is due to several factors: the lack of the kind of entrance pavilion and focal tower that Rogers added on to almost every one of his institutional buildings; the inability to convert the context into a convincingly composed building; and the pressure to compress all of the functional elements into a compact box, leaving the spaces to squeeze out at the top and sides, rather than being stated as sepa-

rate pavilions. Yet within this box, the detailing of the separate elements is often as beautifully crafted and consistent as in any of Rogers' other buildings. One can surmise that by the early 1930s, Rogers had built up both a repertory of forms and details and a staff capable of producing fully elaborated, well-structured, and consistently detailed buildings, even in adverse circumstances.[107]

James Gamble Rogers designed two other educational projects during this period: the Ossining (New York) High School[108] and a series of buildings for Atlanta College (now Clark-Atlanta University). The designs for this latter institution were the result of donations by Edward S. Harkness and two other members of Yale's Class of 1897—Dean Sage and Edward T. Ware.[109] Dean Sage, who had overseen the construction of the Columbia-Presbyterian Medical Center, was the chairman of the board of trustees of Atlanta College, created by the merging of several Baptist schools and missionary institutions.

With the Harkness gift to the school came James Gamble Rogers, who sent Ainslie Ballantyne to inspect the site of the proposed buildings in the fall of 1930; once sufficient funds had been raised to match the Harkness donation, Rogers visited the site himself in February 1931.[110] The program called for the erection of six buildings: a library (already paid for by a grant from the General Education Fund),[111] an administration building (later renamed Harkness Hall), two dormitories, a house for the president, and a recitation hall.[112] Rogers designed all buildings except for the recitation hall, and they were constructed between 1932 and 1933.[113]

All of the Atlanta College buildings are simple brick volumes designed in a Collegiate Georgian style reminiscent of such Rogers buildings as the Southern Baptist Theological Seminary (Figs. 199–201, see Figs. 43, 147–154). The simplicity of the buildings was mandated by the extremely tight budgetary constraints, and Rogers does not seem to have gone out of his way to publicize the group.[114] After the successes of Yale, Northwestern, and their "country cousins," the focus of James Gamble Rogers' and his firm's attention seems to have moved toward another field: the creation of hospitals and medical complexes.

In only one large-scale building does Rogers seem to have attempted to see how far into another stylistic idiom and method of working his institutional architecture could be pushed. The twenty-one-story Abbott Hall dormitory, constructed between 1938 and 1940 on Northwestern's Chicago campus, was the last large building of any kind that James Gamble Rogers designed.[115] It is a limestone-clad block placed on the very perimeter of downtown Chicago along Lake Shore Drive, where it was later joined during the 1950s by Ludwig Mies van der Rohe's Lake Shore Towers, a few blocks farther north.[116]

Contemporary critics and the client all emphasized the modernity of the building, but without making reference to its architectural appearance, which merely lent "a distinctive touch" to the structural marvels of Abbott Hall.[117] The building is 210 feet high and contains 365 rooms housing 700 men and 125 women, two restaurants, a grill, stores, athletic facilities, and offices for staff and students.[118] While its base was meant to fulfill the same kind of socializing function for the Chicago campus as Scott Hall performed in Evanston, its main body was on the scale of a large apartment building. The dormitory was thus "almost a city within itself," a condensed urban scene choreographed for efficiency and comfort.[119] Its character was metropolitan and modern, and its very existence attested the full integration of the educational institution into the life and forms of the city.

The main shaft of Abbott Hall is a fourteen-story, L-shaped building (Figs. 202, 203). The longer of its two side wings, which points straight out to Lake Michigan, is twelve floors tall, while the other wing, which is placed behind the main entrance on the north side of the building, ends after only six floors, allowing the rear section to rise up clear in the middle of the structure. This shaft is then extended with a mechanical tower. The incomplete and unstable composition surmounts a three-story base whose irregular outline follows the major axes of the streets that bound the site.

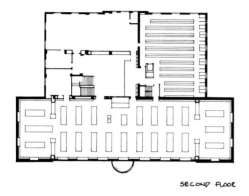

SECOND FLOOR

199. James Gamble Rogers.
Library, Atlanta College (now
Clark-Atlanta University),
1931–33.

200. James Gamble Rogers.
Library, Atlanta College,
1931–33. Plan.

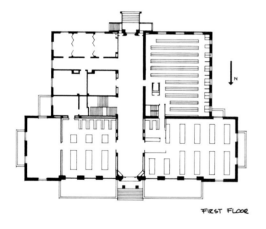

FIRST FLOOR

201. James Gamble Rogers.
Thayer Hall, Atlanta College,
1931–33.

202. James Gamble Rogers.
Abbott Hall, Northwestern
University, Chicago, Illinois,
1938–40.

203. James Gamble Rogers.
Abbott Hall, Northwestern
University, Chicago, Illinois,
1938–40. Detail.

The complicated massing of Abbott Hall is not completely defined by the building's functions. It appears to be rather an attempt to compose large masses into an object that, while not organized around any stable compositional center or building up toward any narrative point, responds to its context and to the character of its programmatic elements. The clarity of the forms and the massiveness of the blocks is accentuated at all times. From the ground, Abbott Hall looks like a series of interlocking blocks, cut from some huge quarry with precision tools and then formed with a smooth hand to create the flowing shapes of the base. The entrance markers, the screens, and the bay windows finally punctuate and accentuate the inherent individual axis of each of these shapes. In Abbott Hall, James Gamble Rogers enlarged his picturesque massing of building forms to a gigantic scale, stripped it of ornament, and turned it into an active participant in the life of a modern metropolis.

CHAPTER SEVEN

Rational Fortresses

James Gamble Rogers' most enduring contribution to the architectural land-scape of the United States can be found in the often elaborate dormitories, libraries, and ceremonial buildings he designed for campuses from Chicago to New Haven. The aura of institutions such as Yale and Northwestern has given his architecture an added importance. Moreover, these institutions have generally regarded Rogers' architecture with respect, preserving its essential features even when uses have changed. Finally, the original function of these buildings was not the sole definer of their forms: the buildings were meant to give physical shape to abstract notions such as knowledge, tradition, and friendship. James Gamble Rogers' best work can today still display the repre-sentational possibilities of architecture in all of its picturesque power.

Yet a large portion of the work produced in the office of James Gam-ble Rogers after 1920 displayed little of the elaborate composition that char-acterized the work in Collegiate Gothic and Collegiate Georgian. Its design was much more constrained by functional parameters and these buildings have been altered, added on to, torn down, and otherwise disfigured, often beyond recognition. Yet hospitals, medical buildings, and clinics formed the mainstay of Rogers' firm by the mid-1930s and created as much publicity for Rogers as the work at campuses such as Yale. The expertise the firm devel-oped in this area is evident in the descendant firm of Rogers, Burgun, Shahide & Deschler, a large office specializing in such projects.[1]

The medical buildings Rogers designed were large and often had lit-tle ornament or superfluous space. Yet they were also intended to be sym-bolic, and their impact on the urban skyline was often pronounced. Moreover, in the designs of these hospitals one can clearly recognize James Gamble Rogers, the Chicago-trained pragmatic organizer of spaces, giving form to the complex demands of his program in a manner that makes specif-ic the overall demands modern society makes on its buildings.

It was Edward Harkness himself who pointed Rogers toward health care. As early as 1910, he wrote to the Presbyterian Hospital Board of New York:

> I have long been interested in that form of charity which has to do with the treatment of human ills, and latterly have become more and more impressed with the extent of the work that a hospital must do in the broadest scientific and practical lines if it at all adequately uses its resources. The scientific development of medicine has especially inter-ested me recently and I have become convinced that its real underlying

promise and mission to humanity lies more particularly in preventing disease than in merely curing it.[2]

With this statement, Harkness prepared the way for the development of the Commonwealth Fund, that nebulous organization started by his mother and himself "to do some good." The fund soon concentrated on health care, and specifically on the integration of scientific research with epidemiological applications: Harkness was interested in the manner in which technology and science could be reintroduced into the mainstream of American society so as to bring about concrete results. That process was embodied, more often than not, in hospitals designed by James Gamble Rogers. Harkness directly made possible the New York Medical Center, Yale-New Haven Medical Center, Sloane-Kettering Memorial Hospital for the Treatment of Cancer and Allied Diseases, and a dozen rural hospitals. He also donated large sums of money to numerous other medical establishments.[3]

Harkness started small, by paying for a hospital in the Yale-in-China program. The latter was a medical program with strong religious overtones headed by Dr. Edward H. Hume, a Yale classmate of Harkness's. In 1913, Harkness gave Yale-in-China $273,414 to build a new hospital in Changsha and paid James Gamble Rogers approximately $5,000 in fees to design the building.[4] On May 2, 1913, Harkness and his financial advisor, Rogers' classmate Samuel Fisher, saw Hume off to China. Rogers commenced designing his first hospital.[5]

Though many alterations were made by local associates, and it is difficult to ascertain the degree to which Rogers' designs were carried out, the building, which was completed in 1915, was essentially a four-story brick structure on to which Rogers added his version of a Chinese pagoda cornice and roof (Figs. 204, 205). The hospital was designed as a long rectangular volume with originally four, but finally only two, wings extending out from the back. There appears to have been virtually no ceremonial space in the building except for a small entrance lobby leading to a long double-loaded corridor. The wings contained combinations of private rooms and open wards, and terminated in solaria and open balconies. Small loggias set them off from the main bar, but few architectural elements were used below the level of the eaves to accent or define the scale of the various elements of the building. Exceptions were the sweeping driveway at the front and a stair framed by curvilinear ramps at the center of the rear facade, which led to stone porches sheltered by pagoda-type tile roofs.[6]

The straightforward planning and extremely simple and conventional detailing of the first four floors of the hospital make the addition of the fanciful Chinese attic all the more startling. Though Rogers did call for downspouts to be decorated with Chinese dragon motifs and designed the

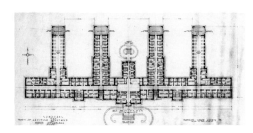

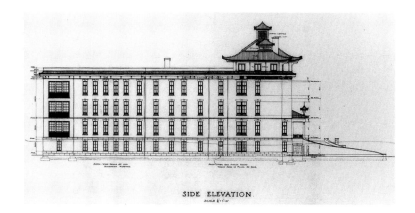

204. James Gamble Rogers.
Yale-in-China Hospital,
Changsha, China, 1913–15.
Plan.

205. James Gamble Rogers.
Yale-in-China Hospital,
Changsha, China, 1913–15.
Side elevation.

SIDE ELEVATION.
SCALE ⅛"=1'-0"

balustrades of the porches as if they were pieces of Chinese lacquerwork, it
was essentially the skyline of the building that added what the architect must
have seen as a contextual cap to the utilitarian hospital. Having fulfilled a
basically technical program on an abstract site on a minimal budget, he then
freed himself to add not his own architectural statement, but an element that
would sanctify the appearance of this formal element to an assumed audience. The architecture was justified as a ritual mask for an otherwise faceless
institution. It was engendered by the characteristics of the site and the program, even when they were completely separate from Rogers' experience.

Rogers had to confront the demands of a hospital program at a vastly
larger scale as Edward Harkness continued his patronage of medical institutions. The first benefactor of Harkness's interest in health care was the Presbyterian Hospital in New York. He and his family had been active in various
Presbyterian charities,[7] and in 1910 Edward Harkness pledged $1.3 miilion
to the hospital so that it might expand its facilities on the East River. In his
gift, he reserved for himself "the privilege of approving any building plans
that may be determined upon and to have a voice in the selection of an architect."[8] It wasn't until eleven years later, however, that James Gamble Rogers
was indeed appointed to build a hospital with the Harkness money. In the
meantime, Harkness had changed the very nature of the institution to which
his donation was made.

After lengthy negotiations with Cornell University failed, he managed to convince the Columbia College of Physicians and Surgeons to agree
to merge with the Presbyterian Hospital. Harkness wanted an institution that
would realize his vision of an integrated complex where research and teaching might be put to practical use. The donor and his family forced the issue
by buying a large plot of land overlooking the Hudson River in Washington
Heights, offering to give the land and a donation increased to nearly $3 mil-

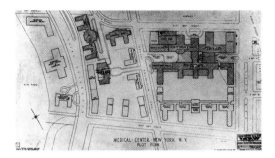

lion for a new medical center. Harkness had to keep goading the two institutions through their lengthy negotiations with each other, but it was not until February 1921 that Columbia had raised enough matching grants and had cleared its own political hurdles so that it could accept the money, the site, and the joint administrative board offered by Harkness to create what was envisioned as a seven-million-dollar combination of research facility, teaching hospital, and general hospital.[9] James Gamble Rogers was appointed in June of that year and immediately started planning the complex with its executive director, C. C. Burlingame.[10]

A year and a half later, Rogers produced sketches for thirty-, forty-, and fifty-story buildings soaring up from the cliffs of the Hudson, and Burlingame proclaimed the process "out of hand."[11] An in-house construction specialist was appointed, the first for an American hospital, who stated that "much time had been wasted in building air castles, and the whole subject had to be brought down to earth."[12] The buildings were redesigned, but still budgeted at $10.5 million (though this budget included a private-patient pavilion not planned in the original conception) (Fig. 206). Harkness and Columbia raised their contributions so that groundbreaking could finally take place on January 1, 1925—almost exactly fourteen years after Harkness made his original gift.

The conception of a "medical center" was unique, as was Rogers' design. This still consisted of a group of "air castles," though they were somewhat lower than he had originally envisioned. Until that time, hospitals had been thought of as low, sprawling complexes organized around a centralized core, in which each ward occupied its own wing. Rogers proposed that hospitals could, like libraries, take advantage of the efficiencies gained by stacking programs on top of each other.[13] He thus continued to apply the lessons he learned in the Chicago School to institutional realms.

A new concept called for a new design process, which justified the bold and unfamiliar architectural results, and Rogers, Burlingame, and their associates went to great lengths to describe the experimental cooperation that produced the final Medical Center.[14] After the establishment of the board and the appointment of James Gamble Rogers, the architect and the board surveyed the existing facilities and interviewed all of the participants in the proposed new center. The needs of each participant were translated into square footage and technical allocations, which were then combined according to flow diagrams reflecting both circulation and service connections.[15] This cumbersome process was necessary because the proposed Medical Center was without direct typological precedents, since it sought to combine usually separate health care facilities in an integrated fashion.

Out of necessity, Rogers produced a design process that, though it might seem rather rational and ordinary to us today, was treated as a progressive alternative to the leisurely discussions between client and designer that were then common practice.[16] The design process was meant to be a fully integrated part of the technology that allowed for the emergence of scientific research and care into the reality of a hospital. As Burlingame said:

> To the architect, it must mean an effort to completely subordinate the old conception of hospital planning and construction to the newer aims and ideals of medicine, and must represent the most advanced step thus far taken in adapting the utilitarian skyscraper to the hospital problems.[17]

That the building should be a skyscraper, or a series of skyscrapers, was supposedly dictated by the size of the site and by the need for technological condensation. The placement and forming of these vertically organized blocks of health care was informed by the need to obtain as much light as possible for the patients, to concentrate connected research facilities, and to buffer certain areas from the noise of the city.

The result was a building organized around two parallel bars running east-west across the site (Figs. 207–209). The northernmost of these volumes, which was directly accessible from 168th Street, contained the Columbia College of Physicians and Surgeons and its facilities for training up to five hundred students. Short and wide wings extended forward from the bar to house the entrance, patient wards, and major teaching rooms. Lecture theaters were placed dramatically on the top floors, where they would not have to support smaller spaces. The southern bar was taller, reaching up to twenty-one floors. It contained the four-hundred-bed Presbyterian Hospital, and its north-south wings were longer and narrower, since they housed patient wards looking back toward lower Manhattan from atop the natural high ridge.

The hospital was connected with the College of Physicians and Surgeons by a "stem" containing the doctors' offices, so that these became the literal bridge between the two institutions. The building was set back from the street on both the west and the south and faced a large courtyard to the south. The Vanderbilt Clinic, added to the design in 1925, and the much

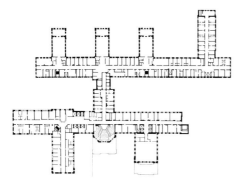

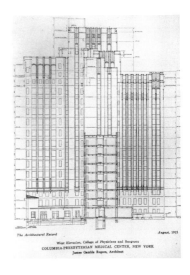

207 James Gamble Rogers. College of Physicians and Surgeons, Columbia-Presbyterian Medical Center, 1921–28. Plan.

208. James Gamble Rogers. College of Physicians and Surgeons, Columbia-Presbyterian Medical Center, 1921–28. West elevation.

209. James Gamble Rogers. Columbia-Presbyterian Medical Center, 1921–28. General view.

lower Harkness Pavilion for Private Patients, continued the hospital to the west, allowing a direct entrance from the more quiet Fort Washington Street for the more genteel patients, while making use of a steep slope on the site to deemphasize the latter structure's relatively modest height (Fig. 210).

The resulting composition of large buildings had very few elements added to its functional mass: a short mechanical tower rose from the center of the hospital, and one-story pavilions formed entrances to the various complexes, but Rogers and his associates strongly emphasized that all architectural decisions were generated almost scientifically by the complex relationships involved—among the various elements of the program, and between the program and its site and method of construction:

> While the Board and its architects agree that they would not be justified in spending one dollar for precious materials, applied decoration, or architectural ornament, exhaustive study has been made and no expense has been spared to provide the ultimate in scientific treatment, service and comfort for the patient. . . . In their outward aspect there is an entire absence in these buildings of that parade of archaeological paraphernalia once customary and obtainable at no great expense. The predominant elements of size and height have been enhanced by such devices of design as can be economically accomplished in utilitarian brick. Mass and form have been made to reflect only the absolute space requirements, with such readjustments as could reasonably be made to enhance the general silhouette. . . . Grandeur has been sought through size, simplicity and austerity. . . . It is a great and grim fortress, benign in purpose, raised high and strong against the assaults of disease."[18]

The Columbia-Presbyterian Medical Center was thus presented as a fact, a direct resultant and realization of the forces that necessitated it. Thus, by the very logic of the process, the buildings became representations of both the direct and the more general function of the complex: a skyscraper fortress embodying man's technological aspirations to keep out the unplanned, invisible forces of nature by replacing them with a concrete and rational object. It was a more businesslike, though no less ambitious, version of the Skyscraper Gothic of Northwestern's Chicago campus.

Though the architectural strategy was essentially the same one Rogers had utilized since the days of his very first independent commissions, its elaboration and connection with the cutting edge of technology and social planning produced an architecture that was startlingly different from that evidenced in his educational work. The difference in appearance overwhelmed the fact that both types of buildings were built responses to and rationalizations of the role of institutions in American society, since both shared a sense of naturalness enhanced by a completely visual manipulation of program elements to cre-

210. James Gamble Rogers. Columbia-Presbyterian Medical Center, 1921–28. View of Service Building, College of Physicians and Surgeons, and Harkness Pavilion.

ate a coherent architectural representation of the institution they served. Whereas the Memorial Quadrangle had seemed a centuries-old Oxbridge embodiment of the Yale myth in sheltered courtyards (though it was in reality made up of simple dormitories arranged according to considerations of site, material, and function), the Columbia-Presbyterian Medical Center became a mountainous ridge infused with modern medical missionary spirit. And whereas in the Chicago campus of Northwestern University Rogers had used architectural styling as a cloak, here he allowed that styling to grow, however tenuously, out of the forms and requirements of the buildings.

The overall composition of the Medical Center was created by the juxtaposition of the different north-south and east-west elements at different heights. The central ridge of the hospital set the highest datum, out of which three crossing towers rose to mark the intersections of the three wings. Each one of the twelve elements that made up the original composition had its own height, and was contrasted with an adjacent element at a different height and of a different orientation. Though the size and placement of these buildings was no doubt dictated by functional requirements, their composition, especially as they originally were seen rising from the cliffs of the Hudson, was turned into an abstract composition of blocks, both spreading out in rationalized ranges and building up to an undefined aspiration: the Columbia-Presbyterian Medical Center resembled a condensation of the kind of "virtual city in itself,"[19] or integrated city-mountain range, into which designers like Raymond Hood, Harvey Wiley Corbett, and Hugh Ferriss only dreamed of transforming Manhattan.[20]

The choice of materials and the detailing of each of the masses enhanced and in fact helped to realize this aspiration. There was virtually no stone or other material added to the skin of the building. Instead, the over four million bricks of the original complex were laid in patterns that established a solid base for the buildings (Fig. 211). This base ended in a corbeled brick cornice, attached to the building with fins that shot up toward piers rising uninterrupted between the windows, to end in finials surrounding the flat roofs. The corners of the wings were kept as solid as the base, so that the vertical thrust so essential to the organization of the buildings seemed carved out of a mountain of repetitive modules of brick. In the spandrels left over in this carving, the brick was laid in raised bands that articulated each floor, further diffusing the focus of the facades.

The inner sides of the two back-to-back ridges are the most solid, and rise up above the openwork wings as stair and mechanical towers. Their brick skins peel away as these functional elements rise to crown the composition. The most striking of these elements is the stack that rises out of a two-story service building to the west of the College of Physicians and Surgeons. This twenty-story shaft is treated as if it were a series of telescoping square

211. James Gamble Rogers.
Columbia-Presbyterian
Medical Center, 1921–28.
Detail.

tubes whose tops are split by deep grooves articulated with brick fins on either side (see Fig. 210). Though the stack is mirrored from certain angles by the northwestern stair tower of the Vanderbilt Clinic, its prominent placement and aggressive detailing make it a landmark of the Medical Center.

While the overall impression of thrusting mountain ranges is accentuated by the treatment of the skin, the relationship of this large complex of buildings to the user or viewer is established not only by the slight manipulation of the top windows on the east and west facades—which are slightly bowed, thus bringing a sense of scale back to the top of the building—but also and principally by the entrances, which are treated as separate elements. Both the hospital and the college entrances are formed by large archways announcing the name and the use of the buildings. The college actually has two entrances, a ceremonial one attached to the central north-south wing, and a clinic entrance set in a separate pavilion placed back from the street as a short, nave-like structure whose two-story arched window above the entrance is set between solid corners.

The Vanderbilt Clinic entrance, set back from the street between the two north-south wings, was a three-story pavilion whose slightly pedimented roofline was clamped down to the ground by four telescoping brick buttresses between which three large arched windows rose above a one-story base. Against this large-scale public gesture for a clinic servicing a larger public, the entrance to the Harkness Pavilion is marked merely by an ornate copper canopy (see Fig. 210). At the same time, the western facade of the Harkness Pavilion, which was the only one of the complex to rise directly from the curb, was treated as a tripartite composition whose central bay of windows was accentuated by more defined versions of the vertical piers that surrounded the rest of the building. It ended in a shallow balcony directly above the canopy. The public face of the buildings is thus always brought down to the scale of entrance, whether by inserting smaller building masses or by a further articulation of the entrance facade.

The interiors were treated forthrightly. The lobbies of the college and the hospital were connected, but a change of level denied any axiality along the entrance axis, and the low, wood-beamed spaces were made completely subservient to the functional double-loaded corridor that formed the cross axis. While all offices, semiprivate rooms, and smaller spaces were kept in the main ridge, the wings were opened up to contain the wards and the main public teaching spaces, here extended from the technological core and liberated into the light and views. The frequent changes in direction and height of the buildings provided areas for use as solaria and gymnasia, and these outdoor spaces for recuperation and relaxation were the only places not fully caught in the brick-and-glass grids. Though hospital planners praised the interiors for their advanced experimentation with materials, colors, and lighting,[21] little of these spaces' streamlined, functional, and wholly artificial character proved of enduring value.

Even before the original buildings of the Medical Center were finished (Columbia-Presbyterian was opened in a series of well-attended ceremonies during the end of 1927 and beginning of 1928), several other institutions had been attracted to the site. Rogers designed the Anna Maxwell Hall of Nursing in 1925 and the Neurological Institute across Fort Washington Avenue in 1927, and these buildings opened in time to extend the composition of the complex farther down the cliffs. There they joined with the imposing bulk of the New York State Psychiatric Institute and Hospital, rising from Riverside Drive far below Fort Washington. Designed by State Architect Sullivan W. Jones, this complex is a momentous ridge of twelve- to fifteen-story buildings capped by up to a ten-story tower (Fig. 212).[22]

Though a 1927 drawing indicates that the original plan had called for the decomposition of the assembled blocks of the original Medical Center into a series of lower and isolated slabs placed in successive ridges farther south and west,[23] all three of the first additions continued the ridge-like, interlocking composition of the hospital and college. Anna Maxwell Hall was essentially a U-shaped dormitory opening up to the river. Eleven stories tall at its eastern side, it extended down the cliff to provide three more stories of public spaces and service rooms placed along the side of the cliff. A loggia underneath a tiled gable stretched between two short towers at the top, while a line of arches applied beneath the cornice pushed the appearance of the building toward Italianate references. A stone base and two layers of brick

212. Sullivan W. Jones. New York State Psychiatric Institute and Hospital, New York, New York, 1928.

applied to either side of the main entrance and rising up the full height of the facade then increased this more delicate and referential reading. The dining room faced the river in a pavilion pulled out ever so slightly from the two cross wings that flanked it. It was marked by a series of Romanesque arches and three small balconies, giving this element the appearance of a small palazzo growing out of the hillside.[24]

As delicate and referential as was Maxwell Hall, so modern was the Neurological Institute. Conceived of as a place for advanced research and the treatment of neurological diseases, it was appropriately placed in front of the more forbidding New York State Psychiatric Institute, but also set back in the quieter, more residential zone formed between the Harkness Pavilion and Maxwell Hall. Its major ridge was treated more plainly than the buildings of the hospital and college, since it lacked both the arched windows at its top and the clear distinction between piers and vertical bands of windows set between rising brick fins. The vertical brick elements were broader and flatter, giving the whole a more grid-like appearance. The two short towers were here placed on top of the twelve-story main block, while the wings cascaded down to the south, ending in semioctagonal bays made up of continuous bands of windows running behind simple brick pilasters. The elaborate corbeling of the brick and the more repetitive nature of the facade in general were contrasted with a more sculptural treatment of the actual building blocks. The result was a composition that, while closely echoing the forms of the first buildings across Fort Washington Avenue, was more abstract and

more energetic, pulling the Medical Center into a modern appearance with virtually no hints of Skyscraper Gothic left to recall any spiritual aspiration or associational values.

The transformation of a complex program on a prominent site into a collection of buildings that translated all of the requirements of the Columbia-Presbyterian Medical Center into a single composition at a huge scale, while still allowing each part to respond to its particular siting, function, and character, was so successful that the center immediately became not only a magnet attracting other health care institutions, but also a model for other medical centers. In New York itself, the Cornell Medical Center on the East Side mimics many of the forms of the Rogers conception: a behemoth of similar size, it was twenty-seven stories tall and also clothed its vertical lines in brick detailed with Neo-Gothic elements (Figs. 213, 214). Yet this complex was much more symmetrical, its blocks larger and less expressive, its detailing more sparing. The Cornell complex thus has little of the expressive power Rogers derived from his picturesque manipulation of the program of the Columbia-Presbyterian Medical Center.[25]

It is perhaps ironic that this, the most stripped-down of Rogers' major works, was perhaps his most innovative. It did not rely on previously established models, but offered a quite radical change of direction in the design of hospitals. Critics were attracted to the Medical Center by the way in which the design both utilized and represented the possibilities and facts of modern building technology and urbanism. Thus the building seemed at the same time natural, an organic extension of its site, as well as a fortress against the destructive forces of nature. Produced, according to one critic

> . . . under very modern conditions of steel-and-concrete architecture, where ground space is supplemented, and in effect magnified, by the utilization of sky space, story on story . . . looking for all the world like a

213. Coolidge, Shepley, Bulfinch & Abbott. New York Hospital-Cornell Medical Center, New York, New York, 1932–34.

214. James Gamble Rogers. Columbia-Presbyterian Medical Center, 1921–28.

gigantic apartment house or Wall Street business block . . . the succession of walls rising from different levels, visually superimposed to seem like a single structure, with a twenty-story base, towering to an incredible pinnacle, [the Medical Center] will perhaps suggest a glorified medieval castle or—more appropriately—the ultimate Thule of New York's new light-giving type of medieval architecture.[26]

As a result of this design, said *Architectural Record* editor Marrion Wilcox, who had earlier commented on the romantic beauties and didactic values of the Memorial Quadrangle, Columbia-Presbyterian "will testify alike to the growing power of human knowledge to minister to the physical and mental ills of man and to the zeal of civilized man to help and cure his less fortunate fellows." In this modernizing effort, the center would cast aside the impositions of style, or any extraneous architectural manipulation. Out of "a series of more manageable small hospitals, each complete in itself yet all attaining the highest efficiency by functioning together," each designed according to its needs and place on the site, a new type of architecture would come. Wrote Wilcox:

> The architecture here will be, not of a conventional style, but such as the internal structure and the purpose of the undertaking require and the location suggests. . . . [T]he walls of steel with facing of brick, stone-colored or gray, will rise sheer and unbroken by dust-catching ledges or cornices . . . [like] those natural features in the landscape which are most impressive architecturally, quite like walls of masonry yet rather like palisades that might have been built in those days when there were giants. . . .[27]

The architecture of Columbia-Presbyterian thus both affirmed the reality, functionality, and place in the metropolis of the program, and transformed it into the realm where the building took on the aspects of a sublime composition of abstract elements that denied the fixed time and place of its insertion: "there is something magical in the play of light and shade and cloud-shadow, that crosses its sheer surfaces. Like some great creation of nature, it's never twice alike . . . an embodiment of calm grandeur."[28] To Erich Mendelsohn, the buildings were the logical result of the "exact science" in "exact technique," which opposed the general "dilettantism" with which New York was groping toward self-expression.[29] Placing his camera below the building, catching its vertical lines and complex juxtaposition of masses, Mendelsohn used the Medical Center as the prime example of realized Modernism: "Down this road lies America's Will to the New, expressed in the ordered strength of its overall composition," he exulted.[30]

Whether or not the Columbia-Presbyterian Center fulfilled the Manifest Destiny of American architecture, its huge size and complex composition vindicated the rational representationalism of James Gamble Rogers' architecture. The result was a building that extended its site and program and presaged the future of architecture as an abstract assemblage of projected volumes, while the functional and site-specific character of each piece was retained as the solid reality of its present condition. Only the complete destruction of this architectural organization by later additions masks the power of this responsible condensation of the modern metropolis.

Rogers continued to design buildings for the Columbia-Presbyterian Medical Center all through the 1930s. During the economic depression of that decade, construction of buildings for educational institutions, which depended mainly on dividends derived from endowments or gifts, fell off sharply, while construction of health care facilities increased, spurred by a combination of economic need and government subsidies.[31] Thus most of the work in his firm during this decade was hospital-related, and the core of this work was the Columbia-Presbyterian Medical Center. After the opening of most of the center in 1928, Rogers was commissioned to design a dormitory there, called Bard Hall, in 1929, a new building for the Eye Institute the following year, and a health and teaching center in 1937. Numerous additions and expansions of the other buildings of the Medical Center provided a steady stream of work and income all during this period.[32]

Bard Hall used the cliffs that had allowed Maxwell Hall to achieve its dramatic sectional variety for the same purpose. One of the firm's employees, architect Charles N. Kent, writing for his alma mater Columbia, summed up the difference between this latest addition to the bastion of medical skyscrapers and the earlier buildings:

> As in the earlier buildings the feeling is definitely modern, but in this case, the striving for verticality has given place to an emphasis on the horizontal elements of the composition. This, together with a somewhat informal and picturesque grouping of masses made possible by the unsymmetrical plan, will result, it is hoped, in a more friendly and domestic feeling than is possible where the vertical elements are strongly emphasized.[33]

The light-colored brick building thus continued the development in the earlier designs for the Medical Center. There, the gothicizing piers had given way more and more to a weaving together of textured bricks to create a tapestry that emphasized the nature of the facade as a thin, repetitive, and malleable skin stretched over the gridded structure and technologically defined functions of the hospital buildings. The adoption of Modernism meant the abandonment of the fiction that a masonry skin could express structural forces at work in the underlying steel skeleton. The building no

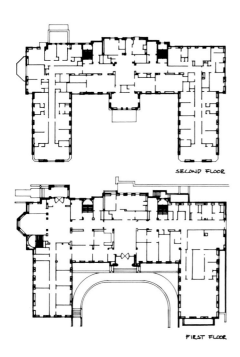

SECOND FLOOR

FIRST FLOOR

215. James Gamble Rogers.
Institute of Ophthalmology,
Columbia-Presbyterian
Medical Center, 1931. Plan.

216. James Gamble Rogers.
Institute of Ophthalmology,
Columbia-Presbyterian
Medical Center, 1921–27.

longer reached from an ornamented base (meant to connect the buildings with the activities of the surrounding streetscape and to state clearly the nature of the institution), past a functional body, toward a shaft aiming at some nonspecific resolution beyond the reaches of construction. What was retained was the impulse toward contextualism, rather than a radical rejection of existing traditions and conditions, and a picturesque massing that sought to arrange the elements of the building into a visually controlled composition. This latter impulse in fact appears to be a reaction against the very rationalizing and standardizing forces of modernization.

The development of this new approach reached a further resolution with the Institute of Ophthalmology, a nine-story structure erected in 1931 (Figs. 215, 216).[34] George Nichols, writing for *The Architectural Record*, described the building in much the same terms of aesthetic functionalism that Kent had used in describing Bard Hall. The U-shaped building might be vaguely symmetrical and might harmonize with the rest of the Medical Center, said Nichols, but

> the widely different requirements of ward and private floors have been harmonized, and the size, shape and fenestration of a plan satisfying these combined requirements have determined the mass and aspect of the building. . . . The exterior is a straightforward expression of the plan and its functions.[35]

Thus the change in floor sizes "allowed" for setbacks on the top three floors, while the need for mechanical exhaust produced "a tower-like terminal feature."[36] This verticality, which was further emphasized by using a darker brick at the base and gradually mixing in more of the yellow brick of the Medical Center towers soaring above the institute (a technique Rogers had used with great success in stone in his buildings at Yale), was then counteracted by the fact that the steel, as it went up the building, "allowed" for closely spaced horizontal bands of brick and chamfered corners.[37] Inside, the rooms were described as marvels of efficiency, easy to clean and light. They utilized the latest synthetic materials and lighting techniques, several of which were outlined in separate articles.[38]

The metamorphosis of traditional Rogers motifs continues in the more minor elements of the facade. The two side wings terminate in semi-hexagonal bay windows, but these bays are four stories tall and grow directly out of both the larger base and the chamfered corners of the wings. They are thus hybrids between the buttresses and the bay windows Rogers was fond of using, but designed at a scale, in relationship to the wall onto which they are placed, that causes them to dissolve the sense of being added on to a flat facade. The entrance retains two carved limestone finials to recall the Gothic entrances down the street, but here they are clamps between three deep-set square windows, while the whole entrance pavilion is no more than a thin undulation in the facade.

The Institute of Ophthalmology was conceived of as a solid block whose dimensions and proportions are defined by the program. The architect then molded this mass by carving away excess and adding on punctuations, but the design remains within the boundaries of the volume generated by the institution. There is no attempt to integrate the object with its site—the building seems to float above the sidewalk, which drops away steeply to the west—or with other building types. No symbolic program has been imposed, so that the object remains self-sufficient. The result is one of the most coherent, strongly composed, and simple designs produced in James Gamble Rogers' office. It is, however, a design that subscribes to the kind of monumental and functional determinism of the built object that Rogers had avoided in his previous work.[39]

A few years later, Rogers designed a much larger hospital building that shares many of the characteristics of the Institute of Ophthalmology. The Memorial Sloan-Kettering Hospital for the Treatment of Cancer and Allied Diseases, constructed on New York's Upper East Side between 1936 and 1939, was made possible by gifts from Edward S. Harkness and the General Education Board, a Rockefeller family charity.[40] Rogers did not necessarily receive the commission as a direct result of the Harkness gift, however. As early as 1932 he was lobbying the hospital, pointing out, first, the experience that he and his partner on the Columbia-Presbyterian Medical Center, Henry

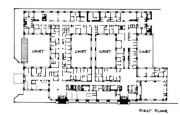

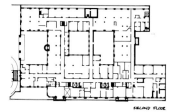

217. James Gamble Rogers and
Henry C. Pelton.
Memorial Sloan-Kettering
Hospital, 1937–39. Plan.

218. James Gamble Rogers and
Henry C. Pelton.
Memorial Sloan-Kettering
Hospital, 1937–39.

C. Pelton (whose contribution appears to have been mainly technical), could offer; second, his connections to Harkness and Rockefeller; and, third, his ability to bring buildings in on budget and on time.[41] Rogers and Pelton finally received the commission in 1937, and Rogers continued on as the sole architect after the death of Pelton at the end of that year.[42]

The building was designed to process twelve thousand patients and filled half a city block with a sprawling base of treatment rooms and offices, out of which a twelve-story volume of patient rooms and operating facilities rose up in a symmetrical series of setbacks (Figs. 217, 218). When it was completed, the building was the largest facility of its kind. It was described by the hospital itself in clinical terms with military inflections. It was designed for "warfare" against cancer, and thus was lean and efficient.[43] "Why this broad expanse of the lower floors? Why this lofty edifice rising high and solitary in a great city block?" asked the director, Dr. James Ewing, rhetorically. "There is no appeal to the emotions," he admitted.

> The appeal is to reason. The architecture has been determined by strict attention to the demands of efficiency. It is the object of this building to enable doctors to get sick people well, as many as possible, and with the least expense of time, energy and morbidity.[44]

"The structural and mechanical specifications for this building make no radical departures from generally accepted hospital construction," explained the hospital, "but they do represent conservative and economical selections of designs and materials and a restraint from over-indulgence in fads and fancies."[45] The Memorial Sloan-Kettering Hospital was supposed to be no more than a translation of its requirements into a three-dimensional object. Whatever stylistic modulations took place in this translation were achieved by emphasizing aspects of the inherent forms: "The architectural character is distinctly modern with a general horizontal motif interrupted by verticals."[46]

The programmatic requirements for the hospital do indeed mandate both the seemingly chaotic collection of spaces on the first three floors, and the slenderness of the top nine floors of the building, which house functions needing daylight. The result is a split between the base and the slab. Rogers organized these conditions into an ordered composition by using abstracted and pared-down elements from his repertoire. The base, for instance, is grouped around a series of courtyards and gardens hidden away from the street, in the manner of the Sterling Library and other Yale buildings. The brick wall of the building meets the ground with a series of stone walls whose curved corners are carved with animal and foliate imagery similar to that found on the Yale School of Graduate Studies. Bay windows are used to break up the monotony of the wall, even if the bays are here nothing but two windows splayed out at a 45-degree angle to form triangles marching up the side of the building.

Yet Rogers added another architectural language on top of both the efficient massing of the building and his own scale-giving choreography of elements and spaces. Those triangular balconies, for instance, are grouped in four pairs that run from the fourth through the ninth floor and end with rounded balconies, so that they appear like paired pilasters of a giant order created by folding and extruding the skin of the building (Fig. 219). The public spaces of the ground floor are expressed through the use of an architectural screen, but here the screen is not one of soaring Gothic windows and buttresses, but a limestone colonnade of square pilasters behind which the ribbon windows and horizontal bands of brick that make up the entire facade run almost without interruption.

James Gamble Rogers here appears to be fighting a rearguard action against changes in architectural taste and convention: by taking his ability to imply architectural forms without stating them, and by stripping down those forms he did use, he was working against the tendency of modern technology, planning, and architectural thinking to make superfluous the sort of elaborate architectural composition at which he excelled. The result is an architecture that turns what had been motifs—like implied columns and screening devices—into monumental gestures at the scale of the urban environment, while dressing the efficiently organized buildings with streamlined versions of the Gothic derivatives with which Rogers was so familiar. There is beauty in the result, though, as in Abbott Hall (see Figs. 202, 203), it is a tense, somewhat uncomfortable beauty.[47]

The James Gamble Rogers firm continued to work on large hospital projects throughout the latter half of the 1930s,[48] but the last buildings with

219. James Gamble Rogers and
Henry C. Pelton.
Memorial Sloan-Kettering
Hospital, 1937–39. Elevation.

which Rogers appears to have been actively involved were a series of health centers paid for by the Commonwealth Fund and erected in rural communities throughout America between 1926 and 1942. These were small and extremely economical buildings whose plans were mass-produced by the Rogers office, originally in joint venture with Henry C. Pelton. They exhibit Rogers' motifs and methods of assembling forms pared down to their essence, to the point where they could be produced far from the hands that had designed them. They extended Rogers' work well outside the reach of the elite institutions of the East Coast and Chicago, and stretched his architecture as far as it could go. After these buildings, there was little further use for an architecture that could translate traditions and context into significant structures. There was only the need for health care or educational facilities.

The "Rural Hospital Program" was started by the Commonwealth Fund in 1925.[49] The fund wanted to redirect its energies away from contributions for the erection of centralized monuments of health care, and sought ways in which it could target specific individuals, projects, and programs. Harkness and the other directors of the board, including Sam Fisher, Malcolm Aldrich, Otto Bannard of the Sterling Trust, and Max Farrand, a history professor at Yale and husband of landscape designer Beatrix Farrand, had always emphasized in their gifts that the hospitals and universities they built were only symbols, focal points and symptoms of more deep-seated problems of morality and epidemiology. The tendency of the Commonwealth Fund was thus away from building and toward abstract, scientific research and education.[50] The Rural Hospital Program itself was a halfway point between the large projects the fund had endowed in the 1920s and its current position as a provider of grants for specific projects and individuals.[51]

In terms of design, these rural hospitals are also halfway between civic structures and science- and need-generated enclosures of wards and operating rooms. H. J. Southmayd, the director of the program, wanted a specialist, not an architect, because "the specialized character of hospital buildings and hospital service are little understood by competent business-men and even architects unless they have had experience in the hospital field."[52] He sought someone to design one standard hospital, to be placed on a five-acre site on the outskirts of a "rural center," not near any industry or cemetery, on high ground, and oriented toward the sun. The architecture of these buildings would then be adapted to the local climate and building materials; also, to smooth the acceptance of these new hospitals (which were not always received with open arms by the communities in which they were placed),[53] a few nonfunctional elements would be added, because, as South-mayd explained, "a modicum of architectural decoration is worth its cost in community good will."[54]

James Gamble Rogers and Henry C. Pelton had the experience to undertake such a design, and they had the confidence, to say the least, of the trustees of the Commonwealth Fund. Though Rogers originally declined the commission, Pelton and he signed a contract with the fund at the beginning of 1926[55] and designed the first "demonstration project" for Farmville, Vir-ginia.[56]

For the next fifteen years, Rogers, initially in conjunction with Pel-ton, designed at least one of these centers a year. The fund would decide on a community in need of improved health care and offer the building on condi-tion that the local medical profession reorganize itself according to the fund's guidelines. Then Rogers & Pelton would send architect Charles Crane from its staff out to find a hilltop site. The description of the Farmville building in the Annual Report of the Commonwealth Fund can stand for that of almost all of the Rogers & Pelton rural hospitals:

> The building is to be of red brick, fireproof in construction, of the Southern colonial style of architecture, and is planned to meet all rea-sonable demands of the community for general hospital care. . . . All facilities and activities are housed under one roof.[57]

Each one of the rural hospitals was a two-story, T-shaped building set on a hill and clad with brick (Figs. 220–223). The main entrance was always marked with a wood porch, and the design of this element was the principal distinguishing feature of each hospital. In Tupelo, Mississippi, the porch was a grand affair of Doric columns holding up a carved wood pediment, while in Farmington, Maine, the porch was an enclosed brick box; in Kingsport, Ten-nessee, the entrance was through a brick screen strengthened at its corners by brick quoins and topped by an arched brick pediment. The only other distinguishing formal elements were the porches and waiting rooms on the side elevations. Often they were treated as two-story cutouts into the brick

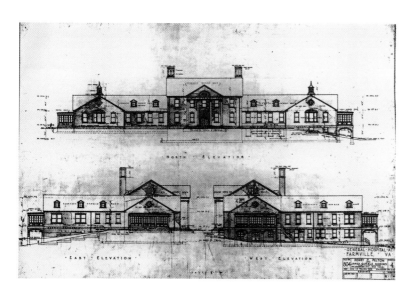

220. James Gamble Rogers.
Rural Hospital, Farmville,
Virginia, 1936.
Elevations.

221. James Gamble Rogers.
Rural Hospital, Farmville,
Virginia, 1936. Plan.

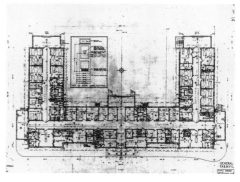

wall. They were composed of wood and glass or covered with mesh grids
that gave the building a scale larger than indicated by the small windows
lighting the remainder of the spaces.[58]

The interior organization of the buildings was similarly standardized.
The spaces were divided into three groups. Immediately upon entering, one
had to turn—as was customary in all of James Gamble Rogers' buildings—
left or right down a double-loaded corridor, which here serviced the emergency rooms and doctors' offices. This was the public part of the hospital,
and the fund prided itself on the modern and cheery appearance of these
spaces.[59] The main entrance axis continued toward the rear of the building,
which was usually inaccessible to the general public, since this wing contained service spaces, culminating in the laundry and mechanical rooms, set
at the farthest remove from the patient rooms and often slightly down the
slope of the hill. The second floor was completely filled with patient rooms.
When necessary, the front wing was extended farther out and down the slope

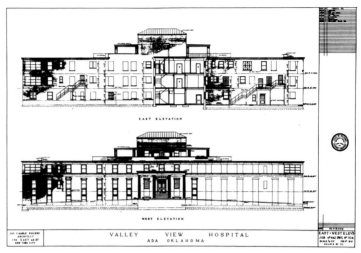

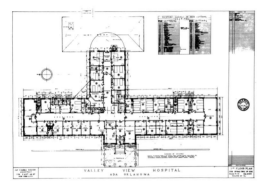

222. James Gamble Rogers.
Valley View Hospital, Ada,
Oklahoma, 1937. Elevations.

223. James Gamble Rogers.
Valley View Hospital, Ada,
Oklahoma, 1937. Plan.

of the hill with lower, telescoping wings.

These hospitals came in two basic sizes, a small "health center" costing around $30,000 and a larger "hospital," usually budgeted at around
$240,000. The larger type might have a third story, and the smaller building
might be only a singular rectangular box, but all of the buildings—from Ada,
Oklahoma, to Ayer, Massachusetts—shared the same basic organization and
appearance.[60] They were essentially solitary and functional pavilions, each
one creating its own realm or campus and each one made to look like a civic
institution by the addition of a Neo-Georgian entrance element. The hospitals exhibited the essence of what James Gamble Rogers did as an architect:
the making of pavilions whose function and meaning were extended into the
landscape and the community through the use of the elements of an architectural style chosen for its social and cultural connotations.

As the three dozen Rural Health Centers were constructed throughout the country, the Depression worsened and the buildings became even

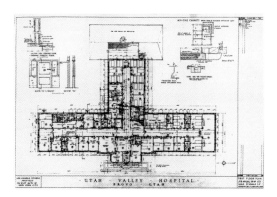

224. James Gamble Rogers.
Utah Valley Hospital, Provo,
Utah, 1938. Plan.

225. James Gamble Rogers.
Utah Valley Hospital, Provo,
Utah, 1938. Elevations.

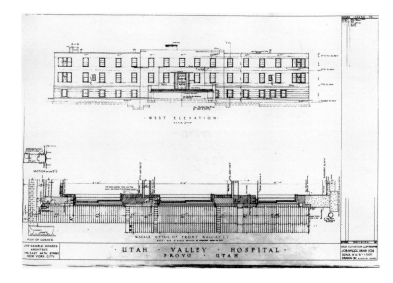

simpler. Some of them were no more than flat-roofed boxes with arched lights over the doorway. In Provo, Utah, Rogers departed strongly from the idiom of the remainder of the hospitals by designing a light-colored brick box banded with limestone whose entrance pavilion was a larger volume set over the two wings (Figs. 224, 225). The strength and simplicity of this hospital seems inspired by the dramatic nature of the mountains rising up behind it in what was then a desolate mining community, but in plan the Provo building was identical with hospitals built in the Midwest or Deep South.[61]

After the start of the Second World War, the building program became severely restricted, to the point where the hospitals were reduced to one story because of the impossibility of obtaining parts for elevators.[62] James Gamble Rogers also saw much of his staff disappear, and he had few larger commissions to keep him busy. Rogers was seventy-three years old when the war broke out, and he continued to work at his profession, as he had almost uninterruptedly for the fifty-five years since leaving Yale. The size of the projects to which he now devoted his attention was almost that of his first houses, though in this case technical requirements and the standardization of the design and construction limited his chances for any experimentation. The era of institutions that needed the services of both a functional organizer of spaces and a composer of validating images was over.

The last record of any involvement James Gamble Rogers had with the design of a building was his successful intervention with the War Board to ensure the construction of the Missouri Delta Community Hospital in Sikeston, Missouri, completed to the specifications of Southmayd and according to the designs of Crane, Ballantyne, and James Gamble Rogers in 1946, only a few months before Rogers' death.[63]

Notes

ABBREVIATIONS USED:

AMB Papers Anita McCormick Blaine Papers, McCormick Family Collection, Wisconsin Historical Society Archives, Madison, Wisconsin.

APS Papers Anson Phelps Stokes Papers, Office of the Secretary Papers, Manuscripts and Archives Collections, Sterling Memorial Library, Yale University, New Haven, Connecticut.

CCAP Papers Corporation Committee on the Architectural Plan Papers, Manuscripts and Archives Collections, Sterling Memorial Library, Yale University, New Haven, Connecticut.

CFA Commonwealth Fund Archives, Rockefeller Archives Center, Pocantico Hills, New York.

JGR Papers James Gamble Rogers Papers, Manuscripts and Archives Collections, Sterling Memorial Library, Yale University, New Haven, Connecticut.

JRA Papers James Rowland Angell Papers, Yale Presidential Papers, Manuscript and Archives Collections, Sterling Memorial Library, Yale University, New Haven, Connecticut.

NUA Northwestern University Archives, Deering Library, Evanston, Illinois.

NYUA New York University Archives, New York University Library, New York, New York.

WDS Papers Walter Dill Scott Papers, Northwestern University Archives, Deering Library, Northwestern University, Evanston, Illinois.

INTRODUCTION

1. John V. Farwell III to author, August 6, 1988.

2. Darnell, Rucker, *The Chicago Pragmatists*, Minneapolis: University of Minnesota Press, 1969.

3. Paul Goldberger, "Romantic Pragmatism. The Work of James Gamble Rogers at Yale," Senior Honors Essay, Yale College, 1972.

4. William James, *Pragmatism. A New Name for Some Old Ways of Thinking*, Cambridge, Mass., London: Harvard University Press, 1978 (1907).

5. Marshall Berman, *All That Is Solid Melts into Air. The Experience of Modernity*, New York: Penguin Books, 1988 (1982). Berman argues that "to be modern and alive is to . . . be overpowered by the immense bureaucratic organizations that have the power to control and often to destroy all communities, values, lives; and yet to be undeterred in our determination to face these forces, to fight to change their world and to make it our own" (p. 13). Berman locates violent opposition in modern art and literature, and one can just as easily locate reformist action in reformist art and architecture.

6. David O. Levine, *The American College and the Culture of Aspiration, 1915–1940*, Ithaca, London: Cornell University Press, 1986, pp. 87–88.

7. Burton J. Bledstein, *The Culture of Professionalism. The Middle Class and the Development of Higher Education in America*, New York: W. W. Norton & Co., 1976.

8. A. McGehee Harvey and Susan L. Abrams, *"For the Welfare of Mankind." The Commonwealth Fund and American Medicine*, Baltimore, London: The Johns Hopkins University Press, 1986, p. 1.

9. T. J. Jackson Lears, *No Place of Grace. Antimodernism and the Transformation of American Culture, 1880–1920*, New York: Pantheon Books, 1981, p. 58.

10. Richard Guy Wilson, "The Great Civilization," in *The American Renaissance: 1876–1917*, New York: Pantheon Books, 1979, pp. 11–74; p. 45; Vincent Scully, *The Shingle Style: Architectural Theory and Design from Richardson to the Origins of Frank Lloyd Wright*, New Haven: Yale University Press, 1955.

11. John Tomsich, *A Genteel Tradition. American Culture and Politics in the Gilded Age*, Stanford: Stanford University Press, 1971, p. 5.

12. Henry Adams, *The Education of Henry Adams. An Autobiography*, Boston: Houghton Mifflin Co., 1961 (1918), p. 343.

13. Tomsich, *Genteel Tradition*, p. 193.

CHAPTER 1

1. William Whitney Ames, *Yale Class Book, 1889*, New Haven: Price, Lee & Adkins, Co., 1889, p. 20.

2. James G. Rogers III, "James Gamble Rogers—Yale Architect," unpublished essay dated 1968, Manuscripts and Archives Collection, Sterling Memorial Library, New Haven, Conn., pp. 4–5.

3. Robert J. Buck, *Trailblazers of the Thomson-Gamble Family*, Asheville, Ky.: 1948, p. 80.

4. For precise figures on the explosive growth in construction in Chicago during this period, see: Gerald Wade Kuhn, "A History of Financing of Commercial Structures in the Chicago Central Business District, 1864 to 1934," Ph.D. diss., Graduate School of Business, Indiana University, 1969; Wesley G. Skogan, *Chicago Since 1840: A Time-Series Data Handbook*, Urbana, Ill.: Institute of Government and Public Affairs, University of Illinois, 1976, p. 6.

5. Clipping files, Chicago Historical Society, Chicago, Ill. J. B. Waller's brother was one of Frank Lloyd Wright's earliest supporters and clients; J. B. Waller became alderman for the 43rd District, which included

Buena Park. See Mary Hartley, *James Breckenbridge Waller and Pioneering in the Wilderness of Politics*, Chicago, private printing, 1921.

6. James Gamble Rogers to Charles Ulysses Gordon, "Buena Park & Graceland: A Choice Part of Chicago," unpublished manuscript dated 1940, Chicago Historical Society, pp. 11–15.

7. The speaker was Henry Cornelius Atkins. Ames, 1889, p. 90.

8. James Gamble Rogers to Howard W. Vernon, n.d., in: *Yale Class of 1889–Fiftieth Reunion*, ed. by Howard W. Vernon, New Haven, 1939, pp. 37–38.

9. See Chapter 5.

10. Rogers, "James Gamble Rogers," pp. 7–9.

11. Though Yale was a pioneer in arts education at the university level, it was not until 1905 that the first professor of architecture was appointed within the School of Fine Arts. It was not until the 1930s that the school achieved professional status. See *Yale School of Architecture*, New Haven: Yale University, n.d.

12. Siegfried Giedion, *Space, Time and Architecture*, Cambridge, Mass.: Harvard University Press, 1941, p. 293.

13. Carl W. Condit, *The Chicago School of Architecture. A History of Commercial and Public Building in the Chicago Area, 1875–1925*, Chicago, London: University of Chicago Press, 1964, pp. 79–94; Thomas E. Tallmadge, *Architecture in Old Chicago*, Chicago: University of Chicago Press, 1941, pp. 185–98.

14. David Van Zanten, one of the most perceptive historians of this period in Chicago architects, points out ". . . the drama of art dealing with the great fact of American society at the end of the 19th century: the emergence of the corporate structures of endeavor," and goes on to point out the increasing convergence of corporate methods of producing architecture in large, highly organized offices, and the predominance of similar corporations as clients for the largest and most visible buildings in American

cities during the turn of the century. Both Alan Trachtenberg, in *The Incorporation of America: Culture & Society in the Gilded Age* (New York: Hill and Wang, 1982), and T. J. Jackson Lears, in *No Place of Grace: Antimodernism and the Transformation of American Culture, 1880–1920* (New York: Pantheon Books, 1981), point out that the emergence of a "corporate architecture" was part of a general movement in American culture during this period. See also David Van Zanten, Introduction, "The Nineteenth Century: The Projection of Chicago as a Commercial City and the Rationalization of Design and Construction," in John Zukowsky, ed., *Chicago and New York: Architectural Interactions*, Chicago: Art Institute of Chicago, 1984.

15. Louis Sullivan, "The Tall Office Building Artistically Considered," *Lippincott's*, March, 1896; reprinted in *Louis Sullivan, Kindergarten Chats and Other Writings*, New York: Dover Publications, 1979, pp. 202–13.

16. For the coherence of the Chicago school, see Condit, *Chicago School*, but also recent biographies of Louis Sullivan and John Root, including: Donald Hoffman, *The Architecture of John Wellborn Root*, Chicago: University of Chicago Press, 1973, esp. Chapter 4, "The Milieu of the Chicago School," pp. 84–97; Robert Twombly, *Louis Sullivan: His Life and Work*, New York: Viking Press, 1986.

17. Mundie suggested, for instance, that the source for the Home Insurance Building skeleton was vernacular construction in the Philippines. Condit, *Chicago School*, p. 81.

18. Theodore Turak, *William LeBaron Jenney. A Pioneer of Modern Architecture*, Ann Arbor, Mich.: UMI Research Press, 1986 (1966), p. 305.

19. Rogers to Gordon, "Buena Park," pp. 11–12.

20. Mundie himself, when naming those assistants he valued most, did not include James Gamble Rogers, and described his own ascension to the position of partner as gradual and wholly the result of his own work. William Bryce Mundie, "Skeleton

Construction—Its Origin and Development Applied to Architecture," unpublished manuscript in the Burnham Collection, Ryerson Library, Art Institute of Chicago, p. 64.

21. Hoffmann, *John Wellborn Root*. Frank Lloyd Wright, who was almost exactly Rogers' contemporary, began "bootlegging," or designing houses by himself while still in the employ of Louis Sullivan, during the same period.

22. Rogers to Gordon, "Buena Park," pp. 14–15.

23. *Prominent Buildings Erected by the George A. Fuller Company, General Contractors*, Chicago, [1894], p. 17.

24. Paul R Coppock, "A Fine House of Courts," *Memphis Commercial Appeal*, May 11, 1975. When the Courthouse Commission of Shelby County, Tennessee, went to Chicago in 1909 to find an architect for their new building, they visited the offices of D. H. Burnham, at that time the largest in the country, and Burnham recommended the then relatively unknown James Gamble Rogers.

25. *Rand McNally & Co.'s Pictorial Chicago*, Chicago: Rand McNally & Co., 1898, plates 60, 61. John Arthur Rogers is listed as the architect of the building; James Gamble Rogers was in Paris during this period.

26. The Burnham firm was certainly not the first office to adopt emerging forms of corporate organization, but it became one of the most successful, and it set the tone for a series of Chicago firms, such as Graham, Anderson & Probst (its successor firm), Holabird & Roche, Perkins & Will, and, later, Skidmore, Owings & Merrill, that were to dominate large-scale architectural design in America. See Thomas Hines, *Burnham of Chicago: Architect and Planner*, Chicago: University of Chicago Press, 1974. Hines is especially eloquent in his descriptions of the relationship of Burnham's work to the Progressive movement on the one hand, and to the increasingly powerful corporate environment on the other hand. If Burnham may be said to have been the foremost architect of the buildings that resulted from

the alliance between corporate America and reform politics (outlined in Trachtenberg, *Incorporation of America*), then Rogers became the architect of the alliance's educational institutions and charities (see Chapter 3).

27. *The Economist*, October 24, 1891, p. 698.

28. Rand McNally, p. 164.

29. *The Economist*, October 24, 1891, p. 698.

30. Rand McNally, p. 164.

31. The most complete description of the Lees Building appears in Robert Cuscaden, "An Elegy for the Lees Building," *Inland Architect* 13 (April, 1969), pp. 22–23. The author notes that the building is "squarely in the commercial, functional, Chicago School tradition. . . . Its clean, uncluttered lines were thrustingly, prominently vertical. . . . Ornamentation was kept to a bare minimum, with just enough of a horizontal demarcation to effect a nice transition from the street level store front and the second floor to the rigidly geometric, soaring upper floors" (p. 22).

32. Charles Hitchcock Sherrill, *Yale College, Yale University. Class of '89 Triennial and Sexennial*, New York, 1896, p. 75.

33. *Year Book of the Society of Beaux-Arts Architects*, 1920.

34. Leonard K. Eaton, *Two Chicago Architects and Their Clients. Frank Lloyd Wright and Howard Van Doren Shaw*, Cambridge, Mass., London: MIT Press, 1969. The author points out that "only a tiny minority of Midwesterners went east to school, and when they returned to their native cities, they constituted a true social elite" (p. 139). Howard Van Doren Shaw graduated from Yale one year after Rogers, went to architecture school at the Massachusetts Institute of Technology, and then worked for Jenney & Mundie. Eaton points out that "a surprising number" of Shaw's clients went to Yale, and since Shaw himself was a Yale man, one begins to suspect something like a British "old boy network" (pp. 168–69). The same can certainly be said of Rogers later on in his career,

though whereas Shaw immediately turned to building for his classmates and their families in the wealthy Lake Forest area, Rogers appears to have relied on connections forged in his neighborhood and through his family.

35. Charles Hitchcock Sherrill, *Yale College, Yale University. Class of '89 Decennial*, New York, 1899, p. 97. For a description of what his experiences in Paris may have been like, see Ernest Flagg, "The Ecole des Beaux-Arts," *Architectural Record* 4 (March, 1914), pp. 25–53.

36. David Van Zanten, *Designing Paris. The Architecture of Duban, Labrouste, Duc, and Vaudoyer*, Cambridge, Mass.: MIT Press, 1987.

37. The three best sources on the Ecole des Beaux-Arts in English are: Donald Drew Egbert, *The Beaux-Arts Tradition in French Architecture. Illustrated by The Grands Prix de Rome*, ed. by David Van Zanten, Princeton: Princeton University Press, 1980; Arthur Drexler, ed., *The Architecture of the Ecole des Beaux-Arts*, New York: Museum of Modern Art, 1977, esp. Richard Chafee, "The Teaching of Architecture at the Ecole des Beaux-Arts," and David Van Zanten, "Architectural Composition at the Ecole des Beaux-Arts from Charles Percier to Charles Garnier," Robin Middleton, ed., *The Beaux-Arts and Nineteenth-Century French Architecture*, Cambridge, Mass.: MIT Press, 1982. See also Richard A. Moore, "Academic *Dessin* Theory in France after the Reorganization of 1863," *Journal of the Society of Architectural Historians* 36 (October, 1977), pp. 145–74.

38. Drawings in JGR Papers.

39. The identification of power with verbal and visual literacy can be traced through the increased importance placed on education and the institutionalization of culture in the latter part of the nineteenth century. As always, Trachtenberg and Lears are indispensable in tracing these developments (see n. 14). See also David O. Levine, *The American College and the Culture of Aspiration, 1915–1940*, Ithaca, London: Cornell University Press, 1986.

40. David Levine, *American College*, comments that at many Ivy League institutions the "goal—and it certainly was an ideal of many other progressive educators—was to provide a valuable intellectual and social experience in a small community for those young people most capable of exercising leadership in society" (p. 141). In broader terms, he states: "The college student was no longer on the fringe of his generation; now he could take his place as a future leader of society, but only after careful selection, generally based on family background, and socialization . . . institutions of higher learning . . . were no longer antithetical to the broad economic and social values of society; indeed, the colleges become the primary champions of those values. The campus became a center for the ethos of an emergent white-collar consumption-oriented middle class" (p. 19).

41. H. Allen Brooks, *The Prairie School: Frank Lloyd Wright and his Midwest Contemporaries*, Toronto: University of Toronto Press, 1972, pp. 28–34.

42. *Prominent Buildings Erected by the George A. Fuller Company, General Contractors*, Chicago, [1894], plates 60, 61.

43. The Chicago Lakeside Directory, the telephone directory of the period, lists James Gamble Rogers in 1893 as having an office in the Ashland Block. After a two-year hiatus, John Arthur Rogers is listed as an architect working in the same building. James Gamble Rogers reappears in 1899 at the same address where John Arthur had been listed. The latter disappears from all listings until he takes over his brother's Chicago office in 1905.

44. *The Economist*, July 8, 1899; April 1, 1905; June 6, 1905. Apparently J. B. Waller had continued disagreements with David Lewis, his partner in this project, whom he finally bought out in 1905.

45. *Directory to Apartments of the Better Class on the North Side of Chicago*, Chicago: Albert J. Pardridge & Harold Bradley, 1917, pp. 52–53. The building has been demolished.

46. *The Economist,* August 17, 1901, p. 199; August 31, 1901, p. 254.

47. Rogers to Gordon, "Buena Park," p. 5.

48. *The Economist,* August 31, 1901, p. 254.

49. *The Economist,* September 14, 1901, p. 312; November 30, 1901, p. 661.

50. For a short discussion of the influence of the Arts and Crafts movement on these various architects, see: Eric Davis, "Dwight Heald Perkins 1894–1904: From the Chicago School to the Prairie School to Chicago's Schools," *Threshold* 5/6 (1991), pp. 24–33; Brooks, *Prairie School,* p. 34ff.; "George W. Maher: A Democrat in Architecture," *The Western Architect* 20 (March, 1914), pp. 25–53.

51. John W. Leonard, *The Book of Chicagoans. A Biographical Dictionary of Leading Living Men of the City of Chicago,* Chicago: A. N. Marquis & Co., 1905.

52. Family Record, Albert Morgan Day, Chicago Historical Society.

53. Francis C. and John V. Farwell Family Records, Chicago Historical Society: conversation with Mrs. Katherine Van Sluyck, August 18, 1987.

54. *The Chicago Bluebook,* Chicago: Chicago Directory Co., 1900, 1901, 1902, 1903, 1904, 1905.

55. Family Records, Albert M. Day and John V. Farwell, Chicago Historical Society.

56. *The Economist,* July 8, 1899, p. 59.

57. Chicago Lakeside Directory (n. 43), 1902.

58. *The Architectural Review* 11, (March, 1904), p. 130.

59. *The Economist,* February 1, 1902, p. 149.

60. The house has been demolished. Photographs can be found in the JGR Papers.

61. "Mr. H. S. Robbins' House at Lake Forest, Ill." *Architectural Record* 22 (August, 1906), pp. 130–36. See also records in the possession of the current owner, Mr. James M. Campbell, Jr.

62. Ralph Mooney Root, "Country Place Types in the Middle West." *Architectural Record* 35 (January, 1924), pp. 1–32. See also Architectural Records, Lake Forest (Ill.) Public Library, and photographs in the JGR Papers.

63. "House at Lake Forest," *Architectural Review* 11, (March, 1904), pp. 127–30. The Architectural Records at the Lake Forest (Ill.) Public Library contain photographs and an interview with Mr. Edison Dick, son of the original owner, and his wife about the original state of the house.

64. "Residence of F. H. Page, Highland Park, Illinois," *Architectural Review* 11, (March, 1904), p. 130. The property also housed a gate lodge designed in a similar style by James Gamble Rogers; see also *The Economist,* February 1, 1902, p. 49.

65. "House of Mr. C. Edward Pope, Lake Forest, Ill.," *Architectural Review* 11 (January, 1904), pp. 80–81.

66. *Ibid.* See also photographs in the JGR Papers.

67. "House at Chicago," *Inland Architect* 16 (February, 1907), plates 19, 20; "Residence No. 5325 Lexington Avenue, Chicago, for Mr. Finch," *The Inland Architect and News Record* 45 (March, 1907); *The Economist,* July 18, 1903, p. 96; Jean F. Block, *Hyde Park Houses,* Chicago: University of Chicago Press, 1978, p. 81.

68. The house, on Chicago's Gold Coast, was completely remodeled during the summer and fall of 1905, after Mrs. Blaine had decided to move back into the city (AMB Papers). Besides the houses mentioned here, records remain for houses designed by Rogers in the period between 1899 and 1905: for George Anderson in Lake Forest (*The Economist,* October 14, 1899, p. 461), for H. Hubbard in Lake Forest (*ibid.,* September 12, 1903, p. 353), for F. C. Lett in Evanston (*ibid.,* February 14, 1903, p. 222), for Arthur Pope in Geneva, Ill. (*ibid.,* February 1, 1902, p. 149; this was one of seven houses, including the Dick and Page houses, announced during the spring of 1902 by *The Economist* as being under design in Rogers' office), and for Lucas Broadhead, one of the owners of the Ashland Block and a friend of the Waller family, near Lexington, Ky. (*ibid.,* July 18, 1903, p. 96). In 1903, Rogers also designed a brick home down the street from the Finch House for George Hamlin, but subsequent alterations have made it almost impossible to recognize the original design (*ibid.,* February 14, 1903, p. 222). According to records provided to the author by John V. Farwell IV, Rogers also designed a house for his father in Libertyville, Ill., during this period.

69. Buck, *Thomson-Gamble Family.*

70. Montgomery Schuyler, "The Buildings of Cincinnati." *Architectural Record* 23 (May, 1908), pp. 340–66; p. 365.

71. *Ibid.,* p. 366.

72. Buck, *Thomson-Gamble Family,* p. 53.

73. Laurel Court, undated photo album in the collections of the Cincinnati Historical Society.

74. Harrison, the son of a local banker, was an avid golfer, and it is interesting to note that one of the ties that later bound Rogers to his most important client, Edward S. Harkness, was a shared passion for that game. Records, Cincinnati Historical Society.

75. "House at Cincinnati, Ohio." *The Brickbuilder* 17, (April, 1908), plate 57; *The Economist,* August 12, 1905, p. 251.

76. *The Economist,* May 13, 1905, p. 748. During the next three years, Rogers continued to travel back and forth between Chicago and New York, but most day-to-day correspondence with the clients in Chicago was through John Arthur Rogers or Charles Philips. See AMB Papers, Architectural Archives, Evanston Historical Society.

77. Daybook, accounting ledger of the Herbert D. Hale, Hale & Rogers, and James Gamble Rogers architectural offices in New York, 1905–12, JGR Papers.

78. A. McGehee Harvey and Susan L. Abrams. *"For the Welfare of*

Mankind." The Commonwealth Fund and American Medicine, Baltimore, London: Johns Hopkins University Press, 1986, pp. 9–14.

79. George W. Pierson, *Yale: The University College, 1921–1937*, New Haven: Yale University Press, 1955, pp. 215–16.

80. The most extensive record of the relationship between Harkness and Rogers can be found in the Edward S. Harkness Papers, CFA. Neither Rogers nor Harkness was prone to expressing, let alone committing to paper, their feelings or any thoughts about their personal life, so that the commissions and travel records have to speak for themselves.

81. Harvey and Abrams, *Commonwealth Fund*, p. 13.

82. There is no record of Harkness having ever demanded that Rogers be the architect of any building he designed, though he did on several occasions suggest that Rogers be called upon to design a building that he was making possible.

83. [Montgomery Schuyler], "A Fifth Avenue Mansion," *Architectural Record* 27 (May, 1910), pp. 383–99, 384.

84. *Ibid.*, p. 383.

85. "A Dignified Type of the City House," *The New York Architect* 5 (March, 1911), pp. 31–32. The third floor contains bedrooms, the fourth, servants' quarters.

86. "Fifth Avenue Mansion," p. 384; The house was budgeted at $250,000 but probably cost considerably more. Docket Books, New York Municipal Archives, 1907, Entry #475. The house is currently used as the headquarters of The Commonwealth Fund and is a protected Landmark. It thus remains almost fully as built and in very good condition. See Paul Goldberger, *Harkness House*, New York: The Commonwealth Fund, 1987.

87. "Lewis F. Dunham of Dupont Powder Company Buys C. W. Harkness' Home on Madison Avenue," *The Madison Eagle*, June 15, 1917, p. 1; "Dunham Land is Purchased," *The Madison Eagle*, March 29, 1929, p.1;

"Harkness Residence," photo album, Classics Collection, Avery Library, Columbia University, New York, NY. The house itself has been demolished.

88. Contract dated June 24, 1913, between James Gamble Rogers and William S. Harkness, JGR Papers.

89. The house is referred to as "Weekend" in the Edward S. Harkness Papers, CFA. It was sold in 1944.

90. Photo album, undated and untitled, JGR Papers.

91. The gardens, but not the house, were published as "Garden on the Estate of Edward S. Harkness, Esq., New London, Conn.," in *Architectural Forum* 27 (October, 1917), p. 90.

92. Author's interview with Mrs. Frank Rogers, June 25, 1987.

93. *Ibid.*, author's interview with Mrs. Katherine Rogers Van Sluyck (n. 53); Daybook, JGR Papers.

94. *Yeamans Hall*, Charleston: Yeamans Hall Club, 1961; Robert P. Stockton, "History of Yeamans Hall," unpublished manuscript, Yeamans Hall, S.C., 1984.

95. Contracts for construction of clubhouse facilities and cottages, dated between May 2, 1928, and August 12, 1930. JGR Papers.

96. "Residence for Richard C. Colt," blueprints dated April 4, 1912, Collection of Arthur Geller, Garrison, N.Y.

97. The home is currently being restored to its original condition by the new owner.

98. *Sweden at Park Avenue: Not to Impress, but to Please*, New York: Swedish National Board of Public Building, 1986, p. 2; Daybook, 1910–11, JGR Papers.

99. *Sweden, op. cit.*; Montgomery Schuyler, "New New York Houses— East Side," *Architectural Record* 30 (November, 1911), pp. 451–74.

100. Schuyler, "East Side," 454–55.

101. *Ibid.*, p. 454.

102. *Ibid.*, p. 455.

CHAPTER 2

1. William James, *Pragmatism. A New Name for Some Old Ways of Thinking*,

Cambridge, Mass., London: Harvard University Press, 1978 (1907), p. 83. The first historian to establish the link between Pragmatist philosophy and the integration of science, aesthetic theory, and social thought was Richard Hofstadter in *Social Darwinism in American Thought*, New York: George Braziller, 1959.

2. Robert Venturi, *Complexity and Contradiction in Architecture*, New York: Museum of Modern Art, 1966, pp. 89–103. Venturi is probably the best modern-day apologist for the kind of transitory, hybrid architecture exemplified by the work of James Gamble Rogers.

3. James Gamble Rogers, "The Architecture of the School of Education Building," *The University Record of the University of Chicago* 8 (November, 1903), pp. 183–86.

4. *Ibid.*, p. 183.

5. *Ibid.*, p. 184.

6. *Ibid.*

7. David Van Zanten, "Architectural Composition at the Ecole des Beaux-Arts from Charles Percier to Charles Garner," in Arthur Drexler, ed., *The Architecture of the Ecole des Beaux-Arts*, Cambridge, Mass.: MIT Press, 1977, pp. 111–324; Richard Chafee, "The Teaching of Architecture at the Ecole des Beaux-Arts," *ibid.*, pp. 61–110; Neil Levine, "The Competition for the Grand Prix of 1824," in Robin Middleton, ed., *The Beaux-Arts and Nineteenth-Century French Architecture*, Cambridge, Mass.: MIT Press, 1982, pp. 62–123; David Van Zanten, *Designing Paris. The Architecture of Duban, Labrouste, Duc, and Vaudoyer*, Cambridge, Mass.: MIT Press, 1988; Reyner Banham, "The Academic Tradition and the Concept of Elementary Composition," in Banham, *Theory and Design in the First Machine Age*, London: The Architectural Press, 1960, pp. 14–22; Richard Chafee, "The Ecole des Beaux-Arts (1819–1968): Transmitter of Academic Tradition," *Journal of the Society of Architectural Historians* 33 (October, 1974), p. 238.

8. The clearest discussion of the source of architectural ideas for

Rogers' generation can be found in Robert Prestiano, *The Inland Architect: Chicago's Major Architecture Journal, 1883–1908*, Ann Arbor, Mich.: UMI Research Press, 1985; see also: Theodore Turak, "William LeBaron Jenney: Teacher," *Threshold* 5/6 (1991), pp. 61–81; James Early, *Romanticism and American Architecture*, New York: A. S. Barnes and Co., 1965; Nikolaus Pevsner, *Some Architectural Writers of the Nineteenth Century*, Oxford: Claredon Press, 1972; Louis Sullivan, *The Public Papers*, ed. by Robert Twombly, Chicago: University of Chicago Press, 1988; *Kindergarten Chats and Other Writings*, New York: George Wittenborn, Inc., 1967 (1918); Claude Bragdon, *The New Image*, New York: Alfred A. Knopf, 1928.

9. Rogers, "School of Eduction," p. 186.

10. *The Architectural Theory of Viollet-le-Duc*, ed. by M. F. Hearn, Cambridge, Mass.: MIT Press, 1990. For a discussion of Viollet-le-Duc's powerful influence on young American architects at the end of the nineteenth century, see Donald Hoffmann, "Frank Lloyd Wright and Viollet-le-Duc," *Journal of the Society of Architectural Historians* 28 (October, 1969), pp. 173–83.

11. Jean F. Block, *The Uses of Gothic. Planning and Building the Campus of the University of Chicago, 1892–1932*, Chicago: University of Chicago Press, 1983, p. 13.

12. Thorstein Veblen, *The Higher Learning in America: A Memorandum on the Conduct of a University of Businessmen*, New York: Huebsch & Co., 1918, pp. 175–76. See also Helen L. Horowitz, *Culture and City: Cultural Philanthropy in Chicago from the 1880s to 1917*, Lexington: University Press of Kentucky, 1976.

13. William Rainey Harper, *The Trend in Higher Education*, Chicago: University of Chicago Press, 1905, pp. 23–24.

14. John Dewey, *Intelligence in the Modern World. John Dewey's Philosophy*, ed. by Joseph Ratner, New York: Modern Library, 1939; Robert B. Westbrook, *John Dewey and American Democracy*, Ithaca: Cornell University Press, 1991. For overviews of progressive education, see: Lawrence Arthur Cremin, *American Education—The Metropolitan Experience*, New York: Harper & Row, 1988; *The Transformation of the School: Progressivism in American Education, 1876–1957*, New York: Vintage Books, 1964. For its connection to a wider political movement, see: Frederick Rudolph, *The American College and University. A History*, New York: Vintage Books, 1965, p. 468ff.; Richard Hofstadter, *The Age of Reform from Bryan to F.D.R.*, London: Jonathan Cape, 1962, p. 154.

15. John Russell Pope, *The Architecture of John Russell Pope*, ed. by Charles Herbert Moore, New York: William Helburn, 1930.

16. For the theoretical underpinnings of this architecture, see: Richard W. Longstreth, "Academic Eclecticism in American Architecture," *Winterthur Portfolio* 17 (Spring, 1984), pp. 55–82; Henry Van Brunt, *Architecture and Society. Selected Essays of Henry Van Brunt*, ed. by William A. Coles, Cambridge, Mass.: Harvard University Press, 1969, esp. pp. 289–304, 305–10, 319–22.

17. The revival of the colonial past started in the centennial year of 1876 and was strengthened by both the massive rise in immigration and the push west at the end of the decade, both of which to many artists necessitated a definition of what it meant to be American. The Shingle Style, as Vincent Scully has pointed out, was the first concrete sign of this movement. It was tied in, at least at its inception, with the Arts and Crafts movement and thus had a certain primitivism. After the turn of the century, a marked change in direction took place: architects turned more toward "high style" and Georgian, as opposed to Queen Anne, models. At this point, the Colonial Revival became more allied with the teachings of Academic Classicism. The high point of this development can be said to have been reached with the wholesale reinvention of Williamsburg as a *locus classicus* of American architecture and urbanism in the 1930s. See: Richard Guy Wilson, "The Great Civilization," in *The American Renaissance 1876–1917*, New York: Brooklyn Museum, 1979, pp. 11–73; Vincent Scully, *The Shingle Style Today, Or, The Historian's Revenge*, New York: George Braziller, 1974; Alan Gowans, *Images of American Living. Four Centuries of Architecture and Furniture as Cultural Expression*, New York: Harper & Row, 1976 (1964), pp. 287–366.

18. The first evidence of this decision, although it is taken for granted in all Corporation Board Minutes and Corporation Committee on the Architectural Plan Minutes of Yale University after 1911, is a letter from John V. Farwell, then a new member of the corporation, to Anson Phelps Stokes, secretary of the university, dated November 9, 1911, in which Farwell says that he is "delighted that Yale is adopting the Collegiate Gothic," APS Papers.

19. For the best discussion of the influence of John Ruskin on American culture, see Roger Stein, *John Ruskin and Aesthetic Thought in America, 1840–1900*, Cambridge, Mass.: Harvard University Press, 1967. John Tomsich, among others, has noted that America had its own medievalist tradition dating back at least to the 1830s, which in many ways was more reactionary than that espoused by Ruskin and his followers. John Tomsich, *A Genteel Tradition. American Culture and Politics in the Gilded Age*, Stanford: Stanford University Press, 1971, p. 51ff.

20. *Buildings and Grounds of Yale University*, New Haven: Yale University, 1979.

21. Montgomery Schuyler, "Architecture of American Colleges. II. Yale," *Architectural Record* 26 (November, 1909), pp. 393–416; p. 403.

22. *Ibid.*, p. 416.

23. Paul Venable Turner, *Campus. An American Planning Tradition*, Cambridge, Mass., New York: MIT Press and Architectural History Foundation, 1984, p. 226ff.

24. Montgomery Schuyler, "The Architecture of the American Colleges," *Architectural Record* 26 (October, 1909), pp. 243–69; 26 (December, 1909), pp. 393–416; 27 (February, 1910), pp. 128–60; 27 (June, 1910), pp. 442–69; 28 (September, 1910), pp. 182–211; 28 (December, 1910), pp. 424–42; 29 (February, 1911), pp. 144–66; 30 (July, 1911), pp. 57–84; 30 (December, 1911), pp. 549–73; 31 (May, 1912), pp. 512–37.

25. Montgomery Schuyler, "Architecture of American Colleges. III. Princeton," *Architectural Record* 27 (February, 1910), pp. 129–60.

26. *Ibid.*, p. 156.

27. Ralph Adams Cram, "Princeton Architecture," *The American Architect*, 96 (July 21, 1909), pp. 21–30.

28. Cram's most notable call to arms was contained in "The Promise and the Fulfillment of Gothic Architecture," published in Ralph Adams Cram, Thomas Hastings, and Claude Bragdon, *Six Lectures on Architecture*, Chicago: Art Institute of Chicago Press, 1917, pp. 3–63.

29. Charles Herbert Moore, *Development and Character of Gothic Architecture*, London: Macmillan, 1890.

30. Paul Frankl, *The Gothic. Literary Sources and Interpretations through Eight Centuries*, Princeton: Princeton University Press, 1963.

31. Moore, *Gothic Architecture*, pp. 22–25. Moore cites Viollet-le-Duc in arguing that the Gothic is essentially a constructional method, but then follows Ruskin in pointing out that a "conventionalizing" sculpture that is an "organic" representation of nature is added on to this skeleton (p. 30). Like Bragdon, he argues that Gothic architecture comes not only out of the logic of construction and the material used, but also out of the desire of the community as a whole. He contrasts such an organic architecture with the imposed forms of Classicism (p. 2ff).

32. Claude Bragdon, "Organic Architecture," in Cram et al., *Six Lectures on Architecture*, pp. 123–44; p. 127; John Dewey, *Art as Experience*, New York: Perigee Books, 1980 (1934).

33. James Gamble Rogers, undated, unidentified notecards, JGR Papers.

34. James Gamble Rogers, "Scrapbook Containing Postcards Collected and Used as Sources or Inspiration for Designs for Yale Buildings," undated, JGR Papers. This method of collecting is, of course, hardly unique. It reaches back to the antiquarian collections architects used in the eighteenth century, and is still in use today in architectural offices. Usually, however, such collections are more *ad hoc* and less specific. This author has not heard of other instances of architects working in the Neo-Gothic or any other revivalist mode by assembling such a type-based catalogue of images.

35. James Gamble Rogers to Samuel Fisher, March 16, 1917, JGR Papers.

36. James Gamble Rogers to Anson Phelps Stokes, October 23, 1919, APS Papers.

37. John H. Wigmore to James Gamble Rogers, July 29, 1925, NUA.

38. See: T. J. Jackson Lears, *No Place of Grace. Antimodernism and the Transformation of American Culture, 1880–1920*, New York: Pantheon Books, 1981; Joel H. Spring, *Education and the Rise of the Corporate State*, Boston: Beacon Press, 1972; E. Digby Baltzell, *The Protestant Establishment. Aristocracy and Caste in America*, New York: Random House, 1964, p. 210ff.

39. James Gamble Rogers to William A. Dyche, October 9, 1930. Minutes of the Board of Trustees, October 28, 1930, NUA.

40. *Ibid.*

41. James Gamble Rogers, Inc., "Deering Memorial Library, Northwestern University. View in Stairwell" (2 variants), undated drawings, Northwestern University Architect's Office Archives, Northwestern University, Evanston, Ill. These drawings may no longer be located in the University Architect's office.

42. James Gamble Rogers, "Notes by the Architect." *The Yale University Library Gazette* 3 (July, 1928), pp. 3–7.

43. Herbert Putnam, "Speech at the Dedication of Sterling Memorial Library," April 11, 1931. Transcript in the JRA Papers.

44. William Harlan Hale, "Art Vs. Yale University," *The Harkness Hoot*, 1, November 15, 1930, pp. 17–32.

45. *Ibid.*, p. 21.

46. *Ibid.*

47. *Ibid.*, pp. 29–30.

48. "Various Artists Vs. Yale University," *The Harkness Hoot*, January 1, 1931, pp. 42–46. Letters of support from Henry-Russell Hitchcock, Lewis Mumford, and even Hugh Ferriss were reprinted. Only Cram, despite his earlier disagreement with Rogers over the design of the Harkness Quadrangle, spoke in his defense.

49. For a somewhat dated but still comprehensive summation of the attribution of what was during this period understood as "the colonial style," see: Hugh Morrison, *Early American Architecture from the First Colonial Settlements to the National Period*, New York: Oxford University Press, 1952, p. 301ff.

50. E. Y. Mullins, *The Seminary Emergency*, Louisville: Southern Baptist Theological Seminary, 1924, p. 7.

51. S. S. Drury, "The Annual Report of the Rector to the Corporation of the School—1933," Archives, St. Paul's School, Sheldon Library, Concord, N.H., p. 9.

52. "The New Schoolhouse," *St. Paul's School Alumni Horae* 16, (July, 1936), pp. 66–67.

53. James Gamble Rogers, Inc., "Memorandum for Comparison Purposes of Analysis of Difference Between the Type of Dormitories Designed for St. Paul's School in Tutor [*sic*] Gothic Architecture and the Type of Exeter Dormitory #6 Designed in Scholastic Georgian Style of Architecture," undated typescript, CFA.

54. Rogers drew up both a Georgian and a Gothic scheme for the building. James Gamble Rogers to John Goetchius, St. Paul's School Corporation, April 4, 1935, JGR Papers; Malcolm P. Aldrich, "Memorandum," report of conference between S. S. Drury and Malcolm

Aldrich, May 28, 1935, CFA.

55. James Gamble Rogers to President E. Y. Mullins, April 18, 1924, Archives, Southern Baptist Theological Seminary, Louisville, Ky. Rogers sent similar letters to each of his clients during the spring of 1924.

56. [George S. Chappell], "Editorial Statement," *The Architect* 1 (October, 1923), p. 1. A Holland Forbes was listed as Editor, J. Gamble Rogers as Chairman of the Board, and Charles Platt, Alfred Granger, George Chappell, and Kenneth Murchison as Associates.

57. [George S. Chappell], "Editorial Comment," *The Architect* 1 (November, 1923), p. 103.

58. George S. Chappell, "Salesmanship and Architecture," *The Architect* 2 (July, 1924), pp. 205–9.

59. Lewis Mumford reached his widest public through his columns in *The New Yorker* from 1932 onward, while Cowley wrote in *The New Republic* (though Mumford also wrote for this magazine; see Elmer S. Newman, *Lewis Mumford. A Bibliography*, New York: Harcourt Brace Jovanovich, 1971, p. 10ff.; Malcolm Cowley, *Think Back on Us. A Contemporary Chronicle of the 1930s by Malcolm Cowley*, ed. by Henry Dan Piper, Carbondale, Ill.: Southern Illinois University Press, 1967.

60. "Preliminary Studies—Northwestern Downtown Campus," *The Architect* 1 (October, 1923), plate facing p.1; "The New Home of the Aetna Life Insurance Co., Hartford, Conn.," *The Architect* 2 (April, 1924), pp. 29–30; Walter McQuade, "Our Feature Film," *The Architect* 10 (July, 1928), p. 441; C. Charles Burlingame, "The Medical Center in New York," *ibid.*, pp. 442–43; George Nichols, "The Development of the Medical Center," *ibid.*, pp. 447–551.

61. George S. Chappell, "To Our Public," *The Architect* 1 (November, 1923), p. 435.

62. George S. Chappell, "A Sermon from the Sanctum," *The Architect* 4 (April, 1925), p. 39.

63. George S. Chappell, "The Selection of our Illustrations," *The*

Architect 2 (September, 1924), p. 493.

64. George S. Chappell, "The Modern Note," *The Architect* 3 (December, 1924), p. 274.

65. George S. Chappell, "A Sermon from the Sanctum," *The Architect* 4 (May, 1925), p. 124.

CHAPTER 3

1. "For the Blaine School," *The Economist*, August 5, 1899, p. 162.

2. Gilbert A. Harrison, *A Timeless Affair. The Life of Anita McCormick Blaine*, Chicago, London: University of Chicago Press, 1979.

3. Ida Cassa Heffron, *Francis Wayland Parker. An Interpretive Biography*, Los Angeles: Ivan Deach, Jr., Publisher, 1934, p. 50.

4. Various "at home" cards and notes that appear to date back to 1898 indicate that Rogers and Mrs. Emmons Blaine had regular social contact either right after or right before Rogers received the commission. AMB Papers.

5. James Gamble Rogers to Anita McCormick Blaine, July 12, 1899. AMB Papers.

6. Mrs. Blaine's fellow trustees were her brother, Stanley McCormick, and Owen Aldis. The latter continuously and vigorously opposed her lavish spending plans for various aspects of her educational pursuits. It was Owen Aldis who, as an agent for the Brooks brothers of Boston, is often credited with having helped give shape to the Chicago School by his early insistence on forthright, undecorated architecture. By the time he was a trustee for the McCormick Estate, he was one of the largest real estate managers in Chicago.

7. *Chicago Institute Academic and Pedagogic. Preliminary Announcement*, Chicago, 1900.

8. Especially relevant are the schools Dwight Perkins designed for the Chicago School Board in the first decade of the twentieth century, such as the Carl Schurz High School, 1908, or the Grover Cleveland Public School, 1909.

9. James Gamble Rogers to Anita McCormick Blaine, May 15 and June

10, 1900. AMB.

10. James Gamble Rogers to Anita McCormick Blaine, June 6 and June 11, 1900. AMB Papers.

11. James Gamble Rogers to Anita McCormick Blaine, August 7, 1900. AMB Papers.

12. Jean F. Block, *The Uses of Gothic. Planning and Building the Campus of the University of Chicago, 1892–1932*, Chicago, London: University of Chicago Press, 1983, pp. 81–83.

13. Harrison, *Anita McCormick Blaine*, p. 87.

14. John Dewey, *Intelligence in the Modern World. John Dewey's Philosophy*, ed. by Joseph Ratner, New York: Modern Library, 1939. For overviews of progressive education, see: Lawrence Arthur Cremin, *American Education—The Metropolitan Experience*, New York: Harper & Row, 1988; idem, *The Transformation of the School: Progressivism in American Education, 1876–1957*, New York: Vintage Books, 1964. For its connection to a wider political movement, see Frederick Rudolph, *The American College and University. A History*, New York: Vintage Books, 1965, p. 468ff.; Richard Hofstadter, *The Age of Reform from Bryan to F.D.R.*, London: Jonathan Cape, 1962, p. 154.

15. Robert B. Westbrook, *John Dewey and American Democracy*, Ithaca: Cornell University Press, 1991, pp. 111–13.

16. James Gamble Rogers, "The Architecture of the School of Education Building," *The University Record of the University of Chicago* 8 (November, 1903), pp.13, 183–86.

17. Records in Papers of President William Rainey Harper, Archives, University of Chicago, Chicago, Ill.

18. Rogers, "School of Education," p. 185.

19. Rogers himself admitted that he had had to adopt his original scheme of completely separate buildings because of the necessity for weather-protected circulation. Rogers, *ibid.*, p. 185.

20. James Gamble Rogers to Anita McCormick Blaine, April 9,

May 7, and May 20, 1901, AMB Papers.

21. "Announcement," dated June 1, 1901, AMB Papers.

22. Photographs, Francis Parker School (original building), Photograph Collection, Chicago Historical Society.

23. Architectural Records, Lake Forest (Ill.) Public Library.

24. The grandest of these buildings was a seven-story apartment building at the corner of Scott and State streets, built by J. B. Waller for $150,000 (*The Economist*, February 14, 1903, p. 206). A small building on Prairie Avenue was apparently a rare combination of offices and apartments (*The Economist*, October 21, 1905, p. 633), while the large $150,000 structure on the corner of Sheridan Road and Buena Street was an apartment block (*The Economist*, May 27, 1905, p. 819).

25. C. W. Westfall, *Lake Forest Historic Building Survey*, Lake Forest, 1981; *The Economist*, June 10, 1905, p. 893; August 5, 1905, p. 216. It appears that Anderson originally intended to erect a stone-clad bank building on this site.

26. Carl Condit, "The First Reinforced-Concrete Skyscraper. The Ingalls Building in Cincinnati and Its Place in Structural History," *Technology and Culture* 9 (January, 1968), pp. 1–33; p. 32; Frank A. Randall, *History of the Development of Building Construction in Chicago*, Urbana, Ill.: University of Illinois Press, 1949, pp. 17, 222–23; Photograph Collection, Chicago Historical Society.

27. *The Economist*, October 12, 1901, p. 434; *The Hyde Park Baptist Record*, October, 1901, frontispiece; Thomas W. Goodspeed, *A History of the Hyde Park Baptist Church 1874–1924*, Chicago: Hyde Park Baptist Church, 1924. It appears that the corner entrance was to have been topped by a spire when funds became available; instead, the money was spent on the addition of a chapter house to the rear of the church. Records of the Hyde Park Baptist Church, Chicago, Ill.

28. *The Economist*, June 18, 1904, p. 862.

29. *The McCormick Works*, Chicago, 1909; Robert Ozanne, *A Century of Labor-Management Relations at McCormick and International Harvester*, Madison, Milwaukee, London: University of Wisconsin Press, 1967, pp. 164–65.

30. *The Inland Architect* 46 (August, 1905), pp.19–20; Archives of the Navistar Corporation, Chicago, Illinois.

31. Under the names of "Rogers and Philips" and "Rogers, Philips and Woodyatt," the firm in which John Arthur Rogers was principal designed a number of houses in Evanston and Winnetka, as well as the Evanston Public Library. The firm continued to work on some of James Gamble Rogers' projects, including the Blaine remodeling, the Francis Parker School, and several of the houses. John Arthur Rogers moved to Winter Park, Florida, in 1913 for health reasons, and established a flourishing practice there. See: *Lakeside Directory of Names. Chicago: 1905–1913*; Family Records, Chicago Historical Society; Architectural Archives, Evanston Historical Society, Evanston, Ill.; AMB Papers; *The Economist*, October 28, 1904, p. 575; April 29, 1905, p. 674; May 6, 1905, p. 711; November 4, 1905, p. 712; November 25, 1905, p. 825; December 8, 1905, p. 895. During 1906, Rogers was listed in both the Chicago and New York telephone directories; by 1907 he was listed only in New York.

32. Author's interview with Mrs. Katherine Rogers Van Sluyck, August 18, 1987.

33. "Herbert D. Hale," *A.I.A. Quarterly Bulletin* 19 (October, 1908), pp. 286–87; "South Boston High School," *American Architect & Building News*, February 21, 1903; "Winchester, Mass. High School," *American Architect & Building News*, July 8, 1904.

34. The profits made from the design of these schools were deposited in a trust set up for Herbert Hale's widow, and these deposits were a clear drain on the finances of the office. According to Mrs. Van Sluyck (n. 32),

this was the main reason Rogers later regretted the partnership that had brought him to New York. Daybook, accounting ledger of the Herbert D. Hale, Hale & Rogers, and James Gamble Rogers architectural offices, 1905–13, JGR Papers.

35. "The Engineering Building, West 39th Street, New York," *Architectural Review* 13 (January, 1905), plates 2–5; "The New Engineering Societies' Building," *Architectural Record* 21 (April,1907), pp. 301–7.

36. "The McCreery Building. A Feat in Rapid Construction," *Architects' and Builders' Magazine* 29 (January, 1907), pp. 150–62; p. 157.

37. Daybook, *op. cit.*

38. *Ibid.*; Adin Benedict Lacey, ed., *American Competitions Published by the T-Square Club*, Philadelphia: T-Square Club, 1907, plate 24.

39. *Ibid.*, plates 37–39.

40. Henry F. Whitney and Elsie Nashburn Whitney, *Biographical Dictionary of American Architects (Deceased)*, Los Angeles: Hennesey & Ingalls, 1970, p. 256.

41. William H. Wilson, *The City Beautiful Movement*, Baltimore: Johns Hopkins University Press, 1989; Manfredo Manieri-Elia, "Toward an 'Imperial City': Daniel H. Burnham and the City Beautiful Movement," in Giorgio Ciucci et al., *The American City From the Civil War to the New Deal*, trans. by Barbara Luigia La Penta, London: Granada Publishing, 1980, pp. 1–142; Thomas Hines, "The City Beautiful Movement in American Urban Planning, 1890–1920," *RIBA Transactions* no. 7 (1985), pp. 19–42; Francesco Dal Co, "From Parks to the Region: Progressive Ideology and the Reform of the American City," in Ciucci et al., *American City*, pp. 143–292; John W. Reps, *The Making of Urban America*, Princeton: Princeton University Press, 1965.

42. Henry Adams, *The Education of Henry Adams. An Autobiography*, Boston: Houghton Mifflin Co., 1961 (1918), esp. pp. 331–45.

43. Sarah Bradford Landau, "Coming to Terms: Architecture Com-

petitions in America and the Emerging Profession, 1789–1922," in Helene Lipstadt, ed., *The Experimental Tradition. Essays on Competitions in Architecture,* New York: Architectural League of New York, Princeton Architectural Press, 1989, pp. 53–78.

44. *Ibid.,* p. 65.; Lois Craig et al., *The Federal Presence: Architecture, Politics, and Symbols in United States Government Buildings,* Cambridge, Mass.: MIT Press, 1978, pp. 239–42. How these private buildings absorbed public imagery is traced in Kenneth Turney Gibbs, "Business Architectural Imagery: The Impact of Economic and Social Changes on Tall Office Buildings, 1870–1930," Ph.D. diss., Cornell University, 1976.

45. Richard Guy Wilson, ed., *Public Buildings. Architecture under the Public Works Administration, 1933–1939,* New York: Da Capo Press, 1986 (1939).

46. N. C. Perkins et al., *The New Courthouse, Shelby County Tennessee. Report of the Commission,* Memphis, Tenn., 1910. Reprinted as *The Courthouse Shelby County Tennessee 1909–1984. A Commemorative,* with an introduction by James E. Roper. Memphis, Tenn., 1984.

47. Paul R. Coppock, "A Fine House of Courts," *Memphis Commercial Appeal,* May 5, 1975, Memphis Public Library Special Collections.

48. Perkins, *New Courthouse* (1984), p. 35. The selection of an architect for a major civic building without a competition was unusual for this period, and the commissioners went to great lengths to justify their choice. See James B. Cook, "The Courthouse Architect," *Memphis Commercial Appeal,* August 24, 1905, p. 6.

49. Perkins, *New Courthouse* (1984), pp. 15–17.

50. *Ibid.,* p. 6.

51. Russell F. Whitehead, "The Old and The New South," *Architectural Record* 30 (July, 1911), pp. 1–56; p. 20.

52. *Ibid.,* p. 20.

53. *Ibid.*

54. "New Orleans' Splendid New Post Office Building Structure Is Now Complete and Awaits Occupancy," *New Orleans Times-Picayune,* February

14, 1915.

55. *Ibid.,* p. 13.

56. *Ibid.,* p. 14.

57. *Ibid.* See also "Post Office, New Orleans, La.," *Architecture and Building* 47 (April, 1915), pp. 131–36.

58. Rollin G. Osterweis, *Three Centuries of New Haven, 1638–1938,* New Haven, London: Yale University Press, 1953, pp. 390–92.

59. George Nichols, "The New Haven Post Office and Court House," *Architectural Record* 31 (September, 1919), pp. 85–90; p. 85.

60. *Ibid.,* p. 86.

61. It is interesting to note that Seymour and the other civic leaders were intent on having a building in New Haven that would be grand and would "in its architecture and construction represent the power, the dignity and the authority of the Federal government." *The New Haven Post-Office Problem.* New Haven: Federated Council of One Hundred, 1910, Archives, New Haven (Conn.) Public Library.

62. *American Competitions, Volume Three 1913,* New York: William Helburn, 1913, plates 37–38, 94–97.

63. *Memphis Commercial Appeal,* November 5, 1966, and March 12, 1910, Memphis Public Library Special Collections. The building is illustrated, but pointedly not discussed, in Whitehead's survey of new Southern architecture: Whitehead, "Old and New South," p. 34.

64. Douglas K. S. Hyland, "History of the Collection of the Memphis Brooks Museum of Art," in Sally Parker Thompson, ed., *Painting and Sculpture Collections—Memphis Brooks Museum of Art,* Memphis, Tenn.: Memphis Brooks Museum of Art, 1984, pp. 11–18; "An Abbreviated Chronicle of Events and Activities of Brooks Memorial Art Gallery (1916–1976)," Vertical File, Memphis Brooks Memorial Art Gallery, Memphis, Tenn.

65. "Brooks Memorial Art Gallery," *Through the Ages,* 1926, pp. 32–35, Vertical File, Memphis Brooks Memorial Art Gallery, Memphis, Tenn.

66. The building was not fin-

ished until 1916 and was immediately too small for the collections. Later additions have severely marred the back, and the interiors can be clearly understood only by viewing an extensive series of photographs available in the Special Collections, Memphis (Tenn.) Public Library.

67. "With Camera and Notebook." *Bridgeport Post,* September 17, 1928, Local Historical Collection, Bridgeport (Conn.) Public Library.

68. *Ibid.;* there appear to have been several more engaging public interiors in the school before it was gutted during its renovation into City Hall.

69. Christopher Gray, "79 Neighborhood/New York's Most Elegant Sidestreet," *Avenue* 6 (April, 1982).

70. *Ibid.*

71. David Mannes, *Music Is My Faith. An Autobiography of David Mannes,* New York: Mannes College of Music, 1949, p. 255.

72. Archives of the Madison Avenue Presbyterian Church, New York, N.Y.

73. Marrion Wilcox, "The Yale Club's New House," *Architectural Record* 38 (September, 1915), pp. 310–42, 312. See also "Club House Buildings," *Architecture and Building* 47 (December, 1915), pp. 425–55.

74. "The New York Yale Club Clubhouse," *Yale Alumni Weekly,* November 2, 1912, pp. 151–52; Docket Books, New York Municipal Archives, 1913, #342.

75. Wilcox, "Yale Club," p. 315.

76. Franklin D. W. Glazier, "The New Yale Club," *Yale Alumni Weekly,* October 29, 1915, pp.165–79; p. 168.

77. Wilcox, "Yale Club," p. 312.

78. *Ibid.,* p. 311.

79. Report of the Building Committee, November 25, 1918, Archives, Connecticut General Life Insurance Company, Bloomfield, Conn.

80. Huntington was the youngest president ever elected to head an American insurance company and presided over an explosive growth of the company. Charles Hitchcock Sherrill, *Yale Class Book,* New

Haven, 1889; *Yale Class of 1889 Quindecennial.* New York, 1904.

81. James Gamble Rogers to Robert Huntington, November 29, 1918 (recto and verso), JGR Papers.

82. Undated sketch; photograph in JGR Papers.

83. Peter Grant, "The Palace on the Park," *Hartford Architectural Conservancy News,* Autumn, 1977, p. 5.

84. *Ibid.; Growth,* November 1, 1924; Archives, Connecticut General Life Insurance Company, Bloomfield, Conn.

85. Bruce Clouette and Michael Kerski, "Historic Preservation Nomination—Elm Street Historic District," *National Register of Historic Places Inventory,* June 28, 1984, p. 2, Item 8.

86. *Ibid.*

87. Grant, "Palace," p. 5.

88. "Connecticut General Moves This Week to Beautiful New Home Overlooking Bushnell Park, Modeled after Palace in Florence," *Hartford Times,* June 17, 1926, p. 13.

89. *Ibid.;* undated photographs, Archives, Connecticut General Life Insurance Company, Bloomfield, Conn.

90. Morgan B. Brainard to James Gamble Rogers, October 19, 1923, JGR Papers.

91. *Ibid.*

92. "The New Home of the Aetna Life Insurance Co., Hartford, Conn.," *The Architect* 2 (April, 1924), pp. 29, 31, plates.

93. James Gamble Rogers, "A Home of Beauty, Utility and Charm," *Hartford Times,* November 10, 1923, p. 4.

94. James Gamble Rogers, "The Loomis Institute, Windsor, Connecticut," *American Competitions* 3 (1913), plates 94–97.

95. Rogers, "Home of Beauty."

96. Gibbs, "Business Architectural Imagery" (n. 44), p. 204. An informal survey of insurance company buildings indicates that they are all either Colonial or Modernist in style.

97. Estimates dated April 28, 1928, and November 1, 1929; contract dated July 30, 1928; authorization for design dated January 19, 1929, JGR Papers.

98. Archives of the Aetna Life Insurance Company, Hartford, Conn.

99. *The Aetna Life Home Office Building, Through the Ages,* vol. 9, no. 1, May 1931, pp. 3–8; p. 5.

100. Contract between Heleman-Harris Co. and James Gamble Rogers, Inc., August 22, 1924, JGR Papers.

101. Marrion Wilcox, "The Crane Company Exhibit Building, Atlantic City, New Jersey," *Architectural Record* 59 (February, 1926), pp. 101–9; p. 102.

102. *Ibid.*

103. *Ibid.,* p. 109.

CHAPTER 4

1. "The Life of Mr. Harkness," *Yale Alumni Weekly,* October 12, 1917, pp. 85–86.

2. Edward S. Harkness to George Parmly Day, Treasurer of Yale University, December 22, 1916, CFA.

3. Edward S. Harkness to George Parmly Day, January 30, 1917, CFA.

4. Brooks Mather Kelsey, *Yale. A History,* New Haven, London: Yale University Press, 1974.

5. By the beginning of the First World War, only Osborn Hall and the Battell Chapel remained on the east side of the campus as open buildings not housing dormitories. Osborn was replaced by the Collegiate Gothic Bingham Hall in 1928.

6. Minutes of the Corporation Committee on the Architectural Plan, June 16, 1913, CCAP Papers.

7. Edward S. Harkness to James Gamble Rogers, February 6, 1917, JGR Papers.

8. *Ibid.* The letter outlines a 6 percent fee for a building costing $1.8 million; Harkness appears to have reviewed all sketches before they were presented to the Yale Corporation. James Gamble Rogers to Edward S. Harkness, March 16, 1917, June 12, 1918, May 16, 1919, among others, JGR Papers.

9. Paul Venable Turner, *Campus: An American Planning Tradition,* Cambridge, Mass., and New York: MIT Press and Architectural History Foun-

dation, 1984, pp. 215–47. Ralph Adams Cram, "The Work of Messrs. Cope and Stewardson," *Architectural Record* 16 (November, 1904), pp. 407–38; Charles W. Dibble, "Architecture, Education and Atmosphere: The Early Years of Princeton University, 1896–1916," thesis, Princeton University, 1974; Montgomery Schuyler, "The Architecture of American Colleges," *Architectural Record* 26 (February, 1910), pp. 126–60; 28, pp. 182–211.

10. In addition to a hospital in Changsha for the "Yale-in-China" program (see Chapter 7), Rogers designed an elegant barn for the Yale crew team just up the river from his and Harkness's homes in New London, Connecticut. See: "The New Boathouse," *Yale Alumni Weekly,* February 2, 1915, p. 543; "Yale Boat House," Yale University Architectural Drawings Collection, Sterling Memorial Library, New Haven, Conn.; "Yale Boat House," specifications dated September 17, 1914, JGR Papers. For an unbuilt theater design by Rogers, see "Yale Theatre New Haven," Yale University Architectural Drawings Collection.

11. James Gamble Rogers to Samuel Fisher, Office of Edward S. Harkness, June 12, 1918, JGR Papers. Rogers actually recommended using Adolph Bernard, who had worked with him for a number of years, as superintendent, and only turned to Nichols the following year.

12. Henry F. Whitney and Elsie Nashburn Whitney, *Biographical Dictionary of American Architects (Deceased),* Los Angeles: Hennesey & Ingalls, 1970, p. 203. *Yale School of Fine Arts Catalogue, 1922–1923;* New Haven: Yale University School of Fine Arts, 1922. William Bottomsley, writing in 1922, claimed that Faelten made sketches of many details of the complex, which were then used to adapt the design. William Lawrence Bottomsley, "The Memorial Quadrangle," *Yale Alumni Weekly,* March 31, 1922, pp. 729–30. Wesley Needham, a draftsman in Rogers' office in the late 1920s, gives Faelten much of the credit in his unpublished manu-

script "The Gothic Architecture of James Gamble Rogers at Yale," Manuscripts and Archives Collections, Sterling Memorial Library, New Haven, Conn.

13. For the relative roles of architects and the designers they employed during this period, see Andrew Saint, *The Image of the Architect*, New Haven: Yale University Press, 1983, pp.1–18.

14. Whitney and Whitney, *American Architects*, pp. 514–15.

15. "Monograph on Architectural Renderers. III. The Work of E. Donald Robb," *The Brickbuilder* 23 (March, 1914), pp. 55–57.

16. Of special interest is Goodhue's imaginary project of 1896, "Traumberg." See Richard Oliver, *Bertram Grosvenor Goodhue*, Cambridge, Mass., and New York: MIT Press and Architectural History Foundation, 1983, pp. 31–35.

17. William H. Goodyear, "The Memorial Quadrangle and the Harkness Memorial Tower at Yale," *The American Architect*, October 26, 1921, pp.298–314; p. 309.

18. The most useful survey of American colleges and universities built during this period is Turner, *Campus*. For a primary, though early source, Montgomery Schuyler's series on "The Architecture of American Colleges," alluded to in Chapter 2, is most useful (*Architectural Record*, December 1909–May 1912).

19. Turner, *Campus*, pp. 227–34.

20. George Nichols, "The Memorial Quadrangle of Yale University and the Harkness Memorial Quadrangle," *Architecture*, October, 1921, pp. 293–96, 299–307; p. 299.

21. James Gamble Rogers to Anson Phelps Stokes, September 18, 1917, APS Papers.

22. Nichols, "Memorial Quadrangle," p. 302.

23. Marrion Wilcox, "The Harkness Memorial Quadrangle at Yale," *Architectural Record*, September, 1921, pp. 163–82; p. 164.

24. James Gamble Rogers, undated, unidentified notecards, JGR Papers.

25. James Gamble Rogers, "The

Harkness Memorial Quadrangle, Yale University. The Architectural Plan," *Architecture* 44 (October, 1921), pp. 287–92; p. 290.

26. Drawings in Yale Architectural Drawings Collections, Sterling Memorial Library, New Haven, Conn.

27. "General Specifications—Glass and Glazing—Harkness Memorial Quadrangle, August 6, 1919," JGR Papers.

28. Rogers, "Harkness Memorial Quadrangle," p. 291.

29. James Gamble Rogers to Samuel Fisher, March 16, 1917, JGR Papers.

30. Donn Barber, "Beauty in University Architecture," *Yale Alumni Weekly*, March 31, 1922, pp. 736–40.

31. *Architectural Record* 50 (September, 1921). Aside from the full issues of *Architectural Record* and articles in *Architectural Forum*, *The American Architect*, and *Architecture*, there were numerous mentions of the building in later professional publications.

32. The citation read: "Student at the Beaux-Arts, architect of the Harkness Tower and Memorial Quadrangle; a lover and creator of beauty, whose dreams come true. He is an artist who is never satisfied, never content with rivaling past efforts when it is possible to surpass them; who admires the best buildings in America and then builds better ones. He has given to Yale and to New Haven structures which unite sublimity and intimacy, majesty and charm. It is needless to talk about him; his towers and walls speak more eloquently than words." *Yale Alumni Weekly*, July 8, 1921, p. 1099.

33. "Extract from the Minutes of the Yale Corporation, November 15, 1920," CCAP.

34. "The Sterling Bequest," *Yale Alumni Weekly*, August 23, 1918, pp. 8–10.

35. Kelsey, *Yale*, p. 373; John A. Carver, Speech at the Dedication of Sterling Memorial Library, April 11, 1931, transcript in JRA Papers.

36. George W. Pierson notes that by the time Angell succeeded Hadley as president in 1921, the selec-

tion committee was "dominated by financiers and industrialists." George W. Pierson, *Yale: The University College, 1921–1937*, New Haven: Yale University Press, 1955, p. 6. Farwell headed the search committee, which rejected such favorites of the more traditional-minded members of the Yale community as Secretary Anson Phelps Stokes in favor of the first non-Yale graduate. Angell was a pupil of John Dewey's who had taught at the University of Chicago for two decades, but there is no direct evidence that he knew either the powerful Chicago financier John Farwell or James Gamble Rogers during the time when Rogers was building the School of Education there for Dewey. Hadley confirmed the reasons for hiring Angell by telling *The Yale Alumni Weekly* that the corporation was looking for a man who knew how to run institutions and had found "a Western man thoroughly familiar with Eastern ideals." One could apply this description to Farwell and Rogers as well. *Yale Alumni Weekly*, February 25, 1921, p. 343.

37. See Chapter 1; Conversation with Katherine Van Sluyck, August 18, 1987.

38. John Farwell to Anson Phelps Stokes, October 3, 1911, APS Papers.

39. John Farwell to Anson Phelps Stokes, November 9, 1911, APS Papers.

40. John Farwell to Anson Phelps Stokes, November 8, 1912, APS Papers.

41. "Report of the Committee on the Supervising Architect," June 6, 1913, APS Papers.

42. John Russell Pope, *University Architecture. Yale University. General Plan for Its Future Building*, New York: William Helburn, Inc., 1919. The corporation originally took the Plan under advisement, and then appointed a team of three architects to review the drawings and proposals. The three were Yale graduate William Adams Delano, classicist Paul Cret, and Bertram Goodhue (see John Farwell to Anson Phelps Stokes, October 29, 1919, APS Papers). These three issued

a report that supported the Pope plan, though they disagreed on "the degree to which this 'Gothicization' should be carried"; they also felt that "as a large part of the charm of this style of architecture is due to its irregularity, lack of formality, quiet seclusion of its courts and the intimacy with which one is brought into contact with small detail . . . , Gothic clothing would not hang appropriately on the frame designed by Mr. Pope" ("Recommendation of the Corporation Committee on the Architectural Plan," November 17, 1919. APS Papers; Bertram Goodhue, William Adams Delano, and Paul Cret to the Corporation Committee on the Architectural Plan, February 7, 1920, pp. 4–6, CCAP Papers). The plan was indeed more axial and formal in its conception. The combination of the disjunction between the plan and appearance of the plan (Pope may have been trying to appease those in the university who favored the Gothic) and the fact that its execution would necessitate wholesale demolition and land acquisition, invalidated many if not most of the aspects of the proposal. Rogers, meanwhile, complained to Sam Fisher about the fact that three architects who had "rated below me" in competitions should be the judges of the plan (James Gamble Rogers to Samuel Fisher, September 20,1920, Samuel Fisher Papers, Manuscripts and Archives Collections, Sterling Memorial Library, New Haven, Conn.).

43. James Gamble Rogers to Samuel Fisher, September 20, 1920, loc. cit.

44. Anson Phelps Stokes to James Gamble Rogers, November 22, 1920, CCAP Papers.

45. James Gamble Rogers to Edward S. Harkness, October 30, 1920, Samuel Fisher Papers, loc. cit.

46. Thomas Farnham, Secretary of Yale University, to James Gamble Rogers, June 14, 1921, CCAP Papers.

47. *New Haven Journal-Courier*, January 24, 1922.

48. Turner, *Campus*, pp. 168–78, 201–2; "Always in Style: A Tour of

Stanford Architecture," *Sandstone and Tile* 11 (Winter-Spring, 1987).

49. *New York Times*, March 12, 1922, sec. II, p. 7.

50. Rogers in fact declined the opportunity to design a war memorial, but otherwise was extremely active in asking architects Delano & Aldrich to change materials and massing of buildings. CCAP Papers, 1921–23.

51. Bertram Goodhue to John V. Farwell, December 15, 1923, CCAP Papers.

52. This final resolution was made possible by a series of land acquisitions behind the library on York Square, which allowed a proposed gymnasium to be moved farther to the west. While members of the Corporation Committee pushed for Rogers as the designer of the dormitory, Farwell realized that the Sterling trustees, independent New York lawyers who had chosen Goodhue because of his fame outside of the Yale environment in which Rogers was a big name, would see the dormitories only as an extension of Goodhue's library complex. Vance McCormick, Member, Corporation Committee on the Architectural Plan, to John V. Farwell, January 27, 1923; John V. Farwell to Otto Bannard, Trustee of the Sterling Estate, January 25, 1923, CCAP Papers.

53. It appears that Fisher, Harkness, and Rogers were at this time already considering a proposal to build a series of new dormitories in the form of colleges (Pierson, *Yale*, p. 216). President George Seymour, "For The Corporation" (no date; Spring, 1929?), claimed to have had his first conversations on the subject in 1922 (CCAP Papers; Extract from Minutes of the Yale Corporation, June 13, 1924, CCAP Papers).

54. In terms of budget the project was certainly the largest Rogers ever worked on. On December 15, 1923, Goodhue estimated the cost of the library at $8 million; by 1927 the total cost of the project, even after substantial cuts in its size, was up to almost $12 million, and final cost may

have been even higher. (The whole Columbia-Presbyterian complex cost around $10 million.) Bertram Goodhue to John Farwell, December 15, 1923, CCAP Papers; John Farwell to Trustees of the Sterling Estate, February 15, 1927. CCAP Papers.

55. The first record of any involvement between James Gamble Rogers and Yale University actually dates back to 1905, when Rogers dropped out of an abortive competition to design a new library for the university because he was "unable to find a solution of the difficulties of the requirements of the proposed new library building" (James Gamble Rogers to President Arthur Twining Hadley, March 18, 1905, Arthur Twining Hadley Papers—Yale Presidential Papers, Manuscripts and Archives Collections, Sterling Memorial Library, New Haven, Conn.).

56. For a complete description of Goodhue's side of this argument, and for the place of the design in his oeuvre, see Oliver, *Goodhue* (n. 16).

57. It is unclear whether the trustees or university officials pushed for Goodhue's appointment, but it was made clear that "the committee" (whether the Building Committee or the Corporation Committee on the Architectural Plan) "wanted a great name" (James J. S. Mayers, Office of Bertram Goodhue, to John Farwell, May 16, 1924, CCAP Papers; John Farwell to Bertram Goodhue, May 17, 1920, CCAP Papers).

58. For three years, the university tried to choose the right site for the library they had decided would be the proper monument to Sterling. Goodhue produced a scheme that he said completed the "classic quadrangle" of the Bicentennial Buildings on the site, but not in the manner of the Pope plan (Bertram Goodhue to John Farwell, May 20, 1920, CCAP Papers). While University Librarian Keogh and the administration argued over the size of the new building and Farwell and James Gamble Rogers discussed the correct place for such an important building in the campus, Goodhue

was left waiting, leading him to ask: "Don't you think that since I am to be the architect of this building I should know what's going on—indeed that my own advice might be of some value?" (Bertram Goodhue to John Farwell, April 22, 1922, CCAP Papers). After all, he pointed out, "he did not think that the Gothic needed the long vistas," especially in its modern, American form (John Farwell to President James Angell, January 20, 1922, JRA Papers). While Goodhue thus repeatedly expressed his eagerness to proceed with the design of the building, appropriately formed to answer its internal requirements irrespective of its location on campus, the university and James Gamble Rogers dismissed his queries. "He is a somewhat high-strung individual," President Angell wrote to Corporation Committee Vice-Chairman Vance McCormick, "so do not worry about his querulous tone" (Angell to McCormick, May 3, 1922, CCAP Papers). Rogers, as Consulting Architect, his in-law Farwell, and their friends in the Yale administration continued to weigh—according to values known only to these fellow Yale graduates—the advantages of placing the new library at the site Pope had proposed, at the head of a proposed east-west axis or on newly acquired land west of York Street. It is not surprising that Rogers claimed that Goodhue, who was not an alumnus, called on him, "thinking that he, Gamble, might be after the contract for designing the new library" (Vance McCormick to John Farwell, May 18, 1922, CCAP Papers).

59. Bertram Grosvenor Goodhue, "Proposed Sterling Memorial Library," 1924, Architectural Drawings Collection, Manuscripts and Archives Collections, Sterling Memorial Library, New Haven, Conn.

60. John Farwell to James Gamble Rogers, February 23, 1923; James Gamble Rogers to John Farwell, August 1, 1923, CCAP Papers.

61. Thomas Farnham, Treasurer of Yale University, to George Church, Trustee of the Sterling Estate, May 13,

1924, CCAP Papers.

62. James J. S. Mayers, Office of Bertram Goodhue, to John Farwell, May 16, 1924, CCAP Papers.

63. John Farwell to J. H. Desibour, December 28, 1923, CCAP Papers.

64. Minutes of the Corporation Committee on the Architectural Plan, May 6, 1920, and May 9, 1924, CCAP Papers.

65. Minutes of Library Committee, October 13, 1920, CCAP Papers.

66. "Conference of Librarians," transcript dated February 20, 1925, CCAP Papers.

67. Yale University press release, February 1, 1926, JRA Papers.

68. Specifications dated November 29, 1927, June 26, 1928, July 25, 1929, December 22, 1929, JGR Papers.

69. Thomas Farnham to Edwin Herr, December 14, 1927, JRA Papers. Farnham pointed out that Lawrie's estimate was far over budget, but recommended giving him approval nonetheless.

70. Minutes of Corporation Committee on the Architectural Plan, January 7, 1927, CCAP Papers.

71. John Farwell to James Rowland Angell, January 12, 1927, CCAP Papers.

72. George Church to Thomas Farnham, March 27, 1925, JRA Papers.

73. John Farwell to James Gamble Rogers, January 21, 1927, CCAP Papers.

74. James Rowland Angell to James Gamble Rogers, September 7, 1929, JRA Papers.

75. Merrily E. Taylor, *The Yale University Library 1701–1978: Its History, Collections and Present Organization*, New Haven: Yale University Library, 1978, p. 14.

76. Minutes of the Corporation Committee on the Architectural Plan, October 7, 1927, CCAP Papers.

77. Daniel T. Webster, "Construction Features and Problems," *Yale University Library Gazette* 3 (July, 1928), pp. 9–13.

78. *Ibid.*

79. James Rowland Angell to Anson Phelps Stokes, September 28,

1927, JRA Papers.

80. James Gamble Rogers to James Rowland Angell, October 22, 1928, JRA Papers.

81. The attendant figures who surround the figure of Alma Mater hold up the tools by which Yale and Sterling Library are built. One of the attendants holds up a hammer and a sickle, held crossed. This communistic emblem has been attributed to the intervention of the craftsmen who worked on the building.

82. "Sterling Subjects—Models"; "Sterling Subjects—Models—Extra"; "Interior Models—Extra Subjects," notebooks containing photographs and drawings used during the construction of Sterling Memorial Library, JGR Papers.

83. Angell and his former secretary, Law School Dean Robert Hutchins, used the fact that Rogers' first design came in considerably over budget to argue for moving the Law School to a site adjacent to Yale-New Haven Hospital, with the thought that combined research into criminology, pathology, and sociology could take place there. The trustees and most of the board of governors objected to this purely scientific vision of the Law School, and Rogers lobbied heavily, along with John Farwell, against the move. They finally won the day by emphasizing the necessity for building up the Sterling group as part of Yale and its traditions. Hutchins left to become president of the University of Chicago in 1929 and became famous as an innovator in eduction. For Angell's role, see Pierson, *Yale*, pp. 166–74. See also: John Farwell to Otto T. Bannard, July 17, 1928, CCAP Papers; James Rowland Angell, "Corporation Statement," May 22, 1928, CCAP Papers; John Farwell to Vance McCormick, December 13, 1928, CCAP Papers; Samuel Fisher to John Farwell, September 4, 1928, CCAP Papers; Note by John Farwell, dated May 16, 1940, inserted into 1928 correspondence on the Law School project, CCAP Papers; James Gamble Rogers to John Farwell, November 28,

1928, CCAP Papers; John Farwell to James Gamble Rogers, November 30, 1928, CCAP Papers; John Farwell to James Gamble Rogers, August 8, 1928, CCAP Papers; Thomas Farnham to John Farwell, June 26, 1928, CCAP Papers; Extract from the Minutes of the Yale Corporation, December 8, 1928, CCAP Papers.

84. "Coming Construction," *Yale Alumni Weekly*, July 31, 1928, pp. 76–78.

85. Program dated November 4, 1925, JRA Papers.

86. James Gamble Rogers to John Farwell, March 30, 1928, CCAP Papers. Rogers claims he told Garver, a Sterling trustee, that "in spite of the fact that any Law School in colonial architecture would have to have stone trimmings instead of wood, I thought that I could build in colonial about 6% cheaper than possible in brick gothic . . ." It was also during this visit that Rogers apparently first recommended against moving the site for the Law School.

87. James Gamble Rogers, "Scheme #1," plans, sections, and elevations for the Sterling Law buildings, dated 1927, Architectural Drawings Collection, loc. cit.

88. "The New Law School Quadrangles," *Yale Alumni Weekly*, May 20, 1927, p. 958.

89. *Ibid.*

90. Howell Cheney to James Rowland Angell, July 29, 1929, JRA Papers.

91. *Description of the Sterling Law Buildings*, New Haven: School of Law, Yale University, 1931, p. 21.

92. *Ibid.*, p. 7.

93. René Chambellan, "Models for the Sterling Law Buildings," folder of photographs, JGR Papers.

94. *Description of the Sterling Law Buildings*, p. 25. Farwell later blamed Hutchins for many of the cost overruns on the building, but claimed that he allowed them to occur because Hutchins took his defeat with such grace. John Farwell to Thomas Farnnam, July 29, 1929, CCAP Papers.

95. The Sterling gift also paid for several other buildings, including a hall of medicine, the Divinity Quadrangle, and a chemistry laboratory. None of these buildings was designed by James Gamble Rogers, though as Consulting Architect and Architect for the General Plan he had an active part in reviewing and changing their design development.

96. Wilbur Cross to John Farwell, November 22, 1923, CCAP Papers.

97. James Rowland Angell to John Farwell, November 27, 1926, CCAP Papers; John Farwell to James Gamble Rogers, December 6, 1926, CCAP Papers.

98. Minutes of the Corporation Committee on the Architectural Plan, January 7, 1927, CCAP Papers.

99. Compare this work, for instance, with the closed forms of the University of Chicago (see Chapter 3), Columbia University (Turner, *Campus*, pp. 177–80), or George Post's 1904 College of the City of New York.

100. [Wilbur Cross], "Preliminary Report on Buildings for the Graduate School," December 1, 1926, CCAP Papers.

101. John Farwell to James Gamble Rogers, December 6, 1926, CCAP Papers.

102. James Gamble Rogers to James Rowland Angell, October 31, 1931, JRA Papers.

103. Vance McCormick to James Rowland Angell, November 2, 1930; Thomas Farnham to George Church, February 12, 1930, JRA Papers.

104. Specifications, Hall of Graduate Studies, dated December 11, 1929, JGR Papers.

105. René Chambellan, "Models for the Hall of Graduate Studies," received by James Gamble Rogers, Inc., June 25, 1931, JGR Papers.

106. See Susan Ryan, "The Architecture of James Gamble Rogers at Yale University," *Perspecta* 18 (1982), pp. 25–50; pp. 40–42.

107. A minor controversy arose after construction was completed when it was discovered that one of the inscriptions carved into the Hall of Graduate Studies read: "He was born with a sense that the whole world was mad." Whether this was a comment on the nature of the typical graduate student, a comment on Wilbur Cross, an affectionate tribute by the stone carvers to Rogers, or, as Rogers claimed, merely a quotation among many others, has never been ascertained, but it certainly goes to show that the whole building process was not completely lost in archaeological pretensions. See Alexander Woollcott, "A Gift of Laughter," *The New Yorker*, November 17, 1934. The most complete, though probably biased, discussion of the controversy can be found in Wesley Needham's "The Gothic Architecture of James Gamble Rogers at Yale" (n. 12), pp. 8–12.

CHAPTER 5

1. The best account of the lengthy process by which the college system came about, which is backed up fully by the Archives of the Corporation Committee on the Architectural Plan, President Angell's Papers, and the Archives of the Commonwealth Fund, though all of these records have probably been edited, can be found in George W. Pierson, *Yale: The University College. 1921–1927*, New Haven: Yale University Press, 1955. The acute housing shortage was of great concern to Angell—and to most of Yale—during the 1920s, and the Memorial Quadrangle was seen by almost all observers as some sort of model for future residential developments. See, for instance, "Living Quarters for Undergraduates," *Yale Alumni Weekly*, January 2, 1925.

2. "The school can become an effective means of overcoming the loss of community, if the school itself is made a social unit. . . . Learning, as Mead says, should come from the conversation of concrete individuals rather than from pale abstractions of thought" (Darnell Rucker, *The Chicago Pragmatists*, Minneapolis: University of Minnesota Press, 1969, p. 99).

3. Pierson, *Yale*, p. 215.

4. *Ibid.*, p. 216.

5. Harkness was always fond of England, traveled there frequently, and eventually gave one of his largest donations ever, $11 million, to aid education in the United Kingdom.

6. Pierson, *Yale*, p. 216. See also James Rowland Angell, "1927 Summer Reports," typescript in JRA Papers.

7. James Gamble Rogers, "Notes on Impressions after Visiting Oxford," typescript, June 9, 1927, CFA.

8. James Gamble Rogers, "The Future of Yale College," typescript dated March 27, 1928, CFA, p. 1.

9. *Ibid.*, pp. 3–4.

10. From the beginning, Angell was in constant battle with Yale College Dean Mendell on the one hand and with the more conservative Yale Corporation on the other hand. It appears that, at the beginning of the process, he was not fully committed to the Harkness and Fisher position, but would have listened to any proposal to rationalize unruly Yale College. See: James Rowland Angell correspondence with Dean Mendell, Yale Corporation and Committee on Re-Organization, 1927, JRA Papers; Pierson, *Yale*, p. 174ff.; Charles Seymour, "Notes on Undergraduate Organization," typescript dated November 30, 1927, JRA Papers. Dean Mendell, an arch-conservative, proposed founding an honors college as a subdivision within the existing college, open only to the academically worthy. This system would not permit any inculcation of the social and moral values so important to Harkness, Fisher, and Rogers. Even more disturbing to Harkness was a strong movement, possibly encouraged by Angell, for the founding of a College of Social Sciences. The student body, then still divided between the humanities-oriented Yale College and the science-oriented Sheffield School, would find a third choice in which they could concentrate on the exciting new parasciences and extensions of the humanities such as economics, political science, and psychology. This was the most pro-gressive and least social option. (Clarence W. Mendell, "Memorandum on Honors College," typescript dated September 12, 1927, JRA Papers.) Angell saw the committee drifting toward the latter direction and realized that the plan would invoke resistance among the corporation. He thus declined to make a formal recommendation to Harkness. Harkness, who had first started discussing these ideas with Fisher in 1924 and was used to having his way as a benefactor, became impatient and, in the spring of 1928, looked elsewhere for the fulfillment of his dream of a modern college dedicated to the preservation of the effective elite, while informing Yale that his offer to fully fund the new college program would expire that July. Angell and Seymour traveled to Eolia to explain the problems they were having and to argue for an extension. "I then expressed great regret that Yale had turned me down," Harkness wrote in his notes on the meeting. "Angell at once interrupted that Yale had not turned me down. Interview closed" (Edward S. Harkness, handwritten notes, meeting with James Angell and Charles Seymour, October 22, 1928, CFA). Less than two months later, Harvard University announced a gift by an anonymous donor to start a residential college system. News quickly leaked out that Harkness, who had no formal connections with Yale's arch-rival, was the donor. Apparently, he had traveled to Cambridge at his own initiative and presented President Lowell with his plan. Unlike Angell, Lowell was in full control of his institution, and was in a position to accept the offer immediately. The result was a series of large residential colleges in the Colonial style, and outrage at Yale University. Angell blamed Harkness for not allowing him to inform the faculty that the college plan (as opposed to the other alternatives) would be fully funded by the donor, and Harkness insisted on stating his offer and its "rejection" for the press. (James Rowland Angell to Alfred Ripley, member, Yale Corpora-tion, January 5, 1929, Office of the Secretary Papers, Manuscripts and Archives Collections, Sterling Memorial Library, New Haven, Conn.) Harkness sent Rogers up to study the Harvard situation and to meet with Lowell, but the actual commissions went to the Boston firm of Coolidge Shepley, Bulfinch & Abbott. (James Gamble Rogers to Edward S. Harkness, March 19, 1929, CFA.) Rogers' real role, however, became the crucial one of mediator between Harkness and Yale to salvage the situation. In the process, he defined much of the character of the plan. As early as the spring of 1928, he had invited Dean Mendell and Seymour over for dinner to explain his plan for eleven residential colleges. "Rogers was convinced that the social and cultural advantages of the English system, rather than its intellectual apparatus, were what mattered," notes Pierson (*Yale*, p. 238). Angell, in an effort to sidestep the faculty, agreed and appointed a committee made up of ex-Secretary Day, Seymour, Fisher, and Rogers to come up with a college plan "without reference to curriculum" (*ibid.*, p. 242).

11. James Rowland Angell to Charles Seymour, September 6, 1929, JRA Papers.

12. James Rowland Angell, "Report of the President's Committee on the Program for Undergraduate Housing," October 4, 1929, JRA Papers.

13. Extract from the Minutes of the Yale Corporation, January 11, 1930, JRA Papers.

14. James Rowland Angell, "Yale's Great New Plans," *Yale Alumni Weekly*, March 1, 1929, pp. 651–55.

15. "Harkness Millions for Yale Housing," *New York Times*, January 13, 1930, pp. 1, 16.

16. Reginald M. Cleveland, "Mister Harkness' Gifts Cover Wide Field," *New York Times*, January 19, 1930, sec IX, p. 5.

17. See n. 14.

18. James Gamble Rogers, "Estimated Costs of Plan for Yale Undergraduate Residential Units," n.d. [1930], CFA.

19. Quoted in *New York Herald Tribune*, December 16, 1926, p. 16.

20. Minutes of the Corporation Committee on the Architectural Plan, December 12, 1930, CCAP Papers. See also: James Gamble Rogers, Inc., "Specifications for Dormitories at Library And York Streets, New Haven, Connecticut," dated December, 1924; "Specifications for Quadrangles at High and Library Streets," dated May 3, 1931, JGR Papers.

21. Extract from the Minutes of the Yale Corporation, December 13, 1930, CCAP Papers.

22. The idea that the Sterling group should include a dormitory that would bridge between the institutional mass of the library and the Memorial Quadrangle was first offered by Rogers in 1922 (Minutes of the Corporation Committee on the Architectural Plan, June 9, 1922, CCAP Papers). The Sterling trustees rejected this idea, but later acquiesced.

23. These tall (more than five stories) dormitory bars are held up by twin buttresses that step back repeatedly and in a pronounced manner. In between, a long arch opens up the ground floor and is tied back to the facade by a central column, which holds up a three-story range of bay windows. The granite skin is detailed with limestone trim, which makes it appear as if it is being stretched away from the mass of the building and is held back only by a tall chimney that is tacked on the side of each bar and rises to a row of crisply cut spires.

24. Wesley E. Needham, "The Gothic Architecture of James Gamble Rogers at Yale," unpublished manuscript, Manuscripts and Archives Collections, Sterling Memorial Library, New Haven, Conn., p. 4.

25. The plans for dormitories on this site and their relationship to the whole plan dated back several years, with some members of the Yale administration arguing for the necessity of placing only institutional buildings in this central part of the campus, while others argued for meeting the pressing need for dormitory rooms.

Administration officials also objected to the overly formal nature of the central axis in the Pope plan. On the other hand, during the 1920s the director of the Department of University Health tried to place the undergraduate clinic on the site, and Rogers suggested placing the Divinity School there. His main concern, as voiced in a letter to John Farwell on August 2, 1928, was to remove the unsightly mixture of existing buildings from this prominent site. With the passage of the College Plan, this question was resolved, since the new building would include both dormitory rooms for at least 250 students, according to Harkness's dictates, and such large-scale civic buildings as a dining hall and a library, which would be in character with the Sterling buildings and the Harkness Educational Building directly to the east. CCAP Papers.

26. Edward S. Harkness to James Rowland Angell, May 25, 1931, JRA Papers.

27. Minutes of the Corporation Committee on the Architectural Plan, November 13, 1931, and December 11, 1931, CCAP Papers.

28. James Gamble Rogers to Vance McCormick, December 18, 1931; Carl Lohmann, Secretary of Yale University, to Ellery Husted, James Gamble Rogers, Inc., June 6, 1933, JGR Papers.

29. James Rowland Angell to John Farwell, February 12, 1931, CCAP Papers.

30. Minutes of the Building Committee, January 13, 1933, JRA Papers.

31. The work of Goodhue in particular comes to mind, because this architect had, by the time he designed the Nebraska State Capitol, come to eschew much of the detailing and compositional language that had marked his earlier Neo-Gothic work. A similar development can be seen, to mention just two of the better-known architects who included Neo-Gothic work in their repertoire, in the work of Raymond Hood and (though here the work is more Neo-Classical)

George Howe. All three of these architects turned toward a Modernist vocabulary through a process of stripping away the arches, finials, stone carving, and picturesque masking that had been evident on their earlier buildings. See: Richard Oliver, *Bertram Grosvenor Goodhue*, Cambridge, Mass., and New York: MIT Press and Architectural History Foundation, 1983; Walter H. Kilham, Jr., *Raymond Hood, Architect. Form Through Function in the American Skyscraper*, New York: Architectural Book Publishing Co., 1973; Robert A. M. Stern, *George Howe: Toward a Modern American Architecture*, New Haven: Yale University Press, 1975.

32. Charles Nagel, "Berkeley College," *Yale Alumni Weekly*, September 28, 1934, pp. 7–10.

33. Correspondence between James Gamble Rogers and Mrs. Charles Seymour, the interior decorator for the house, spring and summer, 1934; frequent reference is made to the "French" feel of the decorations (JGR Papers). See also Nagel, "Berkeley College," p. 9.

34. Correspondence between Charles Nagel, Curator of Decorative Arts, Yale Art Gallery, and Richard Kimball, James Gamble Rogers, Inc., commencing September 10, 1933, JGR Papers.

35. "Berkeley College Iconography," *Yale Alumni Weekly*, October 26, 1934, p. 129.

36. Rogers apparently shared the opinion of Delano, Goodhue, and Cret about the Gothic scheme put forward by Pope for the campus. Farwell later commented that he and Rogers had discussed the variations of style according to the placement of the buildings on campus (CCAP). This attitude was formalized in the plans developed after Rogers' appointment as University Architect. See "Coming Construction," *Yale Alumni Weekly*, July 31, 1928, pp. 76–78.

37. CCAP Papers, 1924–25.

38. John Farwell to James Rowland Angell, January 31, 1930, CCAP Papers.

39. Minutes of the Yale Corporation, April 12, 1930, extract in CCAP Papers.

40. John Farwell to James Rowland Angell, January 31, 1930, op. cit., referencing a conversation between Farwell and George Parmly Day.

41. Quoted in "Quadrangle System Plan Outlined by Chairman of Architectural Committee," *Yale Daily News*, May 7, 1930, p. 1.

42. James Gamble Rogers, Inc., "Specifications for Stone Work, Quadrangles I and I-X, Yale University," July 29, 1930, JGR Papers: "The proportions of color and face finish shall be similar to that used on the Sterling Elm Street dormitories."

43. "Quadrangle System Plan," p. 1.

44. Rogers did design a dormitory for women, but this scheme was not completed until after the war by a different architect at a different site.

45. James Gamble Rogers, "Proposed Building Plans for Yale University Given to President Angell, for the Purpose of Advising the Sterling Trustees," n.d., received by John Garver, Sterling Trustee, October 22, 1926, CCAP Papers.

46. Minutes of the Corporation Committee on the Architectural Plan, June 13, 1930, CCAP Papers.

47. Minutes of the Corporation Committee on the Architectural Plan, April 8, 1932, CCAP Papers.

48. Note on copy of letter from James Rowland Angell to Edward S. Harkness, May 19, 1934, JRA Papers.

49. Memorandum by Malcolm P. Aldrich, October 10, 1935, CFA.

50. The specifications for Timothy Dwight College in fact note at one point: "When in doubt, begin same as Davenport-Pierson" (James Gamble Rogers, Inc., "Specifications for Timothy Dwight College, Yale University," November 9, 1933, JGR Papers).

51. James Grafton Rogers, "Timothy Dwight College," *Yale Alumni Weekly*, October 25, 1935, pp. 7–12.

52. *Ibid.*, p. 10.

53. *Ibid.*, p. 11.

54. James Bryant Connant, quoted in "Yale Announces Gift for Ninth Residential College," *New York Herald Tribune*, June 21, 1934, CFA.

55. In addition to the residential colleges, Rogers also helped to lay out "fraternity row," a meandering path to the south of Davenport and Pierson colleges. Here were housed several of the fraternities and one of the secret societies that had been displaced by the building boom. Rogers designed Beta Theta Thi and Psi Upsilon (1927), Phi Gamma Delta (1930), as well as Delta Kappa Epsilon around the corner on York Street (1926). All of these fraternities were brick structures with limestone trim and appear like extracts not so much from the residential colleges as from Rogers' designs for the Taft and St. Paul's preparatory schools and a house he designed in 1926 in Lake Forest ("William F. Peters House," photographs and description in Architectural Collection, Lake Forest [Ill.] Public Library). The most sophisticated of the series is Psi Upsilon ("Fence Club"), a pinwheeling arrangement of rooms with Georgian interiors on various levels. See: "The New Fraternity Houses," *Yale Alumni Weekly*, April 2, 1926, pp. 771–75; "Fraternity and Sorority Houses," *Yale Alumni Weekly*, July 31, 1928, pp. 32–38; "The New DKE Hall," *Yale Alumni Weekly*, December 11, 1925, pp. 344–45. Specifications and estimates for Psi Upsilon House, dated September 8, 1926, and August 19, 1926, JGR Papers. Finally, Rogers also designed a remarkably modern-looking boathouse for the Yale crew team in Derby, Connecticut, in 1923 (contract for Yale Boathouse, dated February 19, 1923, JGR Papers; Drawings of the Bob Cook Boathouse, Derby, Connecticut, Yale Architectural Drawings Collection, Manuscripts and Archives Collections, Sterling Memorial Library, New Haven, Conn.).

56. Manfredo Tafuri in particular discussed this theme at length. Starting from the premise that "to ward off anguish by understanding and absorbing its causes would seem to be one of the principal ethical exigencies of bourgeois art," he claimed that it is the picturesque, and its attempt to reconcile man with a nature that existed before the advent of capitalism, that provided a pure utopian model. He attached great importance to the development of a rationalized architectural organization in the guise of utopian models by which architects—often against their will—further the aims of capitalism. While proposing a seemingly perfect and seamless world outside of the chaotic "shock" of the urban metropolis, this architecture instead provides sublimation of criticism, memory of a time before capitalism, and hope for a different world. Manfredo Tafuri, *Architecture and Utopia. Design and Capitalist Development*, trans. by Barbara Luigia La Penta, Cambridge, Mass., London: MIT Press, 1976. For a more detailed description of the relationship between the image of a natural, organic architecture as an escape from the city made possible by a scientific understanding and typification of the elements of architecture, see Anthony Vidler, "The Scenes of the Street. Transformation in Ideal and Reality, 1850–1871," in Stanford Anderson, ed., *On Streets*, Cambridge, Mass., London: MIT Press, 1978, pp. 29–112; Anthony Vidler, *Writings of the Walls. Architectural Theory in the Late Enlightenment*, Princeton: Princeton Architectural Press, 1987.

57. Gwendolyn Wright, *Building the Dream. A Social History of Housing in America*, Cambridge, Mass.: MIT Press, 1981, pp. 8–10; Perry Miller, *The New England Mind: The Seventeenth Century*, Cambridge, Mass.: Harvard University Press, 1954 (1939). For a description of the early pilgrim community as a corporate entity with didactic purposes, see Alan Trachtenberg, *The Incorporation of America. Culture and Society in the Gilded Age*, New York: Hill and Wang, 1983, p. 102.

58. Richard Norton Smith, *The Harvard Century. The Making of a University to a Nation*. New York: Simon & Schuster, 1986, p. 94.

59. *The Yale Record*, February 12, 1930.

60. "The New Yale," *Fortune*, March, 1934, pp. 70–81, 148, 153–54, 156, 158; quotation on p. 74.

61. *Ibid.*, p. 73.

62. Richard Rhodes, "Shell Games," in Diana Dubois, ed., *My Harvard, My Yale*, New York: Random House, 1982, pp. 236–46; p. 238.

CHAPTER 6

1. W. P. Howard and J. D. Parish, *A Report on the Competition. H. Sophie Newcomb Memorial College 1911*, New Orleans, n.d., Archives, Howard-Tilton Memorial Library, Tulane University, New Orleans, La.

2. Brandt V. E. Dixon, *A Brief History of H. Sophie Newcomb College 1887–1919*, New Orleans: H. Sophie Newcomb Memorial College, 1928.

3. The project suffered from delays and the inability of the administration to fulfill all of its plans; Rogers was forced to cut costs on the buildings several times. Most critics praised Sophie Newcomb College for its "simple and classic" beauty and proportion, rather than its architectural originality or grandeur. "The Winning Design for the Newcomb College Buildings," *New Orleans Times-Picayune*, February 4, 1912; see also *New Orleans Times-Picayune*, January 14, 1912, and January 9, 1917, Archives, Howard-Tilton Memorial Library, New Orleans, La.

4. James Gamble Rogers to George W. Norton, President, Southern Baptist Theological Seminary, November 16, 1921, Archives, Southern Baptist Theological Seminary, Louisville, Ky.

5. E. Y. Mullins, *The Seminary Emergency*, Louisville: Southern Baptist Theological Seminary, 1924, p. 7.

6. Mullins, *Seminary*, p. 7.

7. *Edgar Young Mullins*, Louisville: Southern Baptist Theological Seminary, n.d., p. 182.

8. Arthur Loomis, Associated Architect, to James Gamble Rogers, Inc., December 8, 1926, Archives, Southern Baptist Theological Seminary, Louisville, Ky.

9. The interior of Norton Hall, meanwhile, is simple, almost Spartan: plain stone floors and brick walls lead up to stucco ceilings, coved at the crossing of axes. The central staircase provides the only vertical relief, and catches the entrance axis from both sides. Only the library was more elaborate. It was conceived as a simple nave, a story and a half high, whose stucco ceiling was marked by a widely spaced grid of wood. A smaller reading room at the lower level was surrounded by a balcony supported on wood columns, providing the most highly varied interior space. The main focus in these rooms comes from the large windows, whose arched expanses flood the space with light, while a small lunette creates its own shaft and a bay window allows for a small seating area overlooking the campus. The interior life of the Southern Baptist Theological Seminary was conceived of as simple, clear, and not given to the frills of the Neo-Gothic education of places like Yale University.

10. James Gamble Rogers to E. Y. Mullins, October 19, 1922; October 24, 1922; December 2, 1922; December 18, 1922, Archives, Southern Baptist Theological Seminary, Louisville, Ky.

11. G. B. Nichols to James Gamble Rogers, August 26, 1924, and February 9, 1927, Archives, Southern Baptist Theological Seminary, Louisville, Ky.

12. James Gamble Rogers, "Plot Plan. Proposed Buildings for the Southern Baptist Theological Seminary Louisville, Kentucky," n.d., Archives, Southern Baptist Theological Seminary, Louisville, Ky.

13. Conversations with Jaime Dwan, Taft School Library, and Ed North, Taft Summer Program, August 11, 1987.

14. Sam Fisher lived in nearby Litchfield, Connecticut. Archives, The Taft School, Hulbert Taft, Jr., Library, Watertown, Conn.

15. Horace Taft, Jr., was Dean of Yale College in the 1970s, and members of the Taft family, both of the Ohio and the Connecticut branches, continue to attend Yale.

16. Samuel Fisher, *Taft and Mr. Taft*, New York, 1928, pp. 10, 29.

17. The original school building was—ironically—designed by Bertram Grosvenor Goodhue in 1911.

18. "The New School," *Taft Alumni Bulletin* 5 (December, 1927), pp. 3–9; "Building Delayed," *The Papyrus*, May 6, 1927, p. 4.

19. "New Taft Infirmary Is Well Equipped," *Taft Alumni Bulletin* 6 (December, 1928), p. 3.

20. August Heckscher, *St. Paul's. The Life of a New England School*. New York: Charles Scribner's Sons, 1980, p. 216ff.

21. S. S. Drury, "St. Paul's School Concord, N.H.," typewritten memorandum to Edward S. Harkness, dated May 15, 1931, CFA. For a thorough description of the Chapel of St. Peter and St. Paul, see William Morgan, *The Almighty Wall. The Architecture of Henry Vaughan*, Cambridge, Mass., and New York: MIT Press and Architectural History Foundation, 1983, p. 89ff. Vaughan also designed several dormitories and classroom buildings on the campus.

22. "Memo for Mrs. Harkness Trip, May, 1941," typewritten memorandum, probably by Malcolm Aldrich, CFA.

23. August Heckscher, in his history of St. Paul's, is as mystified by the whole process as most of the members of the St. Paul's community were at the time. He retells the vice-rector's description of the manner in which the school finally received its gift. Vice-rector C. C. Monie had no idea that the New Schoolhouse might become a reality until an encounter he had in 1934 with two unidentified visitors: "I spotted them, introduced myself, and asked if I could do anything for them. One, it turned out, had been a boy at the school forty years before; the other [Rogers—*au.*] was the father of two former students." The visitors were Edward S. Harkness and the architect James Gamble Rogers. "I invited them to lunch, which they declined; they said they

just wanted to look around, and needed no assistance." Soon afterward began complicated negotiations that were to conclude in the princely gift, providing a new educational center on the former school house site" (Heckscher, *St. Paul's*, pp. 222–23).

24. The building is still in use for almost exactly the same purposes for which it was designed. Later additions, such as an arts center by Hardy Holzman Pfeiffer, have enhanced the axes leading to the Schoolhouse. For a sensitive discussion of the campus, see Robert A. M. Stern, *Pride of Place. Building the American Dream*, Boston: Houghton Mifflin Co., 1986, pp. 58–61.

25. Walter Dill Scott, form letter sent to university officials, August, 1921, WDS Papers; Minutes of the Board of Trustees of Northwestern University, August 22, 1921, p. 3, NUA.

26. Minutes of the Board of Trustees, January 31, 1922, p. 17, NUA.

27. Scott was appointed in October, 1920. He was the first Northwestern alumnus to become president of that institution, thus marking the coming of age of its student body. During his eighteen-year tenure, he increased the endowment from $5.6 million to $26 million and the value of the physical plant from $12 million to $48 million. "Biography—Walter Dill Scott," WDS Papers; R. Brett Ruiz, "The Selling of an Image: 'Northwestern Gothic,'" student paper, Northwestern University, 1980.

28. Minutes of the Board of Trustees, January 31, 1922, NUA.

29. Walter Needham, interview with Jill Pearlman, January 22, 1986, in Jill Pearlman, "The Urban University Campus in the Interwar Years: The Case of Northwestern in Chicago," student paper, Northwestern University, 1986, p. 14.

30. Howard Van Doren Shaw to William Mason, January 27, 1922, WDS Papers.

31. James Gamble Rogers to William A. Dyche, Secretary of Northwestern University, January 21, 1922, WDS Papers.

32. Minutes of the Board of Trustees, April 25, 1922, NUA.

33. Harold F. Williamson and Payson S. Wild, *Northwestern University. A History 1850–1975*, Evanston, Ill.: Northwestern University, 1976, pp. 145–48: for a full discussion of this conflict, see Chapters 15 and 16.

34. George Parmly Day to Walter Dill Scott, August 18, 1921, WDS Papers. For the Farwells, see Chapter 1, note 53.

35. Richard Fairchild, "Northwestern University's Plans for Expansion," *Fort Dearborn Magazine*, May, 1920, p. 13, NUA.

36. James Gamble Rogers to William A Dyche, May 4, 1923; Minutes of the Board of Trustees, June 25, 1923, pp. 12–14, NUA.

37. *Ibid.*, p. 14.

38. *The International Competition for the Chicago Tribune MCMXXII* (abridged reprint), New York: Rizzoli International Publications, 1980 (1922), p. 62.

39. Walter H. Kilham, Jr., *Raymond Hood, Architect. Form Through Function in the American Skyscraper*, New York: Architectural Book Publishing Co., 1973; Paul Goldberger, *The Skyscraper*, New York: Alfred A. Knopf, 1981; Thomas A. Van Leeuwen, *The Skyward Trend of Thought. Five Essays on the Metaphysics of the American Skyscraper*, The Hague: AHA Books, 1986; Louis Sullivan, "The Chicago Tribune Competition," *Architectural Record* 53 (February, 1923), pp. 151–57.

40. Professor H. S. Philbrick to Walter Dill Scott, May 13, 1925, WDS Papers.

41. *Ibid.*

42. Many of the buildings of the McKinlock Campus have been substantially altered by later additions and subtractions. The best overview of the original campus can be found in *The American Architect*, July 20, 1927, pp. 77–115, and in the drawings in the Northwestern University Architect's Office, Northwestern University, Evanston, Ill.

43. Guy Murchie, "Woman's

Vision Comes to Life in McKinlock Group," *Chicago Tribune*, July 21, 1935.

44. "Law School Moves to New Campus," *Northwestern University Alumni News*, January, 1927, pp. 12–13.

45. A later addition to the rear of the building completely encloses the finely detailed cloistered courtyard of the building, thus enhancing the monastic sense of the building, while a 1984 addition tries to mimic some of the gothicizing shapes in glass and metal. Both additions were designed, ironically enough, by the firm of Holabird & Roche.

46. Thorne Hall was envisioned by its donor as a dining hall, and by James Gamble Rogers as completing the courtyard of the law group. The final site was chosen after Thorne became a trustee in 1927. Minutes of the Board of Trustees, 1925–27, NUA.

47. Susan P. Moore, "Thorne Auditorium—A Demonstration in Architectural Acoustics," *American School Board Journal*, January, 1933, NUA. See also *Northwestern University Alumni News* 12 (January, 1932), p. 1.

48. The most complete inventory of twentieth-century plans for the Northwestern Evanston campus is to be found in the unpublished 1980 student paper by Brett Ruiz, "The Selling of an Image" (n. 27).

49. Minutes of the Board of Trustees, Northwestern University, July 8, 1943, p. 224, NUA.

50. "Geo. W. Maher: A Democrat in Architecture," *The Western Architect* 20 (March, 1914), pp. 25–53.

51. The Evanston campus of Northwestern had been caught almost since its founding in a tension between two styles of architecture, two ways of planning, and two attitudes toward the community of which it was part. On the one hand, several of the earlier buildings were isolated Gothic bastions set within what was seen, by such planners as Olmsted & Olmsted who proposed a campus plan in 1909, as a sylvan landscape turning its back on the city. On the other hand, planners such as

Daniel Burnham (1905) and George Maher (1907) sought to discipline the campus by imposing a monumental structure of walkways, roads, and artificial bays to mediate between the grid of the city and a newly planned academic precinct. The buildings proposed in these latter plans were shown in what James Gamble Rogers was later to call "the renaissance style" (James Gamble Rogers to President Walter Dill Scott, July 20, 1925, WDS Papers), and were meant to be abstractions built out of the local materials and architectural elements. None of the grand plans generated between the turn of the century and the Second World War was ever carried out. Instead, the Chicago firm of Bennett, Parsons & Frost devised a more cautious proposal for the future development of the campus in 1926. It was this plan, which left almost all of the existing buildings on the original campus in place and foresaw an expansion to the north and to the west across Sheridan Road, that Rogers approved and used in designing his buildings. Edward Bennett sent a preliminary plan to Rogers on December 14, 1926. Rogers apparently studied the plan and wrote to Scott on August 5, 1927, that he approved (WDS). The only Neo-Georgian building Rogers constructed on the campus is the renovation of the bursar's office, completed in 1922.

52. In publications of Dyche Stadium in the professional press, engineer Gavin Hadden was given equal billing with James Gamble Rogers. See "Dyche Stadium, Northwestern University, Evanston, Ill. " *American Architect*, January 5, 1928, pp. 63–68.

53. Minutes of the Evanston Campus Committee—Women's Quadrangle Division, November 11, 1923, WDS Papers.

54. Minutes of the Evanston Campus Committee—Women's Quadrangle Division, June 4, 1924, WDS Papers.

55. Kappa Delta House Record Drawings, dated March, 1926, Archives of the Northwestern Univer-

sity Campus Architects, NUA.

56. In 1926, Scott proposed erecting a dormitory for women who didn't belong to sororities and thus might be of a different social class. The sororities objected not to the idea of such a dormitory but to its physical presence, complaining that this large new Hobart Hall would overwhelm the delicate scale of "their" courtyards (Minutes of the Board of Trustees, April 15, 1926, NUA). Once again, buildings stood in for social issues. Scott prevailed, and Rogers (1929), Hobart (1929), and Willard (1938) halls were completed. All three were designed by Rogers in the same style as the sororities, though observers noted that he emphasized the "masculine ease and comfort" that would surround these less ladylike women ("Plan Dedication of Dormitory for N.U. Coeds," *Daily Northwestern*, September 20, 1938).

57. As early as July 1925, Rogers had sent Scott plans for a grouping of a chapel, a school of music, a science building, a women's buildings, and a library. Though these designs are now lost, from the description it appears that the library would have held a less central position on the campus. For some reason, Rogers felt that the library should thus be Gothic, or modern, while the central campus should be left in a "Renaissance" style (James Gamble Rogers to President Walter Dill Scott, July 20, 1925, WDS Papers). Scott used these plans to raise funds in the following five years, but in the meantime the Bennett, Parsons & Frost plan had already proposed a Georgian main campus, and Rogers had designed the Sorority Quadrangle in a Gothic style, in keeping with what he perceived as appropriate for its peripheral position.

58. Theodore W. Koch, "First Draft of Possible Arrangement of Floor Space in a University Library—T.W. Koch Fake-It," undated manuscript, Northwestern University Architectural Archives, NUA. Theodore W. Koch to President Walter Dill Scott, December 13, 1929,

WDS Papers.

59. Relationships between architect and client deteriorated rapidly. The Rogers office was turning out variations of Neo-Georgian designs and worrying about the proportions of a proposed central tower, while Koch was claiming that Rogers "has shown no enthusiasm for the project . . . thus far we had nothing but the work of his younger associates, —draughtsmen, rather than architects with experience in original design" (Theodore W. Koch to President Walter Dill Scott, August 15, 1930, WDS Papers). Koch referred to what he claimed had been a similar problem at the Yale Law School, though it is unclear whether he was aware of the true nature of the acrimonious debate about the placement of that building. Koch seems to have had three separate objections to Rogers' work: first, Rogers had modified the plans to be "American Colonial" rather than "Renaissance"; second, he had been unresponsive to Koch's frequent criticisms and suggestions; third, he had delegated too much authority. Certainly Rogers was extremely busy during this period, and his single-minded pursuit of a Georgian scheme betrays a certain lack of communication with his client (James Gamble Rogers to Theodore W. Koch, June 12, 1930, WDS Papers).

60. President Walter Dill Scott to James Gamble Rogers, June 16, 1931; James Gamble Rogers to President Walter Dill Scott, June 26, 1931, WDS Papers.

61. The back of the campus was extended with a landfill in 1962, and Walter Netsch of the Chicago firm of Skidmore, Owings & Merrill added a large, self-contained addition to the rear of Deering Library in 1970. It is now no longer possible to enter the original library from the front. Access to all of its spaces is through an underground tunnel.

62. Theodore W. Koch, "The Charles Deering Library; A Description of the New Building." *Charles Deering Library Bulletin* 1 (January–March, 1932), pp. 3–7.

63. Scott and Lutkin halls were the remnants of the original arts center proposed by Rogers in the 1925 plans. Because of the Depression, all of the buildings had been scaled down, and the plans for a new theological seminary were completely dropped. The scientific functions of the university were accommodated by Holabird and Root, Rogers' successors as Campus Architects, in their 1941 Technological Institute. Lutkin Hall is essentially a small auditorium with an ell of offices and rehearsal spaces attached to one side. Beyond one simple gable that faces the Sorority Quadrangle across the street, the building maintains a low profile. The visual impact of the building is further reduced by the fact that the auditorium is roofed by a symmetrical cross gable, so that the building forms an X shape divorced from its immediate surroundings. One-story entrance blocks and hallways mediate this inwardly turned form, while a small spire marks the center of the crossing. The small detail and the judicious use of carved stone moldings and inscriptions to give a scale and texture to the undifferentiated wall of stone mask the fact that this is one of Rogers' most introspective buildings, cut off from its surroundings and given over to a single function that the architect here, unlike at the Yale Theater, felt no need to announce to the outside world.

64. "Scott Hall," Northwestern University, 1939, NUA, n.p.

65. "Scott Hall Dedication," *Northwestern University Alumni News* 20 (October, 1940), pp. 11–13, 32.

66. *Ibid.,* p. 13

67. Elias Lyman, "Dedication Address," typescript, NUA.

68. James Rowland Angell, *American Education. Addresses & Articles,* New Haven: Yale University Press, 1937.

69. *Colgate Rochester Divinity School—Bexley Hall—Crozer Theological Seminary 1987–1989 Catalog,* Rochester: Colgate Rochester Divinity School, 1987, pp. 7–8; Albert William Beaven, "Address—The Divinity School and the Community," *Colgate-Rochester*

Divinity School Bulletin 5 (November, 1932), pp. 7–19, 9.

70. Beaven, "Address," p. 10.

71. *Ibid.*

72. Howard Moise, "The New Buildings of the Colgate-Rochester Divinity School," *Colgate-Rochester Divinity School Bulletin* 5 (November, 1932), pp. 103–13; p. 106.

73. Payroll Book, James Gamble Rogers, Inc., 1924–26. JGR Papers.

74. Moise, "New Buildings."

75. *Ibid.,* p. 104.

76. *Ibid.,* p. 107.

77. A square tower masks the transition between the bar and the dining hall. To the rear or north, the building is organized into a series of three cross gables. The southernmost gable is the library stack, built up out of closely placed piers. The northernmost section is the original dormitory, and the middle cross-gabled piece is an entrance pavilion and stair hall. The wall of the three-story building is repeated as a lower screen punctuated by larger arched windows that light the library's reading room and the auditorium, both of whose axes run parallel to the main spine of the building. A rambling dormitory building and the president's house are treated as separate elements placed, respectively, to the east and the west of the main building. There are no other elements to this scheme, other than an outdoor amphitheater originally placed by the landscape architect, Allan DeForest, to the rear of the property. A grand axis way which was to have swept up to the building from the south could not be built because of the steepness of the site. The forms of the school thus sit as one singular building above a broad lawn reaching up to the pinnacles of the tower. (See James Gamble Rogers, Inc., "General Plan for Campus—Colgate-Rochester Divinity School," undated plan, Archives, Colgate-Rochester Divinity School, Rochester, N.Y.). This plan was reprinted in the Dedication Book. The reorientation of the site toward the rear makes the building appear even more like a soaring monument,

because one cannot reach it directly. At the same time, the rear entrance is somewhat uncomfortable. The outdoor amphitheater no longer exists and a library addition is currently under construction under the front terrace.

78. Moise, "New Buildings," p. 108.

79. *Ibid.,* p. 109.

80. *Ibid.,* p. 108.

81. Frederick George Reynolds, "Address Representing the Alumni," *Colgate-Rochester Divinity School Bulletin* 5 (November, 1932), pp. 25–27.

82. Edgar Sheffield Brightman, "The Personality of God," *Colgate-Rochester Divinity School Bulletin,* 5 (November, 1932), pp. 46–62; p. 59.

83. Dewey in fact emphasized that art should be filled with a tension based on the continually shifting relationship of objects: "Order is not imposed from without but is made out of the relations of harmonious interactions that energies bear to one another. . . . It comes to include within its balanced movement a greater variety of changes" (John Dewey, *Art as Experience,* New York: Wideview/Perigee, 1980 [1934], p. 14). Both Dewey and William James had tried to reconcile art and religion through theories based on perceptual and experiential complexity. See also Chapters 2 and 3 of this book.

84. *A Noble Landmark of New York. The Fifth Avenue Presbyterian Church: 1808–1958,* New York: Fifth Avenue Presbyterian Church, 1960, pp. 81–83.

85. For the history of the gift by Mrs. Harkness, see the Archives, Connecticut College, New London, Conn.

86. The chapel is more or less in its original condition. For period views and descriptions, see Katherine Blunt, "Harkness Chapel," *Connecticut College for Women Alumni News* 15 (Summer, 1938), pp. 1–2.

87. For the building history, see: Minutes of the New York University Trustees, December 7, 1926, NYUA; Minutes of the Trustees, April 23, 1928, NYUA; Minutes of the Trustees, December 18, 1928, NYUA; "New

York University—Report of the Chancellor—1928," NYUA; contract between James Gamble Rogers, Inc., and New York University, dated April 28, 1928, JGR Papers.

88. John W. Withers, "The New Buildings of the School of Education," *New York University Alumnus*, February 20, 1930, pp. 181–82; Elmer Brown, "Dedication Address, New School of Education," *New York University Daily News*, March 30, 1930, p. 3.

89. Elsie A. Hug, *Seventy-Five Years in Education. The Role of the School of Education, New York University, 1890–1965*, New York: New York University Press, 1965.

90. Architectural historian Carol Krinsky describes the building in terms of its gothicizing verticality and sees the abstraction of the ornament tending toward an Art Deco style. Carol Herselle Krinsky, "150 Years of N.Y.U. Buildings," *New York University Education Quarterly* 12 (Spring, 1981), pp. 18–28; p. 25.

91. James Gamble Rogers, Inc., "Building for Wall Street Center New York University," undated rendering, JGR Papers.

92. The building bears some resemblance to all three of the prizewinners in the 1922 Chicago Tribune Competition: Hood & Howells, Eliel Saarinen, and Holabird & Roche, in that order. Rogers received an honorable mention in this competition with a scheme that was itself closer in design to Cass Gilbert's Woolworth Building in New York. Like many other architects of the period, Rogers seems to have assimilated the results of the competition, which pointed toward a possible synthesis of structural expression and expressive ornamentation. See *The International Competition for the Chicago Tribune MCMXXII* (n. 38), pp. 48–60, 62.

93. Nicholas Murray Butler to Edward S. Harkness, December 11, 1926, Nicholas Murray Butler Papers, Manuscripts Collections, Butler Library, Columbia University, New York, N.Y.

94. Memorandum report, meeting between Edward S. Harkness, Malcolm Aldrich, President Butler, November 26, 1930, CFA. Williamson was corresponding with Rogers as early as 1928 about a proposed new library. James Gamble Rogers to C. C. Williamson, September 12, 1928, Archives, Columbia University Libraries, Manuscripts Collections, Butler Library, New York, N.Y.

95. Nicholas Murray Butler, "The Libraries of Columbia," in *South Hall Columbia University New York*, New York: Columbia University, 1935, pp. 1–5.

96. Memorandum of Meeting, November 26, 1930 (n. 94), CFA.

97. Malcolm Aldrich to President Butler, December 12, 1930, CFA.

98. James Gamble Rogers to President Butler, February 13, 1931, CFA.

99. Cost estimate by Eidlitz & Sons, April 9, 1931; accepted by James Gamble Rogers, Inc., May 19, 1931, JGR Papers.

100. President Butler to Malcolm Aldrich, February 27, 1931, CFA.

101. Eugene Savage "The South Hall Mural," in Butler, *South Hall*, pp. 21–23.

102. Memorandum of Meeting, Malcolm Aldrich and President Butler, April 21, 1932, CFA.

103. Edward S. Harkness to President Butler, May 8, 1931, CFA; Charles N. Kent, James Gamble Rogers, Inc., to C. C. Williamson, April 30, 1931, Charles Clarence Williamson Correspondence, Archives, Columbia University Libraries, Manuscripts Collection, Butler Library, New York, N.Y. Unsigned note, dated February 18, 1935 (Malcolm Aldrich?), CFA.

104. Dr. Helmut Lehman-Haupt to Charles Clarence Williamson, June 12, 1931, Charles Clarence Williamson Correspondence, loc. cit.; see also Edward S. Harkness to President James Rowland Angell, May 20, 1931, JRA Papers.

105. In defense of the final design, it must be noted that the building was designed so that the additional stack area requested by Williamson could be added on top of the building, giving the monumental front a more effective backdrop. Buildings planned to either side of the library would also have helped to justify its awkward setbacks and mix of materials. What works about the building, as Robert A. M. Stern has noted, is the fact that its giant screen of fourteen limestone Ionic columns, stretched for over 200 feet over a solid base, gestures toward the columned front of the Low Library and gives a grand scale to the expanse of the lawn. Robert A.M. Stern, Gregory Gilmartin, and Thomas Mellins, *New York 1930. Architecture and Urbanism between the Two World Wars*, New York: Rizzoli International Publications, 1987, p. 110.

106. Apparently this cornice did cause considerable concern to the designers. The magazine of the Columbia alumni reported that the cornice, originally designed in brick, was rebuilt at considerable expense in stone after the building was nearly completed. "South Hall to Be Dedicated Nov. 30," *Columbia Alumni News*, November 23, 1934, pp. 5–12.

107. The project architect for the Library was Charles Kent, apparently a fairly recent arrival at the James Gamble Rogers office. It is unclear why the commission was handled by this man rather than one of the more senior and seasoned members of Rogers' staff. Kent was a graduate of Columbia College. The sculptor was Rogers' frequent collaborator, René Chambellan. (See René Chambellan, "Models—Butler Library," Columbia University Buildings Collection, Avery Archives, Columbia University, New York, N.Y.)

108. Contract for the construction of Ossining High School, dated February 27, 1929; the building was constructed for $634,000, JGR Papers.

109. The group is identified in a photograph caption of the dedication of the Library in the *The Yale Alumni Weekly*, May 27, 1932, p. 689.

110. John Hope, President of Atlanta University, to Trevor Arnett, President of the General Education Board, October 6, 1930, and January 29, 1931, Archives, Atlanta University, Woodruff Library, Atlanta, Ga.

111. John Hope to Trevor Arnett, February 6, 1931, Archives, Atlanta University, loc. cit. The General Education Board, which had strong ties to the Rockefellers, also paid for the Memorial Sloan-Kettering Hospital that Rogers designed in New York.

112. "Program for Various Buildings, Atlanta University, Atlanta, Georgia," typescript dated February 16, 1931, Archives, Atlanta University, loc. cit.

113. Contract for construction of a library, men's and women's dormitories, administration building, president's residence, and power plant, dated April 13, 1931, JGR Papers.

114. Program information comes from an undated response to Association of American Colleges Architectural Advisory Bureau Questionnaire, Archives, Atlanta University, loc. cit. See also "Atlanta University Library," *Architectural Record* 73 (May, 1932), pp. 325–28. There are no further records of site visits, nor are any plans preserved in the James Gamble Rogers Papers. Rogers' son, Frank, who took over the office, did continue to design buildings for the university and was a member of its board of trustees.

115. "Abbott Hall," miscellaneous unidentified clippings, NUA.

116. Rogers originally had envisioned the dormitory as part of the major axis of the campus, but his plans were altered when Thorne Hall was constructed.

117. "Abbott Hall Dedication," *Northwestern Alumni News* 20 (November, 1940), pp. 10–12.

118. "Abbott Hall," construction documents, Northwestern University Architect's Office Archives, Northwestern University, Evanston, Ill.

119. "Abbott Hall Dedication," p. 10.

CHAPTER 7

1. Rogers associated with hospital architect Henry C. Pelton during the 1930s, and assimilated Pelton's office after his death. Frank Rogers, James Gamble's son, continued the firm as Rogers & Butler after his father's death, designing additions to many of Rogers' buildings. The current firm has no official connections with the Rogers family. A grandson, James Gamble Rogers III, maintains a separate architectural practice.

2. Edward S. Harkness to Robert W. DeForest, Presbyterian Hospital, December 19, 1910, CFA.

3. A. McGehee Harvey and Susan L. Abrams, *"For the Welfare of Mankind." The Commonwealth Fund and American Medicine*, Baltimore, London: Johns Hopkins University Press, 1986.

4. "Records of Contributions to Yale University through January 3, 1940," CFA.

5. *Yale Alumni Weekly* 12, May 2, 1913, p. 830.

6. "Changsha Hunan China," Yale University Architectural Drawings Collection, Sterling Memorial Library, New Haven, Conn.

7. "Edward S. Harkness—Ledger," CFA.

8. Edward S. Harkness to Robert W. DeForest (n. 2).

9. Albert R. Lamb, *The Presbyterian Hospital and the Columbia-Presbyterian Medical Center 1868–1943*, New York: Columbia University Press, 1955, pp. 75–91, 161–64.

10. "Minutes of Meetings of the Board of Managers, The Presbyterian Hospital in the City of New York," vol. 5, October 11, 1927–June 7, 1931. Archives, Columbia-Presbyterian Medical Center, New York, N.Y.

11. Lamb, *Presbyterian Hospital*, p. 181.

12. *Ibid.*, p. 183.

13. The design of hospitals was a source of continual debate from the beginning of the nineteenth century onward. In America, however, unlike in Europe, the sanitary and health arguments for Modernism do not seem to have gained much popularity and thus did not lead to the kind of open, white sanatoria and hospitals that were the harbingers of a new age

in Scandinavia and Holland. The idea of using the skyscraper as a model for the design of hospitals appears to have been Rogers', but it is of course difficult to ascertain, since several large medical complexes were built shortly thereafter. The best, though opinionated, history of hospital design is John D. Thompson and Grace Goldin, *The Hospital: A Social and Architectural History*, New Haven: Yale University Press, 1975.

14. C. Charles Burlingame, "The Medical Center in New York," *The Architect* 10 (July, 1928), pp. 442–43; George Nichols, "The Development of the Medical Center," *The Architect* 10 (July, 1928), pp. 447–551; Janet Peterkin, "Manhattan's Colossus of Medical Centers," *The Modern Hospital* 31 (July, 1928), pp. 1–12.

15. Burlingame, "Medical Center," p. 442.

16. The rationalization of the design process was of course part and parcel of a larger adoption of corporate methods of work in architecture offices during this period. This appears to be one of the first instances, however, when an explicit method of client need analysis was applied at a large scale.

17. Burlingame, "Medical Center," p. 442.

18. Nichols, "Development," p. 451.

19. "First Completed Units of Medical Center Officially Opened to Thousands of Visitors," *United News Letter*, March 3, 1928, pp. 9–10, 14.

20. For the best discussion of such schemes, see: Rem Koolhaas, *Delirious New York. A Retroactive Manifesto for Manhattan*, New York: Oxford University Press, 1978; Hugh Ferriss, *The Metropolis of Tomorrow*, New York: Ives Washburn, 1929.

21. Edward F. Stevens, "Hospital Details and Finish," *The Architectural Forum* 49 (December, 1928), pp. 889–98; King A. Reid, "The Lighting of Hospitals," *ibid.*, pp. 917–24; Walter A. Batson, "Electrical Equipment for Hospitals," *ibid.*, pp. 925–28.

22. It is unclear whether James

Gamble Rogers participated in the design process for the New York State building. Certainly Jones' architecture is a more broadly drawn version of that of the Medical Center, and the planning of the State building was coordinated by the Joint Administrative Board. Henry C. Pelton, who was later to associate with Rogers on numerous hospitals, was the consulting architect for the New York State building. Archives, Columbia-Presbyterian Medical Center, New York, N.Y.

23. Unidentified drawing published in *The Nation-wide-Review*, November 1, 1927, p. 15.

24. The building has been demolished, and few photographs of its interior remain.

25. The New York Hospital-Cornell Medical Center was designed by the Boston firm of Coolidge, Shepley, Bulfinch & Abbott in 1932 and was equally large. It covered forty-five acres of floor space. Its tallest building was twenty-seven stories.

26. Dr. Henry S. Williams, "A Hospital in the Clouds. The Story of New York's New Skyscraper Medical Center," *The World's Work* 53 (February, 1927), pp. 408–18.

27. Marrion Wilcox, "New York's Great Medical Center," *Architectural Record* 58 (August, 1925), pp. 101–15.

28. Walter McQuade, "Our Feature Film," *The Architect* 10 (July, 1928), p. 441.

29. "Aber das New York von Heute baut mit exakter Vernunft exakte Techniks": Erich Mendelsohn, *Russland Europa America. Ein Architektonischer Querschnitt*, Berlin: Rudolf Mosse Buchverlag, 1929, p. 196.

30. "Dieser Weg zerlangt auch Amerikas Willen zum Neuen, ausgedruckt in der ordnenden Kraft seiner Samengezetzgebung": *ibid.*, p. 216.

31. Rosemary Stevens, *In Sickness and in Wealth; American Hospitals in the Twentieth Century*, New York: Basic Books, 1989, pp. 11, 140–69; Charles E. Rosenberg, *The Care of Strangers: The Rise of America's Hospital System*, New York: Basic Books, 1989.

32. Rogers renovated the Harkness Pavilion (1929) and the College of Physicians and Surgeons (1937) but also was the joint-venture architect for several other buildings associated with the Medical Center, such as the Babies Hospital (1928–30). His son continued to work at the Medical Center, eventually replacing several of the original buildings. Lamb, *Presbyterian Hospital*, p. 248ff. See also: Archives, Columbia-Presbyterian Medical Center, New York, N.Y.; JGR Papers.

33. Charles N. Kent, "Bard Hall," *Columbia University Quarterly* 23 (June, 1931), pp. 131–36.

34. Dean Sage to Malcolm Aldrich, November 14, 1933; Malcolm Aldrich to Dean Sage, February 23, 1934, CFA.

35. George Nichols, "The New Eye Hospital Columbia-Presbyterian Medical Center," *Architectural Record* 47 (July, 1932), pp. 15–26.

36. *Ibid.*, p. 16.

37. *Ibid.*

38. James O. Oliver, "Voice Transmission in the Eye Hospital," *ibid.*, pp. 26–29; Henry C. Logan, "Operating Room Lighting in the Institute of Ophthalmology," *ibid.*, pp. 30–32.

39. Ironically, the interior, which supposedly dictated the design of the whole mass of the building, is organized in a way extremely similar to many other James Gamble Rogers buildings. The main entrance axis ends at a rather unceremonious "Service Lobby," and one is forced to turn 90 degrees either way down a double-loaded corridor. This corridor itself then branches out at its termination to allow one to enter the wings. Vertical circulation is suppressed as isolated incidents off of these corridors. The Institute of Ophthalmology is still in use, though it has been extensively renovated and, because of subsequent changes in the context, it is difficult to gauge the original impact of the scale of the building.

40. The hospital is today the Sloan-Kettering Cancer Center. *Milestones of the Memorial Hospital for the Treat-*

ment of Cancer and Allied Diseases, New York: Memorial Hospital for the Treatment of Cancer and Allied Diseases, 1938, pp. 8–13.

41. James Gamble Rogers to Archibald Douglas, Counsel to the Memorial Hospital, April 27, 1932, JGR Papers.

42. James T. Lee, Chairman of the Building Committee, to Harry Pelham Robbins, President, Memorial Hospital, May 6, 1938, Archives, Sloan-Kettering Cancer Center, New York, N.Y.

43. *Prospectus—The New Memorial Hospital*, undated pamphlet [1937], p. 5, Archives, Sloan-Kettering Cancer Center, New York, N.Y.

44. *Years of Progress. Report for Quadrennium 1936–1939*, New York: Memorial Hospital for the Treatment of Cancer and Allied Diseases, 1939, p. 20.

45. *Ibid.*, p. 28.

46. Edwin A. Salmon, "The New Battleground in Cancer War," *The Modern Hospital* 55 (September, 1940), pp. 56–59.

47. See also "The Memorial Hospital for the Treatment of Cancer and Allied Diseases, N.Y.C.," *Architectural Record* 71 (November, 1939), pp. 380–83. The northern facade of the building remains intact, but additions and demolition have altered the remaining facades beyond recognition.

48. James Gamble Rogers may have worked on the King's County Hospital in Brooklyn, 1937, a project that was carried further by his son, but there are no clear records to indicate his involvement with this project. Frank Rogers' projects, many of them additions to his father's buildings, were of a generic quasi-Modernist, quasi-monumental style that one archivist described as "bureaucratic moderne."

49. Harvey and Abrams, *Commonwealth Fund*, pp. 114–17.

50. *Twenty-fifth Annual Report of the Commonwealth Fund*, New York: Commonwealth Fund, 1944.

51. Harvey and Abrams, p. 515ff.

52. Henry J. Southmayd, "Rural

Hospitals," *Nelson's Loose-Leaf Medicine*, vol. 7, part 1, chap. 13, p. 37.

53. The Ku Klux Klan mounted a campaign against the building in Glasgow, Kentucky, and in Farmville the hospital had only four patients after a few years of operation, CFA.

54. Southmayd, "Rural Hospitals," p. 40.

55. James Gamble Rogers to H. J. Southmayd, October 24, 1925; contract between The Commonwealth Fund and James Gamble Rogers, Inc., and Henry C. Pelton, dated October 15, 1931, CFA.

56. Henry C. Pelton to H. J. Southmayd, January 14, 1926, CFA.

57. *Eighth Annual Report of The Commonwealth Fund*, New York: Commonwealth Fund, 1927, p. 63.

58. Construction documents for Rural Hospitals, dated January 10, 1927, through June 14, 1942, CFA.

59. "Beloit Community Hospital Stories," unidentified pamphlet [1930], CFA.

60. Contracts between James Gamble Rogers, Inc., and The Commonwealth Fund, for Rural Hospitals, dated from June 29, 1936, through June 24, 1946, JGR Papers.

61. Utah Valley Hospital, Provo, Utah, undated photographs, CFA.

62. H. J. Southmayd to Barry Smith, President of the Commonwealth Fund, May 22, 1942, CFA.

63. Correspondence between H. J. Southmayd and James Gamble Rogers, May–June, 1942, CFA.

Chronology

List of Buildings Designed by James Gamble Rogers (year denotes date of completion)

1893	Lees Building, Chicago, Illinois
1900	Robert H. Allerton House, Monticello, Illinois (with J. J. Borie)
1900	William H. Hubbard House, Lake Forest, Illinois
1901	Dover Street Houses, Chicago, Illinois (7 houses)
1901	Winthrop Street Houses, Chicago, Illinois (13 houses)
1902	The Vonnah Apartment Building, Chicago, Illinois
1902	Arthur L. Farwell House, Lake Forest, Illinois
1902	Stone Gate, Farwell Estate, Lake Forest, Illinois
1902	A. B. Dick House, Lake Forest, Illinois
1902	H. S. Robbins House, Lake Forest, Illinois
1902	C. E. Pope House, Lake Forest, Illinois
1902	Arthur Pope House, Geneva, Illinois
1902	Fred H. Page House, Highland Park, Illinois
1902	Francis Parker School, Chicago, Illinois (demolished)
1903	H. W. Finch House, Chicago, Illinois
1903	George S. Isham House, Chicago, Illinois
1903	Lucas Broadhead House, Lexington, Kentucky
1904	Winton Block, Chicago, Illinois
1904	George Anderson House, Lake Forest, Illinois
1904	F. C. Lett House, Evanston, Illinois
1904	George Hamlin House, Chicago, Illinois (demolished)
1904	McCormick Reaper Works Men's Club, Chicago, Illinois
1904	School of Education, University of Chicago, Chicago, Illinois
1905	Belfield Hall, School of Education, University of Chicago, Chicago, Illinois
1905	A. M. Day House, Lake Forest, Illinois (remodeling)
1905	Anita McCormick Blaine House, Chicago, Illinois (remodeling)

1905	Charles D. Williams House, Kenilworth, Illinois (with Charles A. Philips)
1905	J. A. Bellows House, Kenilworth, Illinois (with John A. Rogers)
1905	Apartment Building, State and Schiller streets, Chicago, Illinois (demolished)
1905	Gorton School, Lake Forest, Illinois (demolished)
1905	George W. Stewart Apartment Building, Chicago, Illinois (demolished)
1906	Evanston Public Library, Evanston, Illinois (with Charles A. Philips)
1906	Hyde Park Baptist Church, Chicago, Illinois
1906	E. P. Harrison House, Cincinnati, Ohio
1906	Edward Yeomans House, Winnetka, Illinois
1906	Oaklands (McCormick Estate), Toronto, Ontario (remodeling)
1906	James S. Anderson Block, Lake Forest, Illinois
1906	Hofer House, Cincinnati, Ohio
1906	Gymnasium, School of Education, University of Chicago, Chicago, Illinois (demolished)
1908	Laurel Court (Peter G. Thomson House)
1908	Edward S. Harkness House, New York, New York
1909	Charles W. Harkness House, Madison, New Jersey (demolished)
1909	Shelby County Courthouse, Memphis, Tennessee
1910	Central Bank and Trust Building, Memphis, Tennessee
1910	Jonathan Bulkley House, New York, New York
1911	Greenman Memorial Chapel, Elm Grove Cemetery, Mystic, Connecticut
1911	A. Henry Mosle House, Black Point, Connecticut
1913	Charles Neave House, Ossining, New York
1914	James Gamble Rogers House, Black Point, Connecticut
1915	James Gamble Rogers House, New York, New York (remodeling)
1915	New Orleans Post Office and Court House, New Orleans, Louisiana

1915	Yale Club, New York, New York
1915	Sloan House, Garrison, New York
1915	Yale Boat House, Gales Ferry, Connecticut
1915	Yale-in-China Hospital, Changsha, China
1916	New Haven Post Office, New Haven, Connecticut
1916	Brooks Memorial Art Gallery, Memphis, Tennessee
1916	Madison Avenue Presbyterian Church Chapter House, New York, New York
1916	Mannes College of Music, New York, New York
1916	Weekend (Edward S. Harkness House), Manhasset, New York
1917	Bridgeport Central High School, Bridgeport, Connecticut
1917	George E. Ide House, Long Island, New York
1918	Newcomb Hall, Sophie Newcomb College, New Orleans, Louisiana
1918	Josephine Louise House, Sophie Newcomb College, New Orleans, Louisiana
1918	Arts Building, Sophie Newcomb College, New Orleans, Louisiana
1920	Arthur Farwell House, Geneva, Illinois
1921	Harkness Memorial Quadrangle, Yale University, New Haven, Connecticut
1922	Business Office, Northwestern University, Evanston, Illinois
1924	Bob Cook Boathouse, Derby, Connecticut
1924	Harkness Mausoleum, Woodlawn Cemetery, New York, New York
1925	Crane Company Exhibit Building, Atlantic City, New Jersey (demolished)
1925	Parish House, Fifth Avenue Presbyterian Church, New York, New York
1926	Connecticut General Life Insurance Company Home Office Building, Hartford, Connecticut
1926	Norton Hall, Southern Baptist Theological Seminary, Louisville, Kentucky
1926	Mullins Hall, Southern Baptist Theological Seminary, Louisville, Kentucky

1926	Heating Plant, Southern Baptist Theological Seminary, Louisville, Kentucky
1926	Married students' apartment buildings, Southern Baptist Theological Seminary, Louisville, Kentucky
1926	Montgomery Ward Memorial Building, McKinlock Campus, Northwestern University, Chicago, Illinois
1926	Wieboldt Hall of Commerce, McKinlock Campus, Northwestern University, Chicago, Illinois
1926	William F. Peters House, Lake Forest, Illinois
1927	Levy Mayer Hall of Law, Elbert H. Gary Library of Law, McKinlock Campus, Northwestern University, Chicago, Illinois
1927	Sorority Quadrangle, Northwestern University, Evanston, Illinois
1927	Dyche Stadium, Northwestern University, Evanston, Illinois
1927	Featherbed Lane Presbyterian Church, New York, New York
1927	Beta Theta Pi Fraternity, Yale University, New Haven, Connecticut
1927	Delta Kappa Epsilon Fraternity, Yale University, New Haven, Connecticut
1927	Donald J. Bridgman House, Norwalk, Connecticut
1928	Levering Gymnasium, Southern Baptist Theological Seminary, Louisville, Kentucky
1928	Psi Upsilon Fraternity, Yale University, New Haven, Connecticut
1928	College of Physicians and Surgeons and Presbyterian Hospital, Columbia-Presbyterian Medical Center, New York, New York
1928	Vanderbilt Clinic, Columbia-Presbyterian Medical Center, New York, New York
1928	Babies Hospital, Columbia-Presbyterian Medical Center, New York, New York
1928	Harkness Pavilion, Columbia-Presbyterian Medical Center, New York, New York
1928	Service Building, Columbia-Presbyterian Medical Center, New York, New York
1928	Neurological Institute, Columbia-Presbyterian Medical Center, New York, New York
1928	Yeamans Hall Club House and Cottages, Yeamans Hall, South Carolina
1928	Thomas W. Lamont Cottage, Yeamans Hall, South Carolina

1928	Mount Hope Farm (Colonel E. Parmarlee Prentice House), Williamstown, Massachusetts,
1929	Bard Hall, Columbia-Presbyterian Medical Center, New York, New York (demolished)
1929	Anna C. Maxwell Hall, Columbia-Presbyterian Medical Center, New York, New York (demolished)
1929	Alpha Delta Phi Fraternity, Yale University, New Haven, Connecticut
1929	Hobart Hall, Northwestern University, Evanston, Illinois
1929	Rogers Hall, Northwestern University, Evanston, Illinois
1929	Upper School Building, The Taft School, Watertown, Connecticut
1929	Infirmary Building, The Taft School, Watertown, Connecticut
1929	Service Building, The Taft School, Watertown, Connecticut
1929	Power Plant, The Taft School, Watertown, Connecticut
1929	A. Henry Mosle Cottage, Yeamans Hall, South Carolina
1929	Arthur Farwell Cottage, Yeamans Hall, South Carolina
1929	Goetchius Cottage, Yeamans Hall, South Carolina
1929	Scott McLanahan Cottage, Yeamans Hall, South Carolina
1929	Mary M. Moen House, Oyster Bay, New York
1930	Aetna Life Insurance Company Home Office Building, Hartford, Connecticut
1930	School of Education, New York University, New York, New York
1930	Alpha Sigma Phi Fraternity, Yale University, New Haven, Connecticut
1931	Sterling Memorial Library, Yale University, New Haven, Connecticut
1931	School of Law, Yale University, New Haven, Connecticut
1931	University Theatre, Yale University, New Haven, Connecticut (facade)
1931	Institute of Ophthalmology, Columbia-Presbyterian Medical Center, New York, New York
1932	Jonathan Edwards College, Yale University, New Haven, Connecticut
1932	Hall of Graduate Studies, Yale University, New Haven, Connecticut
1932	George R. Thorne Hall, McKinlock Campus, Northwestern University, Chicago, Illinois

1932	Deering Library, Northwestern University, Evanston, Illinois
1932	Colgate-Rochester Theological Seminary, Rochester, New York
1932	Library, Atlanta College, Atlanta, Georgia
1933	Branford College, Yale University, New Haven, Connecticut (remodeling)
1933	Saybrook College, Yale University, New Haven, Connecticut (remodeling)
1933	Trumbull College, Yale University, New Haven, Connecticut
1933	Davenport College, Yale University, New Haven, Connecticut
1933	Pierson College, Yale University, New Haven, Connecticut
1933	Dormitories, Atlanta College, Atlanta, Georgia
1933	Thayer Hall, Atlanta College, Atlanta, Georgia
1933	President's House, Atlanta College, Atlanta, Georgia
1933	Morris Tyler House, Woodbridge, Connecticut
1934	Berkeley College, Yale University, New Haven, Connecticut
1934	Butler Library, Columbia University in the City of New York, New York
1934	James J. Lee House, Brookville, New York
1935	Timothy Dwight College, Yale University, New Haven, Connecticut
1936	Health Center, Ayer, Massachusetts
1936	Rural Hospital and Nurses' Home, Farmville, Virginia
1937	New Schoolhouse, St. Paul's School, Concord, New Hampshire
1937	Valley View Hospital, Ada, Oklahoma
1938	Willard Hall, Northwestern University, Evanston, Illinois
1938	Mary T. Bradley Cottage, Yeamans Hall, South Carolina
1938	Harkness Chapel, Connecticut College for Women, New London, Connecticut
1938	Health Center, Blountville, Tennessee
1938	Health Center, McComb, Mississippi
1938	Health Center, Trenton, Tennessee
1938	Utah Valley Hospital, Provo, Utah
1939	New York Memorial Hospital for the Treatment of Cancer and Allied Diseases, New York, New York (with Henry C. Pelton)

1939	Chrysler Motors Building, New York World's Fair, New York, New York (demolished)
1939	Health Center, Meridian, Mississippi
1939	Hospital and Nurses' Home, Lancaster, South Carolina
1939	King's Mountain Memorial Hospital, Bristol, Virginia
1940	Scott Hall, Northwestern University, Evanston, Illinois
1940	Abbott Hall, McKinlock Campus, Northwestern University, Chicago, Illinois
1940	Illini Community Hospital and Nurses' Home, Pittsfield, Illinois
1941	Lutkin Hall, Northwestern University, Evanston, Illinois
1941	Central Michigan Community Hospital, Mt. Pleasant, Michigan
1943	Jones Country Health Center, Laurel, Mississippi
1946	Missouri Delta Community Hospital, Sikeston, Missouri
1946	Health Center, Gallatin, Tennessee

UNREALIZED AND PARTIALLY REALIZED PROJECTS

1898	"A House for the United State Embassy in Paris" (diploma project)
1899	Chicago Institute, Chicago, Illinois
1906	United States Department of State, Washington, D.C. (competition entry)
1907	Soldiers' Memorial, Allegheny, Pennsylvania (with Herbert D. Hale)
1907	Delaware, Lackawanna & Western Railroad Station, Scranton, Pennsylvania (with Herbert D. Hale)
1911	Sophie Newcomb College, New Orleans, Louisiana
1915	The Yale Theatre, Yale University, New Haven, Connecticut
1921	Sketch Plan for the Future Development of Yale University, New Haven, Connecticut
1922	Chicago Tribune Tower, Chicago, Illinois (competition entry)
1925	Southern Baptist Theological Seminary, Louisville, Kentucky
1925	Chapel, Southern Baptist Theological Seminary, Louisville, Kentucky

1925	President's House, Southern Baptist Theological Seminary, Louisville, Kentucky
1928	Dormitory for the Old Campus, Yale University, New Haven, Connecticut
1933	Women's Dormitory, Yale University, New Haven, Connecticut
no date	Loomis Institute, New London, Connecticut
no date	Building for Wall Street Center, New York, New York
no date	University Chapel, Northwestern University, Evanston, Illinois
no date	Service Building for the Yale & Towne Manufacturing Company, Stamford, Connecticut

Index

Figure numbers appear in italics following page numbers.

A

Academic Classicism, 16–17, 28, 39, 46, 47, 48, 71, 200, 240 n. 17
Adams, Henry, 80
Aldis, Owen, 242 n. 6
Aldrich, Malcolm, 142, 204
Allerton, Robert H., 67
Alundum, 102
Anderson, George, 238 n. 68
Angell, James Rowland, 3, 114, 127, 131, 133, 137, 138, 139–41, 143–44, 150, 158, 171, 192, 193, 246 n. 36, 247 n. 83, 250 n. 10
The Architect, 63–65
Architectural Record, 102, 113, 223, 241 n. 24
Art As Experience (Dewey), 53
Arts and Crafts movement, 26–27, 238 n. 50, 240 n. 17
Ashland Block, Chicago, IL, 14, 16, 18, 237 n. 43; 3
Atterbury, Grosvenor, 16
Austin, Henry, 48

B

Baker, Samuel, 179, 180
Ballantyne, Ainslie, 179–80, 192, 206, 234
Bannard, Otto, 229
Barber, Donn, 64, 113
Beaven, Albert William, 194
Behrens, Peter, 11
Bennett, Parsons & Frost, 188, 255 nn. 51, 57
Berkeley, 153
Bernard, Adolph, 245 n. 11
Bibliotheque Ste.-Geneviève, Paris, 191
Blaine, Anita McCormick (Mrs. Emmons), 67–70, 73, 242 n. 4
Blaine, Emmons, 67
Blondel, Paul, 16, 78
Bragdon, Claude, 43, 53
Brainard, Morgan, 97
Brightman, Edgar Sheffield, 198

Broadhead, Lucas, 14, 238 n. 68
Brooks, Samuel Hamilton, 90
Brown, Sam, Jr., 19
Bulkley, Jonathan, 37
    house, New York, NY, 37–38; *31*
Burlingame, C . C ., 214
Burnham, Daniel H., 11 , 14, 47, 52, 60, 81, 236 nn. 24, 26, 255 n. 51; 3
Burnham & Root, 14; 3
Butler, Nicholas Murray, 202, 203, 204

C

Carrère & Hastings, 48; *37*
Chambellan, René, 121, 126, 132, 133, 137, 257 n. 107
Chapel of St. Peter and St. Paul, Concord, NH, 173
Chappell, George S., 64–65
Chicago School, 2–3, 11–12, 14, 18, 21, 43, 53, 140, 179, 214, 237 n. 31, 242 n. 6
Chicago Tribune Building competition, 119, 179, 257 n. 92; *166*
Choisy, Auguste, 16
City Beautiful movement, x, 15, 80, 81, 117, 243 n. 41
Clark, George Rogers, 9
Cobb, Henry Ives, 44–45, 71
Coffin, Henry Sloane, 140
College of the City of New York, New York, NY, 249 n. 99
Collegiate Georgian style, 60–63, 109, 153–56, 158–59, 207
Collegiate Gothic style, 52, 56–58, 62–63, 103, 105–6, 110, 152, 153, 154, 155, 163, 189, 195, 198, 240 n. 17
Colt , Richard C., 36
    house, Garrison, NY, 36–37; *30*
Columbia College of Physicians and Surgeons, 213. *See also under* ROGERS, JAMES GAMBLE, WORKS: Hospitals
Columbia University, New York, NY, 71, 117
    Low Library, 202, 203
    McKim, Mead & White plan for, 202. *See also under* ROGERS, JAMES

GAMBLE, WORKS: Schools and Collegiate Buildings
Commonwealth Fund, 4, 32, 212, 229
Coolidge, Shepley, Bulfinch & Abbott, 155, 162, 250 n. 10, 259 n. 25; *213*
Cooper, James Fenimore, 112
Cope & Stewardson, 105, 108; *90*
Corbett, Harvey Wiley, 218
Cornell University Medical Center, New York, NY, 213, 222; *213*
Cowley, Malcolm, 64, 242 n. 59
Cram, Goodhue & Ferguson, 106, 107, 108, 163; *93, 102*
Cram, Ralph Adams, ix, 6, 49–50, 52, 54, 55–56, 107, 108, 117, 241 nn. 28, 48; *39*
Cram & Ferguson, 175
Crane, Charles, 230, 234
Cret, Paul, 117, 175, 246 n. 42, 251 n. 36
Cross, Wilbur, 133, 135, 138, 249 n. 107

D

Day, Albert Morgan, 22
    house, Lake Forest, IL, 23, 30; *12, 13*
Day, Anne (Mrs. James Gamble Rogers), 22, 114
Day, Frank Miles, 50, 105, 115; *38*
Day, George Parmly, 154, 177
Day & Klauder, 49, 105, 108, 163; *38, 89*
Deering, Charles, 188
DeForest, Allan, 256 n. 77
Delano, William Adams, x, 246 n. 42, 251 n. 36
Delano & Aldrich, 118
Dewey, John, 1, 2, 3, 46, 53, 70–71, 114, 198, 201, 256 n. 83
Dick, A. B., house, Lake Forest, IL, 25; *16*
Dick, Edison, 238 n. 63
Drury, S. S., 62, 173–74
Duke, James B., house, New York, NY, xi
Durand, J.N.L., 43
Dyche, William, 56

E

Ecole des Beaux-Arts, 3, 11, 15–18, 38, 43, 44, 54, 64, 67, 70, 78, 106, 185, 237 n. 37, 239 n. 7

Eidlitz & Sons, 180
Embury, Aymar, 64
Ewing, James, 227
Exposition Internationale des Arts
        Décoratifs, 102

F

Faelten, Otto, 44, 106, 110, 138, 151,
        179, 180, 192, 245 nn. 12, 58
Farnham, Thomas W., 142
Farrand, Beatrix, 35, 229
Farrand, Max, 229
Farwell, Arthur, 22, 177
    house, Lake Forest, IL, 23–25; 14
Farwell, Francis C., 22, 114
Farwell, John V., 22
Farwell, John V., Jr., 22, 114, 118, 119,
        120, 122, 135, 153, 154, 177,
        240 n. 18, 245 n. 36, 247 nn.
        52, 58, 248 n. 83, 249 n. 94
Farwell, John V., IV, 238 n. 68
Ferriss, Hugh, 218, 241 n. 48
Field, Marshall, 22
    estate, Long Island, NY, 47
Finch, F. H., house, Chicago, IL, 27–28;
        20, 21
Fisher, Samuel, 32, 115, 139–41, 170,
        212, 229, 250 n. 10, 253 n. 14
Flagg, Ernest, 16, 47
French, Robert, 170

G

Garvin, John P., 115
General Education Board, 226
Gilbert, Cass, x, 257 n. 92
Gisors, L.H.G. Scellier de, 16
Goodhue, Bertram Grosvenor, 52, 53,
        54, 107, 116, 118–19, 121, 175,
        246 nn. 16, 42, 247 n. 52, 251
        n. 36
Graham, Anderson & Probst, 236 n. 26
Grand Central Terminal, New York,
        NY, 93
Gropius, Walter, 6, 63
Guadet, Julien, 16

H

Hadden, Gavin, 255 n. 52
Hadley, Arthur, 103
Haight, Charles, 48
Hale, Edward Everett, 78
Hale, Herbert D., 16, 31, 78–79, 81,
        243 n. 34. See also Hale &
        Rogers
Hale, William Harlan, 58–59; 41

Hale & Rogers, 78–86
    Delaware, Lackawanna & Western
        Railroad Station, Scranton, PA
        (project), 79; 57
    Engineering Society Building, New
        York, NY, 79; 56
    McCreery Building, New York, NY,
        79
    Post Office and Court House, New
        Orleans, LA, 83–86; 62–65
    Shelby County Courthouse, Mem-
        phis, TN, 81–83; 58–61
    Soldiers' Memorial, Pittsburgh, PA
        (project), 79
Hamlin, George, 238 n. 68
Hardy Holzman Pfeiffer, 254 n. 24
Harkness, Charles William, 31, 103,
        105
    estate, Madison, NJ, 34
Harkness, Edward S., 4, 31–32, 36, 55,
        62, 80, 103, 105, 107, 115,
        116, 117, 139–43, 150, 158,
        161, 162, 170, 173–74, 199,
        203–4, 206, 211–12, 213–14,
        226, 227, 238 n. 74, 239 nn.
        80, 82, 250 nn. 5, 10, 253 n.
        23
    house ("Eolia") nr. New London, CT,
        34–35, 142
    house, New York, NY, 31–34; 25–27
Harkness, Mrs. Edward S., 32, 119
Harkness, Stephen V., 4, 31
Harkness, William S., house, Glen
        Cove, Long Island, NY, 34
The Harkness Hoot, 58–59, 153; 41
Harper, William Rainey, 46, 75
Harrison, E. P., house, Cincinnati, OH,
        30
Harvard University, Cambridge, MA,
        142, 161–62, 250 n. 10
    Graduate School, 63
    Widener Library, 205
Hastings, Thomas, x
Hefner, Hugh, 23
Heisenberg, Werner, 198
Hitchcock, Henry-Russell, 241 n. 48
Holabird, William, 11
Holabird & Roche, 69, 71, 177, 179,
        236 n. 26, 254 n. 45, 257 n.
        92; 163
Holabird & Root, 256 n. 63
Home Insurance Building, Chicago, IL,
        11
Hood, Raymond, 218, 251 n. 31
Hood & Howells, 179, 257 n. 92

Howe, George, 52, 251 n. 31
Howells, William Dean, 98
Hubbard, H., 238 n. 68
Hume, Edward H., 212
Hunt, Richard Morris, 6, 29
Huntington, Robert, 95, 244 n. 80
Hutchins, Robert, 131, 133, 248 n. 83,
        249 n. 94

I

Inns of Court, London, 127, 184
International Harvester, 188
Isham, George, 22, 67
    house, Chicago, IL, 22–23; 11
Isham, Katherine (Mrs. Arthur Farwell),
        22

J

James, William, 1, 2, 3, 5, 39, 256 n. 83
Jefferson, Thomas, 169
Jenny, William LeBaron, 9, 11–13
Jenny & Mundie, 13, 19, 237 n. 34; 2
Jensen, Elmer C., 13
Jones, Sullivan W., 220; 212

K

Kent, Charles N., 224, 257 n. 107
Keogh, Andrew, 120, 121, 122, 126,
        247 n. 58
King's College Chapel, Cambridge,
        England, 129, 132
Klauder, Charles Z., 120; 103. See also
        Day & Klauder
Koch, Theodore, 188–89, 191

L

Labrouste, Henri, 191
Lake Shore Towers, Chicago, IL, 207
Lawrie, Lee, 121
Lehmann-Haupt, Helmut, 204, 257 n.
        104
Lewis, David, 237 n. 44
Linonia & Brothers, 111
Litchfield, Electus D., 64
Lowell, Abbott Lawrence, 161

M

McCormick, Cyrus, 67, 188
McCormick, Stanley, 242 n. 6
McCormick, Vance, 248 n. 58
McCormick family, 22, 23
McKim, Charles, 202
McKinlock, Alexander, 180
McLean, Robert Craik, 12
Maher, George, 21, 255 n. 51; 10

plan for Northwestern University, 185
Manhattan Building, Chicago, IL, 13; 2
Marble House, Newport, RI, 29
Massachusetts Institute of Technology, Cambridge, MA, 106
Mead, George Herbert, 2, 3
Medici Palace, Rome, 96
Mendell, Charles, 250 n. 10
Mendelsohn, Erich, 223
Michelozzi di Bartolomeo, 96
Mies van der Rohe, Ludwig, 207
Moise, Howard, 194–95, 197–98
Monie, C. C., 253 n. 23
Moore, Charles Herbert, 52–53
Morse, Samuel F. B., 112
Mosle, A. Henry, 35
Mullins, E. Y., 166
Mumford, Lewis, 64, 241 n. 48, 242 n. 59
Mundie, William Bryce, 9, 12–13

N

National Gallery of Art, Washington, DC, 47; 35
Nebraska State Capitol, Omaha, 121
Needham, Wesley, 245 n. 12
Netsch, Walter, 255 n. 61
New York State Psychiatric Institute and Hospital, New York, NY, 220, 221, 259 n. 22; 212
Nichols, George, 87, 88, 106, 110–11, 117
Northwestern University, 56–57. See also under ROGERS, JAMES GAMBLE, WORKS: Schools and Collegiate Buildings

O

Olbrich, Joseph Maria, 21
Olmsted, Frederick Law, 117
Olmsted & Olmsted, 36, 254 n. 51

P

Page, F. H., house, Highland Park, IL, 26; 17
Palazzo Massimi, Rome, 93
Palazzo Massimo, Rome, 96
Parker, Francis Wayland, 68, 71
Pelton, Henry C., 226–27, 229, 258 n. 1, 259 n. 22. See also Rogers & Pelton
Perkins, Dwight, 18, 71, 242 n. 8
Perkins, N. C., 81
Perkins & Will, 236 n. 36
Perret, Auguste, 11
Peruzzi, Baldassare, 96

Philips, Charles A., 31
Pierson, George W., 140
Pope, Arthur, 238 n. 68
Pope, C. Edward, house, Lake Forest, IL, 26–27; 18
Pope, John Russell, x, 46–47, 60, 115, 148, 180; 35, 99, 100
Post, George B., 87 , 249 n. 99
Pragmatist movement, 1, 3–4, 39, 53, 80, 140, 239 n. 1
Prairie School, 18, 21, 192
Presbyterian Hospital, New York, NY, 213. See also under ROGERS, JAMES GAMBLE, WORKS: Hospitals
Price, Bruce, 88
Princeton University, Princeton, NJ, 49–50, 106, 115; 39
    Freshman Dormitories, 50; 38
    Hall of Graduate Studies, 106, 108; 93
    Hamilton Hall, 105; 89
    Holder Hall, 105; 89
    Madison Hall, 105
Pugin, A.W.N., 52
Purcell & Elmslie, 21

Q

Quatremère-de-Quincy, Antoine, 43

R

Reformed Dutch Church, Poughkeepsie, NY, 40
Rice University, Houston, TX, 117, 118
Robb, E. Donald, 54–55, 106–7, 110, 179; 40
Robbins, H. S., 25
    house, 25; 15, 19
Roche, Martin, 11
Rockefeller, John D., 4, 31, 193, 227
Rogers, Bernard Fowler (brother of James Gamble Rogers), 9
Rogers, Burgun, Shahide & Deshler, 211
Rogers, Frank (son of James Gamble Rogers), 258 nn. 114, 1
ROGERS, JAMES GAMBLE, LIFE; 1
    architecture of, characterized, 4–7, 39–66, 102
    birth, 9
    competition designs, 179; 166
    as Consulting Architect to Yale University, 113–15
    at Ecole des Beaux-Arts, 15–18; 5, 6
    education, 10–11
    forebears and youth of, 9

joins office of William LeBaron Jenny, 11; of Burnham & Root, 14; of brother, John Arthur Rogers, 18–19
    moves to New York City, 31
    personality of, 1–2
    postcard album, 54, 168, 241 n. 34
    travels, 11, 139–41
    See also below, ROGERS, JAMES GAMBLE, WORKS (Subentries: Churches; Civic Structures; Commercial Structures; Domestic Architecture; Hospitals; Schools and Collegiate Buildings). See also above, ROGERS, JAMES GAMBLE, LIFE
Churches
    Connecticut College, Harkness Chapel, New London, CT, 199–200; 192, 193
    Fifth Avenue Presbyterian Church, Chapel and Chapter House addition, New York, NY, 199; 191
    Hyde Park Baptist Church, Chicago, IL, 75, 243 n. 27; 53
    Madison Avenue Presbyterian Church, Parish House, New York, NY, 92; 74
Civic Structures
    Brooks Museum of Art, Memphis, TN, 90-91, 244 n. 66; 71
    "House for the United States Embassy at Paris" (thesis design), 16, 17, 33, 73; 5, 6
    Post Office, New Haven, CT, 86–89, 106; 66–68
    Post Office and Court House, New Orleans, LA, 83–86, 89; 32d, 62–65
    Shelby County Courthouse, Memphis, TN, 46, 81–83, 89; 32c, 34, 58–61
Commercial Structures
    Aetna Life Insurance Company, Hartford, CT, 97–101; 81–85
    Central Bank and Trust Building, Memphis, TN, 90, 201; 70
    Connecticut General Life Insurance Company, Home Office, Hartford, CT, 95–97; 78–80
    Crane Company Exhibition Building, Atlantic City, NJ, 101–2; 86, 87

Engineering Society Building, New York, NY. *See under* Hale & Rogers
Lees Building, Chicago, IL, 14–15, 17, 201; *4*
McCormick Reaper Works employees' clubhouse, Chicago, IL, 75–78; *54, 55*
McCreery Building, New York, NY. *See under* Hale & Rogers
Winton Block, Chicago, IL, 75; *52*
Domestic Architecture
Anderson house, Lake Forest, IL, 238 n. 68
apartment house ("The Vonnah"), Chicago, IL, 21; *9*
apartment house, Prairie Avenue, Chicago, IL, 243 n. 24
apartment house, Scott and State streets, Chicago, IL, 243 n. 24
apartment house, Sheridan Avenue and Buena Street, Chicago, IL, 243 n. 24
apartment house for J. B. Waller, 19
Black Point, association houses, nr. New London, CT, 35; *28*
Broadhead house, nr. Lexington, KY, 238 n. 68
Bulkley house, New York, NY, 37–38; *31*
Colt house, Garrison, NY, 36–37; *30*
Day house, Lake Forest, IL, 23, 30; *12, 13*
Dick house, Lake Forest, IL, 25, 29; *16*
Farwell house, Lake Forest, IL, 23–25; *14*
Finch house, Chicago, IL, 27–28; *20, 21*
Hamlin house, Chicago, IL, 238 n. 38
Harkness, Charles W., estate, Madison, NJ, 34
Harkness, Edward S., house ("Eolia"), nr. New London, CT, 34–35
Harkness, Edward S., house, New York, NY, 31–34, 37; *25–27*
Harkness, William S., house, Glen Cove, Long Island, NY, 34
Harrison House, Cincinnati, OH, 30
Hofer house, Cincinnati, OH, 30
Hubbard house, Lake Forest, IL, 238 n. 68
Isham house, Chicago, IL, 22–23; *11*
"Laurel Court." *See* Thomson house
Lett house, Evanston, IL, 238 n. 68
Page house, Highland Park, IL, 26; *17*
Peters house, Lake Forest, IL, 252 n. 55

Pope, Arthur, house, Geneva, IL, 238 n. 68
Pope, C. Edward, house, Lake Forest, IL, 26–27; *18*
Robbins house, Lake Forest, IL, 25, 83; *15, 19*
speculative houses, Dover and Winthrop streets, Buena Park, IL, 19; *7, 8*
Thomson house, Cincinnati, OH, 28-30; *22–24*
Yeamans Hall, association houses, nr. Charleston, SC, 35–36; *29*
Hospitals
Columbia-Presbyterian Medical Center, New York, NY, 213–28, 247 n. 54; *209, 211, 214*
Babies Hospital, 259 n. 32
Bard Hall, 224–25
Columbia College of Physicians and Surgeons, 215, 218, 259 n. 32; *207, 208, 210*
Harkness Pavilion, 217, 219, 221, 259 n. 32; *210*
Institute of Ophthalmology, 224, 225–26, 259 n. 32; *215, 216*
Maxwell Hall of Nursing, 220–21
Neurological Institute, 220, 221
Presbyterian Hospital, 215
Vanderbilt Clinic, 215–16, 219
Yale-in-China Hospital, Changsha, 212–13; *204, 205*
(with Henry C. Pelton) Memorial Sloan-Kettering Hospital, New York, NY, 226–28; *32i, 217–219*
(with Henry C. Pelton) Rural Hospital Program, 229–34; *220–225*
Schools and Collegiate Buildings
Atlanta College (Clark-Atlanta University), 206; *119–201*
Bridgeport Central High School, Bridgeport, CT, 91; *72*
Chicago Institute, Chicago, IL (project), 67–70; *32a, 45* (first plan), *46* (second plan)
Colgate-Rochester Theological Seminary, Rochester, NY, 193–99, 256 n. 77; *185–190*
Columbia University, New York, NY, Butler Library, 200, 202–6, 257 n. 105; *196–198*
Francis W. Parker School, Chicago, IL, 73–74, 76; *51*
Gorton School, Lake Forest, IL, 75

Mannes College of Music, New York, NY, 91–92; *73*
New York University, New York, NY
Building for Wall Street Center (project), 201; *195*
School of Education, 200–201; *194*
Northwestern University
Chicago, IL, campus (McClintock campus), 175–77, 217, 218, 254 n. 42; *164, 165*
Abbott Hall, 207, 210, 228; *202, 203*
Gary Library of Law, 180–84; *171*
Levy Meyer Hall of Law, 180, 184; *171*
Montgomery Ward Building, 180–81, 182; *167*
Thorne Hall, 180, 184–85; *172*
Wieboldt Hall, 180, 181–83; *168–170*
Evanston, IL, campus, 175, 185–92, 254 n. 48
Deering Library, 56–57, 185, 188–91, 255 n. 61; *32g, 175–181*
Dyche Stadium, 185, 186
Lutkin Hall, 185, 191–92, 256 n. 63
Scott Hall, 191–92, 207; *182–184*
Sorority Quadrangle, 185, 186–88, 192; *173, 174*
women's dormitories (Hobart, Rogers, and Willard halls), 255 n. 56
Ossining High School, Ossining, NY, 206
St. Paul's School, New Schoolhouse, Concord, NH, 62–63, 173–75; *44, 160–163*
Southern Baptist Theological Seminary, Louisville, KY, 98, 165–70; *147*
dormitory row, 169
Lawn, 169; *154*
Mullins Hall, 166–67; *148, 149*
Norton Hall, 61, 66, 167–68, 253 nn. 8, 9; *32f, 42, 43, 150–153*
Taft School, Watertown, CT, 170–73; *156–159*
Tulane University, New Orleans, LA, Sophie Newcomb College, 95, 163–65, 166, 253 n. 3; *144–146*
University of Chicago, Chicago, IL, School of Education, 2–3, 40,

42, 46, 70–74, 75, 88, 156; 47–49, 50 (Belfield Hall)
Yale University, New Haven, CT
  Berkeley College, 148–53; 129–132
  boathouse (1915), 245
  boathouse (1923), 252 n. 55
  Branford and Saybrook colleges, 146–47; 124
  College Plan, 139–44, 146, 161–62, 249 n. 1, 250 n. 10, 251 n. 25
  Davenport College, x, 153–58, 171, 32b, 133–135
  fraternity houses, 252 n. 55
  Hall of Graduate Studies, 127, 133–38, 228, 247 n. 107; 116–120
  Harkness Memorial Quadrangle, x, 48, 54, 55, 58, 103–15, 117, 118, 121, 122, 125, 126, 127, 128, 130, 133, 135, 139, 140, 144, 145, 146–47, 152, 153, 155, 162, 168, 170, 218, 223; 32e, 91, 92, 94–96
  Harkness Tower, 75, 110, 111, 112, 121, 136, 138, 162, 197; 98
  Wrexham Tower, 111–12, 147; 97
  Jonathan Edwards College, 145–47; 122, 123
  Pierson College, 153–54, 158, 159, 171; 32b, 136–138
  plan for, 117–18; 101
  Sterling Law School, 127–33, 138, 184; 110–115
  Sterling Memorial Library, 58, 59, 113, 116–27, 128, 131, 133, 138, 147, 148, 150, 188, 202, 203, 228, 247 n. 58; 41, 102, 104–109
  Timothy Dwight College, 158–61; 139–142
  Trumbull College, 147–48, 151; 125–128
  Yale Club, New York, NY, 93–95; 75–79
Rogers, James Gamble, III (grandson of James Gamble Rogers), 258 n. 1
Rogers, John Arthur (brother of James Gamble Rogers), 9, 14, 18–19, 237 n. 43, 243 n. 31
Rogers, Joseph (great-grandfather of James Gamble Rogers), 9
Rogers, Joseph Martin (father of James Gamble Rogers), 9
Rogers, Katherine Gamble (mother of James Gamble Rogers), 9

Rogers & Butler, 258 n. 1
Rogers & Pelton, 229–34; 220–225
Root, John Wellborn, 13–14; 3
Rural Hospital Program, 229–34
Ruskin, John, 48, 53, 240 n. 19

S
Saarinen, Eliel, 257 n. 92
Sage, Dean, 206
St. Paul's Academy, Chapel, 62
San Orso, College of, Aosta, 132
Santayana, George, 198
Schuyler, Montgomery, 28, 37–38, 49, 50, 103, 162, 241 n. 24
Scott, Walter Dill, 3, 175–76, 177, 180, 186, 188, 189, 192, 254 n. 27
Scully, Vincent, 240 n. 17
Seymour, George, 86, 142, 158, 250 n. 10
Seymour, Mrs. Charles, 251
Shaw, Howard Van Doren, 16, 22, 176, 237 n. 34
Shaw, Richard Norman, 23, 78
Shepley, Rutan & Coolidge, 33
Shingle Style, 240 n. 17
Skidmore, Owings & Merrill, 236 n. 26, 255 n. 61
Skyscraper Gothic, 179, 217
Sloan-Kettering Memorial Hospital, See Memorial Sloan-Kettering Hospital under ROGERS, JAMES GAMBLE, WORKS: Hospitals
Stanford University, 117, 118
Sterling, John, 113, 117, 162
Sterling Estate, 116, 119, 122, 127, 139, 144, 229, 247 n. 52, 249 n. 95
Stillman, Mary (Mrs. Edward S. Harkness), 32, 199
Stokes, Anson Phelps, 55, 105, 111, 115, 126
Sturgis, Russell, Jr., 48; 36
Sullivan, Louis, 11–12, 43, 179

T
Taft, Horace, Jr., 253 n. 15
Taft, Horace Dutton, 170–71
Tafuri, Manfredo, 252 n. 56
Tarnsey Act, 80, 86
Thomson, Mr. and Mrs. Peter Gibson, 28, 29
  house, Cincinnati, OH, 28–30; 22–24, 32b
Trinity College, Hartford, CT, 117
Trumbauer, Horace, x, 205
Tuttle, John Donald, 138

U
University of Chicago, Chicago, IL, 117 Noyes Hall, 33 See also under ROGERS, JAMES GAMBLE, WORKS: Schools and Collegiate Buildings
University of Pennsylvania, Philadelphia, PA, 105
University of Pittsburgh, Pittsburgh, PA, 120; 103
University of Texas, Austin, TX, 120
University of Virginia, Charlottesville, VA, 159, 165, 169; 155
University of Wisconsin, Madison, WI, 117

V
Vaughan, Henry, 45, 52, 62, 173, 253 n. 21
Veblen, Thorstein, 45, 46, 59
Venturi, Robert, 39, 239 n. 2
Viollet-le-Duc, Eugène-Emmanuel, 44, 240 n. 10
Voysey, C.F.A., 21

W
Waller, J. B., 9–10, 14, 19
  apartment house for, 19
Waller, Robert A., 14
Waller, William, 14
Ward, Mrs. Montgomery, 180
Ware, Edward T., 206
Warren, Whitney, x
Washington University, 105; 90
Western Association of Architects, 12
Whitehead, Russell F., 86
Wigmore, John J., 56
Wilcox, Marrion, 102, 112, 223
Williamson, C. C., 202, 203, 204
Winthrop, John, 194
Woolworth Building, New York, NY, 257 n. 92
World's Columbian Exposition, 15
Wright, Frank Lloyd, 13, 18, 21, 27, 43, 44, 60, 235 chap. 1 n. 5, 236 n. 21

Y
Yale, Elihu, 111, 112
Yale-in-China program, 212
Yale University, New Haven, CT, 245 n. 10
  Bicentennial Building group, 48, 103, 247 n. 58; 37
  Calhoun College, 148

College Plan, 139–44, 146, 161–62,
        249 n. 1, 250 n. 10, 251 n. 25
Connecticut Hall, 153
Durfee Hall, 48, 104
Farnham Hall, 48, 104
Lawrence Hall, 48, 104; 36
Osborne Hall, 48
Pope plan for, 115, 144, 247 n. 42,
        251 n. 36; 99, 100
Rogers plan for, 117–18; 101
Sheffield Scientific School, 144
student room; 143
Welch Hall, 103; 88
Yale Library, 48. *See also under*
        ROGERS, JAMES GAMBLE,
        WORKS: Schools and Colle-
        giate Buildings

Z

Zantzinger, Borie & Medary, 163–64
Zantzinger, C. C., 16
Zenitherm, 102

Illustration credits

Architectural Record (Courtesy McGraw-Hill, Inc): 25, 27, 49, 56, 64, 70, 75, 76, 77, 86, 87, 94, 97, 199, 200, 207, 210, 213, 214, 215, 216

The Art Institute of Chicago: 9, 16, 17, 20, 21, 24, 27, 36, 37, 38, 39, 40, 60, 65, 67, 68, 88, 164, 168, 169, 170, 171, 208, 217, 218

The Avery Fine Arts and Architecture Library, Columbia University: 81, 82, 83, 191

Aaron Betsky: 7, 11, 23, 28, 29, 30, 31, 33, 34, 35, 42, 43, 44, 48, 49, 50, 54, 61, 62, 63, 66, 67, 71, 72, 74, 80, 84, 85, 90, 91, 96, 106, 107, 108, 109, 112, 113, 114, 115, 118, 119, 120, 130, 131, 132, 135, 136, 138, 140, 145, 146, 149, 151, 152, 153, 154, 155, 158, 159, 160, 161, 165, 167, 173, 174, 177, 178, 184, 187, 188, 192, 202, 203, 209, 211, 212

Chicago Historical Society: 2, 3, 4, 51, 52, 166

Cigna Corporation: 78, 79

Colgate-Rochester Theological Seminary: 185, 186, 189, 190

Columbia University: 196, 197

Connecticut College: 193

Fortune Magazine: 143

Hyde Park Church: 153

Matthew Kupritz: 10

Peter Lipson: 201

Mannes College of Music: 73

Memorial Sloan-Kettering Hospital: 219

Navistar Archives: 55

Northwestern University Archives: 163, 172, 175, 176, 179, 180, 181, 182, 183

Darryl Ohlenbusch: 26, 194, 198

Princeton University: 89, 93

Rockefeller Archive Center: 220, 221, 222, 223, 224, 225

St. Paul's School: 162

Southern Baptist Theological Seminary: 147, 148, 150

The Taft School: 156, 157

Wisconsin Historical Society, McCormick Family Archives: 45, 46, 47

Yale University, Manuscripts and Archives Collections: 1, 41, 92, 99, 100, 101, 102, 111, 121, 123, 125, 127, 134, 137, 141, 142, 143

Yale University, Manuscripts and Archives Collections, James Gamble Rogers Papers: 5, 6, 8, 12, 13, 14, 15, 18, 19, 22, 57, 58, 59, 69, 92, 98, 104, 105, 110, 116, 117, 126, 128, 129, 130, 144, 195, 204, 205, 206